SRA ART Connections

A comprehensive K–5 art program that integrates the four dimensions of art into every lesson.

Level K

Level 1

Level 2

Level 4

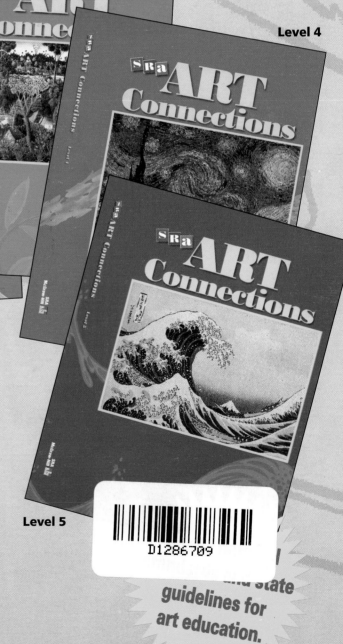

Level 5

D1299005

D1286709

- ● **Art History and Culture**
  Explore the great art, artists, and cultures of the world.

- ● **Aesthetic Perception**
  Develop an understanding and appreciation for art.

- ● **Creative Expression in Art Production**
  Encounter a broad range of art media in a variety of hands-on art activities that give students an avenue for self-expression and self-esteem.

- ● **Art Criticism**
  Enrich critical thinking skills as students learn about the elements and principles of art through examining their own and others' artwork.

Plus *Art Connections* provides resources to **integrate the visual arts** into reading/language arts, math, science, social studies, and technology, as well as the other arts—music, dance, and theater.

...nd state guidelines for art education.

Program Overview

A carefully crafted framework makes the big picture easy to see.

Art Connections, a new K–5 art program from SRA, is designed to show that art is much more than oil paint on canvas. Through this comprehensive program, students can experience the entire spectrum of art education.

- **Student Editions** for every grade level with **Big Book** (22″ x 34″) versions of the student books for K–2.

- **Teacher Editions** for each grade level.

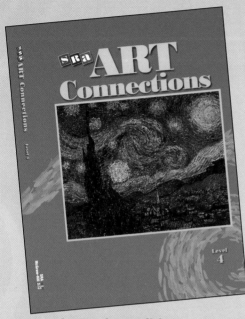

Level 4 Student Edition

Level 4 Teacher Edition

Fine Art Resources

- Overhead Transparency Study Prints (36 per grade level)

- Large Prints (12 per grade level)

- Artist Profiles (1 book per grade level)

- Animals Through History Time Line

- Literature and Art Videos (6 per grade level)

- ARTSOURCE Audio/ Video Resource Package (1 per grade level)

- National Museum of Women in the Arts Collection

Lesson Enrichment Resources

- **Vocabulary Book** (English/Spanish, 36 activities per grade level)

- **Assessment Book** (English/Spanish, 36 assessments per grade level)

- **Art Across the Curriculum Book** (36 Reading/Language Arts, Math, Science, Social Studies, The Arts, and Technology activities per grade level)

- **Technique Tips Flip Chart** (1 17" x 22" book per grade level. Step-by-step photographs of the techniques used in each of the 36 art production activities in the student book.)

- **Test Preparation Book** (1 book per grade level. 12 activities, each based on one of the Large Prints.)

- **Home Connection** (English/Spanish 1 book per grade level. Letters to acquaint families with art concepts and activities.)

- **Lesson Plans** (1 book per grade level)

- **Art Manipulative Kit** (Art-related objects to use when presenting key concepts)

- **Student Artist Portfolio** (Oversized folders for storing artwork)

Multimedia Resources

- **Literature and Art Video Collection** (6 per grade level)

- **2 Listening Cassettes in the Art Manipulative Kit** (Classical music to inspire young artists)

- **ARTSOURCE Audio/ Video Resource Package** (1 per grade level)

- **National Museum of Women in the Arts Collection CD-ROM and Videodisc**

- **Davidson's Multimedia Workshop CD-ROM**

- **National Geographic Picture Atlas of the World CD-ROM**

- **Internet Museum Resource Lists** in the **Teacher Edition**

Mold a lifelong appreciation of art.

Each lesson in the Student Edition integrates objectives from the four art disciplines of aesthetic perception, creative expression, art history and culture, and art criticism.

Grade Levels
K–2 Student Editions

- **Big Book** versions of the student books provide the youngest students with an overview of the topics, so even nonreaders can participate in the learning.

- Thirty-six two-page lessons in each grade level give K–2 students enough information to challenge them, without overwhelming them with details.

22" x 34"

K–2 Student Edition
and Big Book

Unit 1 Lesson 2

Many Kinds of Lines

This painting has thick, thin, smooth, rough, solid, and broken lines. Where do you see a smooth line? Find a broken line.

Joseph Stella. (American). *The Voice of the City of New York/The White Way I.* 1920–22. Oil and tempera on canvas. 88½ × 54 inches. Collection of The Newark Museum, Newark, New Jersey. Purchased 1937 Felix Fuld Bequest Fund.

Seeing like an artist
Draw different kinds of straight and curved lines. Make them move in different directions.

Unit 1

Lines can be **thick** or **thin, smooth** or **rough, solid** or **broken.**

thick   thin   smooth   rough   solid   broken

Create

How many different kinds of lines do you know? Draw an interesting place using many lines.

1. Think of a place you would like to draw.

2. Draw it using thick, thin, smooth, rough, solid, and broken lines.

3. Paint your picture. Use colors you think describe the feeling of the place.

Erika Price. Age 7. Seattle. Oil pastel and watercolor.

Lesson 2

17

Level 2

● Four-page lessons provide more in-depth concept development and background information for older students who are ready for more challenging material.

● Two fine artworks in each lesson encourage students to compare art from around the world.

● **Elements and Principles of Art** such as line, shape, color, form, texture, balance, emphasis, and unity are the focus of *every* unit and lesson to help students understand and appreciate art on a more meaningful level.

Unit 3 Lesson 1

The Color Wheel

Artists use the color wheel to organize colors and understand how they work together.

David Hockney. (English). *Large Interior Los Angeles.* 1988. Oil, ink on cut and pasted paper on canvas. Metropolitan Museum of Art, New York, New York. © David Hockney.

Both paintings on these pages use a wide range of color. David Hockney used a combination of bright primary colors with neutral colors in his painting. Stuart Davis used a mix of bright colors and unusual shapes. Notice how color is the most important element in both paintings.

Unit 3

Stuart Davis. (American). *Report from Rockport.* 1940. Oil on canvas. 24 × 30 inches. Metropolitan Museum of Art, NY, Edith and Milton Lowenthal Collection, Bequest of Edith Abrahamson Lowenthal, 1991/© 1998 Estate of Stuart Davis/Licensed by VAGA, New York, NY.

Both artists use a variety of colors in their artwork.

☑ What colors did the artists use in their artworks?

☑ How did they separate colors in their artworks?

☑ Do the colors in each piece of art create the same feeling?

☑ If both artworks were done in only browns, blacks, and whites, would they communicate the same feelings and moods? Explain your answer.

SEEING LIKE AN ARTIST
Look around your classroom and notice how most objects have a dominant color.

Lesson **1**

Level 4

77

● *Every* lesson starts with 2 forms of **fine art** — painting, sculpture, architecture, fabric art, printmaking, photography, or jewelry, so students see how artists put the elements and principles of art into play.

The Color Spectrum

The colors in the **color spectrum**—red, orange, yellow, green, blue, and violet—appear in the same order in natural light. A rainbow is nature's color spectrum.

Red, yellow, and blue are the **primary colors.** You cannot mix any other colors to make them.

Secondary colors—orange, green, and violet—are created when two primary colors are mixed together. Primary and secondary colors are also called **hues.**

Intermediate colors are made by blending a primary color with a secondary color. Red-orange is an example of one of the six intermediate colors.

This color wheel is made up of three primary, three secondary, and six intermediate colors. Notice how the colors are organized so that you can easily understand how to mix a color.

Practice

Create a geometric design. Use crayon.

1. Use a black marker to draw one large geometric shape touching at least two edges of a sheet of paper. Draw a second geometric shape inside your first shape, then a third shape inside your second shape. Inside each section create geometric patterns.

2. Fill your design with color. In the center shape use primary colors. In the middle shape use secondary colors. In the outside shape use intermediate colors.

Decide Does your design have primary colors at the center, secondary colors in the middle, and intermediate colors on the outside? What changes would you make?

78

Level 4

Unit 3

● **Student artwork** is featured in *every* lesson to help students see that they too can be artists and can integrate the elements and principles of art into the paintings and drawings they create.

Amy Kus. Age 9. Mixed-media.
How did this student artist create a color wheel?

Create

What colors do you imagine you would see if you were a deep-sea diver in the Caribbean Sea? Create an undersea color-wheel drawing.

1. Imagine yourself swimming in the ocean. What creatures would you see?

2. Using pencil, draw a sea creature as large as your hand, adding details such as scales and teeth. Create an environment for your creature. Outline your drawing with black marker.

3. Divide your picture into 12 pie-shaped sections. Color each section as if it were part of a color wheel. Try to create as many of the colors as you can.

Describe What colors did you use in your drawing?

Analyze How did you create the intermediate colors in your drawing?

Interpret What would you choose as a title for your drawing?

Decide Were you successful in keeping your color wheel in sequenced order? Can you think of other themes that could be made into a color wheel?

Lesson **1**

79

● **Create** art activities featuring a wide array of media are incorporated into *every* lesson, so students get frequent hands-on practice building their artistic skills.

The learning curve is drawn with much more than a crayon, a marker, or a paintbrush.

As they move from lesson to lesson, students will discover that every line, brush stroke, and carefully drawn curve they see can lead to a better understanding of artists, their surroundings, and the times in which they lived.

● **Artist Profiles** at the beginning of every unit allow students to meet a master artist, analyze the artist's work, and discuss the techniques and art concepts that were used to create that work.

● **ARTSOURCE lessons** at the end of every unit were developed by the Music Center of Los Angeles County to provide arts integration. These dynamic lessons show how the elements and principles of visual arts can be translated into the performing arts: **music, dance,** or **theater.**

● Performances available on Video- or Audiocassette in the **ARTSOURCE Performing Arts Audio/Video Resource Package.**

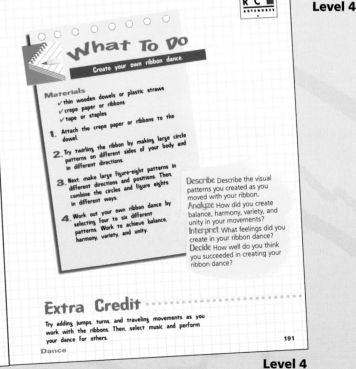

Artists use different types of **forms** to communicate their feelings and ideas and to show how they see the world. They also create forms for use in daily life.
- What is the difference between this sculpture and a drawing?
- Describe the open and solid areas of the sculpture. What basic shape do you see?
- Point out the mother and child in this sculpture. What did Henry Moore do to the figures? Why do you think he did this?
- From how many sides would you view this sculpture? Do you think Moore intended his viewers to observe this sculpture from many angles? Explain why.

Artist Profile

Henry Moore
1898–1986

Sculptor

The English sculptor Henry Moore created many larger-than-life sculptures in stone, wood, and metals such as lead and bronze. He liked to simplify his forms into basic shapes without details. Many of Moore's works have *family* as the theme. He is viewed as one of the greatest and most original sculptors of the twentieth century.

Henry Moore and other sculptors use form to communicate an idea or to create a useful object. In this unit you will learn about using form to express ideas and to understand different ways that artists create forms. Here are the topics you will study.
- Forms
- Additive Sculpture
- Subtractive Sculpture
- Masks
- Functional Forms
- Assembled Forms

105

Level 4

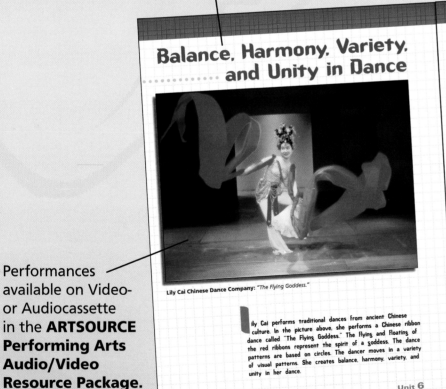

Balance, Harmony, Variety, and Unity in Dance

Lily Cai Chinese Dance Company: "The Flying Goddess."

Lily Cai performs traditional dances from ancient Chinese culture. In the picture above, she performs a Chinese ribbon dance called "The Flying Goddess." The flying and floating of the red ribbons represent the spirit of a goddess. The dance patterns are based on circles. The dancer moves in a variety of visual patterns. She creates balance, harmony, variety, and unity in her dance.

What To Do
Create your own ribbon dance.

Materials
✓ thin wooden dowels or plastic straws
✓ crepe paper or ribbons
✓ tape or staples

1. Attach the crepe paper or ribbons to the dowel.
2. Try twirling the ribbon by making large circle patterns on different sides of your body and in different directions.
3. Next, make large figure-eight patterns in different directions and positions. Then, combine the circles and figure eights in different ways.
4. Work out your own ribbon dance by selecting four to six different patterns. Work to achieve balance, harmony, variety, and unity.

Describe Describe the visual patterns you created as you moved with your ribbon.
Analyze How did you create balance, harmony, variety, and unity in your movements?
Interpret What feelings did you create in your ribbon dance?
Decide How well do you think you succeeded in creating your ribbon dance?

Extra Credit
Try adding jumps, turns, and traveling movements as you work with the ribbons. Then, select music and perform your dance for others.

190   Unit 6

Dance   191

Level 4

● **Museum Profiles** in the unit *Wrapping Up* lessons help students develop an early appreciation of these fascinating and ever-changing places.

Let's Visit a Museum

2. **Picture plane** is the surface of a drawing. There are three parts of a picture plane—foreground, background, middle ground.
3. **Point of View** is the angle from which the viewer sees an object in artwork.
4. **Tactile Texture** is what artists use to show how things actually feel. (rough, smooth, shiny, matte)

Summing Up

Look at *Old Mesilla Plaza* painted by Leon Trousset. The artist used the techniques covered in this unit to create space and texture.

• Has Trousset used all six perspective techniques? Try to identify at least one example of each technique.
• How many different kinds of textures can you find?
• Does the artist use visual texture to imitate the texture of the wagon, ground, and trees, or does he show the texture of the paint?

Space and texture are important elements in paintings and drawings. By using techniques to create space and textures, artists express to others what they see.

The Smithsonian Institution was established in 1846 with funds from the will of the English scientist, James Smithson. Today there are more than 140 million artifacts, exhibits, and works of art at the Smithsonian. It is also a center for research in the arts, sciences, and history. It is made of 16 museums and galleries, several research centers, and the National Zoo. Nine of the museums are located on the National Mall in Washington, DC, between the Capitol and Washington Monument.

163

The Smithsonian Institution

Level 4

Careers in Art
Landscape Architect

• **Alternating rhythm** has a motif that is changed in some way or a second motif is introduced.
• **Flowing rhythm** is created by repeating curved lines or shapes.
3. **Visual movement** is the illusion of motion or change in position. There are two types of visual movement.

Summing Up

Look at the painting by Johnson. He created figures using simplified shapes and repeated areas of color. They create rhythm and movement, which you learned about in this unit.

• Which shapes has Johnson repeated?
• Describe how Johnson created rhythm in his painting.

Shape, rhythm, and movement are important design principles that artists use to communicate to others what they see.

David Barncord is a landscape architect. Landscape architects plan outdoor areas for people. They pay careful attention to protecting the environment. Barncord loved baseball as a boy, but there were no baseball fields near his home. He began laying out his own baseball fields when he was six years old. In his profession he works with architects, engineers, gardeners, building contractors, and various government officials. Barncord got his college degree in landscape architecture. He works long hours and meets many people in his work.

David Barncord, landscape architect

73

Level 4

● **Career Connections** in the unit *Wrapping Up* lessons help students discover that art careers are not always defined by a paintbrush and an easel.

● **More About . . .**
These extra lessons in the back of each book give students an easy-to-access resource for additional information on lesson material in the following areas:

• Art Techniques
• Art Criticism
• Aesthetics
• Art History Around the World
• Art Subject Matter
• Drawing

More About... Art History

A.D. 1000–1800

Leonardo da Vinci.
Mona Lisa.
1503–1505. Italy.

Rembrandt van Rijn.
Self-Portrait.
1660. The Netherlands.

Artist unknown.
Bayon Temple at Angkor Thom.
1100s–1200s. Cambodia.

Artist unknown.
Shrine Head. (Yorub).
1100–1300. Nigeria.

Torii Kiyotada.
Actor of the Ichikawa Clan.
1710–1740. Japan.

Artist unknown.
Chartres Cathedral.
1145–1220. France.

Thomas Jefferson.
Monticello.
1770–1784. United States.

Artist unknown.
Bayeux Tapestry. (Detail).
1070–1080. England.

Artist unknown.
Anasazi culture petroglyphs.
United States.

Artist unknown.
Taj Mahal.
1632–1648. India.

More About...Art History

218

219

Level 4

With this palette of features, every class will have the signature of a true master.

The Teacher Edition for each grade level K–5, contains all the tools needed to add color and texture to every art class. This easy-to-use resource provides the power to deliver a masterful presentation, page by page, lesson by lesson.

● **Three-stage "Focus, Teach, Close" lesson cycle** gives complete directions for presenting each lesson in a format that will reach students most effectively.

● **Self-contained lessons** enable the presentation of topics in any order to suit individual teaching styles and curriculum.

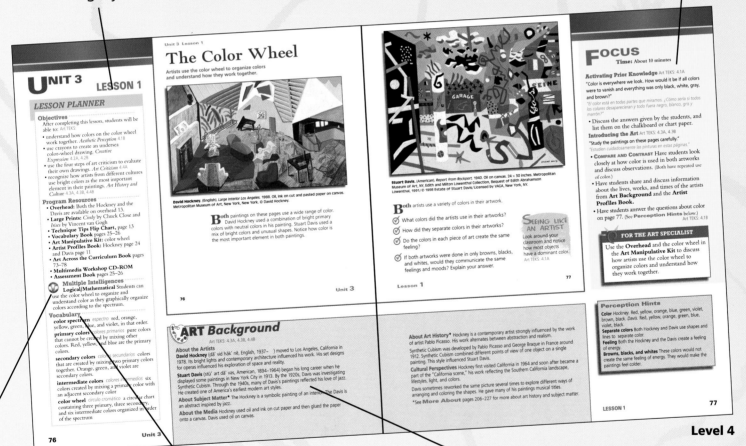

● **Multiple Intelligences** identifies the primary ways of learning in each lesson.

● **Vocabulary** in English and Spanish includes definitions to provide a single-source reference for the new vocabulary words students will master.

● **Art Background** provides the pronunciation of artists' names plus other necessary details to make every art topic more enriching and meaningful.

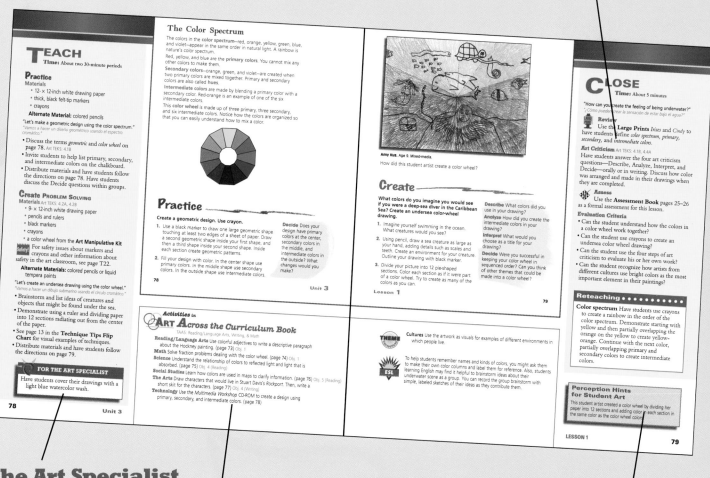

Program Resources
are referenced at point of suggested use to integrate them effectively to enrich each lesson.

For the Art Specialist
gives the art specialist ideas for developing lesson topics even further.

Art Across the Curriculum
provides a preview of the activities in the **Art Across the Curriculum Book** to introduce art lessons into any subject area, so students can understand how art touches and shapes their lives in ways they might never have imagined.

Perception Hints
provide cues to help students identify the specific art concepts being addressed in the artwork from each lesson.

Professional Development
Comprehensive Teacher Edition reference resources at the back of the book include:

- Professional development articles about teaching, assessing, and enriching art education
- Museum Resources
- Program Scope and Sequence
- Program Glossary
- Program Index
- Art Across the Curriculum Index

Teacher Support Materials

With Art Connections, support is never an abstract concept.

These materials help send students' imaginations soaring with each new lesson topic they explore.

Fine Art Resources

Overhead Transparency Study Prints K–5

The 36 transparencies of the fine art in each lesson enable teachers to highlight specific elements of the artwork, so students can develop a better understanding of each concept they're studying, and how those concepts apply to actual pieces of art.

Artist Profiles K–5

This teacher/student resource book profiles the artists covered in each **Student Edition**, so students can better understand each artist's inspiration—and the completed work. Each profile includes a photograph of the artist as well as information about the artist's life and work.

Large Prints K–5 (English/Spanish)

There are 12 Large Prints (22" x 26 1/2") for each grade level featuring art that does not appear in the **Student Edition**. Each one focuses on a specific unit concept to easily integrate additional artwork into every unit. Large Prints are referenced at point of use in the **Teacher Edition** and feature detailed information about the artist, the media, the times, the subject, and the culture on the back of each print in both English and Spanish.

Animals Through History Time Line K–5

Students can use the animal artwork in this 72" x 18" time line to trace how animals have been depicted in art throughout history, as they discover that art has always been a fundamental part of life. On the back of the time line, look for profiles of key museums in the United States.

The National Museum of Women in the Arts Collection

Developed in conjunction with the National Museum of Women in the Arts, this program features 200 works by key women artists. The collection includes 12" x 15" Art Prints, 4" x 5" Art Cards, an Idea Book, a Museum Guide, a Videodisc, and a CD-ROM to enlist a whole range of media to hold students' attention.

Lesson Enrichment Resources

Vocabulary Book K–5

These blackline master books feature an activity for every lesson that focuses on the core art vocabulary at each grade level. Available in *English and Spanish,* students have the opportunity to practice and integrate new vocabulary words immediately.

Assessment Book K–5

These assessment booklets provide assessment alternatives for each lesson at every grade level. Blackline masters appear in both *English and Spanish.*

Art Across The Curriculum Resource Book K–5

The resource book for every grade level includes a one-page blackline master for each of the 36 lessons in the following areas: Reading/Language Arts, Math, Science, Social Studies, The Arts, and Technology.

Technique Tips Flip Chart K–5

This 17- x 22- inch book provides step-by-step photographs of art techniques to support the *Create* activities (art production activities) in the **Student Edition**.

Test Preparation Book K–5

This book contains 12 lessons that focus on reading, writing, and math skills often encountered on standardized tests. Each lesson is based on one of the large prints in the collection for each grade level.

Home Connection K–5

This booklet provides letters to the family explaining what students will be experiencing in each unit of **SRA Art Connections**. Available in *English and Spanish*, these letters also contain suggestions for ways that families can help students appreciate visual arts.

Lesson Plans K–5

This book provides a one-page summary of all information related to each of the 36 lessons in the **Student Edition**.

Student Portfolios

Students can decorate these oversized folders and use them to hold their artwork, measuring what they've learned over the course of the year.

Art Manipulative Kit K–5

With this group of art-related objects, teachers can add a new dimension to their presentations of key art concepts, so students can grasp new concepts more quickly. The Kit includes:

- color wheel
- solid shapes and forms
- flexible curve
- textured materials
- simple balance
- magnifying glass
- mirror
- prism
- Flash Cards to help explain the elements and principles of art
- Listening Cassettes of classical music to help inspire students when it's time to create

Teacher Support Materials

Multimedia Resources

Literature and Art Video Collection K–5

This set of six videos per grade level provides an opportunity to integrate children's literature into art classes, introducing some well-known picture book illustrators as artists. Including the work of Leo Lionni, Jerry Pinkney, Chris Van Allsburg, Trina Schart Hyman, and others, each video is referenced in the Teacher Edition for easy lesson integration.

Listening Cassettes in the Art Manipulative Kit

These classical music selections featuring Bach, Mozart, Handel, Tchaikovsky, Corelli, and Vivaldi are intended to be played during *Create* activities to inspire young artists.

Davidson's MULTIMEDIA WORKSHOP

This multimedia draw-and-paint CD-ROM for elementary students is correlated to activities in the *Art Across the Curriculum* Technology activities. Using computer media, the program provides an engaging alternative for getting young children excited about art projects.

The National Geographic Picture Atlas of the World CD-ROM

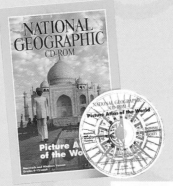

Through this spectacular multimedia CD-ROM, your students have the power to travel to London, Paris, Rome, New York, or any other city where great works of art can be found.

The National Museum of Women in the Arts Collection CD-ROM and Videodisc

This outstanding collection of work by women artists is accessible through CD-ROM and Videodisc technology.

ARTSOURCE Performing Arts Audio/Video Resource Package

These wonderful Theater, Music, and Drama performances produced by The Music Center of Los Angeles County are related to the ARTSOURCE lessons at the end of each unit in the **Student Edition.** The actual performances are captured on audio- or videotape and provided for each grade level.

Learn how to find the Met on the Net . . . and much more.

Here's a list of Internet addresses for museums profiled throughout *Art Connections* and listed on the reverse side of Animals Though History Time Line. Additional museum education resources are listed on pages T30–T33. SRA is not responsible for the content of these Websites, which may contain content and images which may be inappropriate for student use.

Anchorage Museum of History & Art
121 W. Seventh Ave.
Anchorage, AK 99501
Phone: (907) 343-4326
URL: (WWW address): under development

Albright-Knox Art Gallery
1285 Elmwood Ave.
Buffalo, NY 14222
Phone: (716) 822-8700
http://www.akag.org
Information on exhibitions, educational resources, and art library services.

Art Institute of Chicago
111 South Michigan Ave.
Chicago, IL 60603
Phone: (312) 443-3600
http://www.artic.edu
The numerous resources of the Institute are gathered in this site. An excellent art education site containing many links.

Dallas Museum of Art
1717 N. Harwood
Dallas, TX 75201
Phone: (214) 922-1200
http://www.unt.edu/dfw/dma/www/dma.htm
Includes images from the galleries, views of the sculpture garden, and an education resource center.

The Denver Art Museum
100 West 14th Avenue Parkway
Denver, CO 80204
Phone: (303) 640-7591
http://www.artcom.com/museums/nv/af80204-27.htm

The Detroit Institute of Arts
5200 Woodward Ave.
Detroit, MI 48202
Phone: (313) 833-7900
http://www.dia.org
The DIA is the fifth-largest fine arts museum in the United States, with holdings of more than 60,000 works. More than 300 can be viewed at this site.

Guggenheim Museum
1071 Fifth Ave.
New York, NY 10128
Phone: (212) 423-3500
http://math240.lehman.cuny.edu/gugg
The Guggenheim's vast resources are here to sample. Current exhibits, education helps, images, schedules, and links are included.

The Heard Museum
22 E. Monte Vista Road
Phoenix, AZ 85004-1480
Phone: (602) 252-8840
http://www.heard.org/
The website of this museum of native cultures and art concentrates on research help.

High Museum of Art
1280 Peachtree St. N.E.
Atlanta, GA 30309
Phone: (404) 733-4400
http://www.high.org
This site features works from the High's folk art and photo gallery. Exhibit, film series, and membership information are available.

Joslyn Art Museum
2200 Dodge St.
Omaha, NE 68102
Phone: (402) 342-3300
http://www.omaha.org/joslyn.htm
Basic museum information and history.

Kimbell Art Museum
3333 Camp Bowie Blvd.
Fort Worth, TX 76107-2792
Phone: (817) 332-8451
URL: (WWW address): under development

Los Angeles County Museum of Art
5905 Wilshire Blvd.
Los Angeles, CA 90036
Phone: (213) 857-6000
http://www.lacma.org/
Includes images of masterpieces in LACMA's permanent collection, an exhibition schedule, membership information, and the Museum Shop.

The Metropolitan Museum of Art
5th Ave. at 82nd Street
New York, NY 10028
Phone: (212) 879-5500
http://www.metmuseum.org/
This major museum, often called New York's Louvre, features images from 5,000 years of world culture. Images, schedules, history, and educational resources are included.

Museum of Fine Arts, Houston
1001 Bissonnet
Houston, TX 77005
Phone: (713) 639-7300
http://www.mfah.org/
Images of paintings, sculptures, and decorative art, representing all movements and periods.

National Gallery of Art
4th and Constitution Ave. N.W.
Washington, DC 20565
Phone: (202) 737-4215
http://www.si.edu/newstart.htm
Currently accessed through the Smithsonian web site.

National Museum of Women in the Arts
1250 New York Ave. N.W.
Washington, DC 20005-3920
Phone: (202) 783-5000
http://www.nmwa.org/
A 45-minute video tour or individual image clips can be downloaded.

Nelson-Atkins Museum of Art
4525 Oak St.
Kansas City, MO 64111
Phone: (816) 561-4000
http://www.infozine.com/z9611/anel.html
Includes information about museum resources.

Philadelphia Museum of Art
26th St. & Benjamin Franklin Pkwy.
Philadelphia, PA 19130
Phone: (215) 763-8100
http://www.pma.libertynet.org/
View the galleries, resource lists, images, schedules, and historical data.

San Francisco Museum of Modern Art
151 Third St.
San Francisco, CA 94103
Phone: (415)357-4000
http://www.sfmoma.org/
Schedules, education resources, and a self-guided tour of the museum's online gallery.

Seattle Art Museum
100 University Street
Seattle, WA 98101-2902
Phone: (206) 654-3100
Fax: (206) 654-3191
http://www.ci.seattle.wa.us/sam/default.htm
Includes museum information, education resources, and museum technology.

Smithsonian Museums
8th and G Sts. N.W.
Washington, DC 20560
Phone: (202) 357-2700
http://www.si.edu/newstart.htm
The Smithsonian home page is the door to all the museums under its umbrella.

Wadsworth Atheneum
600 Main St.
Hartford, CT 06103-2990
Phone: (860) 278-2670
http://www.courant.com/hartford/hattract/wadswort.htm
Web site under development.

Walker Art Center
Vineland Place
Minneapolis, MN 55403
Phone: (612) 375-7600
http://www.walkerart.org/
Basic site with schedules and mission statement.

White House (Washington, DC)
Pennsylvania Ave.
Washington, DC
http://www.whitehouse.gov/WH/welcome.html
The White House History and Tours link leads to images of art in the White House.

Authors

Senior Author
Rosalind Ragans, Ph.D., Associate Professor Emerita, Georgia Southern University

Willis Bing Davis, Art Department Chair, Central State University, Ohio

Tina Farrell, Director of Visual and Performing Arts, Clear Creek Independent School District, Texas

Jane Rhoades Hudak, Ph.D., Professor of Art, Georgia Southern University

Gloria McCoy, K–12 Art Supervisor, Spring Branch Independent School District, Texas

Bunyan Morris, Demonstration Art Teacher, Marvin Pittman Laboratory School, Georgia Southern University

Nan Yoshida, Former Art Supervisor, Los Angeles Unified School District, California

Contributors

ARTSOURCE Music, Dance, Theater Lessons
The Music Center of Los Angeles County
Education Division, Los Angeles, California

Assessment
Maggie Davis, Lead Teacher, The Performing and Visual Arts Center, Miami Northwestern High School, Miami, Florida

More About Aesthetics
Richard W. Burrows, Executive Director, Institute for Arts Education, San Diego, California

Safe Use of Art Materials
Mary Ann Boykin, Director, The Art School for Children and Young Adults, University of Houston-Clear Lake, Texas

Museum Education
Marilyn JS Goodman, Director of Education, Solomon R. Guggenheim Museum, New York, New York

National Museum of Women in the Arts Collection
National Museum of Women in the Arts, Washington, DC

Contributing Writers

Patricia Carter
Assistant Professor of Art Education, Georgia Southern University, Statesboro, Georgia

Faye Scannell
Art Specialist and Lead Technology Teacher, Bellevue School District, Bellevue, Washington

Marie M. Mennes
Art Supervisor, Dade County Public Schools, Miami, Florida

Jackie Ellett
Elementary Art Teacher, Fort Daniel Elementary School, Dacula, Georgia

Dennis W. Black
High School Art Teacher, Clear Creek Independent School District, Houston, Texas

For more information about SRA products, to place an order, or to follow up on your order, please call SRA Customer Service at 1-888/SRA-4KIDS, from 7 A.M. to 5:30 P.M., Central Time.

SRA Art Connections

Teacher Edition

Level 3

Authors
Rosalind Ragans, Ph.D., Senior Author

Willis Bing Davis
Tina Farrell
Jane Rhoades Hudak, Ph.D.
Gloria McCoy
Bunyan Morris
Nan Yoshida

Contributing Writer
Marie Mennes

Music Center Education Division
The Music Center of Los Angeles County

SRA McGraw-Hill

Columbus, Ohio

A Division of The McGraw-Hill Companies

SRA Art Connections

Table of Contents

Cover Fine Art Credit
Joseph Jean-Gilles. *Haitian Landscape*. Collection of the Art Museum of the Americas, Organization of American States.

Cover Student Art Credits
Heather Byrnes. (age 8) *On the Farm*
Domenique Chery. (age 8) *The Market Place*
Jenna Mooney. (age 8) *A Park in the Future*

SRA/McGraw-Hill

A Division of The **McGraw·Hill** *Companies*

Copyright ©1998 SRA/McGraw-Hill

Printed in the United States of America

Send all inquiries to:
SRA/McGraw-Hill
250 Old Wilson Bridge Road
Suite 310
Worthington, OH 43085

ISBN 0-02-687815-1

2 3 4 5 6 7 8 9 BAN 02 01 00 99 98

SRA Art Connections

Level 3

Authors

Rosalind Ragans, Ph.D., Senior Author

Willis Bing Davis

Tina Farrell

Jane Rhoades Hudak, Ph.D.

Gloria McCoy

Bunyan Morris

Nan Yoshida

Contributing Writer

Marie Mennes

Music Center Education Division
The Music Center of Los Angeles County

SRA McGraw-Hill

Columbus, Ohio

A Division of The McGraw·Hill Companies

JAY

Credits

Cover, Joseph Jean-Gilles, *Haitian Landscape,* Collection of the Art Museum of the Americas, Organization of American States, Washington, DC; **Back Cover**, top Heather Byrnes, Age 8, *On the Farm,* middle Domenique Chery, Age 8, *The Market Place*, bottom Jenna Mooney, Age 8, *A Park in the Future*; **15**, Philadelphia Museum of Art: A.E. Gallatin Collection. ©1998 Estate of Pablo Picasso/Artists Rights Society (ARS), NY. Photo by Graydon Wood; **40**, Photo by Don Perdue; **43**, Photograph courtesy of Kathy Perales; **45**, Smith College Museum of Art, Northampton, MA. Gift of Irene Rich Clifford, 1977; **70**, ©Superstock; **73**, Photo courtesy of The Museum of Fine Arts, Houston, TX; **75**, Alinari/Scala, Art Resource, NY; **100**, Photo by Don Perdue; **103**, Photo courtesy of Andrew Aidt; **130**, Photo by Craig Schwartz, ©1990; **133**, Courtesy of The Walker Art Center, Minneapolis, MN; **135**, *Bayeux Tapestry* (detail) Scala/Art Resource, NY; **160**, Photo courtesy of Tandy Beal & Company; **163**, Photo courtesy of Tommye Scanlin; **165**, Sid Richardson Collection of Western Art, Fort Worth, TX; **190**, Photo courtesy of In the Heart of the Beast Puppet and Mask Theatre ; **193**, Photo courtesy of The Philadelphia Museum of Art, Philadelphia, PA; **214**, *Adena Effigy Figure (Adena Pipe)*, Courtesy of the Ohio Historical Society; *Three Cows and One Horse, ceiling of the Axial Gallery, Lascaux Caves in France*, ©Douglas Mazonowicz/Gallery of Prehistoric Art; *Statues from Abu Temple*, Courtesy of The Oriental Institute of The University of Chicago, Photograph by Victor J. Boswell; *Tutankhamen Mask (Side View)*, ©Brian Brake, Photo Researchers; *Kuang (Gong with Lid)*, Asian Art Museum of San Francisco, The Avery Brundage Collection; **215**, *Colossal Head*, La Venta, Mexico, ©Nathaniel Tarn, Photo Researchers; *Woman Playing Harp*, ©1989 The Metropolitan Museum of Art, NY, Fletcher Fund, 1956, (56.171.38); *Stonehenge*, ©1984 Lawrence Migdale/Photo Researchers, Inc.; *Parthenon*, ©Vladimir Pcholkin/FPG International Corp.; **216**, *Shiva as Lord of the Dance*, The Asia Society, New York, Mr. and Mrs. John D. Rockefeller 3rd Collection/Photo by Lynton Gardiner; *Ravenna Apse Mosaic (Detail)*, Scala, Art Resource, New York; *The Pantheon*, ©Louis Grandadam/Tony Stone Images; *Hagia Sophia*, Constantinople (Istanbul, Turkey), ©The Stock Market/Harvey Lloyd; *The Great Stupa*, ©Hari Mahidhar/Dinodia Picture Agency; **217**, Page from *The Book of Lindisfarne*, Bridgeman/Art Resource, New York; *Pagoda of the Temple of the Six Banyon Trees*, Guangzhou, China, K. Scholz/H. Armstrong Roberts; *Great Mosque at Samarra*, Scala/Art Resource, New York; *Stupa at Borobudur*, Borromeo/Art Resource, New York; **218**, Rembrandt van Rijn, *Self-Portrait*, Andrew Mellon Collection, ©1996 Board of Trustees, National Gallery of Art, Washington, DC; Leonardo da Vinci, *Mona Lisa*, Louvre, Paris, France. Erich Lessing, Art Resource, NY; *Bayon Temple at Angkor Thom*, ©Josef Beck/FPG International Corp.; *Shrine Head*, The Minneapolis Institute of Arts, MN; Torii Kiyotada, *Actor of the Ichikawa Clan*, ©1979/94 The Metropolitan Museum of Art, New York, NY. Harris Brisbane Dick Fund, 1949. (JP3075); **219**, *Chartres Cathedral*, Scala/Art Resource, NY; Thomas Jefferson, *Monticello*, ©The Stock Market/ChromoSohm/Sohm, 1994; *Bayeux Tapestry (Detail)*, Musée de la Reine Mathilde, Bayeux, France. Erich Lessing/Art Resource, NY; *Taj Mahal*, ©The Telegraph Colour Library/FPG International Corp.; *Anasazi Culture Petroglyphs*, ©George H. H. Huey; **220**, Piet Mondrian, *Broadway Boogie-Woogie*, The Museum of Modern Art, New York, NY. Given anonymously. Photograph ©1988 The Museum of Modern Art, NY; Claude Monet, *Impression, Sunrise*, Musée Marmottan, Paris, France. Giraudon/Art Resource, NY; Edgar Degas, *Little Dancer of Fourteen*, Tate Gallery, London, England. Art Resource, NY; Katsushika Hokusai, *The Great Wave off Kanagawa*, The Metropolitan Museum of Art, New York, NY. H.O. Havemeyer Collection, Bequest of Mrs. H. O. Havemeyer, 1929; **221**, Pablo Picasso, *Gertrude Stein*, ©1996 The Metropolitan Museum of Art, New York, NY. Bequest of Gertrude Stein, 1946. (47.106); Chuck Close, *Self-Portrait*, Photograph courtesy Pace Wildenstein Gallery, New York, NY. Photo by Bill Jacobson; Jackson Pollock, *Convergence*, Albright-Knox Art Gallery, Buffalo, New York. Gift of Seymour H. Knox, 1956; Alexander Calder, *Untitled Mobile*, Gift of the Collectors Committee ©1996 Board of Trustees, National Gallery of Art, Washington, DC; Maria Martínez, *Black on Black Pots*, Courtesy of Maria Martínez, ©Jerry Jacka Photography; **228**, Aaron Haupt/Aaron Haupt Photography; **230**, Aaron Haupt/Aaron Haupt Photography; **232**, Stephano Scata/The Image Bar.

SRA/McGraw-Hill

*A Division of The **McGraw·Hill** Companies*

Send all inquiries to:
SRA/McGraw-Hill
250 Old Wilson Bridge Road
Suite 310
Worthington, Ohio 43085

Printed in the United States of America.

ISBN 0-02-688317-1

3 4 5 6 7 8 9 VHP 04 03 02 01 00 99 98

ADDED VOL   SBEN CAR0133

Authors

Senior Author
Dr. Rosalind Ragans, Ph. D.
Associate Professor Emerita
Georgia Southern University

Willis Bing Davis
Art Department Chair
Central State University, Ohio

Tina Farrell
Director of Visual and Performing Arts,
Clear Creek, Independent School
District, Texas

Jane Rhoades Hudak, Ph.D.
Professor of Art
Georgia Southern University

Gloria McCoy
K–12 Art Supervisor, Spring Branch
Independent School District, Texas

Bunyan Morris
Demonstration Art Teacher
Marvin Pittman Laboratory School,
Georgia Southern University

Nan Yoshida
Former Art Supervisor,
Los Angeles Unified School
District, California

 Contributors
ARTSOURCE Music,
Dance, Theater Lessons
The Music Center of
Los Angeles County
Education Division,
Los Angeles, California
Executive Director, Music Center
Education Division–Joan Boyett
Concept Originator and
Project Director–Melinda Williams
Project Coordinator–
Susan Cambigue-Tracey
Arts Discipline Writers:
Dance–Susan Cambigue-Tracey
Music–Rosemarie Cook-Glover
Theater–Barbara Leonard
Staff Assistance–Victoria Bernal
Logo Design–Maureen Erbe

More About Aesthetics
Richard W. Burrows, Executive
Director, Institute for Arts Education,
San Diego, California

Safe Use of Art Materials
Mary Ann Boykin, Visiting Lecturer, Art
Education; Director, The Art School for
Children and Young Adults, University
of Houston-Clear Lake, Houston, Texas

Museum Education
Marilyn JS Goodman, Director of
Education, Solomon R. Guggenheim
Museum,
New York, New York

**The National Museum of Women in
the Arts Collection**
National Museum of
Women in the Arts,
Washington, DC

Contributing Writer
Marie M. Mennes
Art Supervisor
Dade County Public Schools
Miami, FL

Reviewers
Mary Ann Boykin
Visiting Lecturer, Art Education;
Director, The Art School for Children
and Young Adults
University of Houston-Clear Lake
Houston, TX

Judy Gong
Multi-age Classroom Teacher
Pacific Elementary School
Lincoln Unified School District
Stockton, CA

Lori Groendyke Knutti
Art Educator
Harrison Street Elementary School
Big Walnut Elementary School
Sunbury, OH

Grace Baptiste-Hall
Elementary Teacher
42nd Street School
Los Angeles Unified School District
Los Angeles, CA

Nancy L. James
Third Grade Teacher
Dallas Public Schools
Dallas, TX

Steven R. Sinclair
Art Teacher
Big Country Elementary School
Southwest Independent School District
San Antonio, TX

Student Activity Testers
Molly McCloskey
Danielle Kintz
Kelley Krebs
Matthew Cohan
Kyle Harter

TABLE OF CONTENTS

Table of Contents
(continued)

Unit 3   Space and Form

Unit 4   Balance and Emphasis

Table of Contents
(continued)

Unit 5

Texture and Rhythm

Unit 6

Harmony, Variety, and Unity

Table of Contents
(continued)

More About . . .

OVERVIEW

The purpose of these pages is to open students' minds to the idea that visual arts include many components and take many forms. The arts satisfy the human needs for display, celebration, personal expression, and communication. We use the visual arts to enhance our visual environments, to express our innermost feelings, and to communicate ideas. Art is made by people.

Activating Prior Knowledge
Ask students what they think *art* is. Encourage creative, divergent thinking. In visual art, there are many answers to a question.

Questions to Discuss
Have students look at the images on pages 8–9 and name the things that are visual art.

Then ask the following questions:
- Which of these things could you hold in your hands?
- Which one could you walk inside of?
- Which ones would you hang on a wall?
- Which one could you wear on your head?
- Do you have any things at home like the images on these pages?
  (See **Perception Hints** below for answers.)

Perception Hints
- All of the images on these pages are visual art.
- They could hold the sculpture, pottery, and the mask in their hands.
- They could walk inside the architecture, the Parthenon.
- They would hang the painting, the drawing, the print, and the photograph on the wall.
- They could wear the mask on their heads.
- Encourage students to think about things they have at home that fit the categories on these pages. The building they live in is architecture. They have ceramic dishes and other containers. Many of them have things hanging on the walls to enhance their visual environments. A few may have sculpture in the home. Many will have seen sculpture in and around public buildings.

What Is Art?

Art is . . .

Art is made by people
- to communicate ideas.
- to express feelings.
- to give us well-designed objects.

Painting

Painting is color applied to a flat surface.

Henri Matisse. (French). *Woman in Blue.* 1937. Oil on canvas. $36\frac{1}{2}$ x 29 inches. Philadelphia Museum of Art, Gift of Mrs. John Wintersteen/©1998 Succession H. Matisse. Paris/Artists Rights Society (ARS), New York.

Drawing

Drawing is the process of making art with lines.

Wang Chao. (Chinese). *The Three Stars of Happiness, Wealth, and Longevity.* c. 1500. Hanging scroll. Ink and light colors on silk. $62\frac{1}{2}$ x $37\frac{1}{2}$ inches. Kimbell Art Museum, Fort Worth, Texas.

Sculpture

Sculpture is art that fills up space.

Frederic Remington. (American). *Mountain Man.* 1903. Bronze. Carleton Private Collection.

Architecture

Architecture is the art of designing and constructing buildings.

Artist unknown. (Greece). *Parthenon.* 447-438 B.C. Athens, Greece.

8

ART Background

More About Art Terms

Painting is the art of applying color to a surface.

Drawing is the art of creating an image with lines on a surface.

Sculpture is the art of creating three-dimensional images.

Architecture is the art of designing and planning buildings. Architecture includes homes, schools, and other public buildings.

Printmaking is the art of transferring an original image from one prepared surface to another.

Printmaking

Printmaking is the process of transferring an original image from one prepared surface to another.

Thomas Hart Benton. (American). *I Got a Girl on Sourwood Mountain.* 1938. Lithograph. 12½ x 9¼ inches. ©1988 T. H. Benton and R. P. Benton Testamentary Trusts/Licensed by VAGA, New York, NY. Courtesy of the Library of Congress, Washington, DC.

Pottery

Pottery is an object made from clay.

Artist unknown. (Chinese). *Covered Jar.* Ming Dynasty, Jiajing era. c. 1522-1566. Porcelain painted with underglaze cobalt blue and overglaze enamels. The Asia Society, New York, Mr. and Mrs. John D. Rockefeller 3rd Collection/Photo by Lynton Gardiner.

Photography

Photography is a technique of capturing an image of light on film.

Allen E. Cole. (American). *Silas Johnson.* 1920s. Hand-tinted photograph. Western Reserve Historical Society. The Allen E. Cole Collection. Cleveland, Ohio.

Mask

A mask is a covering for the face made by artists to be used in ceremonies, rituals, and other events.

Artist unknown. Abelam (Papua New Guinea). *Yam Mask.* Nineteenth century. Yam fibers. 18¾ x 13⅜ inches. Nelson-Atkins Museum of Arts, Kansas City, Missouri.

. . . and much more.

9

Using the Credit Line

The credit line is a list of important facts about the work of art. It appears below or next to the work of art and contains much useful information. For example, if you are looking at a photo of a piece of sculpture with your students, you can help them understand the size of the work as it relates to their own size. You can help them understand if the work is a six-inch piece they can hold in their hands, or a six-foot piece that would tower over them. Most credit lines have six or more facts in the following order.

- Name of the artist.
- Title of the work. This always appears in italics. If the word *detail* follows the title, it means that the image is part of a larger work of art.
- Year the work was created. A *c* before the date indicates that the piece was made around the year given.
- Medium used by the artist.
- Size of the work: The first number is the height, the second is the width, and if the work is three-dimensional, the third number indicates the depth.
- Location of the work: This tells the museum, gallery, or collection in which the work is housed and the city, state, and country. The names of the donors may also be included.

Photography is the art of making images by exposing film to light.

Pottery is the art of making objects with clay. The finished, dry object must be fired in a kiln to make it strong.

Mask is a three-dimensional face covering.

All of these works have been made by people. There are many beautiful and exciting things in this world that are natural, such as butterflies, flowers, rolling hills, sunsets, waterfalls, ocean waves, and volcanoes. They are not art. To be art, something must be planned and created by a person.

OVERVIEW

The purpose of these pages is to introduce the students to the names of the art concepts they will be learning in this book. Visual art communicates. It has a language for expressing ideas and feelings.

Activating Prior Knowledge

Ask students what they think of when they hear each of the following words: *line*, *shape*, *color*. Encourage them to look around the classroom for examples.

Questions to Discuss

Have students examine the images on pages 10 and 11. Ask them what they can tell about each word by the way it is shown on the page. Encourage them to speculate about the kind of materials that seem to make up the words that are the elements of art. Explore with them possible meanings of the drawing that represent the principles of art, as well. (Share with students information in **Art Background** about the elements and principles of art.)

Art is a language.

The words of the language are the elements of art.

Line

Shape

Color

VALUE

SPACE

FORM

TEXTURE

10

ART Background

About the Elements of Art

Each language has its own system of words and rules of grammar. To learn a new language, you need to learn new words and a new set of rules for putting the words together. The language of visual art also has its own system. The words of the language are the **elements** of art. They are the basic visual symbols in the language of art. Just as there are basic kinds of words such as nouns, verbs, adjectives, and adverbs, there are basic kinds of art elements. These are **line, shape, color, value, space, form,** and **texture.**

These elements are the visual building blocks that the artist puts together to create a work of art. No matter what materials are used, the artwork will contain all of the visual elements. Sometimes one element will be more important than the others.

Artists organize these words using the principles of art.

Rhythm

Balance

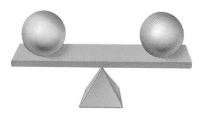

Emphasis

Variety

Harmony

Unity

11

The Principles of Art
Visual images are organized according to rules. In spoken language, these are the rules of grammar. In visual art, the rules for organizing the elements of art are called the **principles** of art. The principles that are included in this book are **rhythm, balance, emphasis, variety, harmony,** and **unity.** These principles are more like guidelines rather than hard-and-fast rules.

OVERVIEW

The purpose of these pages is to introduce the students to the three components that define or make up a work of art: the **subject,** the **composition,** and the **content.**

The **subject** is the image the viewer can easily identify in a work of art. The subject may be one person as the girl in Phillip Evergood's *Her World* and the young man in *David,* or it may be many people. It may be a thing, such as the *Parasol.* It can be an event, such as a party, or watching TV. In recent years, some artists have chosen to create nonobjective art. This is art that has no recognizable subject matter, such as Wassily Kadinsky's *Improvisation #27.* In this work of art, the elements of art become the subject. For more information and additional lessons about subject matter, see pages 222-227.

The **composition** is the way the principles of art are used to organize the elements of art. Notice how Michelangelo has organized line, form, and texture in space to create the feeling that we are looking at a handsome head of a young man with curly hair.

The **content** is the message the work communicates to the viewer. The message may be an idea, such as family unity, or an emotion or feeling, such as joy, loneliness, independence, or weariness. If the work of art is functional, such as *Parasol,* then the function is the meaning. Does the work of art look like it could perform the function it is supposed to?

Every work of art has three parts.

They are

SUBJECT

> The subject is the objects you can recognize. If a work has no objects, the elements of art are the subject.

COMPOSITION

> The composition is how the elements and principles are organized in the artwork.

CONTENT

> The content is the message or meaning of the artwork. When the work of art is functional, then the function of the work is the meaning.

Philip Evergood. (American). *Her World.* 1948. Oil on canvas. 48 x $35\frac{5}{8}$ inches. Metropolitan Museum of Art, New York.

Wassily Kandinsky. (Russian). *Improvisation #27.* 1912. Oil on canvas. $47\frac{3}{8}$ x $55\frac{1}{4}$ inches. Metropolitan Museum of Art, New York, The Alfred Stieglitz Collection, 1949.

12

Michelangelo. (Italian). *David.* (Detail). 1501–1504. Marble. Galleria dell' Accademia, Florence, Italy. Scala, Art Resource, New York.

Artist unknown. Teton, Lakota, (American). *Parasol.* Buckskin, quilled and beaded decoration. $25\frac{1}{2}$ x 23 inches. Courtesy of the Smithsonian National Museum of the American Indian, New York. George H. Bingenheimer Collection. Photo by David Heald.

In which work of art do you think the subject matter is very important?

In which artwork do you think composition is most important?

Which work seems to have the strongest message? Explain?

Which artwork's meaning relates to its function?

13

Activating Prior Knowledge

Ask students when they look at a work of art, what is the first thing they look for. (Students may say they look at color, size, or "what it's about." Some may say they look for the feeling or message they get from it. Give students time to explore this question. It will provide a good context for the discussion of these pages.)

Questions to Discuss

• Read with the students the text on page 12 and look at the images on 12 and 13. Share with them some of the information above. Encourage students to think about their responses during the Activating Prior Knowledge discussion as they look at these images and think about the information you have shared with them.

• Read the questions on page 13 and discuss the answers.
(See **Perception Hints** below for answers.)

• Encourage students to think about subject, composition, and content as they view other works of art they encounter in this text and in their environment.

Perception Hints

• The subject matter is important in *Her World* and *David*.

• Composition is most important in *Improvisation #27.*

• *Parasol* is the work in which the meaning relates to its function.

• Most students will think that *Her World* and *David* have the strongest message. However, it is important to point out that the function of a work is an important message *(Parasol)* and nonobjective work *(Improvisation #27) is* communicating through the elements and principles of art.

UNIT 1

UNIT OVERVIEW

This unit will cover the elements of line and shape. Artists use line in a variety of ways to create a mood and make their art more interesting. Shape is the element of art that is a flat, two-dimensional area.

There are five basic **kinds of lines,** with certain expressive qualities for each. The different kinds of lines and their expressive qualities are covered in Lesson 1.

Line variations are different ways lines vary in appearance. Line variations are covered in Lesson 2.

Simple geometric and free-form shapes are flat, two-dimensional areas. Simple geometric and free-form shapes are covered in Lesson 3.

Complex geometric shapes are made by combining simple geometric shapes. Complex geometric shapes are covered in Lesson 4.

Shapes in architecture are both geometric and free-form. Architectural shapes are covered in Lesson 5.

Shapes are all around us in nature, in the buildings we see, and the furniture we sit on. These and other shapes are covered in Lesson 6.

Introducing Unit Concepts

"Artists use the elements of line and shape in creating all kinds of art."

"Los artistas usan los elementos de la línea y la figura para crear todos los tipos de arte."

Line
• Have students suggest words that come to mind when you say the word *line* (e.g. fishing line, telephone line, wait in line).
• Ask students to draw a line in the air with their fingers. Have them describe the kind of line they created, e.g. straight, bent, curved, or wiggly.

Shape
• Review shapes by asking students to name as many kinds of shapes as they can remember.
• Ask students to put on their "shape eyes" and draw the main shape of an object seen anywhere in the classroom. Have the students try to identify the other objects drawn by their classmates.

An Introduction to
Line and Shape

Artists use line and shape to create all kinds of art.

Pablo Picasso. (Spanish). *Mother and Child.* 1922. Oil on canvas. 100 × 81 cm. The Baltimore Museum of Art: The Cone Collection formed by Dr. Claribel Cone and Miss Etta Cone of Baltimore, Maryland. © 1998 Estate of Pablo Picasso/Artist Rights Society (ARS), New York.

ART Background

About the Artist
Pablo Picasso (pä' blō pē käs' sō, Spanish, 1881–1973) learned to draw before he could talk. In his midteens he could draw with photographic accuracy. An innovator of many artistic styles, Picasso was also a prolific artist. He produced an estimated 50,000 works during his lifetime.

About Subject Matter* The painting is a portrait. The subject of mother and child was a recurrent theme for Picasso. In 1921, his son Paul was born and became the subject of numerous paintings and drawings. He appears in *Mother and Child,* a painting that expresses Picasso's delight with fatherhood and marriage to Olga, his first wife.

About the Media Picasso's *Mother and Child* is oil paint on canvas. He uses the paintbrush and black oil paint as an instrument to draw a variety of lines and shapes.

Artists use a variety of lines to outline objects and show details.

• Which lines outline the objects in *Mother and Child?*

• How do lines show detail in the mother's hair? Where else do you see lines that show detail?

Artists also use geometric and free-form shapes.

• What main shape did Picasso use to draw the mother and child? What kind of shapes are the leaves?

• What complex geometric shape did Picasso use for the child's right foot?

Artist **P**rofile

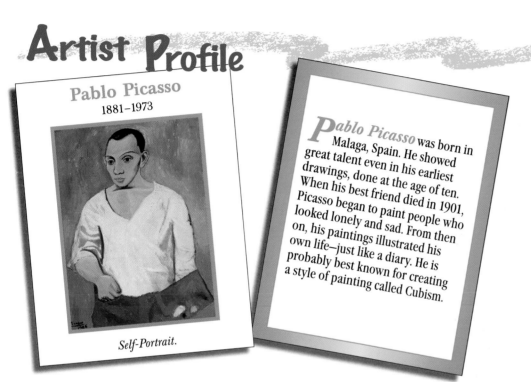

Pablo Picasso
1881–1973

Self-Portrait.

Pablo Picasso was born in Malaga, Spain. He showed great talent even in his earliest drawings, done at the age of ten. When his best friend died in 1901, Picasso began to paint people who looked lonely and sad. From then on, his paintings illustrated his own life—just like a diary. He is probably best known for creating a style of painting called Cubism.

Pablo Picasso and other artists use line and shape to help them create art. In this unit you will learn to use different kinds of lines. You will also learn how shapes are seen in everything around you. You will study:

• Kinds of Lines   • Line Variations   • Geometric and Free-Form Shapes

15

About Art History* *Mother and Child* was painted during Picasso's Classical period, which began around 1921 and lasted about six years. This style of painting and drawing was inspired by a visit to Rome, a city filled with ancient Greek and Roman sculptures and monuments.

Cultural Perspectives Although born in Spain, Picasso lived most of his life in southern France. *Mother and Child* was created shortly after the end of World War I. Newly married, Picasso found himself drifting away from his prewar artist friends and the aggressive expressions of his prewar art. It was at this time that he began to rediscover classical forms and subjects.

*See **More About** pages 206–227 for more about art history and subject matter.

You may wish to point out lines and shapes in the **Video** *Old Henry* to introduce the unit.

Examining the Artwork

"Let's look closely at the painting."
"Vamos a observar detalladamente la pintura."

• Have students look at Pablo Picasso's painting *Mother and Child.* Ask them to describe what they see in the painting.

• Have students answer questions on page 15 pertaining to line and shape in Picasso's painting. (See **Perception Hints** below.)

Artist Profile

Share with students information about the artist, including the self–portrait.

You may wish to provide a notebook that students can use as an **Art Journal** to practice art concepts and record ideas from lesson to lesson.

About Music

Line in music refers to the way a melody moves. *Shapes* also pertains to melodic contour. Have students sing a song and show the movement of the melody with their hands.

Perception Hints

Here are some examples from Picasso's painting of the concepts introduced in Unit 1.

Kinds of lines The curved lines move around the outside edges of the objects to outline them.

Line variations The curved lines show that the mother's hair is wavy. The lines on either side of her part change direction at the point where they disappear below the area that is pulled back. Lines also show detail in the leaves.

Simple geometric and free-form shapes The main shape of the mother and child together is triangular. The leaves are free-form shapes.

Complex geometric shapes The bottom of the child's right foot is a parallelogram.

UNIT 1 Planning Guide

Lesson	Lesson Title	Suggested Pacing	Create Activities	Materials	
1	Lines and What They Express	75 minutes	Draw a weather scene that causes a feeling.	12- x 18-inch white construction paper colored markers sketch paper pencils	
2	Line Variation	75 minutes	Draw a favorite place outdoors using a variety of lines.	12- x 18-inch white construction paper watercolor paints large and small brushes containers of water sketch paper pencils paper towels newspaper	
3	Shapes	75 minutes	Paint a still-life picture using lines to make shapes.	12- x 18-inch white construction paper and still-life objects liquid tempera or watercolor paints paper plates brushes of various sizes containers of water oil pastels paper towels newspaper	
4	Complex Geometric Shapes	75 minutes	Design a robot using geometric shapes.	12- x 18-inch black construction paper 9- x 12-inch construction paper, various colors scissors glue sketch paper pencils	
5	Shapes in Architecture	75 minutes	Draw a building using geometric and free-form shapes.	12- x 18-inch construction paper black felt-tip pens markers, assorted colors	
6	Shapes All Around Us	75 minutes	Draw a portrait using geometric and free-form shapes.	12- x 18-inch colored construction paper dustless chalk oil pastels	
Artsource Lesson	Lines and Shapes in Dance	75 minutes	Create an original eagle dance.	pictures of eagles in different positions	

Test preparation activities using the Large Prints *Fur Traders Descending the Missouri* and *Portrait of a Lady* can be found on pages 8–11 of the Test Preparation Book.

Program Resources (Books)	Art Resources	Literature Resources	*Music Resources
Vocabulary, pp. 1-2 Assessment, pp. 1-2 Art Across the Curriculum Resource Book, pp. 1-6 Technique Tips Flip Chart, p. 1 Lesson Plans Book, p. 2 Home Connection, pp. 5 and 6	Overhead Transparency #1, *Orion in December* and *Bridge over a Pool of Water Lilies* Artist Profile Book, pp. 2, 34 Large Prints, *Fur Traders Descending the Missouri* and *Portrait of a Lady*	**1.** *Time of Wonder* (1985) by Robert McCloskey demonstrates curves and lines found in nature. **2.** *Linnea in Monet's Garden* (1987) by Christina Bjork is a fictional account of a young girl's adventure in Monet's gardens, including facts on the artist's life and work.	"Clair de Lune," from *Suite Bergamasca* by Claude Debussy, p. T359G, CD9:9. One of the most famous pieces for piano, "Clair de Lune" was written in France in the late 1800s.
Vocabulary, pp. 3-4 Assessment, pp. 3-4 Art Across the Curriculum Resource Book, pp. 7-12 Technique Tips Flip Chart, p. 2 Lesson Plans Book, p. 3	Overhead Transparency #2, *Improvisation No. 27* and *The Three Stars of Happiness, Wealth, and Longevity* Artist Profile Book, pp. 24, 52 Large Prints, *Fur Traders Descending the Missouri* and *Portrait of a Lady* **1.** *Knots on a Counting Rope*	(1987) by Bill Martin Jr. and John Archambault has animated watercolor illustrations highlighting the use of portraiture, color, and landscape. **2.** *Lon Po Po: A Red Riding Hood Story from China* (1989) by Ed Young is a Chinese tale, combining ancient Chinese panel art and contemporary watercolors and pastels.	"It Don't Mean a Thing If It Ain't Got That Swing," by Duke Ellington and Irving Mills, p. T246, CD5:19. "It Don't Mean a Thing If It Ain't Got That Swing" is an example of jazz, a twentieth-century musical style that uses improvision.
Vocabulary, pp. 5-6 Assessment, pp. 5-6 Art Across the Curriculum Resource Book, pp. 13-18 Technique Tips Flip Chart, p. 3 Lesson Plans Book, p. 4	Overhead Transparency #3, *Roses, Convolvulus, Poppies and Other Flowers in an Urn on a Stone Ledge* and *Arcanum* Artist Profile Book, pp. 13, 46 Large Prints, *Fur Traders Descending the Missouri* and *Portrait of a Lady*	**1.** *Polar Express* (1985) by Chris Van Allsburg is a magical train ride to the North Pole full of geometric and free-form shapes and illustrates use of modeling, line, and shadow. **2.** *More Shapes and Stories: A Book about Pictures* (1967) by Geoffrey and Jane Gregson offers interesting information about unusual, well-chosen paintings.	*"Eine Kleine Nachtmusik"* (First Movement), by Wolfgang Amadeus Mozart, p. T 359E, CD9:8. *"Eine Kleine Nachtmusik"* is an example of music from the 1700s.
Vocabulary, pp. 7-8 Assessment, pp. 7-8 Art Across the Curriculum Resource Book, pp. 19-24 Technique Tips Flip Chart, p. 4 Lesson Plans Book, p. 5	Overhead Transparency #4, *Sioux Double Saddlebag* and *Mihrab* Artist Profile Book, pp. 55, 56 Large Print, *Fur Traders Descending the Missouri* **1.** *Crow Boy* (1983) by Taro	Yashima has skillful examples of manipulating space, line, and color to create complex shapes in well-designed illustrations. **2.** *The Cut-Outs of Henri Matisse* (1978) by John Elderfield discusses the beginning and evolution of Matisse's cut-outs, including photographs large enough to share or make into slides.	"Lakota Honor Song," p. T129, CD3:40. "Lakota Honor Song" is an example of Native American music.
Vocabulary, pp. 9-10 Assessment, pp. 9-10 Art Across the Curriculum Resource Book, pp. 25-30 Technique Tips Flip Chart, p. 5 Lesson Plans Book, p. 6	Overhead Transparency #5, *Nos. 4, 6, and 8 Fifth Avenue*, and *Sunset Dance-Ceremony to the Evening Sun* Artist Profile Book, pp. 1, 49 Large Prints, *Fur Traders Descending the Missouri* and *Portrait of a Lady*	**1.** *Have You Seen Josephine?* (1986) by Giles Tibo illustrates lines in buildings or everyday shapes of people, nature, and ordinary objects. **2.** *The Inside Outside Book of Washington DC* (1987) by Roxie Munroe is a wordless picture book of intricately sketched historical buildings from this nation's capital, detailing architectural motifs.	"Three Little Words," from *Trio Jeepy*, by B. Kalmar and H. Ruby, p. T215, CD5:40. "Three Little Words" is a jazz piece that features the double bass player Milt Hinton.
Vocabulary, pp. 11-12 Assessment, pp. 11-12 Art Across the Curriculum Resource Book, pp. 31-36 Technique Tips Flip Chart, p. 6 Lesson Plans Book, p. 7	Overhead Transparency #6, *Daniel Crommelin Verplanck* and *Silas Johnson* Artist Profile Book, pp. 6, 7 Large Prints, *Fur Traders Descending the Missouri* and *Portrait of a Lady*	**1.** *Just Plain Fancy* (1990) by Patricia Polacco is about an Amish girl who is horrified when a fancy bird hatches into her simplistic lifestyle. The book uses gestural, skilled color usage applied to different types of line and portraiture. **2.** *On Market St.* (1981) by Anita Lobel uses artistic creativity to reinforce the shapes all around us concept by illustrating a humorous account with free-form shapes.	"In the Good Old Summertime," by George Evans and Ron Shields, p. T305, CD7:31-32. "In the Good Old Summertime" is an American popular song from the early twentieth century.
	Artsource Performing Arts Audio/Video Resource Package: *Eagle Dance* (videocassette)		

*Music references are from **Share the Music,** Macmillan/McGraw-Hill School Publishers

LESSON PLANNER

Objectives

After completing this lesson, students will be able to:

- identify five different kinds of lines and their expressive qualities. *Aesthetic Perception*
- plan and create a weather scene using lines to express a feeling or mood. *Creative Expression*
- use the four steps of art criticism to evaluate their own drawings. *Art Criticism*
- demonstrate knowledge of the life and work of both artists. *Art History and Culture*

Program Resources

- **Overhead:** Both the Burchfield and the Monet are available on overhead 1.
- **Large Prints:** *Fur Traders Descending the Missouri* by George Caleb Bingham and *Portrait of a Lady* by Rogier van der Weyden
- **Technique Tips Flip Chart,** page 1
- **Vocabulary Book** pages 1–2
- **Artist Profiles Book:** Burchfield page 2 and Monet page 34
- **Art Across the Curriculum Book** pages 1–6
- **Multimedia Workshop CD-ROM**
- **Assessment Book** pages 1–2

Multiple Intelligences

Intrapersonal Awareness and expression of different feelings are often created by artists through the use of lines.

Vocabulary

line *linea* a mark drawn by a tool such as a pencil, pen, or paintbrush as it moves across a surface

vertical *vertical* lines that move straight up and down

horizontal *horizontal* lines that move straight across from side to side

diagonal *diagonal* lines that are slanted

zigzag *en zigzag* diagonal lines that connect

curved *curva* lines that bend and change direction slowly

Lines and What They Express

Artists use different kinds of lines to create a mood or feeling in a painting or drawing.

Charles Burchfield. (American). *Orion in December.*
1959. Watercolor and pencil on paper.
$39\frac{7}{8} \times 32\frac{7}{8}$ inches. National Museum of American Art, Washington, DC, Art Resource, NY.

Look at the two landscape paintings on these pages. *Orion in December* was painted by Charles Burchfield. *Bridge over a Pool of Water Lilies* was painted by Claude Monet about sixty years earlier. Both artists have used lines to express a mood felt in nature. Compare the moods of the two paintings.

16 Unit **1**

ART Background

About the Artists

Charles Burchfield (chärlz bûrch' fēld, American, 1893–1967) was born in Ohio. Many of his paintings are on display in museums in Buffalo, New York, where he lived. He favored watercolor to paint his visionary landscapes, often layering colors until the surface of the finished work had the appearance of oil paint.

Claude Monet (klōd mō nā', French, 1840–1926) was one of the first artists to take his paints and canvases outside and paint the subject directly, instead of in a studio. Monet realized that the colors of a subject changed as the day progressed.

About Subject Matter* Both the Burchfield and the Monet are landscape paintings.

About the Media The Burchfield painting is a watercolor, which is a pigment mixed with gum arabic and water. The Monet is an oil painting, which is a ground pigment suspended in oil. (Oil paints can be opaque or transparent.)

Claude Monet. (French). *Bridge over a Pool of Water Lilies.*
1899. Oil on canvas. $36\frac{1}{2} \times 29$ inches. Metropolitan
Museum of Art, New York, New York.

Study both landscape paintings.

☑ Find the vertical lines.

☑ Find the horizontal lines.

☑ Identify the diagonal lines.

☑ Where are the curved lines in each painting?

☑ Find the lines that zigzag.

SEEING LIKE
AN ARTIST

Look outside your
classroom. Look for
things such as trees,
leaves, and grass. Find
lines like the ones you
found in the landscape
paintings.

Lesson **1**   **17**

About Art History★ Burchfield painted during the ragtime and jazz era of American
music. During the 1940s, movie musicals popularized many dance styles.

Monet's painting was done in France during a time when some artists departed from
tradition and painted an "impression" of light and color.

Cultural Perspectives Burchfield loved nature, as did other American artists such as
George Inness and Frederic Church.

Monet painted when people resented tyranny and wanted their rights. Artists wanted
freedom from both the old styles and the strict rules that dominated the world of art.

*See **More About** pages 206–227 for more about art history and subject matter.

Activating Prior Knowledge
"Think about lines you see outside in nature."
*"Piensen acerca de las líneas que pueden observar en la
naturaleza."*

• Have students use their arms to demonstrate
lines seen in a winding road, running water,
tall grass blowing in the wind, and lightning
during a rainstorm.

Introducing the Art
"Let's look closely at the two paintings."
"Vamos a observar detalladamente las dos pinturas."

• **Describe:** Have students describe the subject
matter in each painting. (both: landscapes)
• Share and discuss information from **Art
Background** and the **Artist Profiles Book**.
• Have students answer the questions on page
17. (See **Perception Hints** below.)
• **COMPARE AND CONTRAST** Have students list
the similarities and differences in the two
paintings. (Both are outdoor scenes, show a wooded
area, and show different kinds of lines. Burchfield's
painting is a nighttime scene and shows sky, while
Monet's painting is a daytime scene and shows water.
The horizontal direction of the lines in the Monet gives
a feeling of calm or peace. The strong, vertical lines in
the Burchfield give a feeling of strength and steadiness.)

FOR THE ART SPECIALIST

Use the **Overhead** and the **Large Print**
Fur Traders Descending the Missouri to
demonstrate that lines create a mood or
feeling.

Perception Hints

Vertical lines *Burchfield.* Strong, black vertical lines
emphasize the trees in the middle ground.
Horizontal lines *Monet.* The water lilies are horizontal.
Diagonal lines *Monet.* The tall grass is diagonal.
Curved lines *Monet.* Curved lines illustrate the shape of
the bridge. *Burchfield.* Curved lines emphasize the stars.
Zigzag lines *Burchfield.* Zigzag lines in some areas
indicate the texture of the trees.

TEACH

Time: About two 30-minute periods

Practice
Materials
- 12- × 18-inch paper
- markers

Alternate Materials: pencils

"How can you use lines to show different kinds of weather?"

"¿Cómo se pueden usar las líneas para mostrar diferentes tipos de clima?"

- Review the five different kinds of lines and the expressive qualities of each on page 18.
- Distribute the materials and have students follow the directions on page 18 for using lines to illustrate each of the weather conditions. Have them answer the Decide questions orally.

Create PROBLEM SOLVING
Materials
- 12- × 18-inch white construction paper
- colored markers • sketch paper • pencils

Alternate Materials: pencils, crayons, paints, or oil pastels

"Let's use different kinds of lines to draw a scene."

"Vamos a usar diferentes tipos de líneas para dibujar una escena."

- Have students identify a variety of weather conditions and the mood conveyed by each.
- Review line names and their expressive qualities.

 See page 1 in the **Technique Tips Flip Chart** for visual examples of techniques.

- Distribute materials and have students follow the directions on page 19.
- Review procedures for using markers in **More About Technique Tips** on page 196.

Safety! For safety issues about markers and other information about safety in the art classroom, see page T22.

FOR THE ART SPECIALIST

Have students use a combination of pencils, crayons, paints, or oil pastels to make an expressive media weather scene.

Using Lines

Lines are marks drawn by a tool such as a pencil, pen, or paintbrush as it moves across a surface. There are five different kinds of lines. Each one can make you feel a certain way.

 Vertical lines move straight up and down. They make things look tall, steady, and calm.

 Horizontal lines move straight across from side to side. They give a feeling of calm or peace.

 Diagonal lines are slanted. They look as if they are falling over or getting up. They make things look active.

 Zigzag lines are diagonal lines that connect. They give a feeling of excitement.

 Curved lines bend and change direction slowly. They give a feeling of graceful movement.

Practice

Use different kinds of lines to create a weather chart. Use white paper and markers.

1. Fold a sheet of paper into six equal boxes. Each box will show a different weather condition that occurs in nature—strong wind, rainstorm, and blizzard. Write the name of one of the weather conditions at the bottom of each box.

2. Use different kinds of lines like the ones above to draw the weather condition written at the bottom of each box.

Decide When you look at each box, does it show the feeling of the weather condition? How can you change the lines to improve them?

Activities in ART Across the Curriculum Book

Reading/Language Arts Write a travel advertisement for the places in the painting or a place that you would like to visit. (page 1)

Math Use lines on clocks to tell time. (page 2)

Science Identify a constellation and see it at different times of the year. (page 3)

Social Studies Learn more about different kinds of natural environments like those depicted in the painting. (page 4)

The Arts Understand how lines and movement relate in dance. (page 5)

Technology Use the *Multimedia Workshop* CD-ROM to draw a weather scene that causes you to feel a certain way. (page 6)

Anna Boynton. Age 8. *Twister.* Markers.

How does this student artist's weather scene make you feel?

Create

How do different kinds of weather make you feel? Draw a weather scene that causes you to have a certain feeling.

1. Think about the different kinds of weather where you live. What mood does each create?

2. Select the type of weather condition you would like to draw. Make a rough sketch to plan the scene. Experiment with different kinds of lines. Decide which lines will best express the mood you wish to create.

3. Draw your scene. Be sure to use the right kinds of lines to create a calm or active feeling.

Describe Name the different kinds of lines you used in your drawing.

Analyze Is the scene calm or active? How do the lines show this feeling?

Interpret If you were to change the lines, how would the mood or feeling be different?

Decide Did you successfully use lines to show a calm or active scene? If you could do this drawing over again, how would you change it?

Lesson 1 19

Change Use the paintings to show changes that occur in geographic environments, shifts in seasons, and weather.

Systems Use the paintings as a visual example of our ecosystem and its components.

Patterns Use the paintings as an introduction to the study and understanding of astronomy and the patterns of the stars.

ESL students will need definitions of the five different kinds of lines to be able to participate in the comparison of the two paintings. You may wish to make a chart of the types of lines for ESL students to use as a reference.

CLOSE
Time: About 5 minutes

"What moods can you create with curved, straight, zigzag, and diagonal lines?"

"¿Qué ánimos pueden crear con líneas curvas, rectas, en zigzag y diagonales?"

 Review
Use the **Large Print** *Portrait of a Lady* to have students compare the expressive quality of lines to the works in this lesson.

Art Criticism
Have students answer the four art criticism questions—Describe, Analyze, Interpret, and Decide—orally or in writing. Discuss the use of lines in their drawings.

 Assess
Use the **Assessment Book** pages 1–2 as a formal assessment for this lesson.

Evaluation Criteria
• Can the student name the five different kinds of lines and their expressive qualities?
• Can the student incorporate a variety of lines to create a mood or feeling in a drawing?
• Can the student use the four steps of art criticism to evaluate his or her own work?
• Can the student demonstrate knowledge of the artists' lives and work?

Reteaching ● ● ● ● ● ● ● ● ● ●

Lines Have students look around the classroom to find an example for each of the five lines. Ask them to identify the objects and name the lines in each.

Perception Hints for Student Art
Answers will vary. Students may say the scene makes them feel excited and scared because of the zigzag lines.

Line Variation

Artists can change lines in a variety of ways to make their artwork more interesting.

Wassily Kandinsky. (Russian). *Improvisation No. 27.* 1912. Oil paint. $47\frac{3}{8} \times 55\frac{1}{4}$ inches. Metropolitan Museum of Art, New York, New York.

LESSON PLANNER

Objectives
After completing this lesson, students will be able to:
- identify ways that lines can vary in appearance. *Aesthetic Perception*
- plan and create a landscape painting, using a variety of lines. *Creative Expression*
- use the four steps of art criticism to evaluate their own paintings. *Art Criticism*
- demonstrate knowledge of the lives and work of both artists. *Art History and Culture*

Program Resources
- **Overhead:** Both the Kandinsky and the Wang are available on overhead 2.
- **Large Prints:** *Fur Traders Descending the Missouri* by George Caleb Bingham and *Portrait of a Lady* by Rogier van der Weyden
- **Technique Tips Flip Chart,** page 2
- **Vocabulary Book** pages 3–4
- **Art Manipulative Kit:** flash cards
- **Artist Profiles Book:** Kandinsky page 24 and Wang page 52
- **Art Across the Curriculum Book** pages 7–12
- **Multimedia Workshop CD-ROM**
- **Assessment Book** pages 3–4

Multiple Intelligences
Visual/Spatial Image manipulation and active imagination can occur when students use a variety of lines.

Vocabulary
line variety *variedad lineal* short or long, thick or thin, rough or smooth, and broken or solid.

The following words appear as art in the Student Edition page 22: *short, long, thick, thin, rough, smooth, broken,* and *solid.*

Look at the two paintings on these pages. *Improvisation No. 27* is a nonobjective painting by Wassily Kandinsky. Wang Chao's scroll painting was created around 400 years earlier. Even though both artists used lines, both paintings are very different. Wang used line to describe people and objects. Kandinsky used line as part of the subject.

FOCUS

Time: About 10 minutes

Activating Prior Knowledge

"Think about lines you see in a tree. How do lines in the trunk of the tree look different from lines in its branches?"

"Piensen acerca de las líneas que observan en un árbol. ¿Cómo las líneas en el tronco del árbol se diferencian de las líneas de sus ramas?"

- Discuss student responses and how the lines are different widths.

 # ART *Background*

About the Artists

Wassily Kandinsky (və sēl´ yē kan din´ skē, Russian, 1866–1944) was born in Moscow and gave up a career in law to study painting in Munich, Germany. After looking at one of his paintings resting on its side, he discovered the beauty of colors and shapes on their own as entities. As a result, he was the first artist to abandon recognizable reality and create nonobjective paintings.

Wang Chao (wong chou, Chinese, active 1500–1525) receives little attention in biographies about Chinese artists. Although admired for his expressive style of painting, he is portrayed as an eccentric personality.

About Subject Matter* The Kandinsky is nonobjective. The Wang is narrative.

About the Media The Kandinsky is an oil painting, made of a ground pigment suspended in oil. The Wang is painted with ink, a colored liquid used for drawing and painting.

Wang Chao. (Chinese). *The Three Stars of Happiness, Wealth, and Longevity.* c. 1500. Hanging scroll. Ink and light colors on silk. $62\frac{1}{2} \times 37\frac{1}{2}$ inches. Courtesy of the Kimbell Art Museum, Fort Worth, Texas.

Study both paintings to find a variety of different lines.

✓ Find lines that are long and lines that are short.

✓ Find lines that are thick and lines that are thin.

✓ Do you see any lines that look rough? Where are they? Find the lines that look smooth.

✓ Where do you see lines that move in different directions?

SEEING LIKE
AN ARTIST

Look around your classroom. Find lines like the ones you saw in the paintings.

Lesson **2**

21

About Art History* Kandinsky painted in Munich when artists believed that art should express feelings and experiences rather than scenes and objects.

Wang painted at a time when the ritual and ceremony of Chinese plays included music and costumes to dramatize myths, history, and legends.

Cultural Perspectives Kandinsky painted in Germany until World War I forced his return to Russia. The Russian people were left completely demoralized when they suffered more than 1 million casualties in their battles against the Germans.

Wang's painting illustrates a trio of Taoist deities known as the Three Stars of Happiness, Wealth, and Longevity.

*See **More About** pages 206–227 for more about art history and subject matter.

Introducing the Art

"Let's take a close look at the two paintings."
"Vamos a observar detalladamente las dos pinturas."

• **Describe:** Have students describe the subject matter in each painting. (Kandinsky: nonobjective; Wang: narrative)

• Share and discuss information from **Art Background** and the **Artist Profiles Book**.

• Have students answer the questions on page 21. (See **Perception Hints** below.)

• **COMPARE AND CONTRAST** Have students make a list of the similarities and differences in the two paintings. (Both paintings show a variety of lines and incorporate black brush strokes. Wang's painting shows mostly lines and has people and a limited color scheme. Kandinsky's painting has no people and shows broad, flat areas of bright colors, as well as lines.)

FOR THE ART SPECIALIST

Use the **Overhead** and the **Large Print** *Fur Traders Descending the Missouri* or *Portrait of a Lady* to demonstrate how an artist can change lines in a variety of ways to make his or her artwork more interesting.

Perception Hints

Long and short lines *Wang.* There are long lines in the clothing worn by the men. Short lines make up the texture of the grass.

Thick and thin lines *Wang.* There are thick lines in the collars of the clothing, and thin lines make up the pine needles located at the top.

Rough and smooth lines *Kandinsky.* There are rough, red lines in the central yellow area, and smooth lines in the upper right-hand corner.

Lines that move *Wang.* The eye moves down the mountain, across the shoulders, down the sleeves, and back up to the stick held by the figure at the left.

TEACH

Time: About two 30-minute periods

Practice

Materials
- 9- × 12-inch paper
- crayons

Alternate Materials: pencils

"How can you use crayons in different ways to create line variations?"

"¿Cómo se pueden usar de diferentes maneras los creyones para crear variaciones lineales?"

- Discuss the ways to create variations in line on page 22.
- Distribute materials and have students follow the directions on page 22 for illustrating line variations. Encourage them to experiment with crayons and fill the page with a variety of lines.
- Have them share their answers to the Decide questions.

Create PROBLEM SOLVING

Materials
- 12- × 18-inch white construction paper
- watercolor paints
- large and small brushes
- containers of water
- newspaper
- paper towels
- pencils
- sketch paper

Alternate Materials: broad and thin markers

"Let's use line variations to paint a landscape."

"Vamos a usar variaciones lineales para pintar un paisaje."

- Have students brainstorm a variety of places they might visit. They can look through travel brochures, magazines, and books for ideas.
- Review ways to create variations in line.
- Review procedures for working with watercolor paint in **More About Technique Tips** on page 200.
- See page 2 in the **Technique Tips Flip Chart** for visual examples of techniques.
- Distribute materials and have students follow the directions on page 23.

FOR THE ART SPECIALIST

Have students use broad and thin markers to create a landscape with a variety of lines.

Using a Variety of Lines

Artists can change lines in many ways to make them look different. You saw **line variety** in the two paintings on the previous pages.

Lines can be **long** or **short**.

Lines can be **thick** or **thin**.

Lines can be **rough** or **smooth**.

Lines can be **broken** or **solid**.

Practice

Draw a variety of lines. Use white paper and crayons.

1. Use crayon to make as many different kinds of lines as you can on a sheet of paper.

2. Now use your crayon in different ways to make rough, smooth, thick, and thin lines.

Decide Have you filled your page with a variety of lines? Did you use your crayon in different ways to change how the lines look?

Activities in ART Across the Curriculum Book

Reading/Language Arts Describe characters in *The Three Stars of Happiness, Wealth, and Longevity* using specific words. (page 7)

Math Estimate and measure a variety of lines. (page 8)

Science Learn more about changes caused by weather in a mountain environment like the one depicted in the painting by Wang Chao. (page 9)

Social Studies Study lines in the letters of the alphabet. (page 10)

The Arts Create variations to "Twinkle, Twinkle, Little Star," as an artist would create a variety of lines in an artwork. (page 11)

Technology Use the *Multimedia Workshop* CD-ROM to draw a picture using different kinds of lines. (page 12)

Heather Byrnes. Age 8. *On the Farm.* Watercolors.

What are the different types of lines this student artist used in her landscape?

Create

What does your favorite outdoor place look like? Draw it using a variety of lines.

1. Think about your favorite place. Is it the beach? A lake? A park? A farm? The mountains? What objects would you find there?

2. Using different kinds of lines, make several sketches of the objects you want to include in your landscape.

3. Use watercolor paints to create the landscape. Use large and small brushes to make many different kinds of lines.

Describe Describe the objects you included in your landscape painting.

Analyze List the different kinds of lines you used in your painting.

Interpret How do the lines you used affect the mood or feeling of your painting?

Decide Did you successfully use a variety of lines to paint the objects in your landscape?

Lesson 2 23

"What are some ways you can vary the texture, curve, and width of lines?"

"¿Cuáles son algunas formas de variar la textura, la curva y el ancho de las líneas?"

 Review

Use the **Large Print** *Fur Traders Descending the Missouri* to have students identify line variations.

Art Criticism

Have students answer the four art criticism questions—Describe, Analyze, Interpret, and Decide—orally or in writing.

 Assess

Use the **Assessment Book** pages 3–4 as a formal assessment for this lesson.

Evaluation Criteria

- Can the student use appropriate vocabulary to identify a variety of lines?
- Can the student incorporate a variety of lines in a painting?
- Can the student use the four steps of art criticism to evaluate his or her own work?
- Can the student demonstrate knowledge of both artists' lives and work?

Reteaching • • • • • • • • • • •

Line variations Have students use the flash cards in the **Art Manipulative Kit** to understand and illustrate line variations.

 THEME Connections

Cultures Use the paintings as examples of cultures that are different from our own.

Traditions Use the paintings as vehicles for comparing and contrasting Eastern and Western views regarding traditions.

Perspective Use the paintings as a means to open discussion about the differences in the Eastern and Western perspective.

 ESL

ESL students may need your support to discuss their own artwork. Instead of asking them to describe, analyze, interpret, and decide on their own, ask them specific questions that will allow nonverbal responses such as pointing or saying *yes/no*. For example, you might say: *Find the lines that make your painting feel peaceful.*

Perception Hints for Student Art

The lines are *horizontal, long* and *short, thick* and *thin, solid* and *broken*: area in front of house and on the sides. *Vertical*: grass; *curved*: sun; *zigzag*: hills; *diagonal*: sky.

UNIT 1
LESSON 3

Shapes

Artists use lines to create shapes.

Rachel Ruysch. (Dutch). *Roses, Convolvulus, Poppies and Other Flowers in an Urn on a Stone Ledge.* c. 1745. Oil on canvas. $42\frac{1}{2} \times 33$ inches. The National Museum of Women in the Arts, Washington, DC, Gift of Wallace and Wilhelmina Holladay.

Look at the paintings on these pages. Rachel Ruysch created her painting about flowers around 1745. *Arcanum* was painted by artist Janet Fish more than 200 years later! Both artists have used lines to create the shapes in their paintings.

LESSON PLANNER

Objectives
After completing this lesson, students will be able to:
- identify the use of simple geometric and free-form shapes. *Aesthetic Perceptions*
- plan and create a still-life painting using simple geometric and free-form shapes. *Creative Expression*
- use the four steps of art criticism to evaluate their own paintings. *Art Criticism*
- demonstrate knowledge of the lives and cultures of both artists. *Art History and Culture*

Program Resources
- **Overhead:** Both the Ruysch and the Fish are available on overhead 3.
- **Large Prints:** *Fur Traders Descending the Missouri* by George Caleb Bingham and *Portrait of a Lady* by Rogier van der Weyden
- **Technique Tips Flip Chart,** page 3
- **Vocabulary Book** pages 5–6
- **Art Manipulative Kit:** shapes
- **Artist Profiles Book:** Ruysch page 46 and Fish page 13
- **Art Across the Curriculum Book** pages 13–18
- **Multimedia Workshop CD-ROM**
- **National Museum of Women in the Arts Collection Prints**
- **Assessment Book** pages 5–6

Multiple Intelligences
Body/Kinesthetic The mind/body connection can be made into shapes in art as the student thinks about each shape that his or her hand creates. Shapes can be formed in the air with the hand.

Vocabulary
shapes *figuras* flat, two-dimensional areas that are either geometric or free-form

free-form *forma abstracta* shapes that are uneven and are not regular

geometric *geométrica* shapes that can be defined using mathematical formulas. Examples: circle, square, triangle, oval, and rectangle

ART Background

About the Artists
Rachel Ruysch (rā′ chəl rois, Dutch, 1664–1750) was the daughter of a botanist and a still-life painter, primarily of florals. She tended to use darker colors as she painted with painstaking and precise naturalism. There are only about 100 known paintings that she created in her lifetime.

Janet Fish (jan′ ət fish, American, 1938–) is a still-life painter of everyday, commonplace objects, usually glassware. When arranging a still life, she surrounds herself with objects and selects the ones that are compatible and have interesting color relationships.

About Subject Matter* Both the Ruysch and the Fish are still-life paintings.

About the Media Both the Ruysch and the Fish are oil paintings made of pigments suspended in oil. The medium comes in lush colors and provides a durable finish.

Janet Fish. (American). *Arcanum.* 1990. Oil on canvas. 80 × 50 inches. Courtesy Janet Fish and D.C. Moore Gallery, New York, New York.

Study both still-life paintings to find the following shapes.

- ✓ Find as many round shapes as you can.
- ✓ Find the square shapes.
- ✓ Where are the triangles?
- ✓ Are there any oval shapes? Where?
- ✓ Locate the free-form shapes.

SEEING LIKE AN ARTIST

Think about or look outside and find different shapes found in your environment.

Lesson **3**

25

About Art History* Ruysch's painting was done at a time when most artists specialized in one type of painting and were especially interested in the dramatic use of light. The term *still life* was invented by the Dutch.

Fish is painting during a time in the United States in which many women are working outside the home and gaining equal status in the workplace.

Cultural Perspectives Ruysch painted during a time when the Dutch Republic grew rich through trade with faraway places. There was no aristocracy. Wealthy shopkeepers and merchants commissioned art. Women artists were not taken seriously.

Fish's painting was done during the rock era of American music. Playwrights addressed the concerns of ethnic and other groups.

*See **More About** pages 206–227 for more about art history and subject matter.

FOCUS

Time: About 10 minutes

Activating Prior Knowledge

"Think about lines you use when you write your name. Which letters have lines that come around and close themselves back up?"

"Piensen acerca de las líneas que usan al escribir sus nombres. ¿Qué letras tienen líneas que dan una vuelt entera y se cierran hacia arriba?"

- Call students up to the board to write letters in which the lines create shapes.

Introducing the Art

"Let's look closely at the two paintings."

"Vamos a observar detalladamente las dos pinturas."

- **Describe:** Have students describe the subject matter in the paintings. (both: still lifes)
- Share and discuss information from **Art Background** and the **Artist Profiles Book.**
- Have them answer questions on page 25. (See **Perception Hints** below.)
- **COMPARE AND CONTRAST** Have students make a list of the similarities and differences in the two paintings. (Both still lifes contain floral arrangements, use bright and dark colors, and are realistic in style. Ruysch's painting depicts one floral arrangement, but Fish's painting is filled with many different objects. Ruysch's painting has primarily free-form shapes, while Fish's has a wide variety of both geometric and free-form shapes.)

FOR THE ART SPECIALIST

Use the **Overhead** and the **Large Print** *Fur Traders Descending the Missouri* or *Portrait of a Lady* to demonstrate how artists use lines to create shapes.

Perception Hints

Round shapes *Fish.* Fishbowl, globe, candle.
Square shapes *Ruysch.* Window in background.
Triangles *Fish.* Seashells on the left-hand side.
Oval *Fish.* The top of the goblet.
Free-form Flowers in both.

TEACH

Time: About two 30-minute periods

Practice

"Look around the room and find objects that have geometric and free-form shapes."

"Observen alrededor del salón y busquen objetos que tengan figuras geométricas y abstractas."

- Discuss information about simple geometric and free-form shapes on page 26.
- Illustrate main shapes by tracing the outside edge of an object with your finger.
- Have students follow the directions on page 26 for finding the main shape of an object. Have them answer the Decide question.

Create PROBLEM SOLVING

Materials

- 12- × 18-inch white construction paper
- liquid tempera *or* watercolor paints
- still-life objects
- brushes of various sizes
- paper plates
- containers of water
- paper towels
- oil pastels
- newspaper

Alternate Materials: watercolors

Safety Tip
For safety issues about tempera and other information about safety in the art classroom, see page T22.

"Let's use simple geometric and free-form shapes in a still-life painting."

"Vamos a usar figuras geométricas y abstractas en una pintura de naturaleza muerta."

- Have students identify special objects of various sizes for a still-life arrangement.
- Review simple geometric and free-form shapes.
- Review tips for working with tempera paint in **More About Technique Tips** page 199.

See page 3 in the **Technique Tips Flip Chart** for visual examples of techniques.

- Distribute the materials and have students follow the directions on page 27.

FOR THE ART SPECIALIST

Have students use oil pastels to outline a still life and fill the shapes by smearing different colors.

Using Shapes

Everything has a **shape**. They are flat, two-dimensional areas that are either geometric or free-form.

Here are some simple **geometric** shapes.

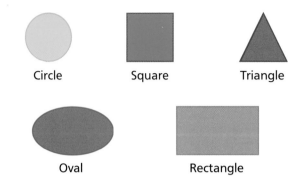

Circle   Square   Triangle

Oval   Rectangle

Free-form shapes are uneven and are not regular. They can look many different ways:

Lines can be used to outline all these shapes.

Practice

Outline geometric and free-form shapes.

1. Find three geometric and three free-form shapes in your classroom.

2. In the air, use your index finger to trace the outline of each object. Close one eye as you trace.

Decide Did you notice how the tip of your finger made a line in the air when you traced the outline of each object?

Activities in
ART Across the Curriculum Book

Reading/Language Arts Write descriptive phrases using shape words.(page 13)

Math Sort a list of objects by their geometric shapes. (page 14)

Science Learn more about flowers and plants like those in the painting by Rachel Ruysch. (page 15)

Social Studies Using a map of the United States, identify areas where the climate would be appropriate to grow flowers similar to those shown in the artworks. (page 16)

The Arts Write a dialogue referring to images in the painting *Arcanum.* (page 17)

Technology Use the *Multimedia Workshop* CD-ROM to draw a picture using geometric and free-form shapes. (page 18)

Kitzia Medina. Age 8. *Still Life.* Watercolors and oil pastels.

What geometric shapes do you see in this student artist's still life?

Create

What are some of the shapes you see in the objects around you? Paint a still-life picture using lines to make shapes.

1. Arrange five objects of different shapes and sizes in a variety of ways. Select the best arrangement.

2. Which object captures your attention most? Outline the shape of that object on your paper. In the same way, add the shapes of the other objects.

3. Begin to fill your shapes with different colors. Use one color at a time in several places on your picture. Continue to do this until your paper is filled with color.

Describe What geometric shapes did you use in your painting? What free-form shapes did you use in your painting?

Analyze What types of lines did you use to create the shapes?

Interpret Look at the first object you drew on your paper. Why did you decide to draw that object?

Decide If you could redo your painting, what would you do differently?

Lesson 3

27

Cultures Use the paintings as a springboard for exploring the Japanese art of ikebana, or flower making.

Identity Use the paintings to discuss what items in a still life would best represent who they (the students) are.

Celebrations Use the paintings to open discussions concerning how and why flowers are used as gifts for celebrations in our society.

ESL students will profit from working with peers during the Create section of the lesson. The support of partners will help them comprehend and discuss the artwork they are creating. If possible, pair each student with a peer who speaks the student's native language.

CLOSE
Time: About 5 minutes

"What is the difference between a geometric shape and a free-form shape?"

"¿Cuál es la diferencia entre una figura geométrica y una figura abstracta?"

Review

Use the **National Museum of Women in the Arts Collection** prints to have students compare the shapes in the prints to those in the lesson.

Art Criticism

Have students answer the four art criticism questions—Describe, Analyze, Interpret, and Decide—orally or in writing. Discuss the use of shapes in their artwork.

Assess
Use the **Assessment Book** pages 5–6 as a formal assessment for this lesson.

Evaluation Criteria

• Can the student identify simple geometric and free-form shapes?

• Can the student incorporate simple geometric and free-form shapes in a still-life painting?

• Can the student use the four steps of art criticism to evaluate his or her own work?

• Can the student demonstrate knowledge of both artists' lives and cultures?

Reteaching ● ● ● ● ● ● ● ● ● ● ●

Shapes Use the **Art Manipulative Kit** to have students create an example of each of the simple geometric and free-form shapes. Ask them to list the names of the shapes.

Perception Hints for Student Art

The geometric shapes in the artwork are as follows: **circles**— the third shape; **oval**— the bottom of the first object; **rectangle**— shapes on right-hand object; **square**— the two objects in the middle.

UNIT 1
LESSON 4

LESSON PLANNER

Objectives

After completing this lesson, students will be able to:

- identify complex geometric shapes. *Aesthetic Perception*
- plan and design a robot using complex geometric shapes. *Creative Expression*
- use the four steps of art criticism to evaluate their own artwork. *Art Criticism*
- demonstrate knowledge of the cultural purpose of both artworks. *Art History and Culture*

Program Resources

- **Overheads:** Both the *Sioux Double Saddlebag* and the *Mihrab* are available on overhead 4.
- **Large Prints:** *Fur Traders Descending the Missouri* by George Caleb Bingham
- **Technique Tips Flip Chart,** page 4
- **Vocabulary Book** pages 7–8
- **Art Manipulative Kit:** shapes
- **Artist Profiles Book** Artists unknown pages 55 and 56
- **Art Across the Curriculum Book** pages 19–24
- **Multimedia Workshop CD-ROM**
- **National Geographic Picture Atlas of the World CD-ROM**
- **Assessment Book** pages 7–8

Multiple Intelligences

Logical/Mathematical Using abstract patterns as they discern the relationships and connections of complex geometric shapes, students can create designs.

Vocabulary

complex geometric shapes *figuras geométricas complejas* shapes formed by combining simple geometric shapes

The following words appear as art in the Student Edition page 30: *diamond, pentagon, hexagon, parallelogram, trapezoid,* and *octagon.*

Complex Geometric Shapes

Artists use complex geometric shapes to create designs.

Look at the artwork on these pages. The double saddlebag was created in North America by a member of the Sioux Indians in 1880. The Mihrab (the focal area in an Islamic house of worship) was created in Iran about 500 years earlier, and is decorated with colorful tiles. Both pieces are decorated with complex geometric shapes.

Artist unknown. Sioux (United States). *Double Saddlebag.* 1875. Buckskin, canvas, glass beads, sinew, and wool. 113.7 × 33 cm. Detroit Institute of Arts, Detroit, Michigan.

ART Background

About the Artists
The saddlebag was created by a member of the Sioux tribe and the mihrab by a Persian artisan. The specific identities of these artists are not known.

Use the **National Geographic Picture Atlas of the World CD-ROM** for more information.

About Subject Matter* The Sioux *Double Saddlebag* is a useful artwork, and the Mihrab is a symbolic architectural structure.

About the Media The saddlebag is made of a variety of materials including buckskin, canvas, glass beads, sinew, and wool. The *Mihrab* is a faience mosaic of glazed clay tiles, cut and embedded in plaster.

About Art History* The Sioux *Double Saddlebag* is decorated with colorful glass "seed" beads that were brought to the tribes by traders about 1840. Sinew, which is a tendon, or cord, was used for beadwork instead of thread.

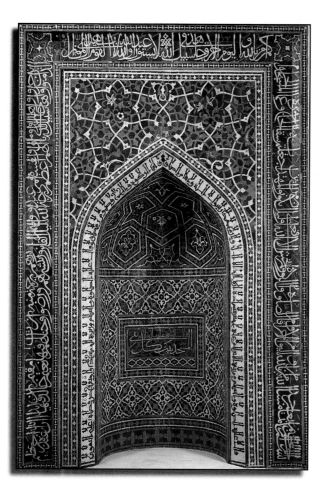

Artist unknown. (Iran). *Mihrab.* 1354. Faience mosaic of glazed terra-cotta cut and embedded in plaster. 11 feet 3 inches × 7 feet 6 inches. Metropolitan Museum of Art, New York, New York.

Study both artworks and find the following complex geometric shapes.

✓ Find the shapes that have six sides.

✓ Point to the large diamond shapes in the saddlebag. Look closely to find smaller diamond shapes in the Mihrab.

✓ Where do you see some star shapes?

✓ Look at the large shapes in the saddlebag. What simple geometric shapes are used to make them?

Lesson 4

SEEING LIKE AN ARTIST

Look at the clothes your classmates are wearing. Are any of them decorated with shapes like the ones you just found in the artwork?

29

The *Mihrab* is a niche in the interior wall of a mosque, which is a house of worship for Muslims. It is large enough to accommodate one standing figure. It indicates the direction of Mecca, a city in Saudi Arabia that is a pilgrimage site because it is the birthplace of Mohammed, the founder of Islam.

Cultural Perspectives Sioux Native American women made lavish personal objects, decorated in geometric fashion. Objects made by men represented famous acts of courage in war. Their nomadic way of life prevented the Sioux from owning and carrying many possessions.

Islamic artists avoid portraying people because they do not want in any way to diminish the greatness of Allah, or God. Instead, artists focus on highly ornate geometric patterns, calligraphy, and stylized plant life.

*See **More About** pages 206–227 for more about art history and subject matter.

FOCUS

Time: About 10 minutes

Activating Prior Knowledge

"Imagine you are riding in a car that slowly comes to a stop. What is the shape of the stop sign on the corner?"

"Vamos a imaginar que van en un carro que se detiene lentamente. ¿Cuál es la forma del símbolo de alto en la esquina?"

• Discuss students' answers, and then draw an octagon on the chalkboard. Have students identify the simple geometric shapes that make it up. (rectangle, two squares, and four triangles)

Introducing the Art

"Let's look closely at the two works of art."

"Vamos a observar detalladamente las dos obras de arte."

• **Describe:** Have students describe the subject matter. (Saddlebag: nonobjective; Mihrab: symbolic)

• Share and discuss information from **Art Background** and the **Artist Profiles Book.**

• Have students answer the questions on page 29. (See **Perception Hints** below.)

• **COMPARE AND CONTRAST** Have students list similarities and differences in the two artworks. (Both objects are functional, have formal balance, and are decorated with complex geometric shapes. The *Mihrab* is divided into many areas of shape and pattern; the saddlebag has shapes in a single area.)

FOR THE ART SPECIALIST

Use the **Overhead** and the **Large Print** *Fur Traders Descending the Missouri* to discuss the questions about complex geometric shapes on page 29.

Perception Hints

Hexagons *Mihrab.* There are hexagon (six-sided) shapes in the area above the central horizontal line and in the rectangular area above the arch.

Diamonds *Saddlebag* and *Mihrab.* The saddlebag has diamond shapes on both sides of the central axis. The mihrab has small diamond shapes in the thin bands that frame the dome and rectangular area on the outside surface.

Stars *Mihrab.* Star shapes can be found inside the domed, hollow area of the mihrab.

Complex geometric shapes *Saddlebag.* Squares, rectangles, and triangles are used to make the complex geometric shapes.

TEACH

Time: About two 30-minute periods

Practice

Materials
- 12- × 18-inch paper
- pencils

Alternate Materials: crayons or markers

"How can you make complex geometric shapes?"

"¿Cómo se pueden hacer figuras geométricas complejas?"

- Discuss simple geometric shapes and how complex geometric shapes are made from them.
- Distribute materials and have students follow the directions on page 30 for creating complex geometric shapes. Have them answer the Decide question with their partner.

Create PROBLEM SOLVING

Materials
- 12- × 18-inch black construction paper
- 9- × 12-inch construction paper, assorted colors
- scissors
- sketch paper
- glue
- pencils

Alternate Materials: wrapping paper, wallpaper, or fabric

 For safety issues about scissors and other information about safety in the art classroom, see page T22.

"Let's use complex geometric shapes to create a robot from our imaginations."

"Vamos a utilizar figuras geométricas complejas para crear un robot de nuestra imaginación."

- Brainstorm ideas for creating robots.
- Discuss and name the different geometric shapes.
- Demonstrate how simple geometric shapes can be combined to create complex geometric shapes.
- See page 4 in the **Technique Tips Flip Chart** for visual examples of techniques.
- Distribute materials and have students follow the directions on page 31.

FOR THE ART SPECIALIST

Have students illustrate a different texture for their robots by using a combination of materials.

Using Complex Geometric Shapes

Complex geometric shapes are made by combining simple geometric shapes such as triangles, squares, and rectangles. You found examples of complex geometric shapes in the two artworks on the previous pages.

Diamond

Pentagon

Trapezoid

Hexagon

Parallelogram

Octagon

Practice

Draw simple geometric shapes to create complex geometric shapes. Use pencil.

1. Fold a sheet of paper into six equal boxes. Print the name of a complex geometric shape at the bottom of each box.

2. Draw one complex geometric shape in each box.

Decide Find the simple shapes in each complex geometric shape.

Activities in
ART Across the Curriculum Book

Reading/Language Arts Identify safety signs with specific shapes. (page 19)

Math Use complex shapes in multiplication problems. (page 20)

Science Identify complex geometric shapes in nature. (page 21)

Social Studies Study the exchange of resources in recent history between two states. Use a bar graph to determine the amounts of exchange. (page 22)

The Arts Use imagination to describe a character traveling in the past with a Sioux double saddlebag. (page 23)

Technology Use the *Multimedia Workshop* CD-ROM to design a robot with geometric shapes. (page 24)

Name the geometric shapes in this student artist's robot.

Ashley Quick. Age 8. *Crazy Robot.* Colored construction paper.

Create

How can you use geometric shapes to create a design? Design a robot using geometric shapes.

1. Imagine a robot you can create with complex geometric shapes.

2. Use your imagination to design a robot using simple and complex geometric shapes.

3. Use your scrap pieces of paper to design a frame or border for your collage.

Describe Describe the robot you created.

Analyze Name the simple and complex geometric shapes you used.

Interpret Give your robot a name.

Decide If you could create this robot again, what would you do differently?

Lesson 4   **31**

Systems Use the artwork to explain our mathematical system for counting as students count the simple and complex geometric shapes.

Connections Use the artwork as a means of explaining the connection between the decoration of items used for special occasions and the decoration of everyday, functional items.

Cultures Use the artwork as a springboard to discuss the cultural characteristics of Native Americans and Iranians.

ESL students will benefit from an introduction to the vocabulary that names complex geometric shapes during the examination of the artwork. For example, you may verbalize the name of the diamond shape as you point to it. ESL students can demonstrate their comprehension of the vocabulary by pointing to appropriate elements in the artwork.

CLOSE

Time: About 5 minutes

"What are some common designs in your surroundings that use simple geometric shapes to make complex geometric shapes?"

"¿Cuáles son algunos diseños comunes en sus ambientes que usan figuras geométricas simples para crear figuras geométricas complejas?"

 Review

Use the **Large Print** *Fur Traders Descending the Missouri* to have students compare the complex geometric shapes to the works in this lesson.

Art Criticism

Have students answer the four art criticism questions—Describe, Analyze, Interpret, and Decide—orally or in writing. Discuss the use of complex geometric shapes in their collages.

 Assess

Use the **Assessment Book** pages 7–8 as a formal assessment for this lesson.

Evaluation Criteria

• Can the student identify the complex geometric shapes?

• Can the student create complex geometric shapes in a collage?

• Can the student use the four steps of art criticism to evaluate his or her own work?

• Can the student demonstrate knowledge of the cultural purpose of each work of art?

Reteaching • • • • • • • • • • •

Complex geometric shapes Use the **Art Manipulative Kit** to have students recognize and create complex geometric shapes.

Perception Hints for Student Art

Circle head
Rectangle arms and legs
Triangle feet
Square the border at the bottom

LESSON PLANNER

Objectives
After completing this lesson, students will be able to:
- identify geometric and free-form shapes in architecture. *Aesthetic Perception*
- draw a building from observation using geometric and free-form shapes. *Creative Expression*
- use the four steps of art criticism to evaluate their own drawings. *Art Criticism*
- demonstrate knowledge of the lives and cultures of both artists. *Art History and Culture*

Program Resources
- **Overhead:** Both the Abbott and the Sharp are available on overhead 5.
- **Large Prints:** *Fur Traders Descending the Missouri* by George Caleb Bingham
- **Technique Tips Flip Chart,** page 5
- **Vocabulary Book** pages 9–10
- **Artist Profiles Book:** Abbott page 1 and Sharp page 49
- **Art Across the Curriculum Book** pages 25–30
- **Multimedia Workshop CD-ROM**
- **Assessment Book** pages 9–10

Multiple Intelligences
Verbal/Linguistic Students' opportunities to discuss and recall what they have observed enhance the study of shapes in architecture.

Vocabulary
architect *arquitecto* an artist whose profession is designing and drawing up plans for cities, buildings, and bridges, and generally supervising the construction of them

architecture *arquitectura* the art form of designing and planning construction of buildings, or other structures for people

Shapes in Architecture

Architects use geometric and free-form shapes to design buildings.

Berenice Abbott. (American). *Nos. 4, 6, & 8 Fifth Avenue.* 1936. Black-and-white photograph. Museum of the City of New York, neg. 87, New York, New York.

Look at the artwork on these pages. Each one includes an image of buildings. *Nos. 4, 6, & 8 Fifth Avenue* is a photograph of three private homes in New York. It was taken by Berenice Abbott in 1936. At about the same time, artist Joseph Henry Sharp painted *Sunset Dance-Ceremony to the Evening Sun.* Both works of art show how geometric and free-form shapes are used in architecture.

32   Unit **1**

ART Background

About the Artists

Berenice Abbott (ber ə nēs' ab' at, American, 1898–1991) was born in Springfield, Ohio, and is known for her photographs of New York City and its changing character throughout the 1930s. She studied photography as a tool for the scientific study of motion.

Joseph Henry Sharp (American, 1859–1953) became deaf from an accident. His interest in Native Americans led him to sketch and record their disappearing cultures. He eventually moved to Taos, New Mexico, and is considered to be "the father of the Taos art colony." He specialized in painting Native American portraits with scientific accuracy.

About Subject Matter* The Abbott is a cityscape. The Sharp is a narrative.

About the Media The Abbott is a photograph, an image recorded with light on a photosensitive surface. The Sharp is an oil painting.

Joseph Henry Sharp. (American). *Sunset Dance-Ceremony to the Evening Sun.* 1924. Oil on canvas. $25\frac{1}{8} \times 30$ inches. National Museum of American Art, Washington, DC/Art Resource, NY.

Study the buildings in both pieces of artwork to find the following shapes.

☑ Point to all the square shapes you see.

☑ Where are the rectangles?

☑ Find the triangles.

☑ Do you see any circles? Where are they?

☑ Find some free-form shapes.

SEEING LIKE AN ARTIST

Go outside your classroom and look at the buildings in the neighborhood. Look for geometric and free-form shapes.

Lesson 5

33

FOCUS

Time: About 10 minutes

Activating Prior Knowledge

"Think about the doors and windows in your home. What shapes are they? What shape is the roof?"

"Piensen acerca de las puertas y ventanas de sus casas. ¿Qué formas tienen? ¿De qué forma es el techo?"

• Discuss students' answers to the questions regarding shapes in the architecture.

Introducing the Art

"Let's look closely at the two artworks."

"Vamos a observar detalladamente las dos obras de arte."

• **Describe:** Have students describe the subject matter. (Abbott: cityscape; Sharp: narrative)

• Share and discuss information from **Art Background** and the **Artist Profiles Book.**

• Have students answer the questions on page 33. (See **Perception Hints** below.)

• COMPARE AND CONTRAST Have students list similarities and differences between the two artworks. (Both are outdoor scenes, have buildings, and show a defined ray of sunlight. Abbott's is black and white and shows a building with one rectangular form and windows. Sharp's includes color, no windows, and many rectangular forms.)

FOR THE ART SPECIALIST

Use the **Overhead** to demonstrate how architects use geometric and free-form shapes to design buildings.

About Art History* Abbott photographed when "little" theaters were founded as an outlet for new writers. Musical theater was popularized by George Gershwin, Jerome Kern, and Cole Porter.

Sharp painted when Realism began to dominate art in America. Artists limited themselves to subject matter that they experienced personally.

Cultural Perspectives Abbott photographed during the Great Depression when Roosevelt's New Deal included the Works Progress Administration.

Sharp painted during a time when the United States government was attempting to assimilate Native Americans with the majority and give up their unique culture. Sharp's paintings helped to preserve part of their culture.

*See **More About** pages 206–227 for more about history and subject matter.

Perception Hints

Squares *Abbott.* The windows in the front of the building at the top right-hand side are square.

Rectangles *Abbott and Sharp.* The buildings in both pictures are rectangular.

Triangles *Sharp.* The archway in the foreground is triangular in shape.

Circles *Abbott.* The headlights and tires on the car.

Free-forms *Sharp.* The orange treetops, bushes, mountains, clouds, and people are free-form shapes.

TEACH

Time: About two 30-minute periods

Practice

Materials
- 9- × 12-inch paper
- pencils

Alternate Materials: markers

"How can you use shapes to draw a building?"

"¿Cómo pueden usar figuras para dibujar un edificio?"

- Discuss information on the simple and complex geometric shapes, as well as free-form shapes on page 34.
- Distribute materials and have students follow the directions on page 34 for using shapes to draw a building. Have them answer the Decide questions with a partner.

Create PROBLEM SOLVING

Materials
- 12- × 18-inch construction paper
- black felt-tip pens
- markers, assorted colors

Alternate Materials: dustless chalk and oil pastels

"Let's use geometric shapes to create a drawing of our school."

"Vamos a usar figuras geométricas para hacer un dibujo de nuestra escuela."

- Have students select an area of the school building they would like to draw, identifying the various shapes they observe in the building.
- Review the use of markers in **More About Technique Tips** on page 196.

 See page 5 in the **Technique Tips Flip Chart** for visual examples of techniques.

- Distribute materials and have students follow the directions on page 35.

Safety! For safety issues about markers and other information about safety in the art classroom, see page T22.

FOR THE ART SPECIALIST

Have the students indicate the different shapes in the building by filling them with dustless chalk or oil pastels.

Shapes in Architecture

Architecture is the art of designing and planning buildings for people. You saw examples of architecture in the artwork on the previous pages. An **architect** is the person or artist who plans and designs buildings. Architects use **geometric** and **free-form shapes** in their designs.

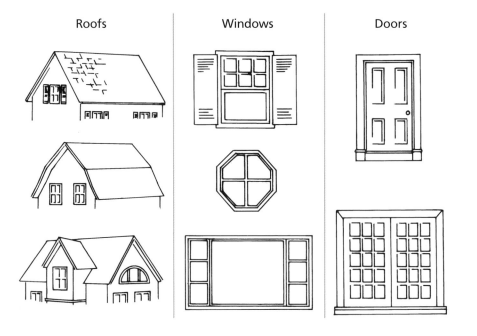

| Roofs | Windows | Doors |

Practice

Illustrate geometric and free-form shapes in architecture. Use pencil.

1. On a sheet of paper, use your pencil to draw a large geometric shape to create the outline of a house or building.

2. Use your imagination to add smaller geometric and free-form shapes to create the roof, windows, and doors.

Decide Is your drawing of a building or house where people live or work? Does it have different kinds of shapes?

Activities in **A**RT **A**cross the Curriculum Book

Reading/Language Arts Use similes to describe architecture. (page 25)

Math Use basic math skills to plan your own party or celebration like the one depicted *in Sunset Dance-Ceremony to the Evening Sun.* (page 26)

Science Identify different kinds of energy shown in the photograph *Nos. 4, 6, and 8 Fifth Avenue.* (page 27)

Social Studies Learn about different types of houses around the world. (page 28)

The Arts Follow steps to create a dance for a celebration like the celebration in *Sunset Dance-Ceremony to the Evening Sun.* (page 29)

Technology Use the *Multimedia Workshop* CD-ROM to draw a building using geometric and free-form shapes. (page 30)

Edwin Vasquez. Age 8. *My School.* Marker

Which parts of this student artist's drawing are examples of free-form and which are geometric shapes?

Create

In the world around you, what buildings are designed with geometric and free-form shapes? Draw a building using geometric and free-form shapes.

1. Walk outside and choose an area of your school building that you would like to draw.

2. Point out all the geometric shapes you see. Now look for the free-form shapes.

3. Draw the area of your school building you selected. Make sure you include all the geometric and free-form shapes you see.

Describe List the simple and complex geometric shapes you used in your drawing. Describe the free-form shapes you used.

Analyze Which shape is used most?

Interpret How could you completely change the appearance of the building with different shapes?

Decide Does your drawing look like your school building? If not, what needs to be changed to improve your drawing?

Lesson 5

35

Communities Use the artworks as visual examples to open a discussion about dwellings in the different communities of the world.

Scale and Structure Use the artworks as a means to discuss differences in the scale and structure in the construction of different styles of buildings.

Energy Use the artworks as a springboard to compare and contrast the uses of energy in buildings in the eastern and western United States.

ESL

ESL students may be hesitant to answer the open-ended questions suggested. Provide support by describing, analyzing, and interpreting the elements in their drawings yourself or inviting an English-speaking peer to do so. Encourage ESL students to point to elements in their drawings as you describe them.

CLOSE

Time: About 5 minutes

"What geometric and free-form shapes are used to design roofs, windows, and doors?"

"¿Qué figuras geométricas y abstractas se usan para diseñar techos, ventanas y puertas?"

LARGE PRINT **Review**
Use the **Large Print** *Fur Traders Descending The Missouri* to have students compare the geometric and free-form shapes used in it.

Art Criticism

Have students answer the four art criticism questions—Describe, Analyze, Interpret, and Decide—orally or in writing. Discuss the use of geometric and free-form shapes in their drawings.

 Assess
Use the **Assessment Book** pages 9–10 as a formal assessment for this lesson.

Evaluation Criteria

• Can the student identify the simple and complex geometric shapes, as well as free-form shapes in architecture?

• Can the student draw, from observation, a building using geometric and free-form shapes?

• Can the student use the four steps of art criticism to evaluate his or her own work?

• Can the student demonstrate knowledge of the lives and cultures of both artists?

Reteaching • • • • • • • • • •

Shapes Have students find at least three examples of architecture in a book. Ask them to draw and list all the geometric and free-form shapes that they see.

Perception Hints for Student Art

Free-form shapes the rope-type fence and the grass.
Geometric shapes the roof, windows, doors, flagpole, bricks, and possibly others.

Shapes All Around Us

Artists use geometric and free-form shapes in portraits.

John Singleton Copley. (American). *Daniel Crommelin Verplanck.* 1771. Oil on canvas. $49\frac{1}{2} \times 40$ inches. Metropolitan Museum of Art, New York, New York.

A portrait is a picture of a person. Look at the portraits on these two pages. *Daniel Crommelin Verplanck* was painted by John Singleton Copley in 1771. About 150 years later, Allen E. Cole used a camera to take the photograph of *Silas Johnson*. Both portraits show geometric and free-form shapes.

36   Unit **1**

LESSON PLANNER

Objectives
After completing this lesson, students will be able to:
- identify geometric and free-form shapes that describe people and objects in art and the environment. *Aesthetic Perception*
- draw a portrait using geometric and free-form shapes. *Creative Expression*
- use the four steps of art criticism to evaluate their own drawings. *Art Criticism*
- demonstrate knowledge of the lives and cultures of both artists. *Art History and Culture*

Program Resources
- **Overheads**: Both the Copley and the Cole are available on overhead 6.
- **Large Prints:** *Portrait of a Lady* by Rogier van der Weyden and *Fur Traders Descending the Missouri* by George Caleb Bingham
- **Technique Tips Flip Chart,** page 6
- **Vocabulary Book** pages 11–12
- **Artist Profiles Book:** Copley page 7 and Cole page 6
- **Art Across the Curriculum** pages 31–36
- **Multimedia Workshop CD-ROM**
- **Assessment Book** pages 11–12

Multiple Intelligences
Interpersonal When students use geometric or free-form shapes to create portraits, they can express moods or feelings.

Vocabulary
portrait *retrato* a picture of a person

free-form shapes *figuras abstractas* shapes that are uneven and irregular, not geometric

geometric shapes *figuras geométricas* math shapes, such as a circle, triangle, rectangle, or square

---

FOCUS

Time: About 10 minutes

Activating Prior Knowledge
"Think about masks. What shapes are used for the eyes, nose, and mouth?"

"Piensen acerca de máscaras. ¿Qué figuras se usan para los ojos, la nariz y la boca?"

- Discuss students' answers and how faces are made of shapes.

ART Background

About the Artists
John Singleton Copley (jon sing' gəl tən käp' lē, American, 1738–1815) is considered to be the greatest American portrait painter of the eighteenth century. His stepfather, who was an artist, gave him his first art lessons. Copley favored truth above elegance. As a result, his portraits accurately revealed the personalities of his subjects.

Allen E. Cole (al' ən kōl, American, 1884–1970) was born in Kearnesville, West Virginia. He was a railroad porter and waiter before moving to Cleveland, Ohio. He learned photography skills in exchange for cleanup and odd jobs. Cole opened his own studio in 1922 in his home, and he became Cleveland's first professional African American photographer. Cole was the first Cleveland photographer to offer tinted prints.

About Subject Matter* Both the Copley and the Cole are portraits.

About the Media The Copley is an oil painting. The Cole is a photograph.

Allen E. Cole. (American). *Silas Johnson.* 1920s. Hand-tinted photograph. Western Reserve Historical Society, Cleveland, Ohio.

Study both portraits to find the following geometric and free-form shapes.

- ✓ Find the circles.
- ✓ Point to the rectangles you see.
- ✓ Are there any triangles?
- ✓ Find the free-form shapes.
- ✓ Where are the oval shapes?

SEEING LIKE AN ARTIST

Look at your face in a mirror, or think about the shape of your face. Place your index finger on the mirror or on your face and use it to trace all the shapes. Name the shapes you traced.

About Art History* Copley painted during a time when new musical forms, such as the symphony and the string quartet, were being developed. The opera reached great heights in the works of Gluck and Mozart.

Cole photographed when artists, such as Georgia O'Keeffe, painted their subjects realistically, with precision, and so stripped of detail that they appeared abstract.

Cultural Perspectives Copley painted during the time when English colonists were establishing homes and public buildings. Life centered on the family.

Cole was a trailblazer in photography within the Cleveland African American community. Western Reserve Historical Society purchased and preserved some of his prints and 27,000 negatives from his estate.

*See **More About** pages 206–227 for more about art history and subject matter.

Introducing the Art

"Let's look closely at the two artworks."
"Vamos a observar detalladamente las dos obras de arte."

- Have students describe the subject matter in the artwork. (both: portraits)
- Using **Art Background** and the **Artist Profiles Book**, have students compare the lives, work, and cultures of both artists.
- Have students answer the questions on page 37. (See **Perception Hints** below.)
- **COMPARE AND CONTRAST** Have students make a list of the similarities and differences in the two artworks. (Both are indoor, realistic, and formally posed portraits. Copley's painting shows deep space through the window opening, while the Cole shows shallow space. Copley's painting includes an animal; Cole's does not. Copley's painting shows the figure emerging from a dark space, while the lighting in Cole's photograph is even.)

FOR THE ART SPECIALIST

Use the **Overhead** and the **Large Prints** *Fur Traders Descending the Missouri* and *Portrait of a Lady* to discuss the questions about shapes on page 37. Demonstrate how an artist uses geometric and free-form shapes in portraits.

Perception Hints

Circles *Cole.* There are circular shapes in the wicker chair.
Rectangles *Copley.* Parts of the column base and the window are rectangular.
Triangles *Cole.* The gentleman's arm on the left-hand side of the photo is bent into the shape of a triangle.
Free-forms *Copley.* The boy, squirrel, and trees are free-form shapes. *Cole.* The boy is free-form shaped.
Ovals *Cole.* The eyes and head are oval-shaped.

TEACH

Time: About two 30-minute periods

Practice

Materials
- $8\frac{1}{2}$- × 11-inch paper
- pencils

"What shapes do you see in an object in your classroom?"

"¿Qué figuras ven en un objeto en su salón de clases?"

- Discuss student answers in reference to the different type of shapes.
- Distribute materials and have students follow the directions on page 38 for drawing the shapes of an object. Have them answer the Decide questions with a partner or on the back of the paper.

Create PROBLEM SOLVING

Materials
- 12- × 18-inch colored construction paper
- oil pastels
- dustless chalk

Alternate Materials: liquid tempera paints

"Let's use geometric and free-form shapes to draw a portrait."

"Vamos a utilizar figuras geométricas y abstractas para dibujar un retrato."

- Think about the different shapes of faces of the people you know.

 See page 6 in the **Technique Tips Flip Chart** for visual examples of techniques.

- Distribute materials and have students follow the directions on page 39.
- Review ways to use dustless, colored chalk in **More About Technique Tips** on page 198.

Safety! For safety issues about chalk and other information in the art classroom, see page T22.

FOR THE ART SPECIALIST

Have students draw a model in liquid tempera paints and fill the shapes with oil pastels.

Using Shapes

Shapes are all around us. You have already seen different shapes in the portraits on pages 36 and 37.

Free-form shapes can be found in nature. Puddles, clouds, and flowers are examples of free-form shapes found in nature. People are free-form shapes.

Geometric shapes are usually found in objects that are made by people. Buildings, furniture, and road signs are some examples.

Most objects have one main shape. Some objects are made of many smaller shapes.

Practice

Draw the shapes of an object. Use pencil.

1. Choose an object from your classroom to draw. Find the smaller geometric or free-form shapes that make it.

2. On a sheet of paper, draw the object by putting together the smaller shapes you see.

Decide Does your drawing have the same shape as the actual object? Did you draw the smaller shapes that make it up?

Activities in ART Across the Curriculum Book

Reading/Language Arts Write a list of questions to ask in an interview with either person in the portraits. (page 31)

Math Use a bar graph to show the collection, recording, and analyzing of data relating to pets like the pet seen in Copley's work. (page 32)

Science Use paper, hands, and light to study shapes in shadows. (page 33)

Social Studies Keeping in mind the colonists as depicted in Copley's work, learn more about American symbols and constitutional rights. (page 34)

The Arts Rather than painting a portrait, create a musical portrait of someone you know by putting different words to a well-known song. (page 35)

Technology Use the *Multimedia Workshop* CD-ROM to draw a portrait using geometric and free-form shapes. (page 36)

What geometric shape is the face in this student artist's portrait?

Carolina Monsure. Age 8. *Self-Portrait.* Oil pastel.

Create

What are the shapes of the faces of some of the people you know? Draw a portrait using geometric and free-form shapes.

1. Ask a classmate to be your model. Select some objects from the classroom to use as props. Have your model use some of these props as they pose for you.

2. Look very carefully at your model. Find the geometric and free-form shapes.

3. Use chalk to draw your model and the props. Use lines to create all the geometric and free-form shapes you see. Fill the shapes with oil pastels.

Describe Identify the shapes you used in your portrait.

Analyze Where did you use the geometric shapes? Where did you use free-form shapes?

Interpret Give your portrait a title. Then, invite your model to give the portrait a title.

Decide Did your portrait turn out as you had hoped? Why or why not? If you were able to do this artwork over again, what would you do to improve it?

Lesson 6 39

THEME Connections

Change Use the artwork to discuss how clothing styles change throughout history.

Models Use the artworks to discuss how each figure is a model or representative of the time period in which they were pictured.

Transitions Use the artworks as a springboard for a discussion regarding the transitions in age that people go through and how they want to be remembered.

ESL

ESL students need visual support to understand new vocabulary. During the discussion, use the artwork from previous lessons as visual support. Point to the elements in the artwork that illustrate the discussion points.

CLOSE
Time: About 5 minutes

"What are the most common geometric or free-form shapes used to draw a portrait?"

"¿Cuáles son las figuras geométricas y abstractas más comunes que se utilizan para dibujar un retrato?"

LARGE PRINT

Review
Use the **Large Print** *Portrait of a Lady* to have students compare shapes used in portraits to those in the artworks in the lesson.

Art Criticism
Have students answer the four art criticism questions—Describe, Analyze, Interpret, and Decide—orally or in writing. Discuss the use of geometric and free-form shapes in their drawings.

Assess
Use the **Assessment Book** pages 11–12 as a formal assessment for this lesson.

Evaluation Criteria
• Can the student identify geometric and free-form shapes?
• Can the student create a portrait using geometric and free-form shapes?
• Can the student use the four steps of art criticism to evaluate his or her own work?
• Can the student demonstrate knowledge of the lives and cultures of both artists?

Reteaching ● ● ● ● ● ● ● ● ● ● ● ●

Shapes Have the students look through this book to find another portrait. Ask them to list the title of the work and identify the geometric and free-form shapes they find.

Perception Hints for Student Art
The face in the portrait is oval in shape.

UNIT 1

LESSON PLANNER

Objectives

After completing this lesson, students will be able to:

- create lines and shapes by representing eagles in various positions through body movements. *Aesthetic Perception*
- express individual interpretations of the eagle's lines and shapes in a dance study. *Creative Expression*
- use the four steps of art criticism to evaluate their own dance study. *Art Criticism*
- demonstrate knowledge about the content of the Eagle Dance. *Art History and Culture*

Program Resources

Artsource Performing Arts Audio/Video Resource Package

Eagle Dance performed by the American Indian Dance Theater. Videocassette Running Time: 0:45.

FOCUS

Time: About 10 minutes

Activating Prior Knowledge

"What do you know about the way Native Americans look at the world of animals and nature?"

"¿Qué conocen acerca de la forma en que los nativos americanos observan el mundo animal y la naturaleza?"

- Discuss how traditional Native Americans imitate animals' actions and qualities through dance movements as a way to understand and honor them.

Introducing the Art

"Look at the picture of the dancer performing the Eagle Dance. How would you describe the eagle's movements?"

"Observen el dibujo del bailarín representando el Eagle Dance (Baile del Águila). ¿Cómo describirían los movimientos del águila?"

- Discuss the mood and feeling of the dancer on page 40. Have students describe the lines and shapes and how the dancer imitates an eagle. Share information from **Art Background**. If you have the *Artsource* videocassette, have students view the performance of the Eagle Dance.
- Show students some photos, drawings, and paintings of eagles. List all the information they know about eagles and their actions.

40 Unit **1**

Lines and Shapes in Dance

American Indian Dance Theatre: Zuni, *"Eagle Dance."*

The eagle is an important symbol for Native Americans. It stands for someone who is strong and wise. Native Americans perform an Eagle Dance. The dancers try to copy the eagle's movements. The dancers' bodies form different shapes and create straight, diagonal, and curved lines.

40   Unit **1**

ART Background

About the Choreographer

Hanay Geiogamah (1943–), Artistic Director of the American Indian Dance Theatre, was raised with the traditions of the Kiowa Tribe. One of Hanay's most comforting memories as a child is of his father performing his morning ritual of preparing for work. He would fix himself coffee, turn on the radio to country-western music, and whistle ancient tribal songs. This gave Hanay a sense that he was a Native American, even though his modern world contrasted with his culture's traditions.

About Subject Matter The "Eagle Dance" varies from region to region, but this interpretation is a blending of two styles: the Northern Plains and the Zuñi Pueblo. The dances reflect the life cycle of the eagle, from its first steps and attempts to fly, through maturity and into the spirit world.

ART SOURCE
ARTSOURCE

What To Do

Create an original eagle dance.

Materials
✔ pictures of eagles in different positions

1. Study the pictures carefully. Then, list everything you know about the eagle.

2. Look closely at the pictures. Try showing their positions with your body.

3. Make a list of actions done by the eagle. Pick one action. Explore how you can show the action with movements of your body.

4. Create a simple dance about the eagle. First, use your body to show three different positions of the eagle. Next, select one or two actions. Do each action for eight counts. End in a "perched" eagle shape.

5. Perform your dance in a group.

Describe Describe the way you made your three eagle shapes.
Analyze Explain how you made your eagle movements to show actions.
Interpret How does your dance express the spirit and strength of the eagle?
Decide How well did you show what an eagle is like? How did you use shape and line?

Extra Credit

Work with a partner. One of you can play a steady beat on a drum. The other can perform the eagle dance.

Dance   41

Cultural Perspectives The American Indian Dance Theatre was founded in 1987 to present American Indian dance and music professionally and to fill the need for experienced traditional performers.

About Dance Dance and music serve as a framework to which American Indian philosophy and tradition are attached. Geiogamah has developed a system for categorizing American Indian dance: seasonal/functional; celebrational/bravura; and spiritual/ceremonial/religious. He researches and collects traditional dances from many of the 430 tribes in the United States and puts this material together in new ways without altering the original intent of the dances.

TEACH

Time: Two 30-minute periods

Materials
• paintings, drawings, or photos of eagles in different positions

"We are going to observe the positions and actions of eagles, and then create eagle dances."
"Vamos a observar las posiciones y las acciones del águila, y luego crearemos bailes de águilas."

• Arrange students so that each has enough space to move without touching others.

• Instruct students to choose ideas from their lists of eagle information and explore how they can depict the eagle using movement.

• Direct students to create a simple dance study about the eagle. First, have them show three different positions of the eagle. Next, have them select one or two actions and do each for eight counts, then end in a "perched" eagle shape.

• Ask student partners to perform their dance studies for each other or for the class. Alternatively, have several people perform simultaneously.

CLOSE

Time: About 5 minutes

"Think about the types of lines and shapes you used to communicate your ideas in an eagle dance."
"Piensen acerca de los tipos de líneas y figuras que usaron para comunicar sus ideas en un baile de águila."

Assess

Have students answer the four art criticism questions on page 41—Describe, Analyze, Interpret, and Decide—orally or in writing.

Evaluation Criteria

• Can the student create lines and shapes by representing eagles in body movements?

• Can the student express the positions and qualities of the eagle through movement?

• Can the student use the four steps of art criticism to evaluate his or her dance?

• Can the student demonstrate knowledge about the content of the Eagle Dance?

UNIT 1

Reviewing Unit Concepts

"Artists use different kinds of lines and shapes to create all kinds of art."

"Los artistas usan diferentes tipos de líneas y figuras para crear todos los tipos de arte."

• Review the definitions of *lines* and *shapes* on pages 42 and 43. Have students draw and label an example of each.

Examining the Artwork

"Let's look closely at the work of art."

"Vamos a observar detalladamente la obra de arte."

• Have the students study Picasso's *Three Women at the Fountain* and answer the questions on page 43. (See **Perception Hints** below.)

Student Portfolio

Have students review all the artwork they have created during this unit and select the pieces they wish to keep in their portfolios.

School Portfolio

You may wish to confer with students to select one of their artworks, possibly a self-portrait, to be included in a school portfolio to record their developing skills from year to year.

Art Criticism Activity

Have students select an artwork from this unit and study it using the four steps of art criticism. (See pages 206–209 for more information about Art Criticism.)

Perception Hints

Lines

Vertical The vertical lines of the woman standing on the left give a feeling of steadiness and solidity.

Horizontal The horizontal lines in the floor and platform give a feeling of calm and rest.

Curved The curved lines of the bent arms give a feeling of movement to the piece.

Line Variation

Length Short and long lines in the fabric.

Curve The lines in the women's hair curve a little.

Shapes

Oval The women's heads.

Rectangle The forearms.

Trapezoid Skirt covering right leg of seated figure.

Parallelogram The main shape of the forearm and hand resting on the leg of the seated figure.

Line and Shape

Reviewing Main Ideas

The lessons and activities in this unit cover different kinds of lines and shapes that artists use in works of art.

1. **Lines** are made when a tool such as a pencil moves across a surface. There are five different kinds of lines. Each one expresses a different feeling.
   • **Vertical** lines make things look tall and calm.
   • **Horizontal** lines give a feeling of calm or peace.
   • **Diagonal** lines make objects seem unsteady.
   • **Zigzag** lines cause a feeling of excitement.
   • **Curved** lines give a feeling of graceful movement.

2. **Line variations** make lines look different. (short or long, thick or thin, rough or smooth, or broken or solid)

3. **Shapes** are flat, two-dimensional areas. There are two types of shapes.
   • Circles, squares, triangles, ovals, and rectangles are *simple geometric shapes.*

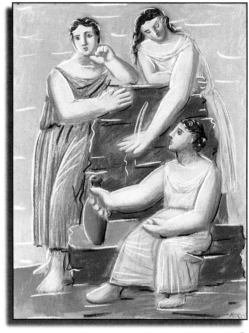

Pablo Picasso. (Spanish). *Three Women at the Fountain.* 1921. Pastel on blue paper. $25 \times 19\frac{1}{8}$ inches. Museum of Fine Arts, Houston, TX; Gift of Miss Ima Hogg and other Trustees of the Varner-Bayou Bend Heritage Fund.

ART Background

About the Artist
Pablo Picasso (pä' blō pē käs' sō, Spanish, 1881–1973) was the eldest child of Dona Maria Picasso and Don Jose Ruiz Blasco. On the night he was born, he was not breathing and appeared not to be alive. The midwife who was assisting at the birth set aside the baby to take care of his mother. Picasso's uncle, however, who had some training in medicine, saved the newborn child.

About Subject Matter* The women in this drawing look as if they have been sculpted from stone. The fullness of their figures is reminiscent of the roundness and solidity of ancient Greek and Roman sculptures.

About the Media *Three Women at the Fountain* is pastel on blue paper. Pastels are pigments held together with gum and molded into sticks. The sensitive shading and bold lines seen in Picasso's drawing are characteristic of this medium.

- **Free-form shapes** are uneven and not regular. People are free-form shapes.
4. **Complex geometric shapes** are made by combining simple geometric shapes. (diamond, pentagon, hexagon, octagon, trapezoid, and parallelogram)
5. **Architecture** is the art of designing and planning buildings. An *architect* is the person who does the planning and designing.

Summing Up

Look at the painting by Picasso. Notice how he used the different lines and shapes you learned about in this unit.

- Find at least three different kinds of lines. What feeling does each express?
- Find two different line variations.
- Where do you see simple and complex geometric shapes?

Line and shape are important elements in drawings, paintings, and prints. By using lines and shapes, artists can describe to others the objects, areas, and details they see.

Careers in Art
Art Educator

Kathy Perales is an art educator. Art educators teach people all about art. They show students how to look at and talk about artworks. They also teach them how to produce their own artwork. Perales lives in Canyon Lake, Texas. She thinks the best part of being an art educator is being able to help students improve their skills. Their excitement as they discover success makes all her hard work worth it. Perales studied art at college to get ready for her exciting career.

Kathy Perales, Art Educator

43

Learning About Careers in Art

Kathy Perales credits a "wonderful" fourth-grade teacher who inspired her to teach. From then on, it was just a matter of combining her love of art with a desire to teach. Her greatest joy is when her students discover they can be successful. Her greatest challenge is convincing students that their work and opinions are valuable. Perales has her students practice substantiating their opinions about what they like in art, and she hopes they will transfer this decision-making ability to other parts of their lives.

- Encourage interested students to find out more about a career as an art educator. Have them interview an art teacher and share their findings with the class.

A Final Thought
"Every child is an artist. The problem is how to remain an artist once you grow up."—Pablo Picasso

About Art History* Picasso's art in the 1920s reflected his classical style inspired by the sculptures of ancient Greece and Rome. Simultaneously, however, he was still creating the flat, geometric forms of Cubism for which he is probably most famous.

Cultural Perspectives Until World War I, Paris was at the center of the world revolution in art. Painters came from all over to live in France. The anti-German feeling among Parisians in 1916, however, was felt in Picasso's circle. Cubism was initially viewed as an anti-patriotic demonstration because a German-born art dealer had been the first to exhibit Cubist paintings.

*See **More About** pages 206–227 for more about art history and subject matter.

UNIT 2

UNIT OVERVIEW

This unit will cover the elements of color and value. Color is the element of art derived from reflected light. Value is the lightness or darkness of a color.

Primary and secondary colors are found in the color spectrum. Primary and secondary colors are covered in Lesson 1.

Value is the lightness or darkness of a color. Value is also covered in Lesson 1.

An **intermediate color** is created by mixing together a primary and a secondary color. Intermediate colors are covered in Lesson 2.

A **color wheel** is the color spectrum bent into a circle. The color wheel is covered in Lesson 3.

Warm and cool colors suggest warmth and coolness in an artwork. Warm and cool colors are covered in Lessons 4–6.

Color contrast is created when warm and cool colors are placed side by side. Color contrast is covered in Lesson 6.

Introducing Unit Concepts

"Artists use the elements of color and value in creating all kinds of art."

"Los artistas usan los elementos del color y del valor para crear todo tipo de obras de arte."

Color

• Ask students to survey at least 20 people of different ages to discover their favorite color. Have students determine the most popular color and report it to the class.

• Have students select a color and make a list of nouns, adjectives, and adverbs that are associated with that particular color. Ask them to write a poem about the color by connecting words from their lists.

Value

• Have students suggest words that come to mind when you say the word *value,* e.g. *worth, respect, ideals.*

• Turn out the lights in the classroom. Shine a flashlight on different objects in the room. Discuss how the color of each object looks in bright light and in dim light.

An Introduction to
Color and Value

Artists use color and value to make their artwork special.

Diego Rivera. (Mexican). *Kneeling Child on Yellow Background.* 1927. Oil on canvas. $25\frac{1}{2} \times 21$ inches. San Francisco Museum of Modern Art, San Francisco, California. Bequest of Elise S. Haas. Photo by Ben Blackwell.

ART Background

About the Artist

Diego Rivera (dē ā' gō rē bā' rä, Mexican, 1886–1957), along with a twin brother, was born on December 8, 1886, in Guanajuato, Mexico. He was a bright and observant child who liked to take apart mechanical objects to see how they worked and then draw them on canvas that covered the walls in his "studio" at home. His interest in mural painting was evident at the young age of four.

About Subject Matter* The land and people of Mexico were most often the focus of Diego Rivera's work. His murals depict the struggle of laborers and peasants in a country dominated by a wealthy upper class. A master portraitist, Rivera was also inspired by the colorful and simple images of his native culture. His painting of the kneeling child is a sensitive portrait of a young Mexican girl.

Artists use **color** to create a certain feeling or emotion in a work of art.

- What colors do you see in *Kneeling Child on Yellow Background?*
- How do the colors make you feel?

Some artists use different **values** of a color to show the highlights and shadows of an object.

- Where did Rivera use light and dark color values on the young girl's face?
- Where else do you see light and dark values of a color?

Artist Profile

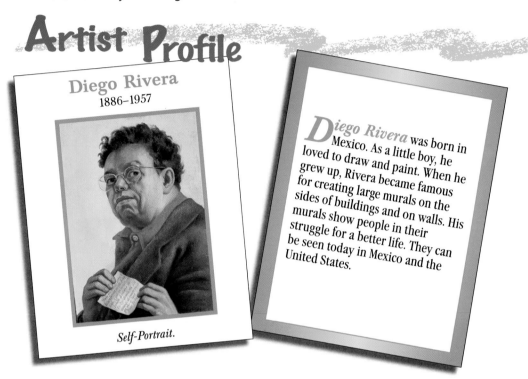

Diego Rivera
1886–1957

Self-Portrait.

Diego Rivera was born in Mexico. As a little boy, he loved to draw and paint. When he grew up, Rivera became famous for creating large murals on the sides of buildings and on walls. His murals show people in their struggle for a better life. They can be seen today in Mexico and the United States.

Diego Rivera and other artists use color and value to help them create art. In this unit you will learn about colors and the feelings they create. You will practice mixing and using colors. You will study:

- Primary and Secondary Colors
- Value
- Intermediate Colors
- Color Wheel
- Warm and Cool Colors
- Color Contrast

45

About the Media *Kneeling Child on Yellow Background* is an oil painting. Oil paint is a slow-drying medium made by mixing colored pigments with linseed oil, allowing artists to work on fine details while the paint is still wet.

About Art History* Rivera painted during a time when Social Realism, prevalent in the 1920s and 1930s, reflected artists' efforts to highlight injustice and motivate reform. Deeply committed to social change, Latino artists in Mexico and the United States created huge murals that celebrated the working class.

Cultural Perspectives Inspired by Mexican folk art, Diego Rivera painted a series of panels that encompassed the entire history of Mexico. Included in these murals were the people of his native Guanajuato, who were among the first to join in Mexico's War of Independence against Spain.

*See **More About** pages 206–227 for more about art history and subject matter.

You may wish to introduce the unit by using the **Video** *Diego* to discuss Diego Rivera and point out primary, secondary, warm, and cool colors.

Examining the Artwork

"Let's look closely at the painting."
"Vamos a observar detalladamente esta pintura."

- Have the students look at Rivera's painting *Kneeling Child on Yellow Background.* Ask them to describe what they see in the painting.
- Have students answer questions on page 45 pertaining to color and value in Rivera's painting. (See **Perception Hints** below.)

Artist Profile

Share with students information about the artist, including his self-portrait.

Encourage students to use their **Art Journals** to practice art concepts and record ideas from lesson to lesson.

About Music

Color in music refers to the distinctive tone qualities, or *timbre,* of different instruments and voices.

Value, while not a musical term, has a parallel in music: the ability of performers to create subtle differences in tone that are sometimes characterized as "warm" or "cool."

- Have students choose warm and cool colors for instruments. (wood blocks—yellow; cymbals—green) Then, point to the colors on the color wheel from the **Art Manipulative Kit** and have the students respond by playing their assigned color.
- Have the students choose a piece of music to match the color value of their artwork in one of the lessons in this unit.

Perception Hints

Secondary colors The little girl's skirt is violet and her waistband is orange.

Warm colors The yellow mat and orange tile floor are warm colors.

Value The flesh color of the young girl's face gets darker under her chin and lighter down the middle of her nose. The violet color in the skirt gets darker inside the folds and lighter at the top of each fold.

UNIT 2 Planning Guide

Lesson	Lesson Title	Suggested Pacing	Create Activities	Materials	
1	**Looking at Color**	75 minutes	Draw a picture using the spectral colors, tints, and shades to illustrate a special occasion that expresses a mood.	12- x 18-inch white paper markers in assorted colors liquid tempera paints paintbrushes paper plates paper towels newspaper water dishes prism from **Art Manipulative Kit**	
2	**Intermediate Colors**	75 minutes	Create a giant color wheel using primary, secondary, and intermediate colors.	12- x 18-inch white construction paper paper towels liquid tempera paints paper plates for palettes brushes of various sizes containers of water scissors newspaper	
3	**Color Wheel**	75 minutes	Create an amusement ride for the Rainbow Park using the colors of a color wheel.	construction paper scissors glue markers sketch paper posterboard	
4	**Cool Colors**	75 minutes	Design a sculpture of an environment using cool colors.	9- x 12-inch construction paper (cool colors) scissors tape or glue oil pastels (cool colors) sketch paper pencils markers	
5	**Warm Colors**	75 minutes	Create an imaginative painting using warm colors.	12- x 18-inch white construction paper brushes of various sizes containers of water oil pastels watercolor paints paper towels sketch paper pencils tape	
6	**Color Contrast**	75 minutes	Create a group mural contrasting warm and cool colors.	12- x 18-inch construction paper (warm colors) large piece mural paper for each team glue liquid tempera paints oil pastels large brushes scissors pencils palettes containers of water scrap paper paper towels newspaper	
Artsource Lesson	**Color and Value in Storytelling**	75 minutes	Tell a folk tale in a rap style.	a tale or story paper and pencils scary music or sounds	

Test preparation activities using the Large Prints *Rhapsody* and *Young Man and Woman in an Inn* can be found on pages 12–15 of the Test Preparation Book.

Program Resources (Books)	Art Resources	Literature Resources	*Music Resources
Vocabulary, pp. 13–14 Assessment, pp. 13–14 Art Across the Curriculum Resource Book, pp. 37–42 Technique Tips Flip Chart, p. 7 Lesson Plans Book, p. 8 Home Connection, pp. 7 and 8	Overhead Transparency #7, *Tar Beach and Boys' Day* Artist Profile Book, pp. 42, 45 Large Prints, *Rhapsody* and *Young Man and Woman in an Inn*	**1.** *Tar Beach* (1991) by Faith Ringgold incorporates facts from the artist's childhood with fiction in this book based on a story quilt. Ringgold's dramatic use of colors demonstrates how color is used to express moods. **2.** *Out of the Blue: Poems about Color* (1993) by Hiawyn Oram is a collection of poems centering around the theme of color.	*"Three Rides in the Park,"* by Linda Williams, p. T118, CD3:22. *"Three Rides in the Park"* is a modern American piece for synthesizer that describes three different rides at the amusement park, the merry-go-round, the ferris wheel, and the roller coaster.
Vocabulary, pp. 15–16 Assessment, pp. 15–16 Art Across the Curriculum Resource Book, pp. 43–48 Technique Tips Flip Chart, p. 8 Lesson Plans Book, p. 9	Overhead Transparency #8, Hat: *Birds and Geometric Patterns* and *Remedial Archaeology and the Like* Artist Profile Book, pp. 54, 57 Large Prints, *Rhapsody* and *Young Man and Woman in an Inn*	**1.** *Little Blue and Little Yellow* (1991) by Leo Lionni is a clever book for putting the concept of combining colors into children's perspective. **2.** *White Rabbit's Color Book* (1994) by Alan Baker demonstrates color changing through use of the character's paints pots.	"Cuequita de los Coyas," p. T179, CD5:3. "Cuequita de los Coyas" is folk dance music from the Andes Mountains played on native flutes.
Vocabulary, pp. 17–18 Assessment, pp. 17–18 Art Across the Curriculum Resource Book, pp. 49–54 Technique Tips Flip Chart, p. 9 Lesson Plans Book, p. 10	Overhead Transparency #9, *La Fortune* and *Brilliant as the Sun Upon the World* Artist Profile Book, pp. 23, 29 Large Prints, *Rhapsody* and *Young Man and Woman in an Inn*	**1.** *A Color Sampler* (1993) by Kathleen Westray discusses primary, secondary, and intermediate colors through classic quilt patterns. **2.** *The Big Orange Splot* (1977) by Daniel M. Pinkwater provides fictional color transformation of a neighborhood tale.	"Variations" (Excerpt), by Andrew Lloyd Webber, p. T230, CD6:9. "Variations" is an example of twentieth-century music, written by the Broadway composer Andrew Lloyd Webber.
Vocabulary, pp. 19–20 Assessment, pp. 19–20 Art Across the Curriculum Resource Book, pp. 55–60 Technique Tips Flip Chart, p. 10 Lesson Plans Book, p. 11	Overhead Transparency #10, *Indefinite Divisibility* and *Sky* Artist Profile Book, pp. 5, 50 Large Prints, *Rhapsody* and *Young Man and Woman in an Inn*	**1.** *The Moon of the Winter Bird* (1992) by Jean Craighead George provides superb examples of the use of cool colors. **2.** *Owl Moon* (1987) by Jane Yolen has watercolor illustrations in exemplary cool colors.	*"Silver Moon,"* by Kitaro, p. T70, CD2:15. *"Silver Moon"* is a contemporary piece using the electronic sounds of the synthesizer.
Vocabulary, pp. 21–22 Assessment, pp. 21–22 Art Across the Curriculum Resource Book, pp. 61–66 Technique Tips Flip Chart, p. 11 Lesson Plans Book, p. 12	Overhead Transparency #11, *Firebirds* and *Rotes Haus* Artist Profile Book, pp. 25, 39 Large Prints, *Rhapsody* and *Young Man and Woman in an Inn*	**1.** *The Firebird* (1993) by Selina Hastings provides rich, warm color illustrations. **2.** *Way Out West Lives a Coyote Named Frank* (1993) by Jillian Lund has vibrant colors of a desert adventure.	"Classical" Symphony (Third Movement), by Sergei Prokofiev, p. T359K, CD9:11. Prokofiev's "Classical" Symphony is a twentieth-century piece that combines modern musical ideas with warm classical tone colors.
Vocabulary, pp. 23–24 Assessment, pp. 23–24 Art Across the Curriculum Resource Book, pp. 67–72 Technique Tips Flip Chart, p. 12 Lesson Plans Book, p. 13	Overhead Transparency #12, *Covered Jar* and *Pistia Kew* Artist Profile Book, pp. 53, 58 Large Prints, *Rhapsody* and *Young Man and Woman in an Inn*	**1.** *Round Trip* (1983) by Ann Jonas provides excellent examples of contrast and creativity. **2.** *The Art of China* (1973) by Shirley Glubok surveys Chinese art with more examples of Ming Dynasty porcelain.	"Variations on the theme 'Pop! Goes the Weasel,'" by Lucien Caillet, p. T47, CD1:34. "Variations on the Theme 'Pop! Goes the Weasel'" features the contrasting tone colors of the string, woodwind, brass, and percussion families of the orchestra.
	Artsource Performing Arts Audio/Video Resource Package: *That Ole' House is Ha'nted* (videocassette)		

*Music references are from **Share the Music,** Macmillan/McGraw-Hill School Publishers

Level 3 Planning Guide   **45B**

LESSON PLANNER

Objectives

After completing this lesson, students will be able to:

- identify primary and secondary colors and tints and shades. *Aesthetic Perception*
- plan and create an illustration of a special occasion, utilizing color to express a mood or an emotion. *Creative Expression*
- use the four steps of art criticism to evaluate their own drawings. *Art Criticism*
- recognize stories and life experiences in each artwork. *Art History and Culture*

Program Resources

- **Overhead:** Both the Russell and the Ringgold are available on overhead 7.
- **Large Prints:** *Rhapsody* by Hans Hofmann and *Young Man and Woman in an Inn* by Frans Hals
- **Technique Tips Flip Chart,** page 7
- **Vocabulary Book** pages 13–14
- **Art Manipulative Kit:** prism
- **Artist Profiles Book:** Russell page 45 and Ringgold page 42
- **Art Across the Curriculum Book** pages 37–42
- **Multimedia Workshop CD-ROM**
- **National Museum of Women in the Arts Collection CD-ROM**
- **Assessment Book** pages 13–14

Multiple Intelligences

Verbal/Linguistic As students mix the three primary colors to create the other colors, they are involved in recognizing and understanding vocabulary, recalling the meanings of terms, and understanding verbal explanations.

Vocabulary

primary colors *colores primarios* colors that cannot be made by mixing other colors—red, yellow, and blue

secondary colors *colores secundarios* colors that are made by mixing two primary colors together

hue *color* another name for *color*

value *valor* the lightness or darkness of a color

shade *sombra* the dark value of a color

tint *tono o tinte* the light value of a color

Looking at Color

Artists mix three primary colors to create many other colors. Color can express different feelings or moods in art.

Shirley Ximena Hopper Russell. (American). *Boys' Day.* 1935. Oil on canvas. $29\frac{5}{8} \times 24\frac{5}{8}$ inches. Honolulu Academy of Arts. Honolulu, Hawaii, Gift of Henry B. Clark, Jr.

Shirley Russell's painting *Boys' Day* is about a holiday celebrated by people flying flags and colorful streamers. Faith Ringgold created the story quilt *Tar Beach.* It tells the story of a third grader who imagines herself flying high above the rooftops of New York. Both artists use color to show the mood of the events they painted.

ART Background

About the Artists

Shirley Russell (shûr' lē rəs' əl, American, 1886–1985) was born in California and moved to Hawaii to teach art at the high school level. For two years, Russell studied art in Paris. Well known for her still lifes and Hawaiian landscapes and seascapes, she exhibited her art in France and in the United States. She died in Honolulu at the age of 98.

Faith Ringgold (fāth ring' gōld, American, 1930–) was born in Harlem. As a little girl, she often missed school due to chronic bouts of asthma. Her mother, a dressmaker, taught her how to create things from fabric. Inspired by this early influence, Ringgold made fabric "story quilts" to tell stories about her life and ancestors.

About Subject Matter* Both the Russell and the Ringgold are narrative pieces.

About the Media The Russell painting is an oil, which is made by suspending pigment in oil. The Ringgold painting is an acrylic, which is a pigment mixed with acrylic resin. It is bordered with quilted fabric.

Faith Ringgold. (American). *Tar Beach.* 1988. Acrylic on canvas bordered with printed, painted, quilted, and pieced cloth. $74\frac{5}{8} \times 68\frac{1}{2}$ inches. Solomon R. Guggenheim Museum, New York, New York. Photograph by David Heald © The Solomon R. Guggenheim Foundation, New York.

Study both paintings to find the following colors.

☑ Find the primary colors—red, yellow, and blue.

☑ Point to the secondary colors—orange, green, and violet.

☑ Where are the light colors? The dark colors?

SEEING LIKE AN ARTIST

Look in a magazine or an advertisement. Find the same colors that you saw in the paintings.

Lesson **1**

47

About Art History* Russell painted in Hawaii at a time when the Royal Hawaiian Band played for the arrival and departure of ships.

Cultural Perspectives Ringgold began painting during the 1960s when African Americans were trying to gain their civil rights. She illustrates the story-telling and quilt-making traditions of her family.

Russell's painting illustrates Boys' Day, a holiday commonly celebrated in Hawaii on May 5. Long streamers of paper carp are displayed, symbolizing the valued qualities of masculinity, fortitude, and persistence.

*See **More About** pages 206–227 for more about art history and subject matter.

FOCUS
Time: About 10 minutes

Activating Prior Knowledge

"Think about the colors you see in the springtime. What colors come to mind?"

"Piensen en los colores que ven en la primavera. ¿Qué colores se les ocurren?"

• Discuss students' responses to primary and secondary colors.

Introducing the Art

"Let's take a close look at the two artworks."

"Vamos a observar de cerca estas dos obras de arte."

• **Describe:** Have students describe the subject matter in each painting. (Both: narratives)

• **COMPARE AND CONTRAST** Have students make a list of the similarities and differences in the two artworks. (Both pieces are outdoor scenes, show deep space, and illustrate a celebration. The Ringgold work is a nighttime scene, while the Russell work is a daytime scene. Ringgold's piece includes many people, while Russell's does not include any.)

• Share and discuss information with the students from **Art Background** and the **Artist Profile Book** about the lives, work, and times of the artists.

• Have students answer the questions on page 47. (See **Perception Hints** below.)

FOR THE ART SPECIALIST

Use the **Overhead** and **Large Prints** *Rhapsody* and *Young Man and Woman in an Inn* to demonstrate how color can express different moods in art.

Perception Hints

Primary colors *Ringgold.* The man at the right-hand side of the table is wearing blue pants and is sitting on a red chair. The woman directly across from him is seated on a yellow cushion.

Secondary colors *Russell.* The earth in the foreground is orange, and the grass in the middle ground is green. The trees in the background, on the left-hand side, are violet.

Light colors *Russell.* The areas in direct sunlight are painted with light colors.

Dark colors *Ringgold.* The buildings in the distance, the roof, and the nighttime sky are painted with dark colors.

TEACH

Time: About two 30-minute periods

Practice

Materials
• paper cut into strips • pencils • shoe boxes

Alternate Method: 2 points for correct answers

"How many color questions can you think of?"

"¿Cuántas preguntas sobre los colores pueden pensar?"

• Discuss color on page 48.
• Distribute materials and have students follow directions on page 48 for a "Color Bee."
• Choose someone from another team randomly to decide if the answer is correct.
• Discuss students' answers to the Decide question.

Create PROBLEM SOLVING

Materials
• 12- × 18-inch white paper • paintbrushes
• markers in assorted colors • water dish
• liquid tempera paints • paper plates
• prism from the **Art Manipulative Kit**
• paper towels • newspaper

Safety! For safety issues about markers, liquid tempera and other information about safety in the art classroom, see page T22.

Alternate Materials: oil pastels or colored pencils

"Let's use the spectral colors, tints, and shades to illustrate a special occasion that expresses a mood."

"Vamos a utilizar los colores del espectro, los tonos y las sombras para ilustrar una ocasión especial que exprese el ánimo."

• Discuss the students' favorite colors and how each one makes them feel.
• Use the prism to show students how light can be separated into colors.
• See page 7 in the **Technique Tips Flip Chart** for visual examples of techniques.
• Distribute the materials and have students follow the directions on page 49.
• Review procedures for mixing shades and tints in **More About Technique Tips** on page 199.

FOR THE ART SPECIALIST

Have students create tints and shades by mixing various colors of tempera with white and then with black.

Using Colors

Colors are used to express different moods or feelings in works of art. **Hue** is another name for color. The three **primary colors** are red, yellow, and blue. They cannot be made by mixing other colors.

The **secondary colors** are made by mixing two primary colors together.

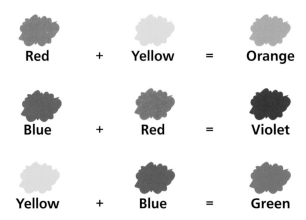

Red	+	**Yellow**	=	**Orange**
Blue	+	**Red**	=	**Violet**
Yellow	+	**Blue**	=	**Green**

Value is the lightness or darkness of a color. Adding white makes a color lighter. Adding black makes a color darker. When the value of a color is lighter, it is called a **tint**. When the value of a color is darker, it is called a **shade**.

Practice

Hold a "Color Bee."

1. Divide into four teams. Think up color questions based on the above information.

2. Write each question on a piece of paper. Fold the papers and put them into a question box.

3. Take turns pulling questions from the box and answering them.

Decide Did each team write questions? Were the questions based on colors and value? Were the teams able to answer the questions?

Activities in
ART Across the Curriculum Book

Reading/Language Arts Identify the different meanings of color words. (page 37)

Math Find shapes in *Tar Beach* and *Boys' Day*, and then create a quilt square. (page 38)

Science Study how color and light are related by using a prism. (page 39)

Social Studies Learn about holidays around the world, like Boys' Day depicted in Shirley Russell's painting. (page 40)

The Arts Understand the mood of music, first looking at how colors create mood in paintings. (page 41)

Technology Use the *Multimedia Workshop* CD-ROM to create a picture of a celebration using color to show mood. (page 42)

Domenique Chery. Age 8. *The Market Place.* Mixed-media.

What mood does this student artist create in her artwork?

Create

What colors do you like? Draw a picture of a special event using the colors that show the feeling of that event.

1. Think of ways that you, your family, and friends celebrate special events. Choose one for your drawing. What objects do you need to include? What colors will you use to show the mood of this event?

2. Draw the event or occasion with colored markers on white construction paper.

3. Fill your paper with color.

Describe What special event did you draw? Describe the people and objects. Point to the tints and shades.

Analyze Name the colors you used. Did you use some colors for special effects?

Interpret What is the mood of your event?

Decide If you could do this drawing again, how would you improve it?

Lesson 1 49

Patterns Use the paintings to study the many interesting patterns found in the quilt border and also in the banners.

Traditions Use the artwork as a springboard to discuss traditions in various cultures.

Celebrations Use Russell's *Boys' Day* as an opportunity to discuss holiday celebrations in different cultures.

When discussing special events, take a moment to quickly sketch elements of these celebrations. ESL students will benefit from seeing a quick sketch that illustrates important parts of celebrations. Pair ESL students with English-speaking peers to discuss special occasions or events.

CLOSE

Time: About 5 minutes

"How can you use color to create a special feeling in a work of art?"

"¿Cómo pueden usar el color para crear un sentimiento especial en una obra de arte?"

Review

Use the **National Museum of Women in the Arts Collection CD-ROM** to have students compare the use of color in other artworks to its use in the works in this lesson.

Art Criticism

Have students answer the four art criticism questions—Describe, Analyze, Interpret, and Decide—orally or in writing. Discuss the use of color in their drawings.

Assess

Use the **Assessment Book** pages 13–14 as a formal assessment for this lesson.

Evaluation Criteria

• Can the student identify the primary and secondary colors and demonstrate mixing tints and shades?

• Can the student use color to create a mood or feeling in a drawing?

• Can the student use the four steps of art criticism to evaluate his or her own work?

• Can the student recognize stories and life experiences in Ringgold's and Russell's artwork?

Reteaching • • • • • • • • • • • •

Color Have students look through the book to find three works of art that incorporate the spectral colors and tints and shades. Ask them to list the title of each work and describe the colors they find.

Perception Hints for Student Art

The artwork creates a happy, party-type mood.

UNIT 2
LESSON 2

LESSON PLANNER

Objectives
After completing this lesson, students will be able to:
- identify the intermediate colors. *Aesthetic Perception*
- create primary, secondary, and intermediate color samples for a class color wheel. *Creative Expression*
- use the four steps of art criticism to evaluate their own color samples and the class color wheel. *Art Criticism*
- identify how artists from diverse cultures utilize intermediate colors. *Art History and Culture*

Program Resources
- **Overhead:** Both *Hat: Birds and Geometric Patterns* and the Wiley are available on overhead 8.
- **Large Prints:** *Rhapsody* by Hans Hofmann and *Young Man and Woman in an Inn* by Frans Hals
- **Technique Tips Flip Chart,** page 8
- **Vocabulary Book** pages 15–16
- **Art Manipulative Kit:** music audiotapes
- **Artist Profiles Book:** Artist unknown page 57 and Wiley page 54
- **Art Across the Curriculum Book** pages 43–48
- **Multimedia Workshop CD-ROM**
- **Assessment Book** pages 15–16

Multiple Intelligences
Visual/Spatial Students can use intermediate colors to express ideas and emotions to relate accurate perception and recognize the relationships of colors.

Vocabulary
intermediate colors *colores intermedios* colors made by mixing a primary color with a secondary color

primary colors *colores primarios* colors that cannot be made by mixing other colors—red, yellow, and blue

secondary colors *colores secundarios* colors that are made by mixing two primary colors together

---

Intermediate Colors

Some artists use intermediate colors in their work to express different ideas and emotions.

Artist unknown. (Peru). **Hat: Birds and Geometric Patterns.** 700–1000. Alpaca and cotton. $4\frac{1}{2} \times 5$ inches. The Seattle Art Museum, Gift of Jack Lenor Larson. Photo by Paul Macapia Seattle, Washington.

Look at the two works of art on these pages. The cap was woven in the South American country now named Peru, sometime between A.D. 700 and 1000. William Wiley's painting was done in the United States almost 1000 years later. Both artists used intermediate colors in their works.

50

ART Background

About the Artist
William T. Wiley (wil′ yəm wī′ lē, American, 1937–) incorporates numerous words and images in his work, which creates many layers of meaning. He often misspells words intentionally in order to convey a double meaning. The text in *Remedial Archaeology and the Like* reveals the artist's personal stories as well as his philosophical statements.

About Subject Matter* *Hat: Birds and Geometric Patterns* is a nonobjective textile. The Wiley is a narrative piece.

About the Media The cap is woven with cotton and alpaca. Alpaca is the wool from an alpaca. The Wiley painting is acrylic and graphite. Acrylic is a pigment mixed with an acrylic vehicle.

William T. Wiley. (American). *Remedial Archaeology and the Like.* 1986. Acrylic and graphite on canvas. 100 × 165 inches. Collection of the Birmingham Museum of Art, Birmingham, Alabama; Museum purchase with funds provided by the National Endowment for the Arts and Museum Store.

Study both artworks to find the intermediate colors.

- ✓ Find the yellow-orange hues. Where are the red-orange hues?

- ✓ What other intermediate colors can you find?

SEEING LIKE AN ARTIST

Look through this unit. Find more examples of the colors you saw in the art on these pages.

Lesson 2   51

About Art History* The *Hat* was woven at a time in Peru when the Incas created varied and sophisticated textiles, and cloth held great value. Cloth at that time was used as a means of exchange.

Wiley created his artwork in the 1970s and 1980s, a time when performance pieces dramatized movement, sounds, images, and music rather than dialogue.

Cultural Perspectives The *Hat* is an example of the Andean textiles that were preserved in the dry desert south of Lima, Peru. This hat may have once adorned an ancient mummy.

Wiley painted during the time in the late 1960s and early 1970s when America's younger generation protested the United States' involvement in the Vietnam War.

*See **More About** pages 206–227 for more about art history and subject matter.

FOCUS
Time: About 10 minutes

Activating Prior Knowledge
"Think about the colors you see in a beautiful bouquet of flowers. Can you describe them?"
"Piensen en los colores que verían en un ramo de flores. ¿Los pueden describir?"

- Discuss students' responses about colors seen in flowers.

Introducing the Art
"Look closely at the two works of art."
"Observen detalladamente estas dos obras de arte."

- **Describe:** Have students describe the subject matter of each piece. (*Hat:* utilitarian object; Wiley: narrative)

- **COMPARE AND CONTRAST** Have students make a list of the similarities and differences in the two artworks. (Both incorporate a variety of shapes and images and utilize the intermediate red-orange color scheme. Wiley's artwork is two-dimensional, is not utilitarian, and shows a broad spectrum of colors.)

- Share and discuss information with the students from **Art Background** and the **Artist Profiles Book** about the lives, work, and times of the artists.

- Have students answer the questions on page 51. (See **Perception Hints** below.)

FOR THE ART SPECIALIST

Use the **Overhead** and the **Large Prints** *Rhapsody* and *Young Man and Woman in an Inn* to demonstrate that some artists use intermediate colors in their work to express different ideas and emotions.

Perception Hints

Yellow-orange *Hat.* The bird shape in the black area at the bottom is yellow-orange.
Red-orange *Hat.* The tassels at the top are red-orange.
Yellow-green *Wiley.* There is yellow-green to the right of the triangular shape in the center of the artwork.
Blue-green *Wiley.* There is a blue-green area above the sun image.
Red-violet *Wiley.* Red-violet can be found in the area above the large S-curve on the right-hand side.
Blue-violet *Wiley.* Blue-violet can be found in the area to the right of the hat that is drawn near the center.

TEACH

Time: About two 30-minute periods

Practice

Materials
- 9- × 12-inch paper folded into six boxes
- magazines
- glue

 For safety issues about glue and other information about safety in the art classroom, see page T22.

Alternate Materials: paper scraps

"How many examples of intermediate colors can you find?"
"¿Cuántos ejemplos de colores intermedios pueden hallar?"

- Discuss how intermediate colors are made on page 52.
- Distribute the materials and have students follow the directions on page 52 for finding intermediate colors. Have them answer the Decide question with a partner.

Create PROBLEM SOLVING

ART MANIPULATIVES While students are creating their artworks, play the music audiotapes from the **Art Manipulative Kit.**

Materials
- 12- × 18-inch white construction paper
- liquid tempera paints
- paper plates for palettes
- brushes of various sizes
- containers of water
- paper towels
- newspaper
- scissors

Alternate Materials: watercolor paints

"Let's use paint to mix the intermediate colors."
"Vamos a usar pintura para mezclar los colores intermedios."

- Review methods for mixing intermediate colors.
- Review procedures for working with tempera paints in **More About Technique Tips** on page 199.
- See page 8 in the **Technique Tips Flip Chart** for visual examples of techniques.
- Distribute materials and have students follow the directions on page 53.

FOR THE ART SPECIALIST

Have students create a new shape using their color samples in order.

Using Intermediate Colors

Intermediate colors are made by mixing a **primary color** and a **secondary color**. There are six intermediate colors—red-orange, yellow-orange, yellow-green, blue-green, blue-violet, and red-violet.

A **color wheel** is an artist's way of organizing these 12 colors.

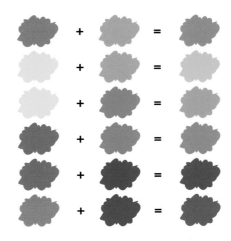

Practice

Find intermediate colors. Use magazines and scissors.

1. Fold a sheet of paper into six equal boxes. Write the name of one intermediate color in each box.

2. Find examples of intermediate colors in magazines. Glue each example into the correct box.

Decide Did you find all six intermediate colors?

Activities in
ART Across the Curriculum Book

Reading/Language Arts Write a poem or paragraph about an intermediate color. (page 43)

Math Learn how to solve problems. (page 44)

Science Study the *Hat* and two other objects to determine what kind of materials they are made of. (page 45)

Social Studies Compare and contrast the United States with Peru. (page 46)

The Arts Create a dance about a favorite color, using the color to help create the mood. (page 47)

Technology Use the *Multimedia Workshop* CD-ROM to create overlapping shapes filled with primary, secondary, and intermediate hues. (page 48)

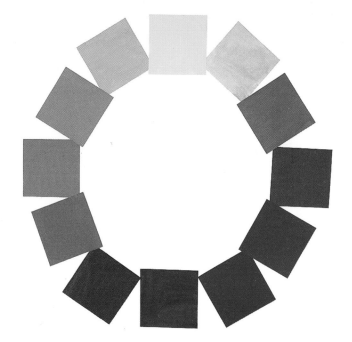

Which colors make you happy? Which colors make you sad?

Ivie Gulbrandson and others. Age 8. *A Color Wheel.* Tempera.

Create

What colors make you feel happy? Sad? Excited? Create a giant color wheel using primary, secondary, and intermediate colors.

1. Cut a large sheet of drawing paper into 12 pieces. Put a large spoonful of red, yellow, and blue paint on a paper plate. Paint three pieces of paper with primary colors. Mix secondary colors and paint three more pieces of paper.

2. Now mix the intermediate colors. Paint the six remaining pieces of paper with these colors.

3. Use your color samples to make a giant temporary class color wheel on the floor.

Lesson 2

Describe Name the primary, secondary, and intermediate colors in the color wheel.

Analyze Compare the intermediate colors in the color wheel. Why do you think some look different?

Interpret How do each of the intermediate colors make you feel?

Decide Which of the intermediate colors came out best? Which would you redo? Why?

53

Discovery Use the artwork as examples of how the eye perceives color.
Patterns Use the artwork as visual examples of how colors are related.
Cultures Use the *Tasseled Cap* to discuss how we learn about ancient peoples and cultures through our discoveries of objects they used.

During the Create section of the lesson, model the steps with your own color wheel as you give directions to the whole class. ESL students will achieve greater comprehension of the vocabulary and process if they follow visual clues in addition to the oral directions.

"How do the intermediate colors look to you?"
"¿Cómo les parecen los colores intermedios?"

 Review
Use the **Large Prints** *Rhapsody* and *Young Man and Woman in an Inn* to have students identify and compare intermediate colors in the prints and in the works in this lesson.

Art Criticism
Have students answer the four art criticism questions—Describe, Analyze, Interpret, and Decide—orally or in writing. Discuss the intermediate colors they mixed for their color samples.

 Assess
Use the **Assessment Book** pages 15–16 as a formal assessment for this lesson.

Evaluation Criteria
- Can the student identify the intermediate colors?
- Can the student use primary and secondary colors to mix intermediate colors and correctly locate placement for the primary, secondary, and intermediate color samples in the large class color wheel?
- Can the student use the four steps of art criticism to evaluate his or her own work?
- Can the student identify how artists from diverse cultures use intermediate colors?

Reteaching • • • • • • • • • • •

Intermediate colors Have students look around the classroom and find six objects with intermediate colors. Ask them to list the objects and name the intermediate colors for each.

Perception Hints for Student Art

Answers will vary, however the student might answer that bright colors make them happy and dark colors make them sad.

UNIT 2
LESSON 3

LESSON PLANNER

Objectives
After completing this lesson, students will be able to:

- identify and perceive the specific arrangement of colors in the color wheel. *Aesthetic Perception*
- create a color wheel ride for "The Rainbow Park." *Creative Expression*
- use the four steps of art criticism to evaluate their own artwork. *Art Criticism*
- compare the background of the two artists. *Art History and Culture*

Program Resources
- **Overhead:** Both the Man Ray and the Jones are available on overhead 9.
- **Large Prints:** *Rhapsody* by Hans Hofmann and *Young Man and Woman in an Inn* by Frans Hals
- **Technique Tips Flip Chart,** page 9
- **Vocabulary Book** pages 17–18
- **Art Manipulative Kit:** color wheel
- **Artist Profiles Book:** Man Ray page 29 and Jones page 23
- **Art Across the Curriculum Book** pages 49–54
- **Multimedia Workshop CD-ROM**
- **Assessment Book** pages 17–18

Multiple Intelligences
Logical/Mathematical Students can understand that the relationships of colors on the color wheel require using logic and mathematical intelligence to discern these relationships and connections.

Vocabulary
color spectrum *colores del espectro* the range of colors that comes from light

color wheel *círculo cromático* a tool for organizing colors that shows the spectrum bent into a circle

FOCUS
Time: About 10 minutes

Activating Prior Knowledge
"Think about the colors you see in a rainbow. See if you can name them in the order in which they appear."

"Piensen en los colores que ven en un arco iris. Fíjense si pueden nombrarlos en el orden en que aparecen."

- Discuss students' responses and how the spectral colors appear in a specific order.

Color Wheel

Artists use the color wheel to get information and ideas about spectral and intermediate colors and how they relate to one another.

Man Ray. (American). *La Fortune*. 1938. Oil on canvas. 24 × 29 inches. © Collection of the Whitney Museum of American Art, New York, New York. © 1998 Artists Rights Society (ARS), New York/ADAGP/Man Ray Trust, Paris.

Look at the works of art on these pages. Both artists have used spectral colors. *La Fortune* was painted by Man Ray in 1938. At about the same time, Calvin Jones created *Brilliant as the Sun upon the World*.

 **ART Background**

About the Artists
Man Ray (American, 1890–1977) was born in Philadelphia. He was a photographer, painter, and filmmaker. In 1917, he invented the "rayograph," a cameraless photographic image that is created by placing objects on photosensitive paper and exposing it to light. He lived in Paris from 1920–1940 and became an established *avant-garde* figure.

Calvin Jones (kal' vin jōnz, American, 1934–   ) began exhibiting his artistic talent while in elementary school in Chicago. After high school he won a full scholarship to the Art Institute of Chicago where he majored in drawing, painting, and illustration.

About Subject Matter* Man Ray's *La Fortune* is a landscape painting. The Jones assemblage is an example of iconography.

About the Media Man Ray's work is an oil painting, which is a pigment mixed with oil. Jones's work is a mixed-media assemblage, which incorporates a variety of media.

Calvin Jones. (American). *Brilliant as the Sun Upon the World.*

Study both works of art to find the following colors.

- ✓ Find the primary colors.
- ✓ Where are the secondary colors?
- ✓ Which artist used intermediate colors?

SEEING LIKE AN ARTIST

Look around you to see how many colors of the spectrum you can find.

Lesson **3**   55

About Art History* Man Ray created art during the Dada movement when artists, protesting the madness of war, created absurd images meant to denounce, shock, and awaken the imagination.

After 17 years as a successful graphic designer and illustrator, Calvin Jones returned to fine art. He is known for his use of bright colors and texture.

Cultural Perspectives Man Ray created art after World War I, a time when the new machine-age technology was being blamed for the terrible destruction of war.

Calvin Jones is an experienced muralist, easel painter, and commercial artist. He has received wide acclaim for his images of the African American experience.

*See **More About** pages 206–227 for more about art history and subject matter.

Introducing the Art

"Let's take a close look at the two artworks."
"Vamos a observar detalladamente estas dos obras de arte."

- **Describe:** Have students describe the subject matter in each artwork. (Ray: fantasy; Jones: iconography)
- **COMPARE AND CONTRAST** Have students make a list of the similarities and differences in the two paintings. (Both works include objects found in nature and incorporate the spectral and intermediate colors. Jones's piece depicts images of animals, while Ray's does not. Jones's is a relief sculpture and uses real texture. Ray's painting is two-dimensional and shows a smooth, visual texture.
- Share and discuss information from **Art Background** and the **Artist Profiles Book** with the students about the lives, work, and times of the artists.
- Have students answer the questions on page 55. (See **Perception Hints** below.)

FOR THE ART SPECIALIST

Use the **Overhead** and the color wheel from the **Art Manipulative Kit** to demonstrate how the colors on a color wheel relate to one another.

Perception Hints

Primary colors *Jones.* The image of the cat, in the lower left-hand corner, is on a red background and is bordered with yellow and blue.
Secondary colors *Man Ray.* There are orange, green, and violet clouds in the sky.
Intermediate colors *Jones.* Intermediate colors can be found in the various fabric pieces incorporated into the design.

TEACH

Time: About two 30-minute periods

Practice

Materials
- 8 $\frac{1}{2}$- × 11-inch paper
- crayons

Alternate Materials: magazines

"How can you create spectral and intermediate colors?"

"¿Cómo se pueden crear los colores del espectro y los intermedios?"

- Discuss the spectral and intermediate colors on page 56, using the Large Prints.
- Use the **Large Prints** *Rhapsody* and *Young Man and Woman in the Inn* to discuss the order of the colors.
- Distribute materials and have students follow the directions on page 56 for creating a color chart. Ask them to answer the Decide orally.

Create PROBLEM SOLVING

Materials
- construction paper
- posterboard
- scissors
- glue
- sketch paper
- markers

Safety! For safety issues about glue and other information about safety in the art classroom, see page T22.

Alternate Material: paints and posterboard

"Let's use the spectral and intermediate colors to create our own color wheel carnival ride."

"Vamos a utilizar los colores del espectro y los intermedios para crear nuestra propia rueda de colores con un círculo cromático."

- Brainstorm ideas for making color wheel carnival rides creative and unique.
- Review the order or placement of the spectral and intermediate colors on the color wheel.

 See page 9 in the **Technique Tips Flip Chart** for visual examples of techniques.

- Distribute the materials and have students follow the directions on page 57.

FOR THE ART SPECIALIST

Have the students use colored tissue paper to create intermediate colors.

Using a Color Wheel

The range of colors that comes from light is called the **color spectrum**. Rainbows are the most famous display of this spectrum in nature. The spectrum that artists use is bent into the shape of a circle. It is called a **color wheel**.

The color wheel includes the six spectral colors and six intermediate colors. Like the colors in the spectrum, these colors are always placed in the same order, no matter which way you turn the wheel.

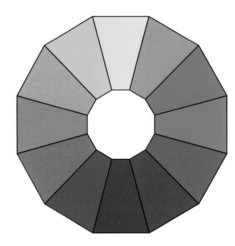

Practice

Make a color chart. Use crayons.

1. Divide paper in half. Label one side "Spectral Colors" and other side "Intermediate Colors."

2. Use crayons to show the colors in order on each side.

Decide Name the spectral and intermediate colors in their correct order.

Activities in ART Across the Curriculum Book

Reading/Language Arts Organize thoughts and ideas, much like the color wheel organizes the spectral colors. (page 49)

Math Solve story problems about the painting *La Fortune*. (page 50)

Science Study the relationship of the sun to Earth, both mentioned in the art title *Brilliant as the Sun Upon the World*. (page 51)

Social Studies Learn about time zones, noting how they are always in the same order, like colors in the color wheel. (page 52)

The Arts Role-play a morning routine, looking first at Calvin Jones's painting. (page 53)

Technology Use the *Multimedia Workshop* CD-ROM to create a color wheel. (page 54)

Michael Dean. Age 8. Tempera.

Name this student artist's color wheel amusement ride.

Create

What is your favorite amusement ride? Create an amusement ride for the Rainbow Park using the colors of a color wheel.

1. Think about an amusement ride you can make using all the colors from a color wheel in order.

2. Be creative. Just remember that the colors have to follow the order of the color wheel.

Describe Name all the colors you used in your ride?

Analyze How did you organize your colors?

Interpret Give your ride a name.

Decide Did you make an interesting ride?

Lesson **3** 57

"How would you describe the color wheel ride?"
"¿Cómo describirían la rueda de colores que crearon?"

 Review Use the color wheel from the **Art Manipulative Kit** to have students compare the order of the colors in their color wheel rides.

Art Criticism

Have students answer the four art criticism questions—Describe, Analyze, Interpret, and Decide—orally or in writing. Discuss the arrangement of color in their rides.

 Assess Use the **Assessment Book** pages 17–18 as a formal assessment for this lesson.

Evaluation Criteria

• Can the student identify the spectral and intermediate colors and place the colors in their proper order?

• Can the student create a nontraditional color wheel ride?

• Can the student use the four steps of art criticism to evaluate his or her own work?

• Can the student compare the two artists' backgrounds?

Reteaching • • • • • • • • • • •

Color wheel Have students look through the book to find a work of art that incorporates all the spectral and intermediate colors. Ask them to write the title of the work and, in the order in which they appear on the color wheel, list the colors and where they are found in the work.

Perception Hints for Student Art

Answers will vary, however an acceptable answer might be "Color Loop."

THEME Connections

Discovery Use the artwork as visual examples of spectral and intermediate colors found in nature.

Patterns Use the artwork as examples of how color patterns can create certain feelings.

Connections Use the artwork as examples of artistic fantasies that stimulate the imagination.

ESL

ESL students may be reluctant to discuss their artwork. To familiarize them with the vocabulary they need to describe their color wheel rides, write the descriptions that other students share on chart paper. Draw a quick sketch to illustrate the concept. Encourage ESL students to refer to the chart when they describe and interpret their own color wheel rides.

LESSON PLANNER

Objectives

After completing this lesson, students should be able to:

- identify the cool colors and their expressive qualities. *Aesthetic Perception*
- plan and create a three-dimensional sculpture using cool colors. *Creative Expression*
- use the four steps of art criticism to evaluate their own sculptures. *Art Criticism*
- compare works by artists from different cultures. *Art History and Culture*

Program Resources

- **Overhead:** Both the Tanguy and the Carr are available on overhead 10.
- **Large Prints:** *Rhapsody* by Hans Hofmann
- **Technique Tips Flip Chart,** page 10
- **Vocabulary Book** pages 19–20
- **Art Manipulative Kit:** color wheel
- **Artist Profiles Book:** Tanguy page 50 and Carr page 5
- **Art Across the Curriculum Book** pages 55–60
- **Multimedia Workshop CD-ROM**
- **National Geographic Picture Atlas of the World CD-ROM**
- **National Museum of Women in the Arts Collection:** prints
- **Assessment Book** pages 19–20

Multiple Intelligences

Intrapersonal Students can understand that using cool colors to suggest controlled emotion calls for inner awareness and individual expression of feelings.

Vocabulary

cool colors *colores frescos o fríos* blue, green, and violet

FOCUS

Time: About 10 minutes

Activating Prior Knowledge

"Think about things in nature that feel cool. What colors are these objects?"

"Piensen en cosas de la naturaleza que sean frías. ¿De qué color son estas cosas?"

- Discuss students' responses and how blues, greens, and violets give a feeling of coolness.

Cool Colors

Artists use cool colors to suggest a calm emotion or feeling. Cool colors often remind people of cool things such as ice, snow, water, or grass.

Yves Tanguy. (French). *Indefinite Divisibility*. 1942. Oil on canvas. 40 × 35 inches. Albright Knox Art Gallery, Buffalo, New York, Room of Contemporary Art Fund, 1945 © 1998 Artists Rights Society (ARS) New York/ADAGP, Paris.

Look at the artwork on these pages. The title of Tanguy's painting is almost a brainteaser. It says the subject of the painting can be divided over and over. Emily Carr turns her sky into a roller coaster. Both artists use cool colors in their art.

 **ART Background**

About the Artists

Yves Tanguy (ēv tän gē', French, 1900–1955) was a self-taught painter who was influenced by a painting by the Surrealist artist Giorgio de Chirico. Tanguy eventually developed a consistent style that depicts a vast and desolate universe.

Emily Carr (em' ə lē kär, Canadian, 1871–1945) was born in Victoria, British Columbia. Two distinct themes run through her work: nature and the cultural heritage of the Canadian West Coast indigenous people. She was noted for her detailed painting of trees.

- .Use the **National Geographic Picture Atlas of the World CD-ROM** to compare the two different cultures of Tanguy and Carr.

About Subject Matter* The Tanguy is a fantasy piece. The Carr is a landscape painting.

About the Media The Tanguy painting is an oil. The Carr is an oil painting on paper.

Emily Carr. (Canadian). *Sky.* 1935. Oil on woven paper. 58.7 × 90.7 cm. National Gallery of Canada. Ottawa, Canada.

Study both works of art to find the following cool colors.

✓ Find the blues.

✓ Find the intermediate colors blue-green and blue-violet.

✓ How do the cool colors affect the mood of each painting?

SEEING LIKE AN ARTIST

Look through magazines to find pictures of blue, green, and violet things in nature. Write down what you see.

Lesson **4**   59

About Art History* Tanguy, a Frenchmen, was a Surrealist, one of a group of artists and poets who created artwork that illustrated dream images. In their art, they wanted to unite the world of dreams and fantasy with everyday reality.

Two artists in particular made an impact on Carr and her art. They were Lawren Harris, whose work consisted of nature scenes of the remote northern West Coast, and Mark Tobey, who helped her translate the inspiration she felt into her painting.

Cultural Perspectives Tanguy was part of Surrealism, a movement that began in the 1920s as a protest against the rationalism that guided Western culture. Their work related to the symbolism developed by Sigmund Freud in his psychological studies of dreams.

During Carr's childhood, there were no true art groups, like the Impressionist painters in France. Instead, the emphasis was on art activity rather than on the actual artwork.

*See **More About** pages 206–227 for more about art history and subject matter.

Introducing the Art

"Look closely at the two artworks."

"Observen detalladamente estas dos obras de arte."

- **Describe:** Have students describe the subject matter in each artwork. (Tanguy: fantasy; Carr: landscape)

- For further examples of artwork created by women, use the **National Museum of Women in the Arts Collection** prints.

- **COMPARE AND CONTRAST** Have students make a list of the similarities and differences in the two artworks. (Both illustrate depth and use cool colors in the background. Tanguy's is very defined, and Carr's is impressionistic. Tanguy's images are imaginary, while Carr's are naturalistic.)

- Share and discuss information with the students from **Art Background** and the **Artist Profiles Book** about the lives, work, and times of the artists.

- Have students answer the questions on page 59. (See **Perception Hints** below.)

FOR THE ART SPECIALIST

Use the **Overhead** and the **Large Print** *Rhapsody* to demonstrate how artists use cool colors to suggest a calm emotion or feeling.

Perception Hints

Blue *Carr.* Blue can be found in the mountains and shades of blue in the sky.

Blue-green *Tanguy.* Blue-green can be found in the middle ground and in the circles.

Blue-violet *Carr.* Blue-violet can be found in the middle of the sky and in the mountains.

Mood *Tanguy* and *Carr.* Both paintings create a calm feeling.

TEACH

Time: About two 30-minute periods

Practice
Materials
- 9- × 12-inch paper
- crayons: blue, green, and violet

Alternate Materials: colored pencils

 For safety issues about crayons and other information about safety in the art classroom, see page T22.

"How can you create a drawing using cool colors?"

"¿Cómo pueden crear un dibujo usando colores frescos?"

- Discuss cool colors on page 60 and ways to mix the cool intermediate colors.
- Distribute the materials and have students follow the directions on page 60 for creating a drawing using cool colors. Have them answer the Decide question on the back of their drawings.

Create PROBLEM SOLVING
Materials
- 9- × 12-inch construction paper (cool colors)
- scissors
- sketch paper
- tape or glue
- pencils
- oil pastels (cool colors)
- markers

Alternate Materials: wood scraps and liquid tempera paints

"How can you create a cool environment?"

"¿Cómo pueden crear un ambiente fresco?"

- Brainstorm ideas for different environments.
- Review the cool spectral and intermediate colors, using the color wheel from the **Art Manipulative Kit.**

See page 10 in the **Technique Tips Flip Chart** for visual examples of techniques.

- Distribute materials and have students follow the directions on page 61.

FOR THE ART SPECIALIST

Have students wearing cool colors use themselves to create a "Cool Sculpture."

Using Cool Colors

Blue, green, and violet are **cool colors**. They remind us of cool things such as grass, water, and ice. Yellow-green, green, blue-green, blue, violet, and blue-violet are cool colors that are related, like members of a family. You can find them on a color wheel to see what they have in common.

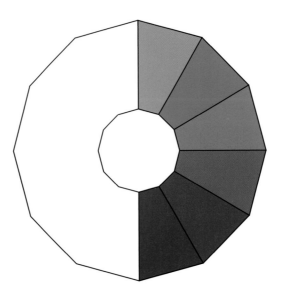

Practice

Create a drawing using cool colors. Use crayons and white paper.

1. Write these words on a sheet of paper: *ocean, sky, grapes, grass, leaves,* and *lettuce.*

2. On the same sheet of paper, create a drawing including each of the objects listed above. Using the correct cool colors, color the objects.

Decide Were you successful at using the cool colors to color your objects?

Activities in
ART Across the Curriculum Book

Reading/Language Arts Understand how to use a play on words, like using the phrase "on cloud nine." (page 55)

Math Write division problems for groups of objects. (page 56)

Science Learn more about clouds, like the ones depicted in *Sky.* (page 57)

Social Studies Learn more about rules and laws, noting that the rules are found in urban and rural places, like the one seen in *Sky.* (page 58)

The Arts Identify sounds that may create a cool feeling, like how cool colors create a similar mood in painting. (page 59)

Technology Use the *Multimedia Workshop* CD-ROM to create a fantasy landscape scene filled with cool colors. (page 60)

Give this student artist's sculpture a name that ties its cool colors with the environment.

Jenna Mooney. Age 8. *A Park in the Future.* Mixed-media.

Create

Where in your environment do you see cool colors? Design a sculpture of an environment using cool colors.

1. Think of ideas dealing with your environment, such as an animal habitat or a playground in the year 3001. Choose an idea and sketch a few things you would find there.

2. Select several pieces of cool-colored paper. Choose one piece for the base. Outline objects you want in your environment on the other sheets of paper and cut them out. Add detail with oil pastels in cool colors. Attach the objects to your base.

Describe Describe your environment. What cool colors did you use?

Analyze What objects did you use in your environment? How did you decide where to place them?

Interpret How did using only cool colors affect the mood of your environment?

Decide If you could redo your sculpture, what would you do? If you could add other colors, what would they be?

Lesson **4** 61

Diversity Use the artwork to discuss the different types of environments where people live.

Scale and Structure Use the artwork to discuss and compare actual size to perceived size.

Models Use the artwork to discuss how color can create a particular feeling, such as peacefulness or excitement, in a room.

Pair ESL students with more fluent English-speaking peers to look through magazines to find blue, green, and violet things in nature. Use this as an opportunity for the ESL student to learn new vocabulary in a low-risk way. The English speaker can write their findings if the ESL student is at the emergent stage of writing in English.

CLOSE

Time: About 5 minutes

"What feelings or moods do cool colors express?"
"¿Qué sentimientos o ánimos expresan los colores frescos?"

Review

Display the students' drawings and compare the use of cool colors in their artwork to their use in the works in this lesson.

Art Criticism

Have students answer the four art criticism questions—Describe, Analyze, Interpret, and Decide—orally or in writing. Discuss the expressive effects of cool colors in their sculptural environments.

Assess

Use the **Assessment Book** pages 19–20 as a formal assessment for this lesson.

Evaluation Criteria

• Can the student identify cool colors and their expressive effects?

• Can the student create a three-dimensional environmental sculpture by manipulating paper and using a variety of cool colors?

• Can the student use the four steps of art criticism to evaluate his or her own work?

• Can the student compare the two artists' works from different cultures?

Reteaching ● ● ● ● ● ● ● ● ● ● ● ●

Cool colors Have students look through the book to find three works of art that use cool colors. Ask them to list the title of each work and describe the cool colors they find.

Perception Hints for Student Art

Answers will vary, however an acceptable answer would be *Cool Play.*

Warm Colors

Artists use warm colors to add warmth to a piece of artwork. Warm colors often remind people of the sun, fire, and light.

Paul Klee. (Swiss). *Rotes Haus.* 1929. Oil on canvas mounted on cardboard. 10 × 10⅞ inches. San Francisco Museum of Modern Art, San Francisco, California. Gift of the Ojerassi Art Trust.

Look at the artwork on these pages. *Rotes Haus* means "red house." *Firebirds* is a **batik** painting, which uses hot wax and colored dyes to create a design on fabric. Both artists have used warm colors in their artwork.

UNIT 2
LESSON 5

LESSON PLANNER

Objectives
After completing this lesson, students will be able to:
- identify warm colors and their expressive qualities. *Aesthetic Perception*
- plan and create an imaginary landscape painting using a variety of warm colors. *Creative Expression*
- use the four steps of art criticism to evaluate their own paintings. *Art Criticism*
- describe how artwork from different cultures use color in a similar way. *Art History and Culture*

Program Resources
- **Overhead:** Both the Klee and the Ragans are available on overhead 11.
- **Large Prints:** *Rhapsody* by Hans Hofmann and *Young Man and Woman in an Inn* by Frans Hals
- **Technique Tips Flip Chart,** page 11
- **Vocabulary Book** pages 21–22
- **Art Manipulative Kit:** color wheel
- **Artist Profiles Book:** Klee page 25 and Ragans page 39
- **Art Across the Curriculum Book** pages 61–66
- **Multimedia Workshop CD-ROM**
- **National Geographic Picture Atlas of the World CD-ROM**
- **Assessment Book** pages 21–22

Multiple Intelligences
Body/Kinesthetic Students can use warm colors and materials to add warmth to a piece of artwork.

Vocabulary
batik *batik* the method of using wax and dye on fabric to create a picture or design

warm colors *colores cálidos* colors that give a feeling of warmth—red-violet, red, red-orange, and yellow

spectral colors *colores del espectro* colors of the rainbow—red, orange, yellow, green,

ART Background

About the Artists
Paul Klee (paul klā, Swiss 1879–1940) was born in Switzerland and studied in Germany. He was an accomplished violinist and painter. He used line and color to imitate the simplicity of children's artwork.

Rosalind Ragans (roz ə lind rā gənz, American, 1933–   ), author of *Art Connections* and *Art Talk,* lives in Georgia where she taught art at the laboratory school of Georgia Southern University. Her love of dance is evident in her unique batik paintings.

Use the **National Geographic Picture Atlas of the World CD-ROM** to discover more about the country where Paul Klee lived.

About Subject Matter* The Klee is an example of iconography, and the Ragans is a portrait.

About the Media The Klee is an oil painting, which is an opaque pigment mixed with oil. The Ragans is a batik, which is a dye and wax-resist on fabric.

Rosalind Ragans. (American). *Firebirds.* 1983. Dye on cotton. 36 × 48 inches. Private collection.

Study both works of art to find the following warm colors.

☑ Find the spectral hues red, orange, and yellow.

☑ Where are the intermediate hues red-orange and yellow-orange?

☑ How would you describe the mood or feeling of each piece?

SEEING LIKE AN ARTIST

Look at what your classmates are wearing. Find examples of the warm hues like those you saw in the artwork.

Lesson 5   **63**

About Art History* Klee painted during a time in 1930s Germany when Hitler banned jazz from the airwaves, confiscated artworks, and burned many American novels.

Ragans created in America during a time when a number of dramatists and choreographers created "performance pieces."

Cultural Perspectives Klee lived in Munich, Germany, during a time when the economic crisis of 1929 opened the door for the Nazi dictator Adolph Hitler, which resulted in the terrible devastation of the Holocaust and World War II.

Ragans worked and created from the 1950s to the present. She was aware of the "women's liberation" movement in America, which addressed the issue of discrimination against women.

*See **More About** pages 206–227 for more about art history and subject matter.

FOCUS

Time: About 10 minutes

Activating Prior Knowledge

"Think about things in nature that feel hot. What colors are these objects?"

"Piensen en cosas de la naturaleza que sean calientes. ¿De qué color son estas cosas?"

• Discuss students' responses and how reds, oranges, and yellows give a feeling of warmth.

Introducing the Art

"Let's look closely at the two artworks."

"Vamos a observar detalladamente estas dos obras de arte."

• **Describe:** Have students describe the subject matter in each artwork. (Klee: iconography; Ragans: portrait)

• **COMPARE AND CONTRAST** Have students make a list of the similarities and differences in the two artworks. (Both artworks illustrate shallow space, utilize the subject as the center of interest, and use warm colors. The Klee has large simple geometric shapes, while the Ragans has free-form shapes. Horizontal and vertical lines make the Klee appear stable and calm, while the diagonal and fluid lines in the Ragans give a feeling of movement.)

• Share and discuss information with the students from **Art Background** and the **Artist Profiles Book** about the lives, work, and times of the artists.

• Have students answer the questions on page 63. (See **Perception Hints** below.)

FOR THE ART SPECIALIST

Use the **Overhead** and the **Large Prints** *Rhapsody* and *Young Man and Woman in an Inn* to demonstrate how artists use warm colors to add warmth to a piece of artwork.

Perception Hints

Red, orange, and yellow *Ragans.* These warm colors can be found throughout the background area.

Red-orange and yellow-orange *Ragans.* These colors can be found in the areas closest to the figures.

Mood *Klee* and *Ragans.* Both artworks have a feeling of warmth.

TEACH

Time: About two 30-minute periods

Practice

Materials
- 9- × 12-inch paper folded into three boxes
- watercolor paints
- paintbrushes
- containers of water

Safety! For safety issues about watercolors and other information about safety in the art classroom, see page T22.

Alternate Materials: crayons

"How can you create a variety of warm colors?"
"¿Cómo se pueden crear una variedad de colores cálidos?"

- Discuss warm colors on page 64 and ways to mix the intermediate warm colors.
- Review procedures for working with watercolors in **More About** Technique Tips on page 200.
- Distribute the materials and have students follow the directions on page 64 for mixing warm colors. Have them answer the Decide question with a partner.

Create PROBLEM SOLVING

Materials
- 12- × 18-inch white construction paper
- oil pastels
- watercolor paints
- brushes of various sizes
- containers of water
- sketch paper
- pencils
- tape
- paper towels

Alternate Materials: dustless chalk

"Let's use warm colors to create an imaginary painting."
"Vamos a usar colores cálidos para crear una pintura imaginaria."

- Brainstorm ways to include three unrelated items as part of a painting.
- Review the warm colors.
- Review procedures for working with paint in **More About Technique Tips** on page 199.
- See page 11 in the **Technique Tips Flip Chart** for visual examples of techniques.
- Distribute materials and have students follow the directions on page 65.

FOR THE ART SPECIALIST

Have students try the wet-on-wet technique of mixing watercolors.

Using Warm Colors

Warm colors are the **spectral colors** yellow, orange, and red that give a feeling of warmth in a work of art. They can be found opposite the cool colors on the color wheel.

Red-violet, red, red-orange, orange, yellow-orange, and yellow are warm colors that are related. They remind many people of warm or hot things like fire and the sun.

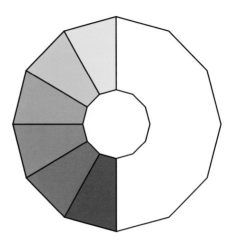

Practice

Mix a variety of warm colors. Use watercolor paints, brushes, and white paper.

1. Fold your paper into three equal parts. Paint the first box red, the middle box orange, and the last box yellow.

2. While the paint is still wet, add different amounts of violet to the red box, then mix.

3. In the same way, add and mix red to the orange, and orange to the yellow.

Decide Did you mix a variety of warm intermediate colors?

Activities in
ART Across the Curriculum Book

Reading/Language Arts Add -er and -est to adjectives. (page 61)

Math Find shapes in Paul Klee's artwork. (page 62)

Science Learn about how things in nature change colors, first studying the warm colors found in nature. (page 63)

Social Studies Identify individuals in history who have worked to ensure freedom. (page 64)

The Arts Learn about the *Firebird* ballet and create a dance to go with the painting *Firebirds*. (page 65)

Technology Use the *Multimedia Workshop* CD-ROM to create a landscape scene colored twice: once with warm colors and once with cool colors. (page 66)

Michael Powell. Age 8. *The Dream*. Oil pastels and watercolor.

What makes this student artwork imaginary?

Create

What colors in your environment give you a feeling of warmth? Create an imaginative painting using warm colors.

1. Use your imagination to create a fantasy landscape that includes three unrelated items such as a matchstick, a bowling pin, and a pair of sunglasses. Make a rough sketch of your idea.

2. Use lines to draw your idea on a sheet of white paper with warm-colored oil pastels.

3. Mix a variety of warm values with watercolor paint. Paint your scene. Remember that the values will get lighter as you add more water to your paint.

Describe Name all the warm colors you used in your landscape.

Analyze What objects did you include in your imaginative painting?

Interpret How did using only warm colors affect the mood of your imaginative painting? If you added cool colors to your painting, how would the mood be different?

Decide If you could do this artwork over again, how would you improve it?

Lesson 5   65

THEME Connections

Discovery Use the artwork as a springboard to name different fruits that are warm-colored.

Energy Use the artwork as examples of energy created in various forms of dance.

Connections Use the artwork to connect the terms *color* and *feeling*.

ESL

Model how to think through a fantasy landscape. Bring in three unrelated objects and demonstrate how you will use these to create a landscape. As you demonstrate, talk about what you're doing. Then, pair ESL students with more fluent peers, and invite them to talk about the objects and landscapes each is going to draw.

CLOSE

Time: About 5 minutes

"What have you learned about how artists use warm colors?"

"¿Qué han aprendido acerca de la manera en que los artistas usan los colores cálidos?"

ART MANIPULATIVES   **Review** Use the color wheel from the **Art Manipulative Kit** to identify warm colors and locate them in both student art and the lesson artworks.

Art Criticism

Have students answer the four art criticism questions—Describe, Analyze, Interpret, and Decide—orally or in writing. Discuss the use of cool colors in their landscapes after the paintings are dry.

 Assess Use the **Assessment Book** pages 21–22 as a formal assessment for this lesson.

Evaluation Criteria

• Can the student identify the warm colors and their expressive qualities?

• Can the student mix a variety of warm colors to use in creating an imaginary painting?

• Can the student use the four steps of art criticism to evaluate his or her own artwork?

• Can the student describe how artists from diverse cultures use color in a similar way?

Reteaching • • • • • • • • • • • • • •

Warm colors Have students identify objects in the classroom for each of the warm spectral and intermediate colors. Ask them to list the objects and the warm colors seen in each.

Perception Hints for Student Art

The huge clock, matches, and centipede make this painting imaginary.

UNIT 2
LESSON 6

LESSON PLANNER

Objectives
After completing this lesson, students will be able to:
- identify color contrast. *Aesthetic Perception*
- create a mural using color contrast. *Creative Expression*
- use the four steps of art criticism to evaluate their group murals. *Art Criticism*
- identify the similarities and differences in the artwork from different cultures. *Art History and Culture*

Program Resources
- **Overhead:** Both the Weber and the *Covered Jar* are available on overhead 12.
- **Large Prints:** *Rhapsody* by Hans Hofmann and *Young Man and Woman in an Inn* by Frans Hals
- **Technique Tips Flip Chart,** page 12
- **Vocabulary Book** pages 23–24
- **Art Manipulative Kit:** flash cards
- **Artist Profiles Book:** Weber page 53 and Artist unknown page 58
- **Art Across the Curriculum Book** pages 67–72
- **Multimedia Workshop CD-ROM**
- **Assessment Book** pages 23–24
- **National Museum of Women in the Arts Collection CD-ROM**
- **Animals Through History Time Line**

Multiple Intelligences
Interpersonal Students in small groups can work together to understand contrast in a work of art.

Vocabulary
contrast *contraste* the difference between two things in an artwork

warm colors *colores cálidos* spectral colors that give the feeling of warmth; red, orange, and yellow

cool colors *colores frescos* spectral colors that give the feeling of coolness; blue, green, and violet

Color Contrast

Artists use contrast in artwork to make colors and subjects stand out.

Idelle Weber. (America). *Pistia Kew.* 1989. Oil on linen. 58 × 59 inches. Schmidt Bingham Gallery, New York, New York.

Look at the artwork on these pages. *Pistia Kew* was painted by Idelle Weber in 1989. The covered jar was created in China about 400 years ago. Both works show contrast of warm and cool colors.

Unit 2

ART Background

About the Artists
Idelle Weber (i'del web' ər, American, 1932–   ) was born in Chicago and studied art in California. Working from photographs, she realistically paints everyday objects seen in the environment. Her paintings force the viewer to pay attention to areas that often go unnoticed and to perceive the world in a new and different way.

*Use the **National Museum of Women in the Arts Collection CD-ROM** to discover other artworks created by women.

About Subject Matter* Both the Weber and the *Covered* Jar are landscapes.

*Use the **Animals Through History Time Line** to compare the time the *Covered Jar* was created with the era of *Pistia Kew* on the time line.

About the Media The Weber is an oil painting, which is an opaque pigment mixed with oil. The Covered Jar is porcelain, which is a hard, white, nonporous, translucent clay. It has been painted and glazed.

Artist unknown. (China). *Covered Jar.* 1522–1566. Porcelain painted with underglaze cobalt blue and overglaze enamels. 18½ inches high, 15¾ inches diameter. The Asia Society, New York, Mr. and Mrs. John D. Rockefeller 3rd Collection/Photo by Lynton Gardiner.

Study both works of art to find the contrast between warm and cool colors.

☑ Find all the cool colors. Are they placed near each other?

☑ Locate all the warm colors. Where are they placed?

☑ Which work has more warm colors?

☑ Find the colors that first catch your attention. Which colors are they?

SEEING LIKE AN ARTIST

Look around your classroom and find examples of cool colors that are near warm colors.

Lesson **6**

67

About Art History* Weber painted during a time when dramatists began to address the concerns of minorities, choreographers began using music not intended for dancing, and rock became a popular form of music.

The Ming Dynasty (1368–1644) was a period of great activity in the arts. An imperial factory was built to keep the court supplied with porcelain and carved lacquer.

Cultural Perspectives Weber painted in America during the Civil Rights and Women's Liberation Movements of the 1960s and 1970s.

The Covered Jar was created during a time when Europeans, like Marco Polo, made the journey to China. However, Europeans were received reluctantly, and the Chinese limited the places where they could trade.

*****See **More About** pages 206–227 for more about art history and subject matter.

FOCUS

Time: About 10 minutes

Activating Prior Knowledge

"Think about flowers growing outside. Why do the flowers attract your attention before you notice the leaves?"

"Piensen en las flores que crecen al aire libre. ¿Por qué las flores atraen la atención antes de que se noten las hojas?"

• Discuss students' answers to the question and how warm colors (red, yellow, and orange flowers) catch the eye's attention when located near cool colors (green leaves).

Introducing the Art

"Let's look closely at the two artworks."

"Vamos a observar detalladamente estas dos obras de arte."

• **Describe:** Have students describe the subject matter in the artwork. (landscape)

• **COMPARE AND CONTRAST** Have students make a list of the similarities and differences in the two artworks. (Both works illustrate underwater scenes, incorporate carp, and are realistic in style. The Weber is a two-dimensional painting that shows a bird's-eye view, while the *Covered Jar* is a three-dimensional form with a view that is at eye level.)

• Share and discuss information with the students from **Art Background** and the **Artist Profiles Book** about the lives, work, and times of the artist.

• Have students answer questions on page 67. (See **Perception Hints** below.)

FOR THE ART SPECIALIST

Use the **Overhead** and the **Large Prints** *Rhapsody* and *Young Man and a Woman in an Inn* to show how artists use contrast to make colors and subjects stand out.

Perception Hints

Cool colors *Weber.* The water (blue) and the leaves (green, yellow-green, and blue-green) are cool colors. They are placed near each other in the painting.

Warm colors *Covered Jar.* The carp (orange, red-orange, and yellow-orange) have warm colors. They are placed apart from each other on the jar. This artwork has the most warm colors.

Color contrast *Weber.* The red-orange color of the fish attracts the eye's attention first because the fish are placed in a background of cool colors.

TEACH

Time: About two 30-minute periods

Practice

Materials
- 9- × 12-inch paper
- oil pastels

Alternate Materials: crayons

"How can you create contrast with warm and cool colors?"

"¿Cómo se pueden crear contraste con colores cálidos y frescos?"

- Discuss the definition of *contrast* on page 68 and how it can be created using warm and cool colors.
- Distribute the materials and have students follow the directions on page 68 for illustrating color contrast. Have them answer the Decide questions on the back.

Create PROBLEM SOLVING

Materials
- large mural paper for every team
- scrap paper
- liquid tempera paints
- pencils
- large brushes
- paper towels
- 12- × 18-inch construction paper (warm colors)
- oil pastels
- palettes
- glue
- containers of water
- scissors
- newspaper

Safety! For safety issues about tempera paints and glue and other information about safety in the art classroom, see page T22.

Alternate Material: construction paper

"Let's contrast warm and cool colors to create a mural of an underwater scene."

"Vamos a hacer un contraste entre colores cálidos y frescos para crear un mural de una escena submarina."

- Have students brainstorm ideas for underwater plants, animals, and objects.
- Review warm and cool colors and techniques for creating color contrast. Use the flash cards from the **Art Manipulative Kit.**
- See page 12 in the **Technique Tips Flip Chart** for visual examples of techniques.
- Distribute materials and have students follow the directions on page 69.

FOR THE ART SPECIALIST

Invite students who are dressed in contrasting colors to stand.

Using Color Contrast

Artists use **contrast** in order to show differences between two things.

The **warm colors** red, orange, and yellow come forward and attract your attention first. So do their related intermediate colors. The **cool colors** blue, green, and violet—and their related intermediate colors—seem to move away from you.

When warm colors are placed next to cool colors, a contrast is created.

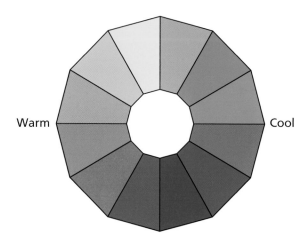

Warm   Cool

Practice

Illustrate color contrast. Use oil pastels and white paper.

1. On a sheet of paper, place cool colors next to warm colors.

2. Mix the intermediate colors by blending the primary and secondary colors. Fill your paper with color contrasts.

Decide Did you fill your paper with color contrasts? Are the warm colors next to the cool colors? Why do you see the warm colors first?

Activities in
ART Across the Curriculum Book

Reading/Language Arts Understand how contrasts are created in writing, first studying contrast in art. (page 67)

Math Study contrasts in temperatures and solve problems. (page 68)

Science Observe objects closely, using a magnifying glass. (page 69)

Social Studies Study how Marco Polo set up trade with China, the origin of the *Covered Jar*. (page 70)

The Arts Working with a partner, role-play things you like to do, showing contrast between the two people. (page 71)

Technology Use the *Multimedia Workshop* CD-ROM to create an imaginary outer space scene filled with warm and cool colors. (page 72)

Laura Littlejohn. Age 8. Mixed-media.

How would the mood of this student artist's artwork change if the background contained warm colors and the creatures were made using cool colors?

Create

What objects in an underwater environment would you find that are warm-colored? Create a group mural contrasting warm and cool colors.

1. Think about the warm and cool colors you see underwater. In a small group, make a list of underwater creatures. Draw the creatures on sheets of warm-colored construction paper. Use warm-colored oil pastels to add color and detail. Cut out the shapes.

2. As a team, paint an underwater scene on a very large sheet of paper. Mix a variety of cool colors to create water and plant life.

3. When the paint is dry, arrange and glue the sea creatures in place.

Lesson 6

Describe Describe the creatures your group created.

Analyze Which cool colors did you use in your mural? Which warm colors did you use in your mural?

Interpret How did the mood or feeling of your mural change when you added the warm-colored sea creatures to the cool background?

Decide If you could do this mural again, what would you do differently?

69

THEME Connections

Exploration Use the artworks as visual examples of plant and animal life found in bodies of water.

Change Use the artworks as visual examples of color opposites.

Cultures Use the artwork as examples of different cultures.

ESL

The group mural project is an especially supportive way for ESL students to feel like a productive part of the class. Prepare all students to appreciate each individual's strengths and weaknesses, especially as these pertain to language development. ESL students can learn a great deal from peers, but only if the relationship is based on trust and supportive interaction.

CLOSE

Time: About 5 minutes

"What have you learned about color contrast?"
"¿Qué han aprendido acerca del contraste de colores?"

Review
Look through the book to find other examples of contrasting colors. Have students compare the use of color contrast in the artwork to its use in the works in this lesson.

Art Criticism
Have students answer the four art criticism questions—Describe, Analyze, Interpret, and Decide—orally or in writing. Discuss the use of color contrast in the print and in their murals.

Assess
Use the Assessment Book pages 23–24 as a formal assessment for this lesson.

Evaluation Criteria
• Can the student identify color contrast?
• Can the student demonstrate color contrast in his or her mural?
• Can the students use the four steps of art criticism to evaluate their group's mural?
• Can the student identify the similarities and differences in the artwork from different cultures?

Reteaching ● ● ● ● ● ● ● ● ● ● ● ●

Color contrast Have students look through the book to find three different works of art that illustrate color contrast. Ask them to list the title of each work and identify the areas where color contrast occurs.

Perception Hints for Student Art

The scene would feel warmer if the background were painted with warm colors.

UNIT 2

LESSON PLANNER

Objectives

After completing this lesson, students will be able to:

- re-create a folk tale in a rap style combined with singing. *Aesthetic Perception*
- express color and value by using tone of voice to match the mood of a story. *Creative Expression*
- use the four steps of art criticism to evaluate their own interpretation of a folk tale. *Art Criticism*
- demonstrate knowledge of the music and storytelling of African American traditions. *Art History and Culture*

Program Resources

Artsource Performing Arts Audio/Video Resource Package

That Ole' House is Ha'nted performed by Dr. Jester Hairston. Videocassette Running Time: 8:19.

FOCUS

Time: About 10 minutes

Activating Prior Knowledge

"Think about a mystery or suspense story you have heard or read. How did you feel as you listened to it or read it?"

"Piensen en un cuento de misterio o suspenso que hayan escuchado o que hayan leído. ¿Cómo se sintieron al escucharlo o al leerlo?"

- Discuss how stories can elicit moods and feelings.

Introducing the Art

"Look at the picture. What mood or feeling does it suggest?"

"Observen la pintura. ¿Qué ambiente o sentimiento sugiere?"

- Have students respond to the picture on page 70 and express any feelings it evokes.
- Read or tell a folk tale that involves mystery or suspense. Use rhythm, emphasis, and dark and light tones of voice to capture moods and feelings. If possible, play scary music softly as background. If you have the *Artsource* videocassette, have students view Jester Hairston's presentation.
- Have students discuss the sequence of events in the story, then identify the techniques of rhythm, emphasis, and value that are used.

70   **Unit 2**

Color and Value in Storytelling

What kind of story might you tell to go with this picture?

dr. Jester Hairston is a grandson of slaves. He retells the stories that he heard and loved as a child. Hairston expresses the moods of a story by using his voice. He uses his voice as artists use colors and values. He makes his voice sound warm or cool. He speaks softly or deeply, in a high or low tone.

70   **Unit 2**

ART Background

About the Storyteller/Composer

Dr. Jester Hairston was born in 1901. After graduating from Tufts University in 1929 with a degree in music, he joined the Hall Johnson Choir and soon became its assistant conductor. The choir was noted for its renditions of African American folk music, especially Spirituals. Since then, Hairston has served the United States as one of its official goodwill ambassadors, lecturing and conducting choirs around the world. Choirs and their audiences are held spellbound by his storytelling skills, and the resulting performances beautifully convey the message of the music.

Cultural Perspectives A grandson of slaves, Hairston has seen and experienced great change in the African American experience during this century.

What To Do

Tell a folktale in a rap style.

Materials
- ✓ a tale or story
- ✓ paper and pencil

1. Read a folktale or a mystery.

2. Talk about the big idea of the story. Then, list what happened in the story in the correct order.

3. Practice telling the story. Use your voice to express feeling. A deep tone can express darkness. A high voice can express lightness. Speak softly or loudly, slowly or quickly, to match the mood of what's happening in the story.

4. Choose one phrase or sentence to sing as a chorus between parts of the story.

5. Take turns telling parts of the story. Sing the chorus together after each part.

Describe What are the different ways you used your voice to tell the story?

Analyze Explain what is different about telling a story in a rap style.

Interpret What moods did you create? How was your tone of voice like the values and colors in a painting?

Decide Did the chorus improve the storytelling? If not, what would you do differently?

Extra Credit

Make up your own story. Then, tell it in a rap style with a chorus. Perform it for others.

Music 71

About Subject Matter Before television, many African American families would sit down together in the evenings and spin tales, especially scary stories. This may go back to the traditional African societies where storytelling is a lively art. In traditional societies, music and song were always a part of storytelling. Many of the characters had their own songs, and often call-and-response choruses were incorporated throughout the telling of a story.

About Storytelling and Music Storytellers of old were often accompanied by musicians. Dr. Hairston has continued this tradition. For example, a familiar African American folk tale was used as a basis for his arrangement of *That Ole' House Is Ha'nted*. The arrangement incorporates dramatic narration, choral singing and vocal effects, and piano accompaniment.

TEACH
Time: Two 30-minute periods

Materials
- a folk tale that involves mystery or suspense
- paper and pencils

"We are going to retell a story using rhythm and the expression of your voices to create feelings and a mood."

"Vamos a contar de nuevo un cuento usando ritmo y la expresión de sus voces para crear sentimientos y un ambiente."

- Outline the events of the story on the chalkboard. Ask volunteers to retell parts of the story in sequence.
- Have students decide on a phrase or chorus they can sing between each part of the story. This should be similar to a rhythmic chorus in a song.
- Have students take turns retelling parts of the story in rap style. Have the full group sing the chorus between each part and at the end.

CLOSE
Time: About 5 minutes

"What did you like about this way of telling a story? If you could change something about the process, what would it be?"

"¿Qué les gustó sobre esta manera de contar un cuento? Si pudieran cambiar algo sobre el proceso, ¿qué sería?"

Assess

Have students answer the four art criticism questions on page 71—Describe, Analyze, Interpret, and Decide—orally or in writing.

Evaluation Criteria
- Can the student participate in retelling a story using rhythm and vocal expression?
- Can the student express the mood of the story by using tone of voice as painters use color and value?
- Can the student use the four steps of art criticism to evaluate his or her interpretation of the story?
- Can the student demonstrate knowledge of the African-American tradition of storytelling?

UNIT 2

Reviewing Unit Concepts

"Artists use primary, secondary, and intermediate colors to express a feeling or mood in all kinds of art. Adding black or white to colors creates value."

"Los artistas usan los colores primarios, secundarios e intermedios para expresar un sentimiento o un ánimo en todos los tipos de arte. Cuando se agrega negro o blanco a los colores, se crea valor."

- Review colors and the techniques artists use to create value on pages 72 and 73. Have the students list the various colors and values seen in clothing worn by their classmates.

Examining the Artwork

"Let's look closely at the work of art."

"Vamos a observar detalladamente esta obra de arte."

- Have the students look at Derain's *The Turning Road, L'Estaque* and answer the questions about color and value on page 73.
  (See **Perception Hints** below.)

Student Portfolio
Have students review all the artwork they have created during this unit and select the pieces they wish to keep in their portfolios.

Art Criticism Activity
Have students select an artwork from this unit and study it using the four steps of art criticism.
(See pages 206–209 for more information about Art Criticism.)

Perception Hints

Primary colors The top part of the tree trunks in the foreground is red. The road on the right side is yellow. Some of the bushes in the bottom left corner are blue.
Secondary colors The treetops, located in the background on the left-hand side, are violet. Orange can be seen in the grassy area in the middle of the painting. The bush at the edge of the bottom left corner is green.
Intermediate colors The tree located in the foreground on the left has a yellow-orange trunk. Blue-green is located in the leaves in the middle of the tree on the right. Blue-violet can be seen at the base of the tree in the middle.
Values Light values can be seen in the sky in the top right. Dark values can be seen below that area in the treetops.
Warm and cool colors Areas of warm and cool colors are seen close together in the lower left and right corners of the painting.

Wrapping Up Unit 2
Color and Value

Reviewing Main Ideas

The lessons and activities in this unit cover color and value. These are used by artists to create certain moods or feelings in works of art.

1. **Primary colors** are pure colors. They are red, yellow, and blue.
2. **Secondary colors** are made by mixing two primary colors together. These are orange, green, and violet.
3. **Value** is the lightness or darkness of a color.
   - A **tint** is made by adding white to a color.
- Adding black to a color creates a **shade.**
4. **Intermediate colors** are made by mixing a primary color and a secondary color. There are six intermediate colors.
5. The **color wheel** is a tool for organizing the twelve colors.

Andre Derain. (French). *The Turning Road, L'Estaque,* 1906. Oil on canvas. 51 × 76¾ inches. Museum of Fine Arts, Houston, Texas. The John A. and Audrey Jones Beck Collection.

ART Background

About the Artist André Derain (än drā' də ran', French, 1880–1954), the artist of *The Turning Road, L'Estaque,* was born in Chatou, France, on June 10, 1880. While studying painting as a young art student, he met the famous artist Henri Matisse. They became joint creators of Fauvism after seeing retrospectives of work by artists van Gogh, Gauguin, and Cezanne.

About Subject Matter* Derain's painting is a landscape, a favorite subject of Fauvist painters. While his earlier landscapes consisted of dots and dashes of exploding color, the forms and figures in this painting are more solidly anchored and sharply outlined.

About the Media *The Turning Road, L'Estaque* is an oil painting. Colored pigments mixed with linseed oil create this slow-drying medium, allowing artists to work on fine details while the paint is still wet.

6. **Cool colors** are blue, green, and violet. They remind us of cool things. Yellow-green, blue-green, and blue-violet are cool colors that are *related*.

7. **Warm colors** are red, yellow, and orange. Red-violet. red-orange, and yellow-orange are warm colors that are related.

8. **Contrast** is used in order to show differences in two things, such as placing a warm color next to a cool color.

Summing Up

Look at the painting by Derain. Notice how he used value and a variety of colors covered in this unit.

- Find the primary and secondary colors.
- Name at least three different intermediate colors.
- Where do you see light and dark values in this landscape?
- Does Derain contrast warm and cool colors anywhere?

Color and value are important elements in paintings and drawings. By using certain colors and values, artists can express a particular feeling or emotion in an artwork.

Let's Visit a Museum

The Museum of Fine Arts in Houston, Texas, is the largest art museum in the Southwest. Its collection contains over 27,000 works of art. There you can see examples of styles of art from different periods in history. There is also a large collection of American decorative arts including furniture, paintings, metals, ceramics, glass, and textiles. If you visit the museum, you can walk in the museum's sculpture garden and see sculptures created by many nineteenth- and twentieth-century artists.

The Museum of Fine Arts, Houston

73

Learning About Museums

The art collection at The Museum of Fine Arts, Houston, ranks as the largest and most outstanding in the Southwest. Renaissance, Baroque, Impressionist, Post-Impressionist, and African Gold art highlight the museum's collection. In addition, a wide variety of programs and classes in the fine arts are offered for adults and children.

- Place students in teams of four art "collectors." Ask each team to decide what type of art they would like to collect and then look through this book to find the artwork for their collection.

TIMELINE For more information about this and other museums, see pages T13, T30–T33, and the back of the **Animals Through History Time Line.**

- The World Wide Web address for the museum is as follows: http://www.mfah.org/

A Final Thought
"The business of the artist is to tell his audience the secrets of their own hearts."—Robin George Collingwood

About Art History* Fauvism was first introduced in a 1905 Paris exhibit. Derived from the French word *fauves,* which means "wild beasts," this style reflected the work of painters who used exaggerated, vibrant colors and loose brush strokes to express their emotional responses to a scene rather than to imitate the actual appearance of nature.

Cultural Perspectives Paris, France, was the center of the art world until World War I. At the turn of the twentieth century, famous artists such as Matisse and Picasso simultaneously effected numerous and rapid changes in artistic styles, many of which the public found hard to understand.

*See **More About** pages 206–227 for more about art history and subject matter.

UNIT OVERVIEW

This unit will cover the elements of space and form. The aspect of space that you will be concerned with in this unit is the illusion of depth in a two-dimensional, or flat, work of art such as a painting, drawing, or print. Form is the element of art that is three-dimensional and encloses space.

Space is the emptiness or area between, around, above, below, or within objects. Space is covered in Lesson 1.

Depth is created when some objects seem to be very close and others seem to be far away. Depth is covered in Lesson 2.

Overlapping occurs when one object covers part of a second object. Overlapping is covered in Lesson 3.

Form is the element of art that is three-dimensional and encloses space. Form is covered in Lesson 4.

Sculpture is three-dimensional artwork made from a variety of materials. Sculpture is covered in Lesson 5.

Jewelry is three-dimensional artwork that is made for people to wear. Jewelry is covered in Lesson 6.

Introducing Unit Concepts

"Artists use the elements of space and form in creating all kinds of art."

"Los artistas usan los elementos de espacio y forma para crear todo tipo de arte."

Space

- Have students brainstorm different meanings of the word *space,* e.g. stars, planets, and parking.
- Have a student stand in the front of the room and hold up one hand. Ask the other students to close one eye and hold up one hand close to their faces. Discuss the reasons their hands appear to be a lot larger than their classmate's.

74   **Unit 3**

Unit 3

An Introduction to Space and Form

Artists use space and form to make all kinds of artwork.

Michelangelo (Italian). *David.* (Detail). 1501–1504. Marble. Galleria dell' Accademia, Florence, Italy. Scala, Art Resource, New York.

74   **Unit 3**

ART Background

About the Artist
Michelangelo (mī′ kəl an″ jə lō′, Italian, 1475–1564) sculpted and painted only figures, using the human form to express an idea rather than tell a story. He was considered one of the greatest sculptors in Italy when he created *David.* This sculpture took four years to complete. Working secretly and diligently in a shed surrounded by a high fence, Michelangelo sculpted the huge figure from a block of marble.

About Subject Matter* *David* is a portrait. Instead of imitating the likeness of a real person, however, Michelangelo created an image of the "ideal" Renaissance man.

About the Media To create *David,* Michelangelo reworked a huge block of marble that had been ruined previously.

Artists create **space** in artworks that are two dimensional and three dimensional.

• Which parts of *David* are behind or partly covered by other parts?

• Describe the area around the sculpture.

Artists create **form** in three-dimensional artwork.

• Which areas of the sculpture are raised? Which parts appear to be farther back?

• If you walked around to the back of this sculpture, how do you think David's head would look on the other side?

Artist Profile

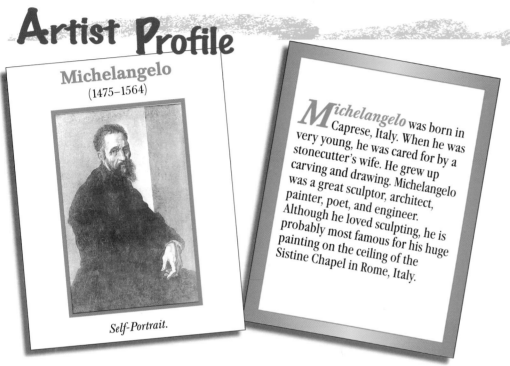

Michelangelo
(1475–1564)

Self-Portrait.

*M*ichelangelo was born in Caprese, Italy. When he was very young, he was cared for by a stonecutter's wife. He grew up carving and drawing. Michelangelo was a great sculptor, architect, painter, poet, and engineer. Although he loved sculpting, he is probably most famous for his huge painting on the ceiling of the Sistine Chapel in Rome, Italy.

*I*n this unit you will learn about and practice techniques to create the appearance of space on a flat surface. You will also learn about three-dimensional forms. Here are the topics you will study:

• Space • Depth • Overlapping • Form • Sculpture

75

About Art History* Michelangelo sculpted in Florence, Italy, during the Renaissance, when great importance was being attached to art. City leaders bestowed commissions, and new programs for public and private works were being undertaken.

Cultural Perspectives Florentines excelled in law, philosophy, literature, science, scholarship, and the fine arts. The Medici family were generous patrons of art and learning. Recognizing the talents of a teenage Michelangelo, the Medicis invited him to study in their palace for three years.

*See **More About** pages 206–227 for more about art history and subject matter.

Form

• Have students name different geometric and free-form shapes. Discuss how form is like a shape because it has height and width, but it also has depth. Form is three-dimensional.

• Ask students to list various objects in their desks that are geometric forms.

You may wish to show the **Video** *When I Was Young in the Mountains* to introduce the concepts of space and form.

Examining the Artwork

"Let's look closely at the sculpture."
"Vamos a observar detalladamente la escultura."

• Have the students look at Michelangelo's *David*. Ask them to describe what they see.

• Have the students answer the questions about space and form on page 75.
(See **Perception Hints** below.)

Artist Profile

Share with students information about the artist, including his self-portrait.

Encourage students to use their **Art Journals** to practice art concepts and record ideas from lesson to lesson.

About Music

Compare positive and negative *space* by having students play eight-beat rhythm patterns. Have one pattern contain rests on the second, third, sixth, and eighth beats, and another pattern, using a different instrument, fill in the rests in the first pattern.

Form in music relates to how music is organized. Many traditional songs, such as "Oh, Susannah," are in AB form.

Perception Hints

Overlapping David's hair partially covers his forehead, ear, and neck.
Space There is empty space under the chin, between the head and neck, and around the outside of the sculpture.
Sculpture This three-dimensional work of art was chiseled from marble. Parts of the hair and ear, the nose, and the chin are raised. The eyes, neck, and certain areas of the hair push back.
Form Because the sculpture is three-dimensional, it can be viewed from all sides. The other side of the form would show the hair on the back of David's head.

UNIT 3 Planning Guide

Lesson	Lesson Title	Suggested Pacing	Create Activities	Materials	
1	**Positive and Negative Space**	75 minutes	Make a stencil print using positive and negative space.	12- x 18-inch colored construction paper liquid tempera paints, any two colors paper plates for palettes tape 6- x 6-inch tagboard scissors small sponges pencils containers of water newspaper paper towels	
2	**Depth**	45 minutes	Create depth in a real or imaginary scene.	12- x 18-inch white construction paper set of watercolor paints brushes of various sizes containers of water sketch paper pencils paper towels tape	
3	**Overlapping**	45 minutes	Create a landscape drawing with overlapping trees and branches.	12- x 18-inch white construction paper pencils sketch paper	
4	**Form**	45 minutes	Create a three-dimensional paper sculpture.	12- x 18-inch colored construction paper oil pastels scissors glue	
5	**Relief Sculpture**	75 minutes	Create a relief tile in clay.	clay, about the size of a baseball, for each student rolling pins or thick dowel rods 6- x 9-inch cardboard frame containers of water and slip pencils and paper clips muslin various textured objects sketch paper slip brushes tape	
6	**3-D Art to Wear**	75 minutes	Create a medallion.	4- x 4-inch cardboard scissors and glue assorted low-relief objects 6- x 6-inch aluminum foil pieces of yarn, ribbon, or string, about 24 inches long hole punch	
Artsource Lesson	**Space and Form in Dance**	75 minutes	Create movements to show the ideas of a poem.		

Test preparation activities using the Large Prints *Warrior Chief, Warriors, and Attendants* and *Silver Llama* can be found on pages 16–19 of the Test Preparation Book.

Program Resources (Books)	Art Resources	Literature Resources	*Music Resources
Vocabulary, pp. 25-26 Assessment, pp. 25-26 Art Across the Curriculum Resource Book, pp. 73-78 Technique Tips Flip Chart, p. 13 Lesson Plans Book, p. 14 Home Connection, pp. 9 and 10	Overhead Transparency #13, *Sleeveless Shirt (two cats)* and *Tree of Life* Artist Profile Book, pp. 59, 60 Large Prints, *Warrior Chief, Warriors, and Attendants* and *Silver Llama*	1. *Black and White* (1990) by David Macaulay has hidden images in shapes, colors, and words that allow students to carefully inspect the award-winning usage of positive and negative space. 2. *The Changling* (1992) by Selma Lagerlof further explores different shapes found in nature, observing positive and negative space of the environment.	"El Pajara campano" (The Bell Bird), arranged by A.R. Ortiz, p. T88, CD2:30. "El Pajara campano" is a traditional Latin American piece for harp that uses overlapping notes.
Vocabulary, pp. 27-28 Assessment, pp. 27-28 Art Across the Curriculum Resource Book, pp. 79-84 Technique Tips Flip Chart, p. 14 Lesson Plans Book, p. 15	Overhead Transparency #14, *Washington's Head-quarters* and *The Piper* Artist Profile Book, pp. 26, 61 Large Prints, *Warrior Chief, Warriors, and Attendants* and *Silver Llama*	1. *Dinosaur for a Day* (1992) by Jim Murphy exemplifies concepts of depth in fantastical illustrations utilizing overlapping and the entanglement of lines to create the perspective illusions. 2. *The Young Artist's Handbook* (1992) by Anthony Hodge shows basic skills required for drawing the lesson techniques and demonstrates them in this elementary reference book.	"Sentry Box," p. T114, CD3:18. "Sentry Box" is an example of traditional fife and drum music from the 1700s.
Vocabulary, pp. 29-30 Assessment, pp. 29-30 Art Across the Curriculum Resource Book, pp. 85-90 Technique Tips Flip Chart, p. 15 Lesson Plans Book, p. 16	Overhead Transparency #15, *The Locust Trees with Maple* and *Haitian Landscape.* Artist Profile Book, pp. 21, 30 Large Prints, *Warrior Chief, Warriors, and Attendants* and *Silver Llama*	1. *The Hidden Jungle* (1992) by Simon Henwood informs of ways to overlap by following the overgrown illustrations of this fun and vibrant jungle tale. 2. *The Ultimate Noah's Ark* (1993) by Mike Wilks has more than 700 creatures that are colorfully woven into the complexity of this story's intricate design along with researched text on each animal.	"Jamaican Jump-Up," by H.C. Mon Solomon, p. T308, CD7:36. "Jamaican Jump-Up" uses steel drums and traditional West Indian folk instruments.
Vocabulary, pp. 31-32 Assessment, pp. 31-32 Art Across the Curriculum Resource Book, pp. 91-96 Technique Tips Flip Chart, p. 16 Lesson Plans Book, p. 17	Overhead Transparency #16, *Spinner* and *The Walking Flower* Artist Profile Book, pp. 4, 27 Large Prints, *Warrior Chief, Warriors, and Attendants* and *Silver Llama*	1. *Sing a Song of People* (1965) by Lois Lenski has 3-D paper constructions that illustrate the lesson concept of shapes and free-form forms. 2. *Things I Can Make with Paper* (1989) by Sabine Lohf has unusual and intriguing crafts that are created from paper and common art supplies in easy-to-read text.	"Doubtful Shepherd," p. T170, CD4:37. The "Doubtful Shepherd" is an example of the musical form AB (same-different).
Vocabulary, pp. 33-34 Assessment, pp. 33-34 Art Across the Curriculum Resource Book, pp. 97-102 Technique Tips Flip Chart, p. 17 Lesson Plans Book, p. 18	Overhead Transparency #17, *Winged Genie* and *The Meeting of Solomon and Sheba/The Gates of Paradise* Artist Profile Book, pp. 16, 62 Large Prints, *Warrior Chief, Warriors, and Attendants* and *Silver Llama*	1. *Gifts* (1995) by JoEllen Bogart is illustrated in Plasticine and pressed onto illustration board. These ingenuitive pages represent 3-D textures, patterns, and details done in relief. 2. *Where the Forest Meets the Sea* (1987) by Jeannie Baker uses clay, paper, and various textured materials to construct outstanding relief collages that can also be used to discuss Australia.	"El Grillo" (The Cricket) by Josquin des Pres, p. T359A, CD9:6. "El Grillo" is an example of music from fifteenth-century Italy.
Vocabulary, pp. 35-36 Assessment, pp. 35-36 Art Across the Curriculum Resource Book, pp. 103-108 Technique Tips Flip Chart, p. 18 Lesson Plans Book, p. 19	Overhead Transparency #18, *Necklace* and *Tuxedo Studs and Cuff Links* Artist Profile Book, pp. 47, 63 Large Prints, *Warrior Chief, Warriors, and Attendants* and *Silver Llama*	1. *A Fish That's a Box* (1990) from the National Museum of American Art is a wide array of 3-D folk art objects from the museum that explain the method and means behind folk art's beginnings. 2. *Play with Models* (1995) by Ivan Bulloch is an informative project book for all ages. 3-D crafts are demonstrated in color illustrations with instructions.	"Caprice in A Minor" (excerpts), by Niccolo Paganini, p. T228, CD6:8. "Caprice in A Minor" is an example of the musical form "theme and variations," in which a simple melody is decorated in different ways.
	Artsource Performing Arts Audio/Video Resource Package: *Hoop Dance* (videocassette)		

*Music references are from **Share the Music,** Macmillan/McGraw-Hill School Publishers

UNIT 3
LESSON 1

LESSON PLANNER

Objectives
After completing this lesson, students will be able to:
- identify and explore positive and negative space. *Aesthetic Perception*
- plan and create a stencil print illustrating positive and negative space. *Creative Expression*
- use the four steps of art criticism to evaluate their own prints. *Art Criticism*
- compare folk art from ancient Peru and modern Poland and their use of positive and negative space. *Art History and Culture*

Program Resources
- **Overhead:** Both the *Sleeveless Shirt (two cats)* and the *Tree of Life* are available on overhead 13.
- **Large Prints:** *Warrior Chief, Warriors, and Attendants* and *Silver Llama*
- **Technique Tips Flip Chart,** page 13
- **Vocabulary Book** pages 25–26
- **Art Manipulative Kit:** flash cards
- **Artist Profiles Book:** pages 59 and 60
- **Art Across the Curriculum Book** pages 73–78
- **Multimedia Workshop CD-ROM**
- **National Geographic Picture Atlas of the World CD-ROM**
- **Animals Through History Time Line**
- **Assessment Book** pages 25–26

Multiple Intelligences
Verbal/Linguistic Students can explore positive and negative space by learning the definitions of these concepts and demonstrating knowledge of those meanings.

Vocabulary
appliqué *aplicación* decoration made from cloth cutouts

positive spaces *espacios positivos* shapes or forms in two- and three-dimensional art

negative spaces *espacios negativos* empty spaces surrounding shapes and forms

---

Positive and Negative Space

Artists use positive and negative space in their artwork.

Artist unknown. Coastal Inca (Peru). *Sleeveless Shirt (two cats).* c. 1438–1532. Wool and cotton. Metropolitan Museum of Art, Nelson Rockefeller Collection, New York, New York.

Look at the artwork on these pages. *Sleeveless Shirt (two cats)* is an **appliqué**, or decoration made from cloth cutouts. The cotton cloth shapes were sewn onto a woolen background. *Tree of Life* is a paper cutout. Positive and negative spaces bring out the design in both works.

76   Unit 3

 ART *Background*

About Subject Matter*
The *Sleeveless Shirt* and the *Tree of Life* are iconographic.

About the Media The *Sleeveless Shirt* is a wool and cotton fabric appliqué. Appliqué employs the technique of attaching fabric shapes onto a fabric background. The *Tree of Life* is a paper cutout.

About Art History* The *Sleeveless Shirt* was created in Peru at a time when the Inca carved huge stones (up to 200 tons!) for the construction of buildings. The stones were so perfectly carved that they fit together without the use of mortar.

*Discuss the **Animals Through History Time Line** in reference to the time of *Sleeveless Shirt.*

Stanistawa Bakula. (Polish).
Tree of Life. 1962. Cut paper.
$12\frac{3}{8} \times 7\frac{1}{2}$ inches. From the Girard
Foundation Collection, in the
Museum of International Folk Art,
a unit of the Museum of New
Mexico, Santa Fe, New Mexico.

Study both works of art to find examples of positive and negative space.

- ✓ What objects do you see in each work? What colors are they?

- ✓ What colors are the negative spaces around the objects in each work?

- ✓ How do the empty spaces in both artworks help make the objects stand out?

SEEING LIKE AN ARTIST

Notice the shapes of clouds. What shapes do you see in the spaces around them?

Lesson **1**   **77**

Tree of Life is an example of a Polish folk art that has passed from one generation to the next for hundreds of years. Originally, the art form began with people using sheep shears to make cutouts from glazed paper. Paper cutouts are often used as decorations for Easter and Christmas holidays.

Cultural Perspectives The *Sleeveless Shirt* was created during a time when the Inca controlled the Andes. Every citizen was employed, and the emperor, thought of as a god, was the absolute ruler of all.

The *Tree of Life* was created in Poland during the 1960s, when, due to poor economic conditions and the oppressive Soviet presence, the people were often at odds with the Polish Communist government.

*See **More About** pages 206–227 for more about art history and subject matter.

Activating Prior Knowledge

"Why is finding a parking place sometimes hard to do?"

"¿Por qué es difícil algunas veces buscar un lugar para estacionar?"

- Discuss students' responses. Explain that the cars are like positive space and the spaces that the cars occupy are like negative space.

Introducing the Art

"Let's take a close look at the two artworks."

"Vamos a observar detalladamente las dos obras de arte."

- **Describe:** Have students describe the subject matter in each artwork. (Both: iconographic)

- **COMPARE AND CONTRAST** Have students make a list of the similarities and differences in the two artworks. (Both pieces depict objects from nature, are symmetrically balanced, and use free-form shapes. The *Sleeveless Shirt* is a functional object made from fabric; it focuses on a single motif. The *Tree of Life* is a decorative piece made from paper; it focuses on a variety of motifs.)

- Use the **National Geographic Picture Atlas of the World CD-ROM** to compare the cultures of the two artworks.

- Share and discuss information with the students from **Art Background** and the **Artist Profiles Book** about the times of the artwork.

- Have students answer the questions on page 77 to identify examples of positive and negative space. (See **Perception Hints** below.)

FOR THE ART SPECIALIST

Use the **Overhead** and the **Large Prints** *Warrior Chief, Warriors, and Attendants* and *Silver Llama* to demonstrate how artists use positive and negative space in their artwork.

Perception Hints

Objects that fill positive space *Sleeveless Shirt.* Black cats. *Tree of Life.* Black trees, birds and roosters.

Negative space *Sleeveless Shirt.* The negative space in the shirt is red-orange. *Tree of Life.* The negative space in the cutout is white.

Empty space The lighter color in the background makes the objects appear to stand out.

TEACH

Time: About two 30-minute periods

Practice

Materials
- 9- × 12-inch paper
- crayons

Alternate Materials: oil pastels

"How can you use shapes to show positive and negative spaces?"

"¿Cómo se pueden usar figuras para mostrar espacios positivos y negativos?"

- Discuss positive and negative space on page 78.
- Distribute the materials and have students follow the directions on page 78. Have them answer the Decide question on the back of their papers.

Create PROBLEM SOLVING

Materials
- 12- × 18-inch colored construction paper
- 6- × 6-inch tagboard   • pencils
- scissors   • containers of water
- liquid tempera paints, any two colors   • tape
- paper plates for palettes   • paper towels
- small sponges   • newspaper

ART MANIPULATIVES Use flash cards from the **Art Manipulative Kit** to illustrate positive and negative space.

Safety! For safety issues about paints and other information about safety in the art classroom, see page T22.

Alternate Materials: oil pastels

"How can you create a print using a positive shape to create negative space?"

"¿Cómo pueden crear un grabado usando una figura positiva para crear un espacio negativo?"

- Have students brainstorm ideas for shapes found in nature.
- Review procedures for working with tempera paints in **More About Technique Tips** on page 199.
- See page 13 in the **Technique Tips Flip Chart** for visual examples of techniques.
- Distribute the materials and have students follow the directions on page 79.

FOR THE ART SPECIALIST

Use a smaller stencil and another color to change the look of the stencil print.

Using Positive and Negative Space

In a work of art, the area that shapes and objects fill is called **positive space**. The empty area around them is called **negative space**.

Negative space can be just as important as positive space. Negative space affects the way shapes and objects look. What objects do you see in the picture below? Can you tell which areas are positive space and which are negative space?

 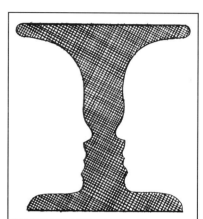

Practice

Create a design with positive and negative space. Use crayons.

1. Fold a piece of paper into two equal parts. Draw a large free-form shape on the outside of each side.

2. Use crayons to color the negative spaces only.

3. Open the paper. How do the negative spaces help you see the shapes that you drew?

Decide Did you color all the space around and between the two shapes?

Activities in ART Across the Curriculum Book

Reading/Language Arts Learn how to use positive and negative meanings, just as artists use positive and negative space in art. (page 73)

Math Solve story problems about *Tree of Life*. (page 74)

Science Understand how heating and cooling objects can cause changes like an artist manipulating positive and negative space. (page 75)

Social Studies Identify positive and negative uses of power. (page 76)

The Arts Create an interesting pose with your body, noting that the pose will create positive space. (page 77)

Technology Use the *Multimedia Workshop* CD-ROM to create a design using positive and negative space. (page 78)

Elizabeth Boger. Age 8. Tagboard, tempera, sponge.

How did this student artist create positive and negative space in her print?

Create

What shapes found in nature do you find interesting? Make a stencil print using positive and negative space.

1. Think about shapes found in nature. Draw one in the middle of stiff paper and cut it out. Keep the paper around it in one piece. This paper will be your stencil.

2. Hold the stencil in place on a large piece of paper. Dip a small piece of sponge into tempera paint and gently press it inside the stencil to make a print.

3. When the print is dry, hold the positive shape in place on the large paper. Dip the sponge into a different color. Then, gently press it around the outside edges of the positive shape.

Describe Point to the positive and negative spaces in the final design.

Analyze Which shape or stencil did you use to create the positive spaces and negative spaces?

Interpret How would your design be different if you had used only the stencil to make it?

Decide If you make another nature print someday, what will you do differently?

Lesson 1

79

THEME Connections

Models Use the artwork as visual examples of animals as a universal source of inspiration for artists in different cultures.

Cultures Use the artwork as visual examples of objects used for a specific function and for decorative purposes.

Identity Use the artwork to discuss how folk art grows out of the interests and ideas of people who are not trained artists.

ESL

ESL students may be hesitant to answer the interpretative question about their artwork. You may wish to phrase the question as an either/or choice so that the vocabulary needed to answer the question is contained in the question itself.

CLOSE

Time: About 5 minutes

"How would you explain the difference between positive space and negative space?"

"¿Cómo explicarían la diferencia entre espacio positivo y espacio negativo?"

LARGE PRINT **Review**

Use the **Large Prints** *Warrior Chief, Warriors, and Attendants* and *Silver Llama* to have students identify positive and negative spaces.

Art Criticism

Have students answer the four art criticism questions—Describe, Analyze, Interpret, and Decide—orally or in writing. After the paint has dried discuss the use of positive and negative spaces in their prints .

Assess

Use the **Assessment Book** pages 25–26 as a formal assessment for this lesson.

Evaluation Criteria

• Can the student identify positive and negative space?

• Can the student create positive and negative space in a print?

• Can the student use the four steps of art criticism to evaluate his or her own work?

• Can the student indicate positive and negative space in the Inca and Polish artworks?

Reteaching ● ● ● ● ● ● ● ● ● ●

Positive and negative space Have students look through the book to find three works of art that use positive and negative space. Ask them to list the title of each work and describe the positive and negative spaces they find.

Perception Hints for Student Art

This student artist created positive space by filling in the apple stencil. She created negative space by sponging along the edge of the apple shape.

UNIT 3
LESSON 2

LESSON PLANNER

Objectives

After completing this lesson, students will be able to:

- identify how artists create depth by the size and placement of objects. *Aesthetic Perception*
- plan and create a real or imaginary scene with a foreground and a background that illustrates depth. *Creative Expression*
- use the four steps of art criticism to evaluate their own paintings. *Art Criticism*
- discuss the art and life of Lee-Smith. *Art History and Culture*

Program Resources

- **Overhead:** Both the Lee-Smith and *Washington's Head-quarters* are available on transparency 14.
- **Large Prints:** *Warrior Chief, Warriors, and Attendants* and *Silver Llama*
- **Technique Tips Flip Chart,** page 14
- **Vocabulary Book** pages 27–28
- **Art Manipulative Kit:** music audiotapes
- **Artist Profiles Book:** Lee-Smith page 26 and Artist unknown page 61
- **Art Across the Curriculum Book** pages 79–84
- **Multimedia Workshop CD-ROM**
- **Assessment Book** pages 27–28

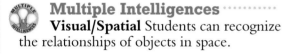 **Multiple Intelligences**
Visual/Spatial Students can recognize the relationships of objects in space.

Vocabulary

depth *profundidad* the feeling of space in a painting or drawing

foreground *frente* the part of the picture that appears closest to the viewer

background *fondo* the part of the picture that seems to be farthest from the viewer

---

Depth

Artists create depth in an artwork by making objects appear close or far away.

Hughie Lee-Smith. (American). *The Piper.* 1953. Oil on composition board. 55.9 × 89.5 cm. Photograph © 1996 Detroit Institute of Arts, Gift of Mr. and Mrs. Stanley J. Winkelman. Licensed by VAGA, New York, New York.

Look at the artworks on these pages. Both artists show deep space by making the objects in the foreground large, and objects in the background smaller.

80   Unit **3**

 **ART** *Background*

About the Artist
Hughie Lee-Smith (hū' ē lē smith, American, 1915–   ) is an African American painter and printmaker. He was born in Eustis, Florida. He worked in Detroit, Michigan, and made murals in his hometown in Ohio and in Detroit, Michigan. Lee-Smith explores a range of topics in his depiction of African American heritage and history. Even though his work is not very well known, he is an important artist. Lee-Smith and other friends of art founded The Cleveland School of Art.

About Subject Matter* The Lee-Smith is a symbolic narrative and *Washington's Head-quarters* is a narrative collage.

About the Media *The Piper* is an oil painting. The artist mixed color from a tube with various types of oil and then applied this smooth mixture to a canvas that had been stretched on a wood frame. *Washington's Head-quarters* is a mixed-media collage.

Artist unknown. (United States). *Washington's Headquarters 1780*. c. 1876. Mixed-media. $21\frac{1}{4} \times 28$ inches. National Museum of American Art. Smithsonian Institution, Washington, DC. Art Resource, New York, New York.

Study both paintings to see how the artists create depth by making objects seem near or far away.

- ☑ Find the objects that seem to be the closest.
- ☑ Which objects seem to be the furthest away?
- ☑ Which objects can you see most clearly?
- ☑ Draw a line with your finger between the front and the back of the scene. Do the objects in the front and the back look the same size?

SEEING LIKE AN ARTIST

Who looks smaller–people close to you or people farther away?

Lesson 2 81

About Art History Hughie Lee-Smith represents one of the many African American artists active during the era of the New Deal's federal art projects (WPA). These artists were underrecognized, yet were catalysts in helping define African American identity.

Washington's Head-quarters was created in the late 1800s, a time when Americans began to place greater importance on the arts and to develop a strong interest in realism.

Cultural Perspectives Lee-Smith's images illustrate his feelings about racial and social isolation and a hopefulness about the restoration and harmony within a social community.

Washington's Head-quarters was probably inspired by the United States Centennial, which was celebrated in 1876, the year that the artwork was completed. A theme of patriotism is apparent.

*See **More About** pages 206–227 for more about art history and subject matter.

FOCUS

Time: About 10 minutes

Activating Prior Knowledge

"Suppose you are looking out your bedroom window. Why do even large-sized objects in the distance all fit within the window frame?"

"Vamos a suponer que se asoman por la ventana de su habitación. ¿Por qué hasta los objetos más grandes en la distancia caben dentro del marco de la ventana?"

- Discuss students' answers to the question and why things in the distance look small even though we know they are actually large.

Introducing the Art

"Let's take a close look at the two artworks."

"Vamos a observar detalladamente las dos obras de arte."

- **Describe:** Have students describe the subject matter in each artwork. (Lee-Smith: symbolic; *Washington's Head-quarters:* narrative)
- **COMPARE AND CONTRAST** Have students make a list of the similarities and differences in the two artworks. (Both works are outdoor scenes, both are realistic in style, and both show depth. Lee-Smith's painting has neutral colors only and illustrates few objects. *Washington's Head-quarters* has many colors and includes a great number of people, as well as a wide variety of objects.)
- Share and discuss information from **Art Background** and the **Artist Profiles Book** about the lives, works, and times of the artists.
- Have students answer questions about depth on page 81. (See **Perception Hints** below.)

FOR THE ART SPECIALIST

Use the **Overhead** and the **Large Print** *Warrior Chief, Warriors, and Attendants* to demonstrate how artists create depth by making objects appear close or far away.

Perception Hints

Foreground *Lee-Smith.* The piper is the closest object; it is in the foreground.
Background *Washington's Head-quarters.* The mountains are the farthest objects. They are in the background.
Size *Lee-Smith* and *Washington's Head-quarters.* In each scene, the objects in the front are larger than the objects in the back.

TEACH

Time: About 30 minutes

Practice

Materials
- 9- × 12-inch construction paper
- colored pencils

Alternate Materials: crayons

"How can you create a feeling of depth?"
"¿Cómo pueden crear una sensación de profundidad?"

- Discuss depth, foreground, and background.
- Distribute materials and have students follow the directions on page 82 to show foreground and background. Have them answer the Decide question on the back of their drawings.

Create PROBLEM SOLVING

Materials
- 12- × 18-inch white construction paper
- pencils
- set of watercolor paints
- brushes of various sizes
- containers of water
- sketch paper
- tape
- paper towels

ART MANIPULATIVES Play music audiotapes from the **Art Manipulative Kit** while students are creating.

Safety! For safety issues about watercolors and other information about safety in the art classroom, see pages T22.

Alternate Materials: oil pastels

"Let's show depth in a painting of a scene."
"Vamos a mostrar profundidad en un dibujo de una escena."

- Have students brainstorm a variety of places they might visit to see animals.
- Review techniques for creating depth.
- Review procedures for working with watercolor paint in **More About Technique Tips** on page 200.
- See page 14 in the **Technique Tips Flip Chart** for visual examples of techniques.
- Distribute materials and have students follow the directions on page 83.

FOR THE ART SPECIALIST

Have students use darker shades of color to add to the feeling of depth.

Creating Depth

Depth in an artwork is created when some objects seem to be very close and others seem to be far away.

Just like in real life, objects in artwork that are larger seem to be closer. Objects that are smaller seem to be farther away.

Just like in real life, objects in artwork that have clear, sharp edges and many details seem close. Objects that have fuzzy edges and little detail seem farther away.

Background

Foreground

Practice

Draw objects in a foreground and a background. Use colored pencils.

1. Near the bottom of your paper, draw an animal or an object. Make it large.

2. Draw the same animal or object near the top of your paper. Make it much smaller.

Decide Which object looks farther away?

Activities in
ART Across the Curriculum Book

Reading/Language Arts Write an in-depth report about the school or community, comparing the meaning of depth in art and news reporting. (page 79)

Math Learn how to estimate numbers in a group. (page 80)

Science Understand how pushing and pulling can change the direction and speed of objects. (page 81)

Social Studies Identify how *Washington's Head-quarters* depicts an important figure in American history. (page 82)

The Arts Identify the musical families of various instruments. (page 83)

Technology Use the *Multimedia Workshop* CD-ROM to create a scene showing plants at the bottom of the screen. (page 84)

Ashley Davis. Age 7. *Playing Wolves.* Pencil and crayon.

How did this student artist show depth in her drawing?

Create

What are some different places where you might find animals? Create depth in a real or imaginary scene.

1. Think about a place where there are lots of animals.

2. Make a rough sketch of the animals and other objects you want in your scene. Show depth by drawing animals and objects larger in the foreground and smaller in the background.

3. Fill your scene with color.

Describe Name the animals and objects you put in the foreground. What did you put in the background?

Analyze Which objects are the largest? Which are the smallest? Why are they different sizes?

Interpret What title would you give your painting?

Decide What did you like best about this drawing? Can you say why?

Lesson **2** 83

THEME Connections

Change Use *Washington's Head-quarters* as a visual example of how clothing styles have changed in America during the last century.

Diversity Use the artworks as visual examples of geographic differences throughout regions of the United States.

Change Use *Washington's Head-quarters* as a visual narrative of early U.S. history.

ESL

ESL students may find it difficult to follow a class discussion without additional visual clues. Use the illustrations provided in the student book to demonstrate what you are talking about or to paraphrase a student response when describing depth in pictures.

CLOSE

Time: About 5 minutes

"How do artists create a feeling of depth in a drawing or painting?"

"¿Cómo crean los artistas una sensación de profundidad en un dibujo o una pintura?"

LARGE PRINT **Review**

Compare: Use the **Large Print** *Silver Llama* to have students compare the techniques used to create the illusion of depth in the print and in the works in this lesson.

Art Criticism

Have students answer the four art criticism questions—Describe, Analyze, Interpret, and Decide—orally or in writing. After the paintings are dry, discuss the ways in which students created depth in their artwork.

 Assess

Use the **Assessment Book** pages 27–28 as a formal assessment for this lesson.

Evaluation Criteria

- Can the student identify two techniques for creating depth?
- Can the student show depth in a painting of a scene?
- Can the student use the four steps of art criticism to evaluate his or her own artwork?
- Can the student tell about the art and life of Hughie Lee-Smith?

Reteaching ● ● ● ● ● ● ● ● ● ● ●

Depth Have students look through the book to find three works of art that create the illusion of depth. Ask them to list the title of each work and describe the techniques the artist used to create a sense of depth.

Perception Hints for Student Art

The flowers are in the foreground. The two wolves pulling on the string are close to the foreground. They overlap the third wolf and the tree. The clouds in the sky are overlapping the sun in the background.

UNIT 3
LESSON 3

Overlapping

Artists overlap objects to make some objects seem close and others far away.

Joseph Jean-Gilles. (Haitian). *Haitian Landscape.* 1973. Oil on canvas. 76 × 122 cm. Collection of the Art Museum of the Americas, Organization of American States, Washington, DC.

Look at the landscape paintings on these pages. Joseph Jean-Gilles has overlapped houses, trees, and gardens. He has created a picture of a farming community. Sylvia Plimack Mangold has added a sense of depth by painting branches that cover each other. This makes the trees in front look closer to the viewer.

84

Unit **3**

LESSON PLANNER

Objectives

After completing this lesson, students will be able to:

- describe how artists create the illusion of depth by overlapping objects. *Aesthetic Perception*
- plan and create a drawing that shows depth by overlapping. *Creative Expression*
- use the four steps of art criticism to evaluate their own drawings. *Art Criticism*
- compare works by artists from different cultures. *Art History and Culture*

Program Resources

- **Overhead:** Both the Jean-Gilles and the Mangold are available on overhead 15.
- **Large Prints:** *Warrior Chief, Warriors, and Attendants*
- **Technique Tips Flip Chart,** page 15
- **Vocabulary Book** pages 29–30
- **Art Manipulative Kit:** music audiotapes
- **Artist Profiles Book:** Jean-Gilles page 21 and Mangold page 30
- **Art Across the Curriculum Book** pages 85–90
- **Multimedia Workshop CD-ROM**
- **National Museum of Women in the Arts Collection:** cards
- **Assessment Book** pages 29–30

Multiple Intelligences
Logical/Mathematical Students can observe and identify the relationships between near and distant objects.

Vocabulary

overlap *superponer* the placement of one object over another so that part of the second object is hidden

depth *profundidad* the appearance of distance on a flat surface

ART Background

About the Artists

Joseph Jean-Gilles (zhō zəf zhän gil lēs, Haitian, 1943–) now lives in Florida, but his native land is never far from his mind. He studied art at Centre d'Art in Port-au-Prince, Haiti, until 1967 and has been painting scenes of his homeland ever since.

Sylvia Plimack Mangold (sil' vē ə pli' mak man' gōld, American, 1938–) paints daily and relies on images in her immediate environment as sources of inspiration—the floors and walls of her studio and the landscape of the Hudson River Valley.

About Subject Matter* Both the Jean-Gilles and the Mangold artworks are landscape paintings.

About the Media The Jean-Gilles works mainly in oil on canvas. The Mangold painting is an oil, which is a slow-drying medium that comes in lush colors and provides a durable finish.

Sylvia Plimack Mangold. (American). *The Locust Trees with Maple.* 1990. Oil on linen.
Courtesy, Brooke Alexander Gallery, New York, New York.

Study both paintings to see how overlapping
creates a feeling of depth.

- Find objects in each painting that overlap.

- Which branches in *The Locust Trees with Maple*
  look closer to you? Which look farther away?

- What objects cover parts of the houses in *Haitian
  Landscape*? What objects do the houses cover?

- Describe the objects in *Haitian Landscape* that look
  closest to you. Which look farthest away?

**SEEING LIKE
AN ARTIST**

Look out a window
and find examples of
objects that overlap.

Lesson 3

85

About Art History* Jean-Gilles's painting is representative of the unique Haitian style of
art that was developed by self-taught artists.

Mangold's painting was created during a time of American performance art, when artists
created pieces that emphasized sounds, images, movement, and music.

- Use the **National Museum of Women in the Arts** cards to learn more about other
  women artists.

Cultural Perspectives Haitian life focuses on family, religion and the interdependence
of people and nature. Haitians, like Jean-Gilles, have a rich tradition of folk painting.

Mangold has followed in the tradition of American artists who closely observe and depict
an aspect of nature in a realistic style.

*See **More About** pages 206–227 for more about art history and subject matter.

FOCUS

Time: About 10 minutes

Activating Prior Knowledge

"Suppose you are sitting in a movie theater. Why can't you
see all of the person in front of you?"

*"Vamos a suponer que están sentados en un cine. ¿Por qué no
pueden ver completamente a la persona en frente de ustedes?"*

- Discuss students' answers to the question and
  how objects that are closer to the viewer cover
  part of objects that are farther away.

Introducing the Art

"Let's take a close look at the two paintings."
"Vamos a observar detalladamente las dos pinturas."

- **Describe:** Have students describe the subject
  matter in each painting. (both: landscapes)

- **COMPARE AND CONTRAST** Have students make
  a list of the similarities and differences in the
  two paintings. (Both paintings are outdoor scenes,
  show depth, and are realistic in style. Jean-Gilles's
  painting has many colors, includes people and houses, and
  is a spring or summertime scene. Mangold's painting has
  limited colors, illustrates only trees, and is a winter scene.)

- Share and discuss information from **Art
  Background** and the **Artist Profiles Book**
  about the lives, work and times of the artists.

- Have students answer questions about
  overlapping on page 85.
  ·(See **Perception Hints** below.)

FOR THE ART SPECIALIST

Use the **Overhead** and the **Large Print**
Warrior Chief, Warriors, and Attendants to
discuss how overlapping makes some
objects seem close and others far away.

Perception Hints

Overlapping *Jean-Gilles.* The trees in front overlap the
hills in the middle ground. Grass and bushes overlap the
houses. The houses overlap the hills behind them.
Mangold. The branches of the trees overlap.
Closest *Mangold.* The branches that overlap. **Farthest**
Mangold. The branches that are overlapped.
Objects that cover houses Plants and hills. **Objects the
houses cover** Brown hills.
Closest *Jean-Gilles.* The plants and hills at the bottom of
the artwork. **Farthest** *Jean-Gilles.* The trees and hills at the
top of the artwork.

TEACH

Time: About 30 minutes

Practice

Materials
- 9- × 12-inch paper
- pencils or crayons

Alternate Materials: markers

"How can you draw shapes that overlap?"

"¿Cómo pueden trazar figuras que se superponen?"

- Discuss how to overlap shapes to create depth. Emphasize that an object in the foreground may partially conceal an object in the background.
- Distribute materials and have students follow the directions on page 86 for illustrating depth by overlapping. Have them answer the Decide questions with a partner.

Create PROBLEM SOLVING

Materials
- 12- × 18-inch white construction paper
- pencils
- sketch paper

 Play music audiotapes from the **Art Manipulative Kit** while students work.

Alternate Materials: fine-line black felt-tip markers

"Let's create depth by overlapping trees in a landscape drawing."

"Vamos a crear profundidad al superponer árboles en un dibujo de un paisaje."

- Discuss different parts of the tree.
- Review overlapping as a technique for creating depth in an artwork.

 See page 15 in the **Technique Tips Flip Chart** for visual examples of techniques.

- Distribute materials and have students follow the directions on page 87.

Creating Overlapping

Overlapping occurs when one object covers a part of a second object. Overlapping makes the object in front seem to be closer to the viewer.

When objects overlap, they create **depth**, or the appearance of distance, on a flat surface. The one in front appears to be closer to the viewer. The second object seems to be farther away.

Practice

Draw shapes that overlap. Use pencil or crayon.

1. Create a feeling of depth in a design by overlapping geometric shapes.

2. Draw one large shape. Then, draw a second shape so that part of it is hidden behind the large shape.

3. Add other shapes.

Decide Do some shapes look like they are in front? Do others look like they are behind?

Activities in

ART Across the Curriculum Book

Reading/Language Arts Write a poem about a tree like the ones in the painting *The Locust Trees with Maple.* (page 85)

Math Study shapes created by overlapping. (page 86)

Science Identify characteristics of the seasons, noting how seasons often overlap and do not change instantly. (page 87)

Social Studies Compare and contrast the Haitian culture with the United States, looking first at the painting *Haitian Landscape.* (page 88)

The Arts Create a dialogue for two of the people in *Haitian Landscape.* (page 89)

Technology Use the *Multimedia Workshop* CD-ROM to create a scene using overlapping that shows objects close and far away. (page 90)

Nick Rogers. Age 8. *The Forest*. Pencil.

How did this student artist create a feeling of depth?

Create

How do the trees look when you are walking toward them? Create a drawing of overlapping trees and branches.

1. Think about the different parts of a tree. How do the branches look? Sketch some, using different kinds of lines.

2. Draw some trees, making each tree's branches and leaves overlap to create a feeling of depth.

3. Fill your page, and touch all edges of the paper with your lines and shapes.

Describe Where did you use overlapping in your drawing?

Analyze How did overlapping help you create a feeling of depth?

Interpret How would your drawing change if the trees did not overlap?

Decide How is your drawing like the paintings shown in this lesson? How is it different?

Lesson **3**   **87**

Relationships Use the Jean-Gilles work as a visual example of how people are dependent upon farmers for the food we eat.

Cultures Use the Jean-Gilles as a springboard to read stories from the book *The Magic Orange Tree and Other Haitian Folktales,* collected by Diane Wolkstein.

Change Use the paintings as visual examples of the appearance of trees during different seasons of the year.

For the first step of drawing overlapping trees and branches, you may wish to create a chart as students share their ideas about trees. Write the different parts of a tree and draw a quick sketch. Model the idea of a rough sketch and how to use it to create the final drawing.

CLOSE

Time: About 5 minutes

"What have you learned about the use of overlapping in a painting or drawing?"

"¿Qué han aprendido acerca del uso de la superposición en una pintura o un dibujo?"

 Review
Use the **Large Print** *Warrior Chief, Warriors, and Attendants* to have students compare how the print and the works in this lesson use overlapping.

Art Criticism

Have students answer the four art criticism questions—Describe, Analyze, Interpret, and Decide—orally or in writing. Discuss the use of overlapping in their drawings.

 Assess
Use the **Assessment Book** pages 29–30 as a formal assessment for this lesson.

Evaluation Criteria

• Can the student describe how artists use overlapping as a technique for creating depth?

• Can the student incorporate overlapping in a drawing?

• Can the student use the four steps of art criticism to evaluate his or her own work?

• Can the student compare the artwork and lives of the two featured artists?

Reteaching ● ● ● ● ● ● ● ● ● ● ●

Overlapping Have students look outside and find five objects that overlap other objects. Ask them to list the objects in front and the objects they overlap.

Perception Hints for Student Art

This student artist created a feeling of depth by overlapping branches.

Form

Artists use three-dimensional forms to create sculptures.

Fernand Leger. (French). *The Walking Flower.* 1951. Ceramic. $26\frac{1}{2} \times 20\frac{1}{2} \times 15$ inches. Albright-Knox, Buffalo, New York.

Look at the sculptures on these pages. *The Walking Flower* is a clay sculpture. *The Spinner* is a metal mobile. Form is an important element in both these sculptures.

88   Unit **3**

UNIT 3
LESSON 4

LESSON PLANNER

Objectives
After completing this lesson, students will be able to:
- identify three-dimensional forms used by artists. *Aesthetic Perception*
- plan and create a sculptural form with paper. *Creative Expression*
- use the four steps of art criticism to evaluate their own sculptures. *Art Criticism*
- describe the lives and artwork of Alexander Calder and Fernand Léger. *Art History and Culture*

Program Resources
- **Overhead:** Both the Léger and the Calder are available on overhead 16.
- **Large Prints:** *Warrior Chief, Warriors, and Attendants* and *Silver Llama*
- **Technique Tips Flip Chart,** page 16
- **Vocabulary Book** pages 31–32
- **Art Manipulative Kit:** 3-D form
- **Artist Profiles Book:** Léger page 27 and Calder page 4
- **Art Across the Curriculum Book** pages 91–96
- **Multimedia Workshop CD-ROM**
- **National Geographic Picture Atlas of the World CD-ROM**
- **Assessment Book** pages 31–32

Multiple Intelligences
Visual/Spatial Students can view sculpture from different angles in order to perceive the various forms used in the creation of an artwork.

Vocabulary
shape *figura* a flat, two-dimensional area

two-dimensional *bidimensional* something that can be measured by height and width

form *forma* the element of art that is three-dimensional and encloses space

three-dimensional *tridimensional* something that can be measured by height, width, and depth

sculpture *escultura* three-dimensional work of art created out of wood, stone, metal, or clay by carving, welding, casting, or modeling

---

ART Background

About the Artists
Alexander Calder (a leg zan' dər kôl' dər, American, 1898–1976) was born in Philadelphia. Both his father and grandfather were sculptors. He was playful and innovative. He invented mobiles—a new art form of sculptures in motion. He also created wire sculptures of animals, toys, and a variety of three-dimensional artworks.

Fernand Léger (fer nän' lā zhā', French, 1881–1955) was born in Normandy of peasant stock. As a young man, he studied architecture. Then, inspired by the geometric basis of Picasso's Cubism, he painted forms that are reminiscent of machines. In the last years of his life, he translated his mechanical forms into ceramic sculpture.

- Use the **National Geographic Picture Atlas of the World CD-ROM** to learn about France.

About Subject Matter* The Calder is a nonobjective sculpture. The Léger is a symbolic sculpture.

Alexander Calder. (American). *The Spinner.* 1966. Aluminum, steel, and oil paint. 235 × 351 inches. Collection Walker Art Center, Minneapolis, Gift of Dayton Hudson Corporation, Minneapolis, Minnesota.

Study both sculptures to find the following forms.

- ✓ Find a form that has a shape like a circle.
- ✓ Locate forms that look like triangles.
- ✓ Find free-forms in these sculptures.

SEEING LIKE AN ARTIST

Look around your classroom. Find objects that have forms like the ones you found in the artwork.

Lesson **4**

89

About the Media The Calder work is an aluminum and steel sculpture. The Léger work is a sculpture made from clay.

About Art History Calder began creating mobiles in the 1930s during the ragtime and jazz era of American music.

Léger began to paint in France in the early 1900s, a time when postimpressionist artists, such as Paul Cezanne, were interested not only in light but also solid forms.

Cultural Perspectives Léger was mobilized into the Engineer Corps of France during World War I. His wartime experiences contributed to his interest in social themes and machine forms.

*See **More About** pages 206–227 for more about art history and subject matter.

FOCUS
Time: About 10 minutes

Activating Prior Knowledge
"Think about three-dimensional geometric shapes that you see in buildings."
"Piensen acerca de figuras geométricas tridimensionales que ven en los edificios."

- Discuss students' responses and how two-dimensional geometric shapes can be seen in three-dimensional forms.

Introducing the Art
"Let's take a close look at the two sculptures."
"Vamos a observar detalladamente las dos esculturas."

- **Describe:** Have students describe the subject matter in each artwork. (Calder: nonobjective; Léger: symbolic)
- Use the 3-D forms from the **Art Manipulative Kit** to demonstrate 3-D forms.
- **COMPARE AND CONTRAST** Have students make a list of the similarities and differences in the two sculptures. (Both sculptures are nonobjective in style, use basic and free-form, three-dimensional forms, and have appendages that radiate from a central point. The Calder is a monumental, kinetic form made from metal. The Léger is a relatively smaller, stabile form made from clay.)
- Share and discuss information from **Art Background** and the **Artist Profiles Book** about the lives, work, and times of the artists.
- Have students answer questions about forms on page 89. (See **Perception Hints** below.)

FOR THE ART SPECIALIST

Use the **Overhead** and the **Large Print** *Silver Llama* to demonstrate how artists use three-dimensional forms to create sculptures.

Perception Hints

Sphere *Léger.* The red form in the center of the sculpture has a shape like a circle.
Triangular Forms *Calder.* The black base at the bottom of the sculpture consists of triangular forms. Together, the triangular forms create a pyramid.
Free-forms *Léger.* The entire sculpture is free-form.

TEACH

Time: About 30 minutes

Practice

Materials

- 9- × 12-inch paper

Alternate Materials: newspapers

"How can you create a three-dimensional form with a two-dimensional piece of paper?"

"¿Cómo pueden crear una forma tridimensional con una hoja de papel bidimensional?"

- Discuss techniques for manipulating paper.
- Distribute materials and have students follow the directions on page 90 for creating a three-dimensional form. Have them answer the Decide question with a partner.

Create PROBLEM SOLVING

Materials

- 12- × 18-inch colored construction paper
- oil pastels
- scissors
- glue

Safety! For safety issues about oil pastels and other information about safety in the art classroom, see page T22.

Alternate Materials: tagboard and colored markers

"Let's change the paper in a variety of ways to create a three-dimensional paper sculpture."

"Vamos a cambiar el papel en una variedad de formas para crear una escultura tridimensional."

- Review the basic three-dimensional forms.
- Review techniques for manipulating paper, curling, folding, tabbing.

 See page 16 in the **Technique Tips Flip Chart** for visual examples of techniques.

- Distribute materials and have students follow the directions on page 91.

FOR THE ART SPECIALIST

Have students think of found objects they could add to their 3-D sculptures.

Using Form

Shapes and forms are similar. They both can be geometric or free-form. But they are different, too. **Shapes** are flat and are **two-dimensional** (2-D). They can be measured in only two ways: height and width.

Forms are not flat. They are **three-dimensional** (3-D) and can be measured in three ways: height, width, and depth.

Below are five basic forms. You saw them in the sculptures in this lesson. Which shapes do these forms remind you of?

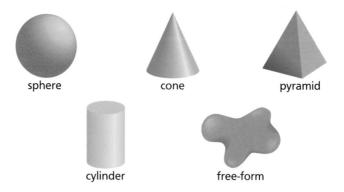

sphere   cone   pyramid

cylinder   free-form

Sculpture is art that is three-dimensional. The form of the sculpture is the positive space. The negative space is the area all around the form.

Practice

Make a form. It will have three dimensions. Use paper.

1. Tear a piece of paper in several places without tearing it completely apart.

2. Fold, bend, curl, and twist the paper to make a form. Notice that it has three-dimensions: height, width, and depth.

Decide Does your paper form have spaces inside and all around it?

Activities in ART Across the Curriculum Book

Reading/Language Arts Learn how to look up different meanings of a word in a dictionary, noting how forms and shapes are similar in art. (page 91)

Math Identify three-dimensional forms and predict patterns. (page 92)

Science Learn about the power of wind. (page 93)

Social Studies Understand the concept of freedom in the United States, first looking at the freedom of Calder's mobile parts to move in the air. (page 94)

The Arts Show movements that reflect the freedom of Calder's mobile to move through space. (page 95)

Technology Use the *Multimedia Workshop* CD-ROM to create a three-dimensional sculpture. (page 96)

Pernandas Freeman. Age 8. *Musical Free Shape.*
Construction paper and oil pastels.

How do you know this paper sculpture is 3-D?

Create

What objects around you have three dimensions? Create a three-dimensional paper sculpture.

1. Think about different ways of shaping paper.

2. Cut out a large free-form shape from a piece of construction paper. Decorate it with a variety of lines and shapes.

3. Turn your 2-D shape into a 3-D sculpture. Make several deep cuts along the outside edges toward the inside.

4. Join opposite points of the cut pieces together. Glue the points together.

Lesson 4

Describe Point to the three dimensions in your sculpture. Identify the positive and negative spaces.

Analyze How did you change the paper to create a 3-D form?

Interpret What does your sculpture make you think of? Why are the negative spaces important to it?

Decide Which do you like better—your 2-D design or your finished sculpture?

91

THEME Connections

Scale and Structure Use the artwork as a springboard to discuss forms used in a playground.

Relationships Use the artwork as visual examples of the relationship between two-dimensional shapes and three-dimensional forms.

Patterns Use the subject of the lesson as an opportunity to point out the geometric shapes that appear in nature, such as the cylinder of a tree trunk and the circle of the sun.

ESL

ESL students may have difficulty following oral directions without some kind of visual support. Consider modeling the steps in creating the sculpture with the whole class. To review, write the steps on the chalkboard along with a quick sketch before asking students to complete the activity.

CLOSE

Time: About 5 minutes

"What have you learned about the way artists use forms to create art?"

"¿Qué han aprendido acerca de las maneras en que los artistas usan las formas para crear arte?"

LARGE PRINT **Review**

Use the **Large Prints** *Warrior Chief, Warriors, and Attendants* and *Silver Llama* and the works in this lesson to have students compare the use of forms.

Art Criticism

Have students answer the four art criticism questions—Describe, Analyze, Interpret, and Decide—orally or in writing. Discuss the use of forms in their sculptures.

Assess

Use the **Assessment Book** pages 31–32 as a formal assessment for this lesson.

Evaluation Criteria

• Can the student use appropriate vocabulary to identify the basic forms?

• Can the student incorporate a variety of forms in a three-dimensional paper sculpture?

• Can the student use the four steps of art criticism to evaluate his or her own work?

• Can the student describe the lives and artworks of Alexander Calder and Fernand Léger?

Reteaching • • • • • • • • • • • •

Forms Have the students look around the classroom and identify an object for each of the basic forms. Ask them to list the basic forms with the corresponding objects.

Perception Hints for Student Art

This sculpture appears to be 3-D because of the shadows and apparent overlapping.

Relief Sculpture

Artists create relief sculptures by making raised forms on flat surfaces. Reliefs often are used for decoration.

Lorenzo Ghiberti. (Italian). *The Meeting of Solomon and Sheba/The Gates of Paradise.* 1425–52. Gilded bronze. Scala/Art Resource, NY.

Look at the artwork on these two pages. The bronze panel has figures that seem to be almost freestanding. This type of relief is called high relief. The *Winged Genie,* carved in Assyria around 850 B.C., is an example of low relief. Its design is slightly raised above the background.

92   Unit **3**

UNIT 3
LESSON 5

LESSON PLANNER

Objectives
After completing this lesson, students will be able to:

- identify the difference between relief and freestanding sculpture. *Aesthetic Perception*
- plan and create a ceramic relief tile. *Creative Expression*
- use the four steps of art criticism to evaluate their own relief tiles. *Art Criticism*
- compare works by artists from different cultures. *Art History and Culture*

Program Resources
- **Overhead:** Both the Ghiberti and *Winged Genie* are available on overhead 17.
- **Large Prints:** *Warrior Chief, Warriors, and Attendants*
- **Technique Tips Flip Chart,** page 17
- **Vocabulary Book** pages 33–34
- **Art Manipulative Kit:** 3-D forms
- **Artist Profiles Book:** Ghiberti page 16 and Artist unknown page 62
- **Art Across the Curriculum Book** pages 97–102
- **Multimedia Workshop CD-ROM**
- **National Geographic Picture Atlas of the World CD-ROM**
- **Animals Through History Time Line**
- **Assessment Book** pages 33–34

Multiple Intelligences
Body/Kinesthetic Students can use fine motor skills as they manipulate materials to create relief tiles.

Vocabulary
freestanding *autoestable* a three-dimensional work of art surrounded by negative space

relief sculpture *escultura en relieve* a work of art in which forms project from a flat surface

FOCUS

Time: About 10 minutes

Activating Prior Knowledge

"Imagine that you are holding a quarter in your hand. How does the surface of the coin feel?"

"Vamos a imaginar que ustedes sostienen un quarter en sus manos. ¿Cómo se siente la superficie de la moneda?"

- Discuss students' responses and how coins have a raised surface.

 **ART** *Background*

About the Artists
Lorenzo Ghiberti (lō rent' sō gē bâr' tē, Italian, 1378–1455) won the competition to design the doors of the Baptistry of Florence. He created a greater illusion of space through perspective and sculptural means than had ever before been possible.

- Use the **National Geographic Picture Atlas of the World CD-ROM** to learn more about Italy.

About Subject Matter* Both the Ghiberti panel and the *Winged Genie* are narrative relief sculptures.

- Use the **Animals Through History Time Line** to compare the animal art created around the same time period as the Ghiberti.

About the Media The Ghiberti relief is gilt bronze. Gilding is the process of applying gold leaf to a surface. The *Winged Genie* is carved from alabaster.

Artist unknown. (Assyria). *Winged Genie.* c. 883–859 B.C. Alabaster. 91 inches high. Brooklyn Museum of Art, New York, New York.

Study both artworks to find the following areas of relief.

- Find the areas that appear to be raised. Trace them with your finger.
- Where are the flat background areas?
- Which relief seems to be the highest?
- Which work has a background that seems to go backward in space?
- In which work do the figures seems most lifelike?

SEEING LIKE AN ARTIST

Look closely at both sides of a coin. Which areas are raised? Why do you think the background is empty?

Lesson 5

93

About Art History* Ghiberti sculpted in Florence, Italy, during the Early Renaissance. City leaders bestowed commissions, and new programs for artworks were undertaken.

The *Winged Genie* was created during a time when the power of Assyrian kings was often depicted in nonhuman forms. Their favorite pursuits of war and hunting were recorded and narrated in numerous relief carvings.

Cultural Perspectives Ghiberti sculpted during a time in Florence when members of the Medici family were generous patrons of art and learning. Florentines excelled in law, philosophy, literature, science, scholarship, and the fine arts.

The *Winged Genie* was created during a time when the Assyrians had experienced centuries of warfare against their neighbors.

*See **More About** pages 206–227 for more about art history and subject matter.

- **Describe:** Have students describe the subject matter in each sculpture. (both: narratives)
- Use the 3-D forms from the **Art Manipulative Kit** to demonstrate freestanding forms/sculpture.
- **COMPARE AND CONTRAST** Have students make a list of the similarities and differences in the two sculptures. (Both have areas that are raised from a flat surface, include the human form, and have the center of interest in the middle. The Ghiberti panel illustrates perspective, includes many figures, and has areas of high and low relief. The *Winged Genie* has a flat background and a single figure that is in low relief.)
- Share and discuss information about the artworks from **Art Background** and the **Artist Profiles Book.**
- Have students answer questions about relief on page 93. (See **Perception Hints** below.)

FOR THE ART SPECIALIST

Use the **Overhead** and the **Large Print** *Warrior Chief, Warriors, and Attendants* to demonstrate how artists create relief sculptures by making raised forms on flat surfaces.

Perception Hints

Relief *Winged Genie.* The figure in the center of the panel is raised and in relief.
Relief *Ghiberti.* This work has two central figures, Solomon and the Queen of Sheba, who are grasping hands, while the raised figures around them are engaged in conversation.
Flat *Winged Genie.* All the area surrounding the figure is flat.
Highest Relief The relief in *The Meeting of Solomon and Sheba* seems to be the highest.
Background The background in *The Meeting of Solomon and Sheba* appears to go back into space.
Lifelike Figures The figures in *The Meeting of Solomon and Sheba* seem lifelike.

TEACH

Time: About two 30-minute periods

Practice

Materials
- 9- × 12-inch paper
- glue
- yarn

Alternate Materials: oil or clay

"How can you use yarn to create areas of relief?"
"¿Cómo pueden usar hilo para crear áreas de relieve?"

- Discuss the use of yarn to create relief sculpture.
- Distribute materials and have students follow the directions on page 94 for creating relief. Have them verbally answer the Decide questions with a partner.

Create PROBLEM SOLVING

Materials
- clay, about the size of a baseball, for each student
- rolling pins or thick dowel sticks
- muslin
- 6- × 9-inch cardboard frame • sketch paper
- pencils • tape
- paper clips • containers of water and slip
- various textured objects • slip brushes

Safety! For safety issues about clay and other information about safety in the art classroom, see page T22.

Alternate Materials: glue and foil relief

"Let's use clay to create a relief tile."
"Vamos a usar arcilla para crear un azulejo de relieve."

- Review guidelines for facial proportions.
- Review procedures for working with clay in **More About Technique Tips** on page 205.
- See page 17 in the **Technique Tips Flip Chart** for visual examples of techniques.
- Distribute materials and have students follow the directions on page 94.
- Use paper clips to carve away clay.
- Allow clay to dry for approximately 6–7 days.

FOR THE ART SPECIALIST

Have students insert a paper clip in the back of their clay tile while still soft and hang when dry.

Creating Relief Sculpture

Artwork in which forms stand out from a flat surface is called **relief sculpture**.

Most three-dimensional sculptures are **freestanding**. They have empty, negative space all around them. Relief sculptures, however, are not freestanding. The background is flat. The positive areas are raised up from the background.

Coins are one example of relief that we see every day. What other examples can you think of?

Practice

Write your name in relief. Use glue and yarn.

1. Make a design with thick lines of yarn glued onto a piece of paper.

2. Allow the glue to dry for a few hours.

Decide Feel the letters of your name. Do they stand out from the surface of your paper?

Activities in
ART Across the Curriculum Book

Reading/Language Arts Write a description of yourself. (page 97)

Math Create a graph about physical characteristics noting how each person stands out like a figure in a relief sculpture. (page 98)

Science Learn about muscles. (page 99)

Social Studies Study how people communicated over long distances, using the Ghiberti as an example. (page 100)

The Arts Imagine you are a person in *The Meeting of Solomon and Sheba* and create a dialogue for your character. (page 101)

Technology Use the *Multimedia Workshop* CD-ROM to create a tile relief sculpture with three-dimensional forms. (page 102)

Brittny Thomas. Age 9. *This is Me.* Clay.

How is this student artist's relief sculpture different from one that is freestanding?

Create

What would you like to show in a self-portrait? Create a self-portrait in relief tile.

1. Think about making a self-portrait of your face or your whole body. Draw a self-portrait on paper for practice.

2. Roll out a slab of clay. Draw your portrait into it with a pencil. Design a frame and press it into the clay around your portrait. Carve away from the area around the portrait but not the frame. Be careful not to carve all the way through the slab.

3. Use scrap pieces of clay to add details.

Lesson 5

Describe What shapes did you use? Describe the textures.

Analyze Which areas are in relief? Where are the negative spaces?

Interpret What words would you use to describe your self-portrait? How would the work change if there were no raised areas?

Decide What do you like best? Why?

95

CLOSE

Time: About 5 minutes

"What do you know now about relief sculpture?"
"¿Qué saben ahora acerca de la escultura en relieve?"

LARGE PRINT **Review**

Use the **Large Print** *Warrior Chief, Warriors, and Attendants* and the works in this lesson to have students compare areas of relief.

Art Criticism

Have students answer the four art criticism questions—Describe, Analyze, Interpret, and Decide—orally or in writing. Discuss the areas of relief in their self-portrait tiles.

Assess

Use the **Assessment Book** pages 33–34 as a formal assessment for this lesson.

Evaluation Criteria

- Can the student identify the difference between relief and freestanding sculptures?
- Can the student create areas of relief in an expressive self-portrait?
- Can the student use the four steps of art criticism to evaluate his or her own work?
- Can the student compare the Ghiberti panel and the *Winged Genie*?

Reteaching • • • • • • • • • • • •

Relief Have the student look outside and find five examples of relief. Ask them to list their examples and describe the areas of relief they find.

THEME Connections

Cultures Use the artwork as visual examples of how art can communicate information about the cultures in which it was created.

Systems Use the artwork as visual examples of how ancient cultures were dependent upon art to record significant events in history.

Energy Use the artwork *Winged Genie* to discuss ways of symbolizing strength and power, such as bulging muscles used to symbolize physical strength.

ESL

You may wish to use the self-portraits of ESL students to review or introduce vocabulary about body parts. Depending on the level of English proficiency of your students, you may wish to introduce the more finely detailed vocabulary for body parts, such as eyelashes, forehead, wrist, and so on.

Perception Hints for Student Art

This student artist's sculpture is created on a flat surface and is two-dimensional. A freestanding sculpture is three-dimensional.

UNIT 3
LESSON 6

3-D Art to Wear

A jeweler creates decorative three-dimensional forms to wear.

Artist unknown. (Morocco). *Necklace.* Twentieth century. Beads and silver alloy. 14 inches long.

Compare the necklace from Morocco to the tuxedo studs and cuff links. They are all forms of three-dimensional art, or jewelry. These pieces of jewelry also have raised areas and a variety of materials.

Unit **3**

LESSON PLANNER

Objectives
After completing this lesson, students will be able to:
- identify three-dimensional forms in jewelry. *Aesthetic Perception*
- plan and create a medallion in relief. *Creative Expression*
- use the four steps of art criticism to evaluate their own artwork. *Art Criticism*
- learn about jewelry from the two cultures, *Art History and Culture*

Program Resources
- **Overhead:** Both the *Necklace* and the Sandkühler are available on overhead 18.
- **Technique Tips Flip Chart,** page 18
- **Vocabulary Book** pages 35–36
- **Art Manipulative Kit:** flash cards
- **Artist Profiles Book:** Artist unknown page 63 and Sandkühler page 47
- **Art Across the Curriculum Book** pages 103–108
- **Multimedia Workshop CD-ROM**
- **National Geographic Picture Atlas of the World CD-ROM**
- **Assessment Book** pages 35–36

Multiple Intelligences
Intrapersonal Students can focus their concentration inwardly and express their individual creativity.

Vocabulary
jeweler *joyero* an artist who designs and creates jewelry

jewelry *joyas* three-dimensional ornaments, such as rings, bracelets, and earrings

---

FOCUS

Time: About 10 minutes

Activating Prior Knowledge

"Think about the different kinds of jewelry that you have seen people wear for decoration. Can you name some? Can you describe how they look?"

"Piensen acerca de los diferentes tipos de joyas que hayan visto que las personas usan para decoración. ¿Pueden nombrar algunas? ¿Pueden describir cómo son?"

- Discuss students' answers to the questions and how jewelry can be made from a variety of materials and three-dimensional forms.

🎨 ART Background

About the Artist
Iris Sandkühler (Ī' ris Sand' kū lər, American 1958–   ) was born in Bingen, West Germany. Her family emigrated to the United States when she was twelve years old. In college she studied glassblowing. She teaches full-time at Georgia Southern University and continues to make jewelry, sculpture, and write.

The *Necklace* was made by an unknown Berber artist in the Rif region of Morocco. The Berbers of North Africa live in the rugged Atlas, Rif, and Kabylia mountains and in the arid lands at the edge of the Saharan desert. Berber silversmiths are primarily male and Jewish.

About Subject Matter* Both pieces of jewelry are utilitarian objects. The Sandkühler pieces were made for conductor Joseph Robbins for a special performance in Australia.

About the Media Both pieces of jewelry are made with a variety of materials, including silver, coral beads, and stones.

Iris Sandkühler. *Tuxedo Studs and Cufflinks.* 1994. The Joseph Robbins Collection.

Study both works of art.

- ✓ Find areas where the designs are raised.
- ✓ Find the jewelry that has beads made from coral.
- ✓ How will the necklace sound when worn?
- ✓ Which piece has a variety of raised jewels?

SEEING LIKE AN ARTIST

Look around your classroom. Is anyone wearing jewelry? What color is it? What materials is it made of?

Lesson **6**

97

About Art History* In the past, jewelry was worn as personal adornment, for religious purposes, or to show a person's rank or nobility. People who create jewelry may concentrate on metalworking, gem-cutting, or making glass plates. The most common forms of jewelry are necklaces, earrings, bracelets, and rings. In prehistoric times these items were made of pebbles, bones, and animal teeth and antlers. After the invention of metalworking, metal and stones could be combined in jewelry pieces.

Cultural Perspectives The twentieth-century Moroccan necklace was created in a land where the people are mainly farmers or belong to nomadic tribes. Women wear veils to cover their faces and do not mix with men in the open-air markets.

Iris Sandkühler's jewelry echoes the beaches on which she finds some of the glass she uses. Beach glass is shards of glass worn smooth by the sand and water of the ocean.

*See **More About** pages 206–227 for more about art history and subject matter.

Introducing the Art

"Let's take a close look at the pieces of jewelry."

"Vamos a observar detalladamente las joyas."

- Use the **National Geographic Picture Atlas of the World CD-ROM** to learn about the areas where these artworks are from.
- **Describe:** Have students describe the subject matter in each piece. (both: utilitarian)
- **COMPARE AND CONTRAST** Have students make a list of the similarities and differences in the two jewelry pieces. (Both incorporate round shapes, and have formal balance. The *Studs and Cuff Links* incorporate metal and stones and are meant to be worn on clothing. The Moroccan necklace is meant to be worn around the neck.)
- Share and discuss information about the works and times of the artworks from **Art Background** and the **Artist Profiles Book.**
- Have students answer questions about form on page 97. (See **Perception Hints** below.)

FOR THE ART SPECIALIST

Use the **Overhead** to demonstrate decorative three-dimensional art to wear.

Perception Hints

Raised designs *Necklace.* Rectangular pieces are found throughout the necklace with raised designs. *Studs and Cuff Links.* Raised metal piece on one spot of each stud and cuff link.

Coral *Necklace.* The dark orange beads are strung in three rows.

Sound *Necklace.* It will jangle when worn.

Raised jewels *Tuxedo Studs and Cuff Links.* Circular and oval shapes are found throughout the studs and cuff links.

TEACH

Time: About two 30-minute periods

Practice

Materials

- assorted low-relief objects such as paper clips, yarn, toothpicks, buttons, pasta, and cardboard
- 8- × 8-inch heavy-duty aluminum foil

Alternate Materials: objects found in nature

"How can you create areas of relief on a flat surface?"

"¿Cómo pueden crear áreas de relieve sobre una superficie plana?"

- Discuss the use of objects to create a foil relief.
- Distribute the materials and have students follow the directions on page 98 for demonstrating areas of relief. Have them answer the Decide question with a partner.

Create PROBLEM SOLVING

Materials

- 4- × 4-inch cardboard
- scissors   • hole punch
- glue
- assorted low-relief objects
- 6- × 6-inch heavy-duty aluminum foil
- pieces of yarn or ribbon (about 24 inches)

Safety! For safety issues about glue and other information about safety in the art classroom, see pages T22.

Alternate Materials: wood or pasta

"Let's use a variety of objects to create a medallion that is in relief."

"Vamos a usar una variedad de objetos para crear un medallón que está en relieve."

- Use flash cards from the **Art Manipulative Kit** to review shapes.
- Review ways to create areas of relief.
- Review techniques for smoothing the foil to emphasize the relief areas.
- See page 18 in the **Technique Tips Flip Chart** for visual examples of techniques.
- Distribute materials and have students follow the directions on page 99.

FOR THE ART SPECIALIST

Have students present a fashion show and explain their jewelry pieces.

Designing and Making Jewelry

A piece of **jewelry** is three-dimensional artwork that is made for people to wear. A **jeweler** is an artist who designs and makes jewelry. The art of making jewelry has been around for about 4000 years. Rings and necklaces are forms of jewelry. Can you think of any other forms?

A variety of materials can be used to make jewelry. Gold, silver, and gemstones are used most often. Jewelry can also be made with wood, glass, leather, beads, and paper. Can you think of any other materials that can be used to make jewelry?

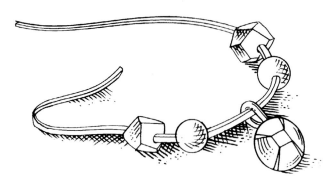

Practice

Use a found object and foil to practice making a foil relief.

1. Place foil on top of an object such as a button to get the feel of stretching foil gently. Start in the middle and use your fingertips to gently press and smooth the foil across the flat surface and over the ridges.

2. Remove the foil from the object and you will have the object's impression.

Decide Does the impression of the object show in the foil?

Activities in

ART Across the Curriculum Book

Reading/Language Arts Learn about Morocco. (page 103)

Math Count the value of coins, understanding the value and beauty of coins and necklaces. (page 104)

Science Learn about recycling, noting jewelry. (page 105)

Social Studies Understand the importance of maintaining a budget to afford such nice things as the necklace or tuxedo cuff links. (page 106)

The Arts Identify songs that go with holidays or special occasions. (page 107)

Technology Use the *Multimedia Workshop* CD-ROM to design a medallion in relief. (page 108)

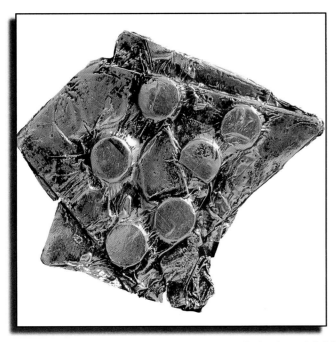

Megan Stein. Age 8. *Raised Rounds.* Posterboard, aluminum foil, ink.

What makes this medallion a relief?

Create

What type of jewelry would you like to wear? Create a medallion.

1. Think about small objects that have interesting shapes.

2. Cut cardboard into a geometric shape. Arrange objects in different ways on top. Glue down your favorite arrangement.

3. When dry, cover the surface with foil.

4. Punch a hole at the top of your design. Pass a piece of yarn or ribbon through the hole and tie the ends.

Describe What objects did you use to create the areas of the relief?

Analyze Why are some areas lower than other areas?

Interpret When would you wear your medallion?

Decide If you could create another medallion, what would you change?

Lesson 6

99

CLOSE
Time: About 5 minutes

"How can you use three-dimensional design to create jewelry?"

"¿Cómo pueden usar un diseño tridimensional para crear joyas?"

Review
Use the **Overhead** to have students identify areas of relief.

Art Criticism
• Have students answer the four art criticism questions—Describe, Analyze, Interpret, and Decide—orally or in writing. Discuss the use of relief in their medallions.

Assess
Use the **Assessment Book** pages 35–36 as a formal assessment for this lesson.

Evaluation Criteria
• Can the student identify three-dimensional forms in jewelry?
• Can the student create areas of relief in a piece of jewelry?
• Can the student use the four steps of art criticism to evaluate his or her own work?
• Can the students relate facts about the jewelry from the two cultures?

Reteaching ● ● ● ● ● ● ● ● ● ● ● ●

Relief Have the students look around the classroom to find five areas of relief. Ask them to list the objects and describe the relief areas.

THEME Connections

Cultures Use the artwork as visual examples of jewelry from different countries.

Origins Use the artwork to discuss the locations of various natural resources used in creating art.

Patterns Use the artwork as visual examples of different shapes used to create pieces of art.

ESL

Hands-on projects provide a lot of support for ESL students. To maximize language learning, encourage all your students to talk about what they are doing. You may wish to pair or group students while they work to ensure that everyone has a chance to talk about their work.

Perception Hints for Student Art

The round shapes are raised from a flat surface creating a relief.

LESSON PLANNER

Objectives

After completing this lesson, students will be able to:

• express the ideas of a poem through dance. *Aesthetic Perception*

• create shapes and forms by using the movements of the body. *Creative Expression*

• use the four steps of art criticism to evaluate their own interpretation of the poem. *Art Criticism*

• demonstrate knowledge about the content of the Hoop Dance. *Art History and Culture*

Program Resources

Artsource Performing Arts Audio/Video Resource Package

Hoop Dance performed by the American Indian Dance Theater. Videocassette Running Time: 3:37.

FOCUS

Time: About 10 minutes

Activating Prior Knowledge

"What things have you seen in nature that are beautiful?"

"¿Qué cosas han visto en la naturaleza que son hermosas?"

• Discuss students' answers and talk about the importance of nature and having respect for all living things.

Introducing the Art

"Let's look at the picture of the hoop dancer."

"Vamos a observar la pintura del bailarín de aro."

• Discuss information on page 100. Explain to students that the hoop was originally designed by Native Americans to teach and tell stories about the creation of animals and plants on Earth. Share information from **Art Background** with students. If you have the *Artsource* videocassette, have students view a performance of the Hoop Dance.

• Have students brainstorm and list animals, plants, terrain, and so on, that could be included in the creations of the hoop dancer.

Space and Form in Dance

American Indian Dance Theatre: *"Hoop Dance."*

n artist creates shapes and forms with paint on paper. A dancer creates shapes and forms through movement. This dancer is dancing the Native American "Hoop Dance." The dancer uses reed hoops to create forms in the air. He creates the form of a butterfly, a turtle, flowers, a snake, and a globe.

ART Background

About the Choreographer

Hanay Geiogamah is the Artistic Director of the American Indian Dance Theatre. Geiogamah is an Associate Professor of Theatre Arts and American Indian Studies at the University of California at Los Angeles. He plans to create an American Indian musical comedy and write and direct an American Indian film.

About Subject Matter Geiogamah explains, "When I was a boy, I saw trees and butterflies, eagles and squirrels, and I saw how they were all connected and that they were related and even a part of me. As I got older, I began to understand that life is a continual flow of creation. When I started dancing, I discovered that my hoops had stories in them and the shapes I made could reflect and teach and honor the forces in life that connect all of us to each other."

What To Do

Create movements to show the ideas in a poem.

Materials
None

1. Read the Navajo poem aloud. Its theme is a love of nature.

2. Talk about what you think the poem means.

3. Work with a partner. Design a movement to show each line in the poem. You are creating forms and shapes with the movements of your body.

4. When you are ready, perform the poem while your partner says the lines. Then, say the lines while your partner performs the poem.

In beauty, I walk
With beauty before me.
I walk with beauty
  behind me.
I walk with beauty
  beside me.
I walk with beauty
  above me.
I walk with beauty
  below me.
With beauty all around
  me, I walk.
With beauty within me,
  I walk.
It is finished in beauty.

Describe What gestures did you make to show the idea of each line?

Analyze Explain how your movements create forms and shapes.

Interpret Identify the feelings that you created through your poem.

Decide How well did you succeed in matching your movements to the words of the poem?

Extra Credit ·····································

Design a costume to be worn as you perform the poem. Use things that you can find at home or school.

Dance   101

Cultural Perspectives There are 430 tribes of Native Americans in the United States today. Each has its own culture, which includes language, traditions, music, and dance.

About Dance Dance and music serve as a framework to which American Indian philosophy and tradition are attached. Hanay Geiogamah, Artistic Director of the American Indian Dance Theatre, developed a system for categorizing American Indian dance: seasonal/functional; spiritual/ceremonial/religious; and celebrational/bravura. Each group of Native Americans has its own dances and music that fit into these categories.

TEACH

Time: Two 30-minute periods

"We are going to explore ways that we can create forms of nature through movements."

"Vamos a explorar las maneras en que podemos crear formas naturales a través de movimientos."

• Have students read the poem on page 101 and discuss its theme of appreciation of nature.

• Have students work with partners to design movements that express the lines of the poem. For example, for the first two lines, students could walk forward while raising their arms. For the third line, they could walk backward, lowering their arms.

• Have partners find different ways they can represent ideas and creatures in the natural world. Have them select ideas that express lines of the poem and put the movements together using four counts to move slowly from one idea to the next.

• You may wish to have both partners perform while a narrator reads the poem.

CLOSE

Time: About 5 minutes

"What would you add or change about your work in creating a dance?"

"¿Qué le agregarían o le cambiarían a su trabajo acerca de un baile?"

Assess
Have students answer the four art criticism questions on page 101—Describe, Analyze, Interpret, and Decide—orally or in writing.

Evaluation Criteria

• Can the student demonstrate an ability to express ideas about the poem and nature through dance?

• Can the student create shapes and forms through movement?

• Can the student use the four steps of art criticism to evaluate his or her performance?

• Can the student demonstrate knowledge about the Hoop Dance?

UNIT 3

Reviewing Unit Concepts

"Artists show depth and use the technique of overlapping to create space in paintings and drawings. They show three-dimensional forms in sculptures."

"Los artistas muestran profundidad y usan la técnica de superposición para crear espacio en las pinturas y los dibujos. Ellos muestran las formas tridimensionales en las esculturas."

- Review the techniques that artists use to create space and form listed on pages 102 and 103. Have the students write down the techniques and examples found in the classroom.

Examining the Artwork

"Let's look closely at the work of art."

"Vamos a observar detalladamente la obra de arte."

- Have the students study Henry Moore's *Knife Edge Mirror Two Piece* and answer the questions on page 103. (See **Perception Hints** below.)

Student Portfolio

Have students review all the artwork they have created during this unit and select the pieces they wish to keep in their portfolios.

Art Criticism Activity

Have students select an artwork from this unit and study it using the four steps of art criticism. (See pages 206–209 for more information about Art Criticism.) Have students work alone or in pairs and present their findings orally or in writing.

Perception Hints

3-D The sculpture has height, width, and depth, which means that it is three-dimensional.

Freestanding The sculpture has empty, negative space all around it.

Shapes and forms The positive forms represent landscape, people, and animals. Flat planes and swelling forms shape the sculpture. Negative space surrounds the artwork.

Space and Form

Reviewing Main Ideas

The lessons and activities in this unit cover the techniques that artists use to create space and form.

1. **Positive space** is the area that shapes and forms fill.
2. **Negative space** is the empty area between and around the shapes or objects.
3. **Depth** in an artwork is created when some objects seem to be very close and others seem to be far away.
   - **Foreground** is the part of the picture that appears closest to the viewer.
   - **Background** is the part that appears farthest away.

Henry Moore. (British). *Knife Edge Mirror Two Piece.* 1977–1978. Bronze. $210\frac{1}{2} \times 284 \times 143$ inches. © 1996 Board of Trustees, National Gallery of Art, Washington, DC. Gift of the Morris and Gwendolyn Cafritz Foundation.

🎨 ART *Background*

About the Artist

Henry Moore (hen' rē môr, English, 1898–1986) was born in Castleford, England. When Moore was ten, he decided he wanted to become a sculptor. At 18 he left home to join the army in World War I. Upon returning from the war, Moore worked as a schoolmaster and began studying art. By the age of 23, he was a serious sculptor. He felt his ability to perform the hard, physical labor needed for sculpting came from his mother.

About Subject Matter*

Frequently, Moore mixed his figures with shapes and textures from nature. He focused on making the simplest form of the subject he carved. He wanted his sculpture to be an artwork of the open air with the sky as the background.

4. **Overlapping** is when one object covers a part of a second object.

5. **Shapes** are flat and two-dimensional. They can be measured by height and width.

6. **Forms** are shapes that are three-dimensional. They can be measured by height, width, and depth. (spheres, cones, pyramids, cylinders, and free-forms)

7. **Relief sculpture** is artwork in which forms stand out from a flat surface.

8. **Freestanding sculpture** is three-dimensional and has negative space all around it.

  • **Jewelry** is three-dimensional art that people wear as decoration. A *jeweler* is the artist who designs and makes it.

Summing Up

Look at the sculpture by Moore. Notice how he uses some of the techniques you learned about in this unit.

• How do you know this work of art is three-dimensional?

• Is it relief sculpture or freestanding sculpture? Explain your answer.

• What shapes and forms do the positive and negative spaces remind you of?

Space and form are important elements in works of art. By using techniques to create space and form, artists express to others what they see.

Careers in Art
City Planner

Andrew Aidt is a city planner for Kettering, Ohio. City planners plan the development of new cities or changes in existing cities. They must determine what the future population will be. They also consider what people will need in terms of housing, schools, parking space, and parks, and where these facilities should be. The main purpose of his work is to create environments that are both pleasant and practical.

Andrew Aidt, city planner

103

Learning About Careers in Art

One aspect of the city planner's job is to design areas in which people can play. In large cities, homes and large buildings have been erected to meet the needs of growing populations. Open land has disappeared. In almost every city, large plots of land are set aside for public parks and recreational playgrounds in which adults and children can spend their leisure time.

• Ask students if they have a park, playground, or community center in their neighborhood or city. Have them discuss the different aspects they enjoy most about these recreational areas.

• Have students list items found in their ideal playground. Allow them to share their answers.

• Encourage interested students to find out more about a career as a city planner. Have them share their findings with the class.

A Final Thought

"Art is an extension of language—an expression of sensations too subtle for words."—Robert Henri

About the Media Henry Moore first made drawings from his thoughts. If he liked the drawing, he then made a small model from plaster. His last step was to carve the sculpture in stone or wood. However, he usually used bronze for his large sculptures.

About Art History* Moore abandoned sculpture that was beautiful or perfect. He resorted to sculpting simpler forms. In the 1930s, many sculptors were making forms that looked real. However, Moore and a few of his artist friends began creating sculpture that was more abstract, or simpler, in form.

Cultural Perspectives Moore's paintings of people in underground shelters during World War II first attracted the public eye. He is best known, however, for sculptures he completed in 1953 and 1965.

*See **More About** pages 206–227 for more about art history and subject matter.

UNIT 4

UNIT OVERVIEW

This unit will cover the principles of balance and emphasis. Balance is the principle of design that deals with equally arranging visual elements in a work of art. Emphasis is the principle of design that stresses one element or area in a work of art to make it attract the viewer's attention first.

Formal balance is the way of organizing parts of a design so that equal or similar elements are placed on opposite sides of a central axis. Formal balance is covered in Lessons 1 and 2.

Symmetry is a type of formal balance in which two halves or sides of a design are identical. Symmetry is covered in Lesson 3.

Approximate symmetry is a special kind of formal balance that happens when both sides of a design are *almost* exactly the same. Approximate symmetry is covered in Lesson 4.

Emphasis is a technique that artists use to draw attention to a particular area in an artwork. Emphasis is covered in Lessons 5 and 6.

Introducing Unit Concepts

"Artists use the principles of balance and emphasis in designing all kinds of art."

"Los artistas usan los principios de equilibrio y énfasis en el diseño de todos los tipos de arte."

Balance

• Have students stand perfectly still on one leg. Discuss why it was difficult to do.

• Ask students to think of going to the circus. Have them identify the various circus acts that require the body's balance, e.g. acrobatics, tightrope walking, and riding a unicycle.

Emphasis

• Ask students to try to get your attention without using their voices or leaving their seats. Have them identify the different methods used by their classmates.

• Have them list ten different kinds of food. Ask them to identify, in some way, their favorite foods, e.g. circle, underline, make bolder, or highlight with color.

Unit 4 An Introduction to Balance and Emphasis

Artists use balance and emphasis to design works of art.

Artist unknown. (Greek). *Parthenon.* 447–438 B.C. Marble. 237 × 110 × 60 feet. The Acropolis, Athens, Greece. Scala, Art Resource.

ART Background

About Subject Matter*
The Parthenon's center is divided into two rooms. One was the treasury, and the other room once housed a large ivory and gold statue of Athena. The outside of the building is surrounded by 46 columns.

About the Media The Parthenon is made entirely of Pentelic marble. It measures 237 feet long and 110 feet wide. The marble was hauled to Athens from 11 miles away in order to build this temple.

Artists use **balance** in their artwork to give equal weight to both sides of a design.

- How are the left and the right sides of the Parthenon the same?
- Are both sides *exactly* the same? If not, what are some differences?

Artists use **emphasis** in their artwork to create a center of interest.

- Which area of the building attracts your attention first?

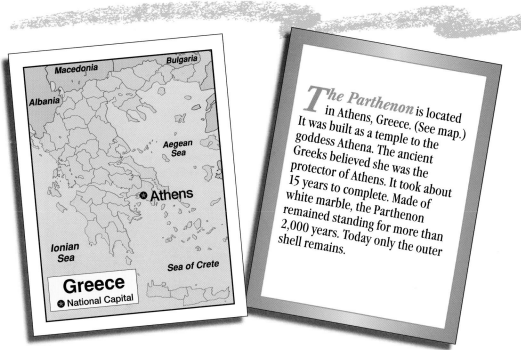

The Parthenon is located in Athens, Greece. (See map.) It was built as a temple to the goddess Athena. The ancient Greeks believed she was the protector of Athens. It took about 15 years to complete. Made of white marble, the Parthenon remained standing for more than 2,000 years. Today only the outer shell remains.

The Parthenon architects and other artists use balance and emphasis in their designs. In this unit you will learn about techniques that artists use to create balance and emphasis. The topics are:

- Formal Balance • Symmetry • Approximate Symmetry • Emphasis

105

About Art History* Masters of painting and sculpture, Greeks also excelled in architecture. Much of what we know today about Greek civilization and myths is derived from their art. The frieze in the outer wall shows the people of Athens celebrating the anniversary of the founding of Athens.

Cultural Perspectives About A.D. 500, the Parthenon became a Christian church. In the mid-1400s, it became a mosque when Turkish Muslims captured Athens. In 1687, while the Turks were using it to store gunpowder, the gunpowder exploded, damaging the central part of the building. Only ruins remain.

*See **More About** pages 206–227 for more about art history and subject matter.

- Place a group of objects in a shallow box. Make sure that one object is much larger than the rest. Have students identify which object they notice first and why.

 You may wish to use the **Video** *The Forest Dwellers: Native American Arts of the Pacific Northwest* to discuss masks and how students can identify balance and emphasis.

Examining the Artwork

"Let's look closely at the ancient Greek building."
"Vamos a observar detalladamente la antigua edificación griega."

- Have students look at the Greek Parthenon. Ask them to describe what they see.
- Have the students answer the questions on page 105 pertaining to balance and emphasis in the Parthenon.
  (See **Perception Hints** below.)

Art Profile
Use the map of Ancient Greece to talk about the location of Athens and other major cities that have pieces of art that help tell the story of Ancient Greece.

Encourage students to use their **Art Journals** to practice art concepts and record ideas from lesson to lesson.

About Music
Balance in music is usually associated with symmetrical forms such as ABA—music having three sections with the middle one different from the two outer sections. Have students sing an example of this by singing *Au Clair de la Lune.*

Students can also sing a round, such as *Frère Jacques,* and try to balance the sound between parts.

UNIT 4 Planning Guide

Lesson	Lesson Title	Suggested Pacing	Create Activities	Materials	
1	**Formal Balance**	75 minutes	Use formal balance in a drawing.	12- x 18-inch white construction paper colored markers oil pastels	
2	**Formal Balance in Masks**	75 minutes	Create a papier-mâché mask using formal balance.	assorted cardboard tubes and boxes containers of water and glue liquid tempera paints newspaper sketch paper tape pencils brushes paper towels paper plates	
3	**Symmetry**	75 minutes	Use symmetry to create a personal totem.	9- x 12-inch construction paper, assorted colors scissors glue black markers stapler (optional) pencils sketch paper	
4	**Approximate Symmetry**	75 minutes	Use approximate symmetry in a self-portrait.	12- x 18-inch construction paper flexible mirror from **Art Manipulative Kit** liquid tempera paints paper plates for palettes paper towels brushes of various sizes pencils containers of water newspaper	
5	**Emphasis**	75 minutes	Contrast light and dark values to emphasize an area of interest.	12- x 18-inch black construction paper colored dustless chalk music audiotapes from **Art Manipulative Kit**	
6	**Emphasis Through Contrast in Shapes**	75 minutes	Contrast shapes to create emphasis in a paper collage.	9- x 12-inch construction paper, assorted colors 12- x 18-inch black construction paper scissors pencils glue black felt-tip pens oil pastels sketch paper	
Artsource Lesson	**Balance and Emphasis in Pantomime**	45 minutes	Mirror some daily activities with a partner.		

Test preparation activities using the Large Prints *Red Figured Amphora* and *Taj Mahal* can be found on pages 20–23 of the Test Preparation Book.

Program Resources (Books)	Art Resources	Literature Resources	*Music Resources
Vocabulary, pp. 37–38 Assessment, pp. 37–38 Art Across the Curriculum Resource Book, pp. 109–114 Technique Tips Flip Chart, p. 19 Lesson Plans Book, p. 20 Home Connection, pp. 11 and 12	Overhead Transparency #19, *Jar* and *Victorian Parlor II* Artist Profile Book, pp. 38, 64 Large Prints, *Red Figured Amphora (vase)* and *Taj Mahal*	**1.** *Grandfather's Journey* (1993) by Allen Say illustrates the formal balance of photography and life experiences and provides excellent lesson examples of art and cross-cultural experiences. **2.** *Snow White and the Seven Dwarfs* (1972) by Nancy Ekholm Burkert has beautiful and mystic illustration demonstrating balance in each image, either alone or as a two-page spread. Lavish artwork enhances the classic tale.	"Alouette," p. T333, CD8:35. "Alouette" is a folk song in a balanced (ABA, or same - different–same) musical form.
Vocabulary, pp. 39–40 Assessment, pp. 39–40 Art Across the Curriculum Resource Book, pp. 115–120 Technique Tips Flip Chart, p. 20 Lesson Plans Book, p. 21	Overhead Transparency #20, *Yam Mask* and *Dancing Headdress Frontlet* Artist Profile Book, pp. 11, 65 Large Prints, *Red Figured Amphora (vase)* and *Taj Mahal*	**1.** *Masks and Mask Makers* (1961) by Kari Hunt explores masks from various cultures in black and white photographic illustrations, researching their purposes and people. **2.** *Masks Tell Stories* (1993) by Carol Gelber studies the uses of masks throughout time for ceremonies, celebrations, theater, and daily life.	"From Morning Night to Real Morning," collected by Steven Feld, p. T301, CD7:29. "From Morning Night to Real Morning" is a collection of sounds from the Papua, New Guinea rain forest.
Vocabulary, pp. 41–42 Assessment, pp. 41–42 Art Across the Curriculum Resource Book, pp. 121–126 Technique Tips Flip Chart, p. 21 Lesson Plans Book, p. 22	Overhead Transparency #21, *Symmetrical View of a Totem* Artist Profile Book, p. 66 Large Print, *Taj Mahal*	**1.** *Brother Eagle, Sister Sky* (1991) by Chief Seattle is full-color art in fine-line pen-and-ink and dye illustrations that have the message of environmental protection revered by Native Americans. **2.** *Cherokee Summer* (1993) by Diane Hoyt-Goldsmith shares the personal account of a 10-year-old girl and her daily life and history of her tribe while teaching about the Trail of Tears, as well.	"Ema, ma," p. T300, CD7:28. "Ema, ma" is a Pygmy folk dance song from the Central African Republic.
Vocabulary, pp. 43–44 Assessment, pp. 43–44 Art Across the Curriculum Resource Book, pp. 127–132 Technique Tips Flip Chart, p. 22 Lesson Plans Book, p. 23	Overhead Transparency #22, *Portrait of a Boy* and *Her World* Artist Profile Book, pp. 12, 67 Large Print, *Red Figured Amphora (vase)*	**1.** *My Painted House, My Friendly Chicken, and Me* (1994) by Maya Angelou has crisp photography that captures the expressions and textures in the many faces of a Ndebele culture in South Africa. **2.** *Portraits* (1995) from Editions Gallimard provides playful and accessible learning to students that examines the many styles and ways of creating portraits.	"Oh Lord, I Want Two Wings," p. T89, CD2:31. "Oh Lord, I Want Two Wings" is an example of an African American spiritual.
Vocabulary, pp. 45–46 Assessment, pp. 45–46 Art Across the Curriculum Resource Book, pp. 133–138 Technique Tips Flip Chart, p. 23 Lesson Plans Book, p. 24	Overhead Transparency #23, *Tokyo Street with Pachinko Parlor II* and *Waiting* Artist Profile Book, pp. 9, 20 Large Print, *Taj Majal*	**1.** *Jabberwocky* (1989) by Lewis Carroll has fanciful illustrations of the classic poem brimming with detail yet are concentrated with fanciful focus and emphasis. **2.** *A Weekend with Degas* (1992) by Rosabianca Skiri-Venturi provides personal insight for students into the life and work of Degas.	"Deta, Deta," p. T69, CD2:12. "Deta, Deta" is a children's song from Japan.
Vocabulary, pp. 47–48 Assessment, pp. 47–48 Art Across the Curriculum Resource Book, pp. 139–144 Technique Tips Flip Chart, p. 24 Lesson Plans Book, p. 25	Overhead Transparency #24, *Apache Crown Dance* and *The Sun Breaks Through* Artist Profile Book, pp. 15, 18 Large Print, *Taj Mahal*	**1.** *Klara's New World* (1992) by Jeanette Winter has dramatic illustrations depicting the use of emphasis through contrasting shapes in this immigration tale of a Swedish family in the 1800s. **2.** *June 29, 1999* (1992) by David Wiesner has masterful watercolor illustrations demonstrating contrasting shapes for emphasis in the story of a third-grade science experiment.	"Seneca Stomp Dance," p. T201, CD5:21. The "Seneca Stomp Dance" is an example of Native American music.
	Artsource Performing Arts Audio/Video Resource Package: *Life Cycle* (videocassette)		

*Music references are from **Share the Music,** Macmillan/McGraw-Hill School Publishers

LESSON PLANNER

Objectives

After completing this lesson, students will be able to:

- identify formal balance in a work of art. *Aesthetic Perception*
- plan and create a drawing using formal balance. *Creative Expression*
- use the four steps of art criticism to evaluate their own artwork. *Art Criticism*
- compare works by artists from different cultures. *Art History and Culture*

Program Resources

- **Overhead:** Both the Pippin and the *Jar* are available on overhead 19.
- **Large Prints:** *Vase: Red Figured Amphora* from Ancient Greece and *Taj Mahal*
- **Technique Tips Flip Chart,** page 19
- **Vocabulary Book** pages 37–38
- **Art Manipulative Kit:** balance
- **Artist Profiles Book:** Pippen page 38 and Artist unknown page 64
- **Art Across the Curriculum Book** pages 109–114
- **Multimedia Workshop CD-ROM**
- **National Geographic Picture Atlas of the World CD-ROM**
- **Assessment Book** pages 37–38

Multiple Intelligences

Body/Kinesthetic Students can use their bodies to identify balance, as well as to manipulate materials and tools.

Vocabulary

formal balance *equilibrio formal* a way of organizing parts of a design so that equal or similar elements are placed on opposite sides of a central axis

FOCUS

Time: About 10 minutes

Activating Prior Knowledge

"Think about looking at a butterfly. How can you describe the wings?"

"Piensen acerca de observar una mariposa. ¿Cómo pueden describir las alas?"

- Discuss students' responses to the question and how the wings look the same on both sides.

Formal Balance

Sometimes artists use formal balance in the design of their art.

Horace Pippin. (American). *Victorian Parlor II*. 1945. Oil on canvas. $25\frac{1}{4} \times 30$ inches. The Metropolitan Museum of Art, New York, New York, Arthur Hoppock Hearn Fund, 1958.

Compare the artwork on these pages. *Victorian Parlor II* was painted by folk artist Horace Pippin. Folk artists learn from the people and works of art around them rather than by studying at school. The *Jar* was created almost 900 years before *Victorian Parlor II*, yet both works make powerful use of formal balance.

ART Background

About the Artists

Horace Pippin (hôr′ əs pip′ pən, American, 1888–1946) was born in Pennsylvania. A self-taught artist, Pippin painted subjects found through personal experience.

Although the specific artist of the Northern Song *Jar* is unknown, it is representative of the incised, embossed, and molded decoration characteristic of the pottery of this period.

- Use the **National Geographic Picture Atlas of the World CD-ROM** to learn more about China.

About Subject Matter* The Pippin is an interior still-life painting and the North China *Jar* is a ceramic container decorated with a floral landscape design.

About the Media The Pippin is an oil painting. The North China *Jar* is made from stoneware clay, which is a clay body that is fired at a high temperature.

Artist unknown. China. *Jar.* Northern Song Period, twelfth century. Stoneware with sgraffito design in slip under glaze. 12½ inches. The Asian Society, New York. Mr. and Mrs. John D. Rockefeller 3rd Collection/Photo by Lynton Gardiner.

Study each artwork to find the following examples of formal balance.

✓ Draw a line down the middle of each artwork with your finger. Describe the matching objects or shapes you see on either side of the line.

✓ Describe colors that are repeated in the same way in Pippin's artwork.

✓ What areas are *exactly* the same on both sides of each piece?

✓ Which areas are similar but *not* exactly the same?

SEEING LIKE AN ARTIST

Look for a building in your neighborhood that has the same colors and forms on its left and right halves. What is similar but not exactly the same?

Lesson **1**

107

About Art History* Pippin's painting was created during the Big Band era of American music. At the same time, in literature, playwrights Tennessee Williams and Arthur Miller were gaining international fame.

The stoneware *Jar* was created during the Northern Song Period (A.D. 960–1279) when the arts, and especially the art of pottery, flourished.

Cultural Perspectives Pippin's painting was created after World War II, when the United States emerged as a superpower. The long period of hostility, known as the Cold War, began then between the Soviet Union and the United States.

The North China *Jar* was created in China during a time of cultural and political insularity when the Chinese had little contact with the outside world and national traditions were emphasized.

*See **More About** pages 206–227 for more about art history and subject matter.

Introducing the Art

"Let's look closely at the two artworks."
"Vamos a observar detalladamente las dos obras de arte."

- **Describe:** Have students describe the subject matter in each artwork. (Pippin: interior still life; North China *Jar:* floral)

- **COMPARE AND CONTRAST** Have students make a list of the similarities and differences in the two artworks. (Both works of art include florals, show contrast, and illustrate formal balance. The Pippin is a two-dimensional painting that illustrates many objects and uses bright colors. The North China *Jar* is a three-dimensional container that illustrates floral designs.)

- Share and discuss information about the lives, work, and times of the artists from **Art Background** and the **Artist Profiles Book.**

- Have students answer the questions about formal balance on page 107.
(See **Perception Hints** below.)

FOR THE ART SPECIALIST

Use the **Overhead** and the **Large Prints** *Vase: Red Figured Amphora* and *Taj Mahal* to demonstate how artists use formal balance in the design of their art.

Perception Hints

Central axis *Pippin.* The vase of flowers, table, wall, and rug are in the center of the painting along the central axis. *Jar.* The curvilinear leaf shapes are on the left and right sides of the container.
Colors *Pippin.* The yellow in the lamp on the left side is repeated in the books on the right side of the painting.
Formal balance *Jar.* The curvilinear, black shapes near the top are exactly the same on both sides.
Formal balance *Pippin.* Although the chairs are similar, they are not exactly the same. The chair on the left side gives a side view, while the chair on the right side gives a frontal view.

TEACH

Time: About two 30-minute periods

Practice

Materials
- 9- × 12-inch paper
- pencils

Alternate Materials: markers

"How can you illustrate formal balance?"

"¿Cómo pueden ilustrar el equilibrio formal?"

- Discuss ways to create formal balance using shapes, lines, and colors on page 108.
- Use photographs to show students examples of formal balance.
- Distribute the materials and have students follow the directions on page 108 for illustrating formal balance. Have them answer the Decide question on the back.

Create PROBLEM SOLVING

Materials
- 12- × 18-inch white construction paper
- colored markers
- oil pastels

 Safety! For safety issues about markers and oil pastels, and other information about safety in the art classroom, see page T22.

Alternate Materials: liquid tempera paints

"Let's show formal balance in a drawing."

"Vamos a mostrar el equilibrio formal en un dibujo."

- Review ways to create formal balance.
- See page 19 in the **Technique Tips Flip Chart** for visual examples of techniques.
- Distribute materials and have students follow the directions on page 109.

FOR THE ART SPECIALIST

On chart paper, use lines, shapes, and colors to illustrate ways to create formal balance in a work of art. Use the balance scale from the **Art Manipulative Kit** to illustrate balance.

Using Formal Balance

Formal balance is a way of organizing a design so that equal or very similar elements are placed on opposite sides of an imaginary, central dividing line. You saw examples of formal balance in the artwork on pages 106 and 107.

On a seesaw, if your partner is much bigger than you, you will stay up in the air. The seesaw is *not* balanced. But if your partner is about your weight, the seesaw will be balanced. There is about the same amount of weight on both sides.

There are different kinds of balance in a work of art. One kind is formal balance. This is created when objects, shapes, lines, and color match on both sides of a design.

Practice

Illustrate formal balance. Use pencil.

1. Fold a piece of paper in half and then open it up again. Use pencil to draw some geometric and free-form shapes on the left-hand side.

2. Repeat the same design on the right side to create formal balance.

Decide Does your design look the same on both sides?

Activities in ART Across the Curriculum Book

Reading/Language Arts Plan a debate. (page 109)

Math Solve problems so that both sides of an equation are equal, like sides of an artwork that is formally balanced. (page 110)

Science Classify objects found in nature as having formal balance or not having formal balance. (page 111)

Social Studies Identify two things people could have used the Chinese jar for 800 years ago, then list ways we carry things today. (page 112)

The Arts Create a dance with balance. (page 113)

Technology Use the *Multimedia Workshop* CD-ROM to design a room with formal balance. (page 114)

Keegan Faught. Age 9. *House for Horace Pippin's People.* Marker and oil pastel.

Where did this student artist use formal balance?
Where did he add objects that do not use formal balance?

Create

**How do buildings show formal balance?
Use formal balance in a drawing.**

1. Look at the artwork *Victorian Parlor II* by Horace Pippin. Think about how the outside of this house might look.

2. On a large piece of paper, draw the outside of the house. Use formal balance in your picture.

3. Fill the house with color. Add trees and plants. Use formal balance in your landscape, also.

Describe What shapes did you use? Describe the lines. Name the colors.

Analyze How did you create formal balance in your drawing?

Interpret How would the mood or feeling of your drawing change if you had not used formal balance?

Decide If you could redo this drawing, what would you do differently?

Lesson 1

109

CLOSE

Time: About 5 minutes

"Were you able to create formal balance in your drawing?"
"¿Fueron capaces de crear equilibrio formal en su dibujo?"

LARGE PRINT **Review**
Use the **Large Print** *Taj Mahal* to have students compare the use of formal balance to the works in this lesson.

Art Criticism
Have students answer the four art criticism questions—Describe, Analyze, Interpret, and Decide—orally or in writing. Discuss the use of formal balance in their drawings.

Assess
Use the **Assessment Book** pages 37–38 as a formal assessment for this lesson.

Evaluation Criteria
• Can the student identify and describe formal balance in a work of art?
• Can the student illustrate formal balance in a drawing?
• Can the student use the four steps of art criticism to evaluate his or her own work?
• Can the student compare works by these two artists from different cultures?

Reteaching ● ● ● ● ● ● ● ● ● ● ●

Formal balance Have students look around the classroom to find examples of formal balance. Ask them to list the examples and how formal balance is seen in each.

THEME Connections
Connections Use Pippin's painting as a springboard for students to describe their own homes, orally or in writing.
Discovery Use the North China *Jar* as a motivation to study parts of a flower.
Models Use *Victorian Parlor II* as a visual example of interior design.

ESL
ESL students will benefit from working with a peer instead of alone to create a drawing showing formal balance. For the Practice activity, pair children to illustrate formal balance. Have one student draw a geometric or free-form shape on one side of the paper. The other student can repeat the design on the other side. Pairs of students could share their drawing with another pair to further increase opportunities to practice oral language.

Perception Hints for Student Art

The house, windows, chimneys, flower boxes, trees, and swings are organized using formal balance. The door, the clouds, and the sun do not use formal balance.

Formal Balance in Masks

Artists from different cultures use formal balance in the design of masks.

Artist unknown. Abelam (Papua New Guinea). *Yam Mask.* Nineteenth century. Yam fibers. $18\frac{3}{4} \times 13\frac{3}{8}$ inches. Nelson-Atkins Museum of Art, Kansas City, Missouri. Gift of the May Dept. Stores Co.

Look at the three-dimensional masks on these pages. The *Yam Mask* was woven from basketry materials. The *Dancing Headdress Frontlet* is carved in wood from a maple tree. Beautiful abalone shells are pressed into the wood for decoration. Both artists have used formal balance to design their masks.

UNIT 4
LESSON 2

LESSON PLANNER

Objectives

After completing this lesson, students will be able to:

- identify how artists use formal balance and exaggerated features in a mask. *Aesthetic Perception*
- plan and create a papier-mâché mask using formal balance. *Creative Expression*
- use the four steps of art criticism to evaluate their own masks. *Art Criticism*
- compare works by artists from different cultures. *Art History and Culture*

Program Resources

- **Overhead:** Both the *Yam Mask* and the *Dancing Headdress Frontlet* are available on overhead 20.
- **Large Prints:** *Vase: Red Figured Amphora* from Ancient Greece and *Taj Mahal*
- **Technique Tips Flip Chart,** page 20
- **Vocabulary Book** pages 39–40
- **Art Manipulative Kit:** distortion mirror
- **Artist Profiles Book:** Artist unknown page 65 and Edensaw page 11
- **Art Across the Curriculum Book** pages 115–120
- **Multimedia Workshop CD-ROM**
- **National Geographic Picture Atlas of the World CD-ROM**
- **Assessment Book** pages 39–40

Multiple Intelligences

Intrapersonal Students can identify emotions by interpreting the features of the masks.

Vocabulary

culture *cultura* how a group thinks, believes, and acts

exaggeration *exageración* to increase or enlarge an object or figure, or one of its parts, to communicate ideas and feelings

mask *máscara* a covering worn over all or part of the face used to hide or disguise one's identity

---

ART Background

About the Artists

The *Yam Mask* is worn in special ceremonies in Papua New Guinea. Men dance and parade through their village wearing this costume. The mask represents piglike creatures.

The *Headdress Frontlet* characterizes the Haida tale of a man who killed a powerful sea monster. By wearing the monster's skin, he is able to catch many fish to feed his village.

- Use the **National Geographic Picture Atlas of the World CD-ROM** to learn more about the New Guinea area.

About Subject Matter* Both the *Yam Mask* and the *Dancing Headdress Frontlet* are examples of iconography (symbolism).

About the Media The *Yam Mask* is made from yam fibers. The *Dancing Headdress Frontlet* is carved from maple wood and decorated with abalone.

Albert Edward Edensaw.
Kaigani Haida. *Dancing Headdress Frontlet.* 1860–1870. Maple and abalone shell. $6\frac{1}{4} \times 5\frac{7}{8} \times 2\frac{1}{4}$ inches. The Seattle Art Museum, Seattle, Washington. Gift of John H. Hauberg. Photo by Paul Macapia.

Study both masks to find examples of formal balance.

- What shapes do you see in the middle of each mask?
- Find shapes or objects on the left side that you also see on the right.
- Find areas that are *exactly* the same on both sides.
- Which areas are *not* exactly the same on both sides?
- How would you describe the expression on each mask?

SEEING LIKE AN ARTIST

Look at posters and signs in your school to find examples of formal balance.

Lesson **2**   **111**

About Art History* The *Yam Mask* was created for ceremonial functions.

The *Dancing Headdress Frontlet* was created during a time when Native American artists, in an effort to communicate with the mysterious forces of nature, used natural materials to create pieces for practical and religious purposes.

Cultural Perspectives The Abelam of Papua New Guinea, are governed by means of a yam cult. Yams, which can grow up to 12 feet long, are endowed with animalistic qualities. Farmers do not eat their own yams. They exchange them with other clansmen.

The mild climate and abundant food from the sea afforded the Haida leisure time to create art objects. Produced mostly by men, the figures portrayed in the artwork were owned by the individuals and marked their social rank.

*See **More About** pages 206–227 for more about art history and subject matter.

Activating Prior Knowledge

"Can you think of a time when you dressed up in a costume and wore a mask? Describe the mask.

"¿Pueden pensar en alguna ocasión en que se disfrazaron y usaron una máscara? Describan la máscara."

- Discuss students' answers. Masks are worn in order to change the appearance of the persons wearing them.

Introducing the Art

"Let's look closely at the two masks."
"Vamos a observar detalladamente las dos máscaras."

- **Describe:** Have students describe the subject matter in each mask. (symbolic)
- **COMPARE AND CONTRAST** Have students make a list of the similarities and differences. (Both are three-dimensional, include an animal image, and have formal balance. The *Yam Mask* is made from one material and is worn on the face. The *Headdress Frontlet* is made with a variety of materials and is worn on the head.)
- Share and discuss about the lives, work, and times of the artists from **Art Background** and the **Artist Profiles Book.**
- Have students answer the questions about formal balance on page 111.
(See **Perception Hints** below.)

 FOR THE ART SPECIALIST

Use the **Overhead** and the **Large Prints** *Vase: Red Figured Amphora* and *Taj Mahal* to demonstrate how artists from different cultures use formal balance in masks.

Perception Hints

Central axis *Yam Mask.* A narrow, raised strip is found along the middle of the mask. *Headdress Frontlet.* Nose, mouth, and inlay are found along the middle.
Shapes *Yam Mask.* Eyes and designs are seen on both sides. *Headdress Frontlet.* Eyes, eyebrows, ears, hands, feet, and pieces of abalone are seen on both sides of the mask.
Formal balance *Yam Mask.* The hair, eyebrows, eyes, and whiskers are exactly the same on both sides.
Formal balance *Headdress Frontlet.* The figure of the whale in the very front is not the same on both sides.

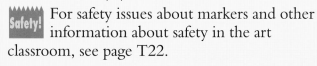
Practice

Materials
- 9- x 12-inch paper
- colored markers

Safety! For safety issues about markers and other information about safety in the art classroom, see page T22.

Alternate Materials: oil pastels

"In what ways can you exaggerate shapes to create a special feeling in a mask? How can you use these shapes to create formal balance?"

"¿De qué manera pueden exagerar las figuras para crear una sensación especial en una máscara? ¿Cómo pueden usar estas figuras para crear equilibrio formal?"

- Discuss ways to create formal balance on page 112.
- Demonstrate exaggeration using the distortion mirror from the **Art Manipulative Kit.**
- Have students follow the directions on page 112. Ask them to answer the Decide questions on the back.

Create PROBLEM SOLVING

Materials
- newspaper
- pencils
- sketch paper
- assorted cardboard tubes and boxes
- tape
- containers of water and glue
- liquid tempera paints
- paper plates
- brushes of various sizes
- paper towels

Alternate Materials: cut-paper collages

"Let's use formal balance to create a papier-mâché mask."

"Vamos a usar equilibrio formal para crear una máscara de cartón piedra."

- Review ways to create formal balance.
- Review procedures for working with papier-mâché in **More About Technique Tips** on page 204.
- See page 20 in the **Technique Tips Flip Chart** for visual examples of techniques.
- Distribute materials and have students follow the directions on page 113.

FOR THE ART SPECIALIST

Have students add objects such as seeds, beans, or buttons when their masks are dry.

Using Formal Balance in Masks

People from around the world have many different **cultures**, or customs. Many have been making and wearing masks for thousands of years. **Masks** are sculptured faces. We believe ancient hunters wore animal masks in good-luck ceremonies before the hunt. Storytellers and actors wore masks to play different characters. Warriors used them for protection. Masks are still being made and worn today.

Masks' features often are **exaggerated**, or made bigger, to show strong feelings. Which features are exaggerated on the masks below? What feelings do they seem to express?

The masks below have **formal balance**. They have the same elements on both sides of a central, imaginary dividing line.

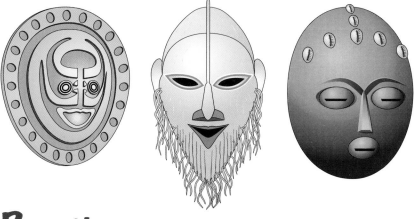

Practice

Design a simple paper mask with exaggerated features formally balanced. Use colored markers.

1. Fold a piece of paper in half and then open it up again to mark the middle of the mask.

2. Think of a feeling you want the mask to express. Sketch exaggerated features that express it, using free-form and geometric shapes. The features on each side of the fold should look alike in some way.

Analyze Which features did you exaggerate? Why did you choose to exaggerate them? Which are formally balanced?

Activities in
ART Across the Curriculum Book

Reading/Language Arts Write endings to sentences to show exaggerations to communicate strong feelings or ideas. (page 115)

Math Learn how division can show balance among equal parts. (page 116)

Science Study the animals represented in the masks, and understand that the artwork reflects animals found in the artists' environments. (page 117)

Social Studies Design a flag for your school, for your family, or for yourself that may show animals or colors that are symbolic. (page 118)

The Arts Understand using exaggerated expressions to show feelings. (page 119)

Technology Use the *Multimedia Workshop* CD-ROM to create a formally balanced mask with exaggerated features. (page 120)

Max Manofsky. Age 8. *M. M. M. Dracula.*
Papier-mâché and tempera.

What part of this student artist's
mask shows exaggeration?

Create

What features in a mask would show formal balance? Create a papier-mâché mask using formal balance.

1. Think of how you want to use your mask and what it will express. Make a few sketches until you get one you like.

2. Look at your sketch. Then, cut pieces of cardboard tubes and boxes to form the features. Tape or glue them in place onto your base, formally balancing some forms.

3. Apply torn strips of newspaper dipped in paste to the mask.

4. When your mask is dry, paint it. Balance colors and lines.

Describe Name the forms and colors that you used.

Analyze What gives the mask formal balance? Which features are most exaggerated? Why did you choose to exaggerate them?

Interpret What feeling does the finished mask express?

Decide Which elements of the mask do you like best? How is the finished mask different from your sketch?

Lesson 2

113

CLOSE

Time: About 5 minutes

"How can you create formal balance in a mask?"
"¿Cómo pueden crear equilibrio formal en una máscara?"

Review
Use the **Overhead** to have students compare the use of formal balance in their masks.

Art Criticism
Have students answer the four art criticism questions—Describe, Analyze, Interpret, and Decide—orally or in writing. Discuss the use of formal balance in their masks after the paint has dried.

Assess
Use the **Assessment Book** pages 39–40 as a formal assessment for this lesson.

Evaluation Criteria
• Can the student identify formal balance in a work of art?
• Can the student use formal balance in a three-dimensional mask?
• Can the student use the four steps of art criticism to evaluate his or her own work?
• Can the student compare the artworks from two cultures in this lesson?

Reteaching • • • • • • • • • •

Formal balance Have students look through the book to find three different works illustrating formal balance. Ask them to list each of the works and describe how formal balance is used.

Perception Hints for Student Art
The mask's large eye holes and teeth show exaggeration.

UNIT 4
LESSON 3

LESSON PLANNER

Objectives
After completing this lesson, students will be able to:
- identify symmetry used by Native Americans in totem pole carvings. *Aesthetic Perception*
- plan and create a three-dimensional totem using symmetrical balance. *Creative Expression*
- use the four steps of art criticism to evaluate their own totems. *Art Criticism*
- identify qualities in the totems in this lesson that pinpoint the culture. *Art History and Culture*

Program Resources
- **Overhead:** Both totems from this lesson are available on overhead 21.
- **Large Print:** *Taj Mahal*
- **Technique Tips Flip Chart,** page 21
- **Vocabulary Book** pages 41–42
- **Art Manipulative Kit:** balance scale
- **Artist Profiles Book:** Artist unknown page 66
- **Art Across the Curriculum Book** pages 121–126
- **Multimedia Workshop CD-ROM**
- **Assessment Book** pages 41–42

Multiple Intelligences
Visual/Spatial Students can recognize the use of symmetry in sculptures, such as totem poles.

Vocabulary
symmetry *simetría* a type of formal balance in which two halves, or sides, of a design are identical

central axis *eje central* an imaginary line that divides a work of art in half

FOCUS
Time: About 10 minutes

Activating Prior Knowledge
"Think about flying a kite. What do you notice about the way most kites are designed?"

"Piensen acerca de volar un papagayo. ¿Qué les llama la atención acerca de la manera en que se diseñan algunos papagayos?"

- Discuss students' responses and how kites are usually designed with symmetrical balance.

Symmetry
Symmetry is a special type of formal balance in which both sides of a piece of artwork are exactly the same.

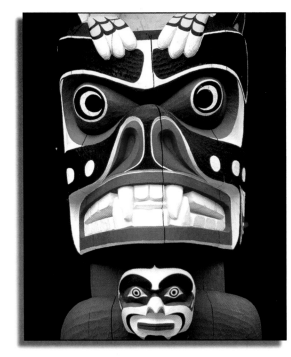

Artist unknown. *Symmetrical View of a Totem Pole.* Photo. © Ron Watts/Westlight. Stanley Park. Vancouver-B.C., Canada.

A totem is the sacred symbol of an animal whose spirit represents and protects a family clan. They were placed in front of homes. The totems on both these pages were carved into tall, wooden poles by artists. Animals most often used in totems include the thunderbird, raven, eagle, bear, frog, wolf, and beaver.

ART Background

About the Artists
Although the specific artists who created these totems are unknown, they characterize the tall, wooden carvings created in the Northwest. Totem poles used stylized creatures to tell a particular family's story. Today, totem poles serve as historical documents recording the wealth, social position, or importance of the person who commissioned them. The way a totem's eyes are made determines where it is from.

About Subject Matter* Both of the three-dimensional, wooden totem poles are examples of iconography.

About the Media Both totem poles are carved from wood. Fir, hemlock, and giant cedar trees were abundant along the Pacific Ocean in the Northwest.

Artist unknown. *Symmetrical View of a Totem Pole.*
Photo. © Matthew McVay/Tony Stone Images, Inc.
Stanley Park. Vancouver-B.C., Canada.

Study both sculptures to find examples of symmetry.

☑ What single shape or object do you see in the center of each carving?

☑ Find the shapes that are exactly the same on both sides of the center line.

☑ What colors are repeated in exactly the same place on both sides of the center?

SEEING LIKE AN ARTIST
Look at the artwork in this book to find other examples of symmetry.

Lesson **3**

115

"Let's look closely at the two totem poles."
"Vamos a observar detalladamente los dos postes de tótem."

• **Describe:** Have students describe the subject matter in each sculpture. (iconographic)

• **COMPARE AND CONTRAST** Have students make a list of the similarities and differences in the two totem poles. (Both are symmetrical and are brightly colored; the designs are different.)

• Share and discuss information about the lives, work, and times of the artists from **Art Background** and the **Artist Profiles Book.**

• Have students answer questions about symmetry on page 115.
(See **Perception Hints** below.)

FOR THE ART SPECIALIST

Use the **Overhead** and the **Large Print** *Taj Mahal* to demonstrate how symmetry is a special type of formal balance in which both sides of a piece of artwork are exactly the same.

Perception Hints

Center The nose is in the center.
Shapes Teeth, eyes, mouth, and all designs are exactly the same on both sides.
Colors Red, green, and orange are repeated on both sides.

About Art History* Northwest Coast carvers were given a relatively high social standing because they had to be members of certain secret societies to carve some of the pieces they made.

Cultural Perspectives Social rank in the community was based on family among the Native Americans of the Northwest Coast. Each family had certain privileges, such as the exclusive rights to particular animal crests, dances, and songs.

*See **More About** pages 206–227 for more about art history and subject matter.

TEACH

Time: About two 30-minute periods

Practice

Materials
- a balance scale from the **Art Manipulative Kit**
- a variety of found materials

Alternate Materials: paints

"How can you show perfect balance with found objects?"

"¿Cómo pueden mostrar equilibrio perfecto con los objetos?"

- Review the definition of *symmetry* on page 116.
- Distribute materials and have students follow the directions on page 116 to demonstrate perfect balance. Ask them to answer the Decide question verbally with a partner.

Create PROBLEM SOLVING

Materials
- 9- × 12-inch construction paper, assorted colors
- scissors
- pencils
- glue
- sketch paper
- black markers
- stapler (optional)

 Safety! For safety issues about markers and other information about safety in the art classroom, see page T22.

Alternate Materials: crayons and brown craft paper

"Let's create a personal totem that shows symmetry."

"Vamos a hacer un tótem personal que muestre simetría."

- Have students brainstorm a variety of animals they could illustrate.
- Review ways to cut symmetrical shapes from paper by putting together two pieces of paper and cutting both at the same time.

See page 21 in the **Technique Tips Flip Chart** for visual examples of techniques.

- Distribute materials and have students follow the directions on page 117.

FOR THE ART SPECIALIST

Have students attach their totems to a bulletin board by stacking them on top of each other.

Using Symmetry

These artists used symmetry to design the faces and bodies of the animals on the totems. **Symmetry** is a special type of formal balance in which two halves of a design are identical, mirror images of each other. The two halves are divided by a **central axis**, which is an imaginary dividing line. Everything on one side of the central axis is balanced by the other side.

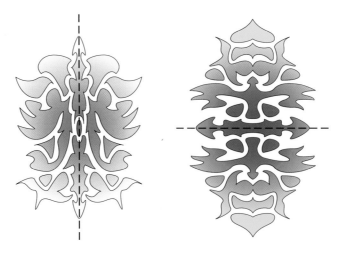

The formal balance of the designs on the totems gives a feeling of calm and dignity. The tall vertical form adds a feeling of importance. Artists use symmetry when they want designs to look formal and important.

Practice

Use a balance scale to create perfect balance. Use a variety of materials.

Practice formal balance by adding and taking away a variety of materials on each side of the scale.

Decide Can you create perfect balance?

Activities in ART Across the Curriculum Book

Reading/Language Arts Understand the symbolic meaning of certain animals in stories as well as art on the totem poles. (page 121)

Math Identify symmetry in geometric shapes and free-form shapes. (page 122)

Science Learn about the different trees named after fruit and nuts. (page 123)

Social Studies Study the different Native American tribes, including the Kwakiuti who created the totem poles seen in this lesson. (page 124)

The Arts Understand how symmetry can be found in music and create new lyrics to "Twinkle, Twinkle, Little Star" that show symmetry. (page 125)

Technology Use the *Multimedia Workshop* CD-ROM to create a totem pole with symmetry. (page 126)

Find the central axis in this student artist's totem.

Donald Nguyen. Age 9. *Creatures of the Night*. Cut paper.

Create

What images would you put on a totem pole? Use symmetry to create a totem.

1. Think of a real or imaginary creature. Make several sketches.

2. Fold a sheet of paper in half. The fold will be your central axis.

3. Using small pieces of colored paper, cut out shapes to represent features such as eyes. Place these features on your totem using symmetry. Glue the pieces into place.

4. Use symmetry to add other details.

5. Join the edges of your paper together to form a cylinder.

Describe What creature did you choose for your totem? What kinds of shapes are used?

Analyze How did you create symmetrical balance?

Interpret What kind of feeling does the formal balance give your totem?

Decide If you could create another totem, what would you do differently?

Lesson **3**   **117**

THEME Connections

Models Use the artwork as models of animals and their symbolic characteristics.

Origins Use the artwork as visual examples of how nature inspires artistic expression.

Cultures Use the artwork to learn more about the culture of these artists.

ESL

ESL students may have difficulty following oral directions without some kind of visual support. Consider modeling with the whole class the steps in creating a totem. To review, write the steps on the chalkboard with a quick sketch before asking the students to complete the activity.

CLOSE
Time: About 5 minutes

"What have you learned about creating symmetry?"
"¿Qué han aprendido acerca de crear simetría?"

Review

Display the students' totems around the room and have students compare the use of symmetry to the works in this lesson.

Art Criticism

Have students answer the four art criticism questions—Describe, Analyze, Interpret, and Decide—orally or in writing. Discuss the use of symmetry in their totem sculptures.

Assess

Use the **Assessment Book** pages 41–42 as a formal assessment for this lesson.

Evaluation Criteria

• Can the student identify the use of symmetry in Native American totem pole carvings?

• Can the student cut out and glue shapes symmetrically onto a three-dimensional paper totem?

• Can the student use the four steps of art criticism to evaluate his or her own work?

• Can the student identify the cultural group of the artists of the two totems?

Reteaching ● ● ● ● ● ● ● ● ● ● ●

Symmetry Have students look through magazines to find three examples of symmetry. Ask them to cut them out and glue them onto a sheet of paper.

Perception Hints for Student Art

The central axis in this totem runs through the center of the mouths and noses and between the eyes.

Approximate Symmetry

Artists can use symmetry to balance their designs.

Artist unknown. (Egypt). *Portrait of a Boy.* Second century A.D. 38 × 19 cm. Encaustic on wood. The Metropolitan Museum of Art, New York. Gift of Edward S. Harkness, 1918.

Look at the portraits on these pages. *Portrait of a Boy* is a painting from an Egyptian mummy case created more than 1,800 years ago. *Her World* was painted in 1948. Both artists have used approximate symmetry to create these portraits. When something is symmetrical, it is the same on both sides. Approximate symmetry means that something is almost the same on both sides.

118

Unit **4**

LESSON PLANNER

Objectives

After completing this lesson, students will be able to:

- identify how artists use approximate symmetry to create portraits. *Aesthetic Perception*
- plan and create a self-portrait with approximate symmetry. *Creative Expression*
- use the four steps of art criticism to evaluate their own paintings. *Art Criticism*
- compare the lives of the two artists. *Art History and Culture*

Program Resources

- **Overhead:** Both the *Portrait of a Boy* and the Evergood are available on overhead 22.
- **Large Print:** *Vase: Red Figured Amphora* from Ancient Greece
- **Technique Tips Flip Chart,** page 22
- **Vocabulary Book** pages 43–44
- **Art Manipulative Kit:** mirror
- **Artist Profiles Book:** Artist unknown page 67 and Evergood page 12
- **Art Across the Curriculum Book** pages 127–132
- **Multimedia Workshop CD-ROM**
- **Assessment Book** pages 43–44

Multiple Intelligences

Logical/Mathematical Students can observe the relationship between symmetry in art and symmetry in nature.

Vocabulary

approximate symmetry *simetría aproximada* a type of formal balance when both sides of a design are *almost* exactly the same

---

FOCUS

Time: About 10 minutes

Activating Prior Knowledge

"Think about combing your hair in the morning. Is your hair arranged in *exactly* the same way on both sides?"

"Piensen acerca de cepillarse el cabello en las mañanas. ¿Está arreglado su cabello igual en ambos lados?"

- Discuss students' answers to the question and how our heads have approximate symmetry.

118 Unit 4

ART Background

About the Artists

Portrait of a Boy. Egyptians painted mummy portraits on wood using the encaustic technique, which preserved the portraits for a very long time. After the death of the portrayed person, these wood pieces were placed inside his or her mummy case.

Philip Evergood (fil′ əp ev′ ər gud, African American, 1901–1973) was born in New York City and educated in England. His paintings varied from simple human themes to ones that were allegorical. During the Depression, he created social protest paintings.

About Subject Matter* Both *Portrait of a Boy* and the Evergood are portraits.

About the Media *Portrait of a Boy* is an encaustic painting, which is paint mixed with melted beeswax. The Evergood is an oil painting. Oil is a slow-drying medium that comes in lush colors and provides a durable finish.

Philip Evergood. (American).
Her World. 1948. Oil on canvas.
$48 \times 35\frac{5}{8}$ inches. The Metropolitan
Museum of Art, New York.

Study each painting to find the following examples
of approximate symmetry.

☑ Which features on the left side of the face are
exactly the same as the ones on the right?

☑ Locate the shapes that are almost the same on
both sides of the face.

☑ In which portrait is the hair the same on both sides
of the middle?

SEEING LIKE
AN ARTIST

Look at a friend's
face to find examples
of approximate
symmetry.

Lesson **4**   **119**

About Art History* *Portrait of a Boy* was created in the Roman Empire, which included
Egypt and Greece, during the Greek and Roman Classical period of the second century A.D.
Narrative images were painted on walls and ceramic vases.

Evergood's painting was created in the 1940s when President Roosevelt's New Deal social
program, which included the Works Progress Administration (WPA), provided funds to
writers, artists, and theater groups for numerous projects.

Cultural Perspectives The Roman Empire included many different people with their
own customs, religions, and cultures.

Evergood was politically active during the Great Depression. His paintings reflect his social
concerns of isolation and prejudice.

*See **More About** pages 206–227 for more about art history and subject matter.

Introducing the Art

"Let's look closely at the two paintings."
"Vamos a observar detalladamente las dos pinturas."

• Have students describe the subject matter in
each painting. (both: portraits)

• **COMPARE AND CONTRAST** Have students
make a list of the similarities and differences
in the two paintings. (Both paintings include a
single figure, depict young adolescents, and are realistic
in style. *Portrait of a Boy* is an image of a young boy,
illustrates the portrait to the shoulders only, and shows
shallow space. Evergood's painting is an image of a girl,
illustrates the full figure, and shows deep space.)

• Share and discuss information about the lives,
work, and times of the artists from **Art
Background** and the **Artist Profiles Book.**

• Have students answer the questions about
approximate symmetry on page 119.
(See **Perception Hints** below.)

FOR THE ART SPECIALIST

Use the **Overhead** and the **Large
Print** *Vase: Red Figured Amphora*
to demonstrate how artists can use
approximate symmetry to balance
their designs.

Perception Hints

Symmetry *Portrait of a Boy.* The hair, eyebrows, and nose
are the same on both sides of the face.
Approximate Symmetry *Evergood.* The shape of the
eyes is almost the same on both sides of the face.
Approximate Symmetry *Portrait of a Boy.* The boy's hair
is almost the same on both sides.

TEACH

Time: About two 30-minute periods

Practice

Materials
- 9- × 12-inch paper
- pencils

Alternate Materials: crayons

"How can you show approximate symmetry in a drawing of a face?"

"¿Cómo pueden mostrar simetría aproximada en un dibujo de una cara?"

- Discuss the use of guidelines to create facial proportions on page 120.
- Distribute the materials and have students follow the directions on page 120 for illustrating approximate symmetry. Ask them to answer the Decide question on the back.

Create PROBLEM SOLVING

Materials
- 12- × 18-inch construction paper
- flexible mirror from the **Art Manipulative Kit**
- liquid tempera paints
- paper plates for palettes   • pencils
- brushes of various sizes   • paper towels
- containers of water   • newspaper

 For safety issues about tempera and other information about safety in the art classroom, see page T22.

Alternate Materials: oil pastels and watercolor paints

"Let's use approximate symmetry in a self-portrait painting."

"Vamos a usar simetría aproximada en un autorretrato."

- Review facial proportions.
- Review ways to create approximate symmetry.
- Review procedures for working with paint in **More About Technique Tips** on page 199.
- See page 22 in the **Technique Tips Flip Chart** for visual examples of techniques.
- Distribute materials and have students follow the directions on page 121.

FOR THE ART SPECIALIST

On a large piece of rolled paper, create a classroom self-portrait collage.

Using Approximate Symmetry

Approximate symmetry is a special kind of formal balance that happens when both sides of a design are *almost* exactly the same. The human face has approximate symmetry. Both sides are almost exactly the same.

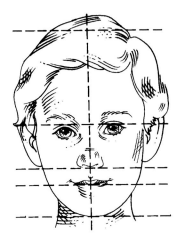

When drawing a portrait, it is helpful to draw the shape of the head first. Look at the **guidelines** in the face above. You can see that the eyes are placed about halfway between the top of the head and the bottom of the chin. Where do you find the tops of the ears? The nose? The mouth? What about your own face?

Practice

Illustrate approximate symmetry. Use pencil.

1. Create the shape of a head by drawing a large oval shape. Draw a line *down* the middle and also *across* the middle of the shape.

2. Look at the guidelines in the diagram above to help you place the eyes, nose, mouth, and ears.

Decide Does the face show approximate symmetry?

Activities in
ART Across the Curriculum Book

Reading/Language Arts Identify adjectives associated with animals, noting how Egyptians used animals as symbols in writing. (page 127)

Math Learn about approximate measurements. (page 128)

Science Understand how scientists use clues, like the picture of the Egyptian boy to draw conclusions about what happened long ago. (page 129)

Social Studies List forms of transportation and determine whether each form could be used in the time of the Egyptian boy and/or today. (page 130)

The Arts Describe how you would act out an activity you do everyday. (page 131)

Technology Use the *Multimedia Workshop* CD-ROM to draw a self-portrait with approximate symmetry. (page 132)

How did this student artist create approximate symmetry?

Daria Crenshaw. Age 8. *Self-Portrait of Daria.* Tempera.

Create

What parts of your face show approximate symmetry? Use approximate symmetry in a self-portrait.

1. Look at your face in the mirror. Notice how it is almost exactly the same on both sides.
2. Draw a self-portrait using approximate symmetry.
3. In the spaces around your portrait, draw objects that are important to you.
4. Add color.

Describe What shapes did you use to create the face? What objects are included in the background?

Analyze How did you create approximate symmetry in the face?

Interpret How would the face look if you had not used approximate symmetry?

Decide If you had painted this self-portrait a year ago, what objects would you have included?

Lesson **4**   121

THEME Connections

Models Use the paintings as visual examples of children as subjects in works of art.

Scale and structure Use the artwork as visual examples of measurement used in facial proportions.

Connections Use the artwork as a springboard to discuss the five senses: sight, hearing, smell, touch, and taste.

ESL

When asking students to create self-portraits and share them, be sensitive to physical differences that may be present in the students in your class. Dealing with issues of skin color, hair type, or other physical characteristics associated with race must be handled sensitively and positively in order to avoid any feelings of bias or discrimination on the part of the students.

CLOSE

Time: About 5 minutes

"What have you learned about approximate symmetry?"
"¿Qué han aprendido sobre simetría aproximada?"

Review
Use the **Large Print** *Vase: Red Figured Amphora* to have students compare the use of approximate symmetry to the works in this lesson.

Art Criticism
Have students answer the four art criticism questions—Describe, Analyze, Interpret, and Decide—orally or in writing. Discuss the use of approximate symmetry in their works after the paintings are dry.

Assess
Use the **Assessment Book** pages 43–44 as a formal assessment for this lesson.

Evaluation Criteria
• Can the student identify how artists use approximate symmetry to create portraits?
• Can the student show facial proportions with approximate symmetry in a self–portrait painting?
• Can the student use the four steps of art criticism to evaluate his or her own work?
• Can the student compare the lives of the two artists?

Reteaching ● ● ● ● ● ● ● ● ● ● ● ●

Symmetry Have students look through the book to find three different works of art that illustrate approximate symmetry. Ask them to list the title of each work and describe how approximate symmetry was created.

Perception Hints for Student Art

The lines in the background are similar, but not exactly the same.

LESSON PLANNER

Objectives

After completing this lesson, students will be able to:

- identify how artists use emphasis to create a center of interest in a work of art. *Aesthetic Perception*
- plan and create a night-scene drawing showing emphasis. *Creative Expression*
- use the four steps of art criticism to evaluate their own drawings. *Art Criticism*
- compare works by artists from different cultures. *Art History and Culture*

Program Resources

- **Overhead:** Both the Jacquette and the Degas are available on overhead 23.
- **Large Print:** *Taj Mahal*
- **Technique Tips Flip Chart,** page 23
- **Vocabulary Book** pages 45–46
- **Art Manipulative Kit:** music audiotapes
- **Artist Profiles Book:** Jacquette page 20 and Degas page 9
- **Art Across the Curriculum Book** pages 133–138
- **Multimedia Workshop CD-ROM**
- **Assessment Book** pages 45–46

Multiple Intelligences

Interpersonal Students can share opinions as a group to identify the emphasis in a work of art.

Vocabulary

center of interest or *focal point* *centro de interés* the area of a work of art that attracts the viewer's attention first

contrast *contraste* to set in opposition in order to show or emphasize differences

emphasis *énfasis* the principle of design that stresses one element or area in a work of art over another

value *valor* the lightness or darkness of a color or object

Unit 4 Lesson 5

Emphasis

Artists use emphasis in their artwork to create a center of interest.

Yvonne Jacquette. (American).
Tokyo Street with Pachinko Parlor II.
1985. Oil on canvas. $85\frac{5}{16} \times 55\frac{3}{16}$ inches.
Courtesy, Yvonne Jacquette and the D C Moore Gallery.

Look at the artworks on these pages. Yvonne Jacquette painted *Tokyo Street with Pachinko Parlor II* in 1985. French artist Edgar Degas created his artwork about 100 years earlier. Both artists used emphasis to create a center of interest in their work. They did this by showing a contrast of light and dark values.

ART Background

About the Artists

Edgar Degas (ed' gär dā gä', French, 1834–1917) was best known for his paintings in theatrical, orchestral, or race-course settings. Because he was nearly blind for the last 20 years of his life, he turned to sculpture as a means of personal expression.

Yvonne Jacquette (ē von' jac ket', American, 1934–) was born in Pittsburgh, Pennsylvania, and studied art at the Rhode Island School of Design. She takes photographs from airplanes or tall buildings as a resource for her paintings.

About Subject Matter* The Degas is a portrait, and the Jacquette is a cityscape.

About the Media The Degas is a pastel drawing, which is a pigment held together with gum and molded into sticks. The Jacquette is an oil painting, which is an opaque, slow-drying medium that comes in lush colors and provides a durable finish.

Edgar Degas. (France). *Waiting.* c. 1882. 19 × 24 inches. Pastel on paper. Norton Simon Museum, Jointly owned by the Pasadena, California, and The J. Paul Getty Museum Malibu, Pasadena, CA.

Study both artworks to find areas of emphasis.

☑ Find which areas attract your attention most.

☑ Where do you see the lightest areas?

☑ Find the darkest areas.

☑ Do the two artworks give you different feelings? Describe the differences.

SEEING LIKE AN ARTIST

Look outside your window at night. Find objects or areas that are emphasized with light and attract your attention.

Lesson 5 123

About Art History* Degas created art in France during the Impressionist movement (early 1860s to 1886), when artists departed from tradition and expressed their "impressions" through changes in light and color.

Jacquette's painting was created during a time when rap music was popular in America, and dance was choreographed with experimental multimedia such as film and light.

Cultural Perspectives Degas painted during a time when the French people resented tyranny and wanted their rights and freedom. Artists wanted freedom from the old styles and strict rules for creating artwork.

Jacquette's painting was created when the control of nuclear arms was a hotly debated issue between America and the Soviet Union, and efforts were being made to reduce the threat of a nuclear war.

*See **More About** pages 206–227 for more about art history and subject matter.

FOCUS

Time: About 10 minutes

Activating Prior Knowledge

"Think about sitting in a dark movie theater. Why does the movie screen catch your attention?"

"Piensen acerca de estar sentados en un cine oscuro. ¿Por qué la pantalla atrae su atención?"

• Discuss students' responses to the question and how a light area attracts attention when surrounded by a dark area.

Introducing the Art

"Let's look closely at the two artworks."

"Vamos a observar detalladamente las dos obras de arte."

• **Describe:** Have students describe the subject matter in each artwork. (Degas: portrait; Jacquette: cityscape)

• **COMPARE AND CONTRAST** Have students make a list of the similarities and differences in the two artworks. (Both works give a feeling of movement, include people, and are realistic in style. Degas's drawing is an indoor scene, contains few objects, and has neutral colors. Jacquette's painting is an outdoor scene and contains many objects and many bright colors.)

• Share and discuss information about the lives, work, and times of the artists from **Art Background** and the **Artist Profiles Book.**

• Have students answer questions about emphasis on page 123.
(See **Perception Hints** below.)

 FOR THE ART SPECIALIST

Use the **Overhead** and the **Large Print** *Taj Mahal* to demonstrate how artists use emphasis in their artwork to create a center of interest.

Perception Hints

Center of Interest *Jacquette.* The brightly colored building at the top of the painting attracts the eye's attention first.
Light Areas *Degas.* The lightest areas are found in the bent figure of the ballet dancer.
Dark Areas *Jacquette.* The darkest values are found around the outside edges and bottom half of the painting.

TEACH

Time: About two 30-minute periods

Practice

Materials
- 9- × 12-inch white paper
- black crayons
- pencils

Alternate Materials: collage: light-colored shapes on dark paper

"How can you use black crayon to create emphasis?"
"¿Cómo pueden usar creyón negro para crear énfasis?"

- Discuss emphasis through a contrast in values on page 124.
- Distribute materials and have students follow the directions on page 124 for illustrating emphasis. Ask them to answer the Decide question on the back.

Create PROBLEM SOLVING

Materials
- 12- × 18-inch black construction paper
- colored dustless chalk
- Music audiotapes from the **Art Manipulative Kit**

 For safety issues about chalk and other information about safety in the art classroom, see page T22.

Alternate Materials: crayon batik

"Let's contrast light and dark values to emphasize an area of interest."
"Vamos a contrastar valores claros y oscuros para enfatizar el área de interés."

- Have students brainstorm where they might see areas of light at night.
- Review ways to create emphasis through a contrast in values.
- See page 23 in the **Technique Tips Flip Chart** for visual examples of techniques.
- Distribute materials and have students follow the directions on page 125 while listening to the audiotapes.

FOR THE ART SPECIALIST

Have students use another medium to create interest in a different way.

Understanding Emphasis

Sometimes an artist wants you to look immediately at a certain area in a work of art. This area is called the **center of interest**. An artist uses **emphasis** to draw your attention there. Often, the center of interest shows the artist's main idea.

Contrast is one way to emphasize a center of interest. This can be used when there is a great difference between two things, such as a contrast in **value**. This is shown in the following examples. The area with strong value contrasts, lightness or darkness of a color, will attract your attention first.

Practice

Contrast values to illustrate emphasis. Use pencil and black crayon.

1. Draw a shape several times until a small piece of paper is filled. Keep the shapes about the same size.

2. Pick one to be the center of interest. Color it with black crayon, leaving the rest of the shapes uncolored to create emphasis.

Analyze Which shape attracts your attention first? Why?

Activities in
ART Across the Curriculum Book

Reading/Language Arts Write a comparison of two things that are different, first looking at how artists use contrast to emphasize things. (page 133)

Math Study a graph that shows information about games. (page 134)

Science Distinguish between things that take a short time to change or a long time to change. (page 135)

Social Studies Understand how compromise is used to solve problems. (page 136)

The Arts Evaluate ways you could create light and heavy sounds to show emphasis. (page 137)

Technology Use the *Multimedia Workshop* CD-ROM to create contrast with emphasis in a scene. (page 138)

Mara Santiago. Age 8. Dustless chalk.

What did this student artist use as the center of interest in her night scene?

Create

What would you emphasize in a night scene? Contrast value to show the center of interest in a drawing.

1. On black paper, use a piece of colored chalk to draw a picture of your house or apartment at night. Choose one object or a small group of objects you want to emphasize.

2. To make your chosen object the center of interest, color it with light colors.

3. Use dark values for contrast to color the rest of the objects in your picture.

Describe What objects did you include in your drawing? Where are the light areas? Where are the dark areas?

Analyze How did you use emphasis to create a center of interest?

Interpret How would the mood or feeling of your artwork change if you had used light values only?

Decide What else could you draw and show a center of interest?

Lesson 5

125

"How did you create a center of interest in your drawing?"
"¿Cómo crearon un centro de interés en sus dibujos?"

Review
Display the student artwork and have students compare their use of emphasis to the works in this lesson.

Art Criticism
Have students answer the four art criticism questions—Describe, Analyze, Interpret, and Decide—orally or in writing. Discuss the use of contrast to create emphasis in their artwork.

Assess
Use the **Assessment Book** pages 45–46 as a formal assessment for this lesson.

Evaluation Criteria
- Can the student describe how emphasis creates a center of interest in a work of art?
- Can the student emphasize a center of interest by contrasting values in a night scene?
- Can the student use the four steps of art criticism to evaluate his or her own work?
- Can the student compare the works by artists from different cultures?

Reteaching ● ● ● ● ● ● ● ● ● ●

Emphasis Have students look through the book to find three different works of art that contrast values to emphasize an area of interest. Ask them to list the title of each work and describe the areas of emphasis they find.

Perception Hints for Student Art
A candle in the window is the center of interest.

THEME Connections

Discovery Use Degas's drawing as a springboard to discuss careers in the visual and performing arts.

Relationships Use the artwork as a springboard to review pairs of opposites such as light and dark.

Cultures Use the artwork to discuss differences and similarities of artwork from different cultures.

ESL

ESL students may feel shy or hesitant to answer the interpretative question about their artwork. You may wish to phrase the question as an either/or choice so that the vocabulary needed to answer the question is contained in the question itself.

LESSON PLANNER

Objectives

After completing this lesson, students will be able to:

- identify how artists contrast shapes to emphasize the center of interest in a work of art. *Aesthetic Perception*
- plan and create a leaf collage emphasizing the center of interest through contrasting shapes. *Creative Expression*
- use the four steps of art criticism to evaluate their own collages. *Art Criticism*
- compare the cultures of the two artists. *Art History and Culture*

Program Resources

- **Overhead:** Both the Houser and the Freilicher are available on overhead 24.
- **Large Print:** *Taj Mahal*
- **Technique Tips Flip Chart,** page 24
- **Vocabulary Book** pages 47–48
- **Art Manipulative Kit:** flash cards
- **Artist Profiles Book:** Houser page 18 and Freilicher page 15
- **Art Across the Curriculum Book** pages 139–144
- **Multimedia Workshop CD-ROM**
- **Assessment Book** pages 47–48

Multiple Intelligences
Verbal/Linguistic Students can explore contrasting shapes through discussion, instruction, and definitions.

Vocabulary

contrast *contraste* to set in opposition in order to show or emphasize differences

emphasis *énfasis* the principle of design that stresses one element or area in a work of art over another

FOCUS

Time: About 10 minutes

Activating Prior Knowledge

"Think about looking up at the sky at night. What objects do you see? Which objects do you notice first?"

"Piensen acerca de mirar hacia el cielo en la noche. ¿Qué objetos ven? ¿Qué objetos notan primero?"

- Discuss students' responses and how the moon attracts the attention first because it is the largest shape and because it is bright against a dark sky.

Emphasis Through Contrast in Shapes

Artists can contrast shapes to create a center of interest in a work of art.

Allan Houser. (American). *Apache Crown Dance.* 1953. Casein. $24\frac{5}{8} \times 36\frac{1}{2}$ inches. The Denver Art Museum, Denver, Colorado.

Look at the paintings on these pages. Allan Houser painted *Apache Crown Dance* in 1953. About 40 years later, Jane Freilicher painted *The Sun Breaks Through*. The subject matter in each is very different, but both artists used emphasis to create a center of interest. They did this by showing a contrast in the size of the shapes.

ART Background

About the Artists

Jane Freilicher (jān frī' lik ər, American, 1924–) was born in Brooklyn, New York, and has committed herself to a lifetime of painting. Even though she does not consciously paint images for symbolic reasons, she feels that everything she has painted is a symbol.

Allan Houser (al' ən hau' zər, American, 1915–1994) was born on a small farm in Oklahoma. Native Americans are the primary focus of his paintings, and he strived toward realism. Houser experimented and worked in a variety of media.

About Subject Matter* The Freilicher is a still-life painting, and the Houser is a narrative painting.

About the Media The Freilicher is an oil painting, which is a slow-drying medium that comes in lush colors and provides a durable finish. The Houser is painted with casein, pigment blended in a protein derived from milk and an emulsifying agent.

Jane Freilicher. (American). *The Sun Breaks Through.* 1991. Oil on linen. 47 × 49½ inches. Private Collection. Courtesy, Fischbach Gallery, New York.

Study both paintings to find areas of emphasis.

☑ Where do you see the active shapes?

☑ Which areas or objects attract your attention most?

☑ Find the artwork that has small shapes in the center of interest.

☑ Which painting uses large shapes in the center of interest? Where are the smaller shapes in this work?

SEEING LIKE AN ARTIST

Look around on the ground outside. Find an object completely surrounded by shapes that are the opposite size.

Lesson **6**

127

About Art History* Houser's painting was created in 1950s America when many artists continued to paint in the realistic manner that was dominant before World War II.

Freilicher's painting was created in America during the 1990s when dance was choreographed with experimental multimedia such as light and electronic music.

Cultural Perspectives Houser's painting was created shortly after America's involvement in the Korean War and during the time when Senator Joseph McCarthy claimed that a Communist conspiracy, aimed at undermining American democracy, existed within the government.

Freilicher's painting was done when the control of nuclear arms was a hotly debated issue between America and the Soviet Union, and efforts were being made by these two countries to reduce the threat of nuclear war.

*See **More About** pages 206–227 for more about art history and subject matter.

Introducing the Art

"Let's look closely at the two paintings."

"Vamos a observar detalladamente las dos pinturas."

- **Describe:** Have students describe the subject matter in each painting. (Freilicher: still life; Houser: narrative)
- **COMPARE AND CONTRAST** Have students make a list of the similarities and differences in the two paintings. (Both paintings show outdoor scenes, illustrate depth, and are realistic in style. Freilicher's painting also shows an interior scene, does not depict any people, and has smaller shapes as the center of interest. Houser's painting does not show an interior scene, depicts a great number of people, and has larger shapes as the center of interest.)
- Share and discuss information about the lives, work, and times of the artists from **Art Background** and the **Artist Profiles Book.**
- Have students answer questions about emphasis through contrast in shape on page 127. (See **Perception Hints** below.)

FOR THE ART SPECIALIST

Use the **Overhead** and the flash cards from the **Art Manipulative Kit** to demonstrate how artists can contrast shapes to create a center of interest in a work of art.

Perception Hints

Active shapes *Houser.* The Apache dancers, located in the center, are the active shapes.

Small shapes *Freilicher.* The flowers on the table are the small shapes in the center of interest.

Center of interest *Houser.* The Apache dancers attract the most attention.

Emphasis *Freilicher.* The flowers, which are the small shapes in the center of interest, are emphasized by the large shapes of the table, curtain, and landscape. *Houser.* The Apache dancers, which are the large shapes in the center of interest, are emphasized by the circle of people who are smaller in shape.

TEACH

Time: About two 30-minute periods

Practice

Materials
- 9- × 12-inch paper
- crayons

Alternate Materials: colored pencils

"How can you illustrate emphasis through contrast in shape?"

"¿Cómo pueden ilustrar énfasis a través del contraste en una figura?"

- Discuss techniques for creating emphasis through contrast in shape on page 128.
- Distribute materials and have students follow the directions on page 128 for creating emphasis through contrast in shape. Ask them to answer the Decide questions on the back.

Create PROBLEM SOLVING

Materials
- 9- × 12-inch construction paper, assorted colors
- 12- × 18-inch black construction paper
- scissors
- pencils
- glue
- sketch paper
- oil pastels
- black felt-tip pens

Safety! For safety issues about glue and oil pastels, and other information about safety in the art classroom, see page T22.

Alternate Materials: stamp printing

"Let's contrast shapes to create emphasis in a paper collage."

"Vamos a contrastar figuras para crear énfasis en un collaje de papel."

- Have students brainstorm different leaves to draw.
- Review ways to create emphasis through contrast in shapes.
- See page 24 in the **Technique Tips Flip Chart** for visual examples of techniques.
- Distribute materials and have students follow the directions on page 129.

FOR THE ART SPECIALIST

Have students create emphasis by adding a dark shape on the largest leaf.

Emphasis Through Contrasts

Using **emphasis** through contrast in shape is one way to create a center of interest in a work of art.

Artists can emphasize a center of interest by **contrasting** values. They can also create emphasis by contrasting shapes and sizes. A large shape, for example, will stand out if it is surrounded by small shapes.

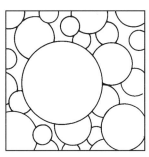

A free-form shape will attract attention first if it is surrounded by geometric shapes.

Practice

Illustrate contrast in shape. Use crayon.

1. Fold a piece of paper into two equal parts. On the left side, draw a free-form shape. Draw geometric shapes around it.

2. On the right side, draw a large circle. Draw smaller circles around it.

Decide Which shapes first attract your attention? Why?

Activities in
ART Across the Curriculum Book

Reading/Language Arts Learn more about antonyms, first noting how opposites are used in art to show contrast. (page 139)

Math Create contrasting sets of multiplication and division facts. (page 140)

Science Understand how parts are related to the whole. (page 141)

Social Studies Learn more about the Apache culture that is depicted in *Apache Crown Dance.* (page 142)

The Arts Write and perform a circle dance, which includes a group of dancers, as in *Apache Crown Dance.* (page 143)

Technology Use the *Multimedia Workshop* CD-ROM to create a design that shows emphasis through the contrast of shapes. (page 144)

Carla Sutton. Age 8. *Falling Leaves*. Construction paper.

Which leaf is emphasized in this student artist's collage?

Create

What would you emphasize in a collage of leaves? Contrast shapes to show emphasis in a collage.

1. Think of leaves from trees, houseplants, or other plants you remember. Sketch some that have different shapes.

2. Draw leaves on different colors of paper. Draw one leaf very large and the others much smaller. Cut them out.

3. The large leaf will be your center of interest. Arrange all the leaves on a piece of black construction paper. Fill the page. Glue the leaves down. Add details with oil pastels.

Describe What shapes did you use in your collage? Name the colors. Describe the lines. Where is the center of interest?

Analyze How did you emphasize the center of interest?

Interpret How would the feeling of your collage change if all the shapes were the same size?

Decide Which shapes do you like best? Why? Which ones would you change? Why?

Lesson 6 **129**

THEME Connections

Celebrations Use *Apache Crown Dance* as a springboard to describe the celebration that may be occurring.

Identity Use Freilicher's painting as a springboard to discuss annual and perennial flowers.

Traditions Use Houser's painting as a visual example of Native American traditions.

ESL

You may wish to pair an ESL student with a more proficient peer to create the collage. By working together on a project, the ESL student will have the opportunity to practice oral language in a less threatening way. Working on a hands-on project will give the students a concrete topic to talk about and interpret.

CLOSE

Time: About 5 minutes

"Were you able to create a center of interest in your collage?"

"¿Fueron capaces de crear un centro de interés en sus collajes?"

LARGE PRINT **Review**

Use the **Large Print** *Taj Mahal* to have students compare the use of emphasis to the works in this lesson.

Art Criticism

Have students answer the four art criticism questions—Describe, Analyze, Interpret, and Decide—orally or in writing. Discuss the use of emphasis through contrast in shapes in their collages.

Assess

Use the **Assessment Book** pages 47–48 as a formal assessment for this lesson.

Evaluation Criteria

• Can the student identify how artists contrast shapes to emphasize the center of interest?
• Can the student incorporate emphasis, through contrast in shape, in a collage?
• Can the student use the four steps of art criticism to evaluate his or her own work?
• Can the student compare the cultures of the two artists?

Reteaching • • • • • • • • • • • •

Emphasis Have students look outside to find three objects emphasized by contrasting shapes. Ask them to list the objects and how they are emphasized.

Perception Hints for Student Art

The yellow leaf near the center is emphasized.

Objectives

After completing this lesson, students will be able to:

- demonstrate the process of achieving balance in a performance with a partner. *Aesthetic Perception*
- express individual interpretation in miming everyday activities. *Creative Expression*
- use the four steps of art criticism to evaluate their own performance. *Art Criticism*
- demonstrate knowledge about the art of mime. *Art History and Culture*

Program Resources

Artsource Performing Arts Audio/Video Resource Package

Life Cycle performed by The Chameleons—Keith Berger and Sharon Diskin. Videocassette Running Time: 6:25.

FOCUS

Time: About 10 minutes

Activating Prior Knowledge

"What are some of the activities you do every day?"

"¿Cuáles son algunas de las actividades que hacen diaria?"

- Have students explain specifically how and when they do the activities.

Introducing the Art

"Look at the picture of the mimes. What activity do you think they could be doing?"

"Vamos a observar el dibujo de las pantomimas. ¿Qué creen que pudieran estar haciendo?"

- Discuss with students the information on page 130. Have students describe the mimes and their activity. Share information from **Art Background** about the art of mime. If you have the *Artsource* videocassette, have students view the performance by Sharon Diskin and Keith Berger.
- Discuss how everyday activities may vary from one person to another. Give an example of combing one's hair. The movement will be different depending on whether the hair is short or long, curly or straight, tangled or smooth, and if a comb, brush, or pick is used.
- Have the class select three everyday activities for all to mime as practice.

130   **Unit 4**

Balance and Emphasis in Pantomime

The Chameleons: Sharon Diskin and Keith Berger.

a mime tells a story without words. Mimes communicate with the movements of their bodies and the expressions on their faces. Sometimes a mime copies another person. The two people are balanced, as one does just what the other does. The mime is like your image in a mirror.

130   Unit 4

ART Background

About the Artists

Keith Berger and Sharon Diskin are known as "The Chameleons," masters of traditional mime illusions. Their piece *Life Cycle* follows the relationship of two characters, one female and one male, from infancy through childhood, adolescence, courtship, marriage, parenthood, middle age, old age, death, and rebirth.

About Subject Matter Mime is the art of dramatic representation by movement and gestures only, without words. The first use of mime as a part of organized theater was in the Orient. The Greeks were probably the first to use mime as an art form in and of itself, though strongly connected to dance. During the Middle Ages, mimes became traveling jesters and were also part of church dramas. Today, Frenchman Marcel Marceau is the best-known mime, and the style continues to evolve.

What To Do

Mirror some of your daily activities with a partner.

Materials
None

1. Work with a partner. Face each other and practice moving as though you are the mirror image of your partner. Take turns.

2. Choose four simple, everyday activities to mime. Each partner can lead two activities. You might comb your hair, put on clothes, draw a picture, or make a sandwich. Move very slowly, using clear gestures and movement.

3. Perform your mirror study for others. Work as a team. You and your partner should do exactly the same things.

Describe How did you use mime to show everyday activities?

Analyze Explain how you made certain that you and your partner balanced each other.

Interpret Tell how your actions expressed the mood or feeling of an everyday activity.

Decide Were you satisfied with your activities? Were you more successful as a leader or as a follower? Why?

Extra Credit

Choose an everyday activity to mime. Design it so that it has a beginning, a middle, and an end. Perform it for others.

Theater 131

Cultural Perspectives When studying any period of history, you can extend your understanding of the people and the times by knowing about their daily activities. For example, in pioneer times, the activities might include driving oxen, chopping wood, making butter, and building fences; in today's times, activities might include driving a car, watching TV, or working out.

About Theater The principles of balance and emphasis are important in the theater. Actors must always be sensitive to the balance of energy between themselves and other actors. The director of a play must always make sure that certain aspects of a performance are emphasized.

TEACH
Time: About 30 minutes

"You're going to mime everyday activities with a partner. One person will clearly mime the activity and the other will mirror what is being done."

"Ustedes van a imitar las actividades diarias con un compañero. Una persona hará la actividad claramente y la otra persona imitará lo que está haciendo."

- Have partners brainstorm and choose four simple everyday activities to mime. One will begin as the leader and the other will copy everything the leader does. Explain that the goal is for partners to move exactly together so that an observer could not easily tell who is leading and who is following. Have partners move for one or two minutes and then switch roles.

- Encourage students to keep focused on working as a team.

- Point out that activities can vary according to cultural influences (such as ways of cooking) and the ages of the people doing the activities.

- Have partners perform their activities for others, taking turns as leader and follower.

CLOSE
Time: About 5 minutes

"What might you do to make your miming more believable and clearer?"

"¿Qué podrían hacer para lograr que su imitación sea más clara y real?"

Assess
Have students answer the four art criticism questions on page 131—Describe, Analyze, Interpret, and Decide—orally or in writing.

Evaluation Criteria
- Can the student work with his or her partner to show balance and emphasis in their mime explorations?

- Can the student demonstrate an ability to interpret everyday activities through mime?

- Can the student use the four steps of art criticism to evaluate his or her performance?

- Can the student demonstrate knowledge about the art of mime?

UNIT 4

Reviewing Unit Concepts

"Artists use formal balance, approximate symmetry, and symmetry to create balance in all kinds of art. They contrast value and shape to create emphasis."

"Los artistas usan el equilibrio formal, la simetría aproximada y la simetría para crear equilibrio en todos los tipos de arte. Ellos contrastan valor y figura para crear énfasis."

• Review ways that artists create space and emphasis on pages 132 and 133. Have the students write down examples found in their environment.

Examining the Artwork

"Let's look closely at the work of art."

"Vamos a observar detalladamente la obra de arte."

• Have students look at Noguchi's *Cronos*. Ask them to describe what they see in the sculpture related to the concepts learned in this unit and answer the questions on page 133 about balance and emphasis.

(See **Perception Hints** below.)

Student Portfolio
Have students review all the artwork they have created in this unit and select the pieces they wish to keep in their portfolios.

Art Criticism Activity
Have students select an artwork from this unit and study it using the four steps of art criticism. (See pages 206–209 for more information about Art Criticism.)

Perception Hints

Balance

Approximate symmetry The overall form is designed with approximate symmetry. For example, the left side of the lower horizontal, curved form has a small opening in the rounded end, while the right side does not.

Symmetry The outside, main structure of the sculpture is symmetrical.

Center of interest The objects in the middle of the sculpture create the center of interest.

Emphasis

Value The darkness of the wood against the light background emphasizes the sculpture's forms.

Shape The smaller forms grouped together in the center are emphasized by the larger, main form.

Wrapping Up Unit 4

Balance and Emphasis

Reviewing Main Ideas

The lessons and activities in this unit cover the techniques that artists use to create balance and emphasis.

1. **Formal balance** is a way of organizing a design so that equal or very similar elements are placed on opposite sides of a central dividing line. Many *masks* are examples of formal balance.

2. **Symmetry** is a type of formal balance in which both sides of a design are *exactly* the same. The two halves are divided by a *central axis,* an imaginary dividing line.

3. **Approximate symmetry** is a special kind of formal balance in which both sides of a design are *almost* exactly the same.

4. **Emphasis** is the way artists create a **center of interest** in their artwork. Following are two common ways to create emphasis.

• **Contrast in value** — A light area will attract attention if there are darker areas around it.

• **Contrast in shape** — Large shapes will stand out if they are surrounded by smaller shapes.

Isamu Noguchi. (American). *Cronos.* 1947. Wood, string, metal. $86\frac{1}{4} \times 22 \times 31$ inches. Collection Walker Art Center, Minneapolis, Minnesota, Gift of the artist, 1979.

ART *Background*

About the Artist
Isamu Noguchi (ē sä' mū nō gū' chē, American, 1904–1988) was born in Los Angeles. His father was Japanese and his mother, American. Sensitive to the environment, Noguchi learned the principles of garden design during visits to China and Japan. He has had tremendous influence and input in the creation and aesthetic design of parks, playgrounds, and public plazas.

About Subject Matter* *Cronos* is a nonobjective sculpture utilizing abstract forms only.

About the Media *Cronos* was created from wood. The appearance of wood is dependent on the kind of tree from which it is derived and how it is treated by the artist. The surface can be sanded smooth or left rough. The color can be altered using paints, stains, or varnishes.

Summing Up

Cronos is a wooden sculpture by American artist Isamu Noguchi. In this sculpture, Noguchi used the techniques of balance and emphasis covered in this unit.

- Which type of formal balance did the artist use to design this sculpture? Give a reason for your answer.
- Find the center of interest in this sculpture.
- Which of the two techniques did Noguchi use to create emphasis?

Balance and **emphasis** are important design principles in art. By using techniques to create emphasis, artists can create a center of interest in their artwork.

Let's Visit a Museum

The Walker Art Center, located in Minneapolis, Minnesota, is famous for its collection of 8,000 pieces of twentieth-century art. The collection includes paintings, sculpture, videos, prints, drawings, and photographs. The Walker Art Center also has a varied educational program that appeals to people of all ages. Beside the museum is the Minneapolis Sculpture Garden. It covers 11 acres and is one of the largest urban sculpture parks in the country. It is a popular tourist attraction.

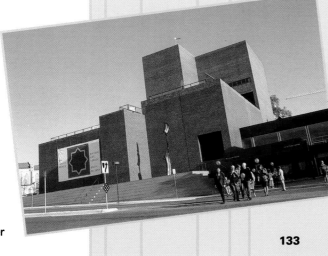

The Walker Art Center

133

Learning About Museums

The Walker Art Center is housed in an award-winning building designed by architect Edward Larrabee Barnes. Internationally acclaimed for its major exhibitions of twentieth-century art, the Walker Art Center also presents vanguard music, dance, theater, and film. Initially a small, regional museum, the center has evolved into a major national and international artistic resource. Many of its exhibitions travel to major museums.

- In small groups, have students look through this book and identify twentieth-century artwork that could be considered for exhibition at the Walker Art Center.

- *TIMELINE* For more information about this and other museums, see pages T13, T30–T33, and the back of the **Animals Through History Time Line.**

- The World Wide Web address for the museum is as follows: http://www.walkerart.org/

A Final Thought

"To live a creative life, we must lose our fear of being wrong."—Joseph Chilton Pearce

About Art History* Noguchi was influenced by the art of the Constructivists, whose aim was to construct art, not create it. Up to the early 1900s, sculpture was traditionally created by taking away or building up from the mass of the raw material. Influenced by Picasso's Cubist paintings, however, Constructivist sculptures emphasized space rather than mass. Wood, metal, glass, and plastic were used to construct forms.

Cultural Perspectives During America's Great Depression, Noguchi worked for Roosevelt's Federal Art Project. He was one of 10,000 artists who were paid to produce six works of art per year. During a ten-year period, more than 100,000 works of art were created by artists in this program.

*See **More About** pages 206–227 for more about art history and subject matter.

UNIT OVERVIEW

This unit will cover the element of texture and the principle of rhythm. Texture is the element of art that refers to how things feel or how things appear to feel if touched. Rhythm is the principle of design that repeats elements to create the illusion of movement.

Tactile texture is texture that is perceived through the sense of touch. Tactile texture is covered in Lessons 1 and 2.

Visual texture is texture that is perceived through the sense of vision. Visual texture is covered in Lessons 1 and 3.

Random rhythm is the repetition of a motif in no particular order, with no particular spacing. Random rhythm is covered in Lesson 4.

Regular rhythm is the repetition of identical motifs using the same intervals of space between them. Regular rhythm is covered in Lesson 5.

Alternating rhythm is the repetition of motifs by changing position, content, or spaces between them. Alternating rhythm is covered in Lesson 6.

Introducing Unit Concepts

"Artists use the element of texture and the principle of rhythm to create all kinds of art."

"Los artistas usan el elemento de la textura y el principio del ritmo para crear todos los tipos de arte."

Texture

• Look up the word *texture* in the dictionary and read the definition. Have students brainstorm and list on the chalkboard a variety of "texture words" based on the definition.

• List a variety of objects that have pronounced textures (cactus, sandpaper, roads). Have students use texture words to describe how the surface of each might feel to the touch.

• Ask students to write a limerick using a texture word as the theme.

Unit 5

An Introduction to
Texture and Rhythm

Artists create texture and rhythm to show how things move and feel.

Artist unknown. *Bayeux Tapestry.* Detail of *Norman Cavalry Charging in the Battle of Hastings.* 1070–1080. Embroidered wool on linen. 20 inches high × 231 feet. Musée de Peinture, Bayeux, France. Art Resource, New York, New York.

ART Background

About the Artist
The *Bayeux Tapestry* was commissioned in the eleventh century by Odo, the bishop of Bayeux, to be hung in the cathedral at Bayeux.

About Subject Matter* The *Bayeux Tapestry* is a narrative representing the invasion and conquest of England by William the Conqueror.

About the Media The *Bayeux Tapestry* is made of colored, woolen thread worked on canvas or linen cloth.

Artists can create **texture** in a work of art to show how things feel, or look as if they might feel if touched.

- If you were able to touch the surface of the *Bayeux Tapestry,* how do you think it would feel?

Artists use **rhythm** in their artwork to create a feeling of movement.

- What shapes or objects do you see more than once?
- What shapes or objects look like they are moving?

Artist Profile

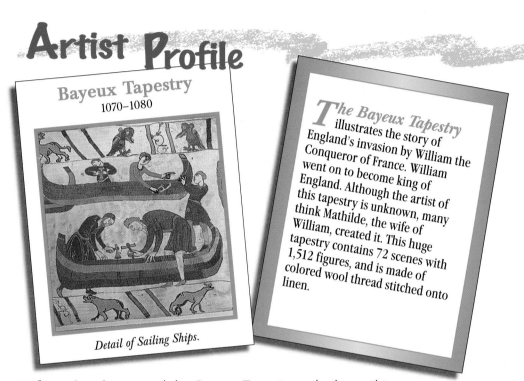

Bayeux Tapestry
1070–1080

Detail of Sailing Ships.

The Bayeux Tapestry illustrates the story of England's invasion by William the Conqueror of France. William went on to become king of England. Although the artist of this tapestry is unknown, many think Mathilde, the wife of William, created it. This huge tapestry contains 72 scenes with 1,512 figures, and is made of colored wool thread stitched onto linen.

The artist who created the *Bayeux Tapestry* and other artists use texture and rhythm to show how things move and feel. In this unit you will learn and practice the techniques that artists use to create texture and rhythm in their artwork. The topics are:

- Tactile Texture
- Visual Texture
- Random Rhythm
- Regular Rhythm
- Alternating Rhythm

135

About Art History* The Romanesque period, in which the *Bayeux Tapestry* was created, is represented by a wave of narrative sculpture, monumental mural painting, and illuminated manuscripts created to inform and educate the illiterate.

Cultural Perspectives In 1066, King Edward of England died. Because he had no children, the English had to choose a new king. Harold, an earl under Edward, and William, Duke of Normandy and distant relative of the king, both vied for the throne. Although Harold was crowned, William invaded and defeated him at the Battle of Hastings, ending the rule of Saxon kings. The English accepted William as their first Norman king.

*See **More About** pages 206–227 for more about art history and subject matter.

Rhythm

- Ask students to identify and list at least two objects in the room that are seen over and over again.
- Beat out on a tabletop two different rhythms. Have students describe what they hear and the differences between the two different rhythms.

You may wish to show the **Video** *Abuela* and identify the different textures and rhythms.

Examining the Artwork

"Let's look closely at the tapestry."
"Vamos a observar detalladamente el tapiz."

- Have students look at the *Bayeux Tapestry.* Ask them to describe what they see in the textile.
- Read the definition of *texture.* Have students answer the questions on page 135 pertaining to texture and rhythm in the tapestry. (See **Perception Hints** below.)

Art Profile

Share with students information about the art, including the size and the medium that gives it texture.

Encourage students to use an **Art Journal** to practice art concepts and record ideas from lesson to lesson.

About Music

Texture in music generally refers to combining melody and harmony to create layers of sound. It can also be used in describing the effect of layering together several different rhythm patterns. Demonstrate layered texture by having the children sing a round, such as *Row, Row, Row Your Boat.*

UNIT 5 Planning Guide

Lesson	Lesson Title	Suggested Pacing	Create Activities	Materials	
1	**Texture**	45 minutes	Create a mixed-media collage with a variety of textures.	9- x 12-inch stiff paper or cardboard assorted fabrics and paper of varied textures scissors glue	
2	**Tactile Texture**	75 minutes	Design and stitch an appliqué banner.	assorted pieces of colorful felt or other fabric burlap and yarn tapestry needles glue and scissors markers and tape pencils sketch paper music audiotapes from **Art Manipulative Kit**	
3	**Visual Texture**	75 minutes	Draw a still life of shiny objects showing their visual texture.	12- x 18-inch construction paper 9- x 12-inch aluminum foil oil pastels glue scissors shiny still-life objects	
4	**Random Rhythm**	75 minutes	Design wrapping paper using random rhythm.	12- x 18-inch colored construction paper containers of water flat brushes liquid tempera paints sketch paper paper plates paper towels potatoes pencils grapefruit spoons newspaper	
5	**Regular Rhythm**	45 minutes	Design a quilt to illustrate regular rhythm.	6- x 6-inch tagboard 12- x 18-inch colored construction paper scissors glue pencils sketch paper	
6	**Alternating Rhythm**	75 minutes	Design a mural featuring alternating rhythm.	cardboard, pencils, yarn, glue, scissors, and markers 18- x 24-inch colored paper liquid tempera paints toothpicks or craft sticks paintbrushes sketch paper palettes paper towels water containers newspaper	
Artsource Lesson	**Texture and Rhythm in Dance**	75 minutes	Make up movements in response to sounds.	a drum or other musical instrument	

Test preparation activities using the Large Prints *Henry VIII* and *The Hunt of the Unicorn, II, The Unicorn Dips His Horn into the Stream to Rid It of Poison* can be found on pages 24–27 of the Test Preparation Book.

Program Resources (Books)	Art Resources	Literature Resources	*Music Resources
Vocabulary, pp. 49–50 Assessment, pp. 49–50 Art Across the Curriculum Resource Book, pp. 145–150 Technique Tips Flip Chart, p. 25 Lesson Plans Book, p. 26 Home Connection, pp. 13 and 14	Overhead Transparency #25, *Feather Headdress* and *Shirt Section* Artist Profile Book, pp. 69, 70 Large Prints, *Henry VIII* and *The Hunt of the Unicorn*…	1. *It Could Still Be a Rock* (1993) by Alan Fowler includes many textures and forms found in large photographs of objects in nature. 2. *Play with Models* (1995) by Ivan Bulloch is an informative project book for all ages. 3-D crafts are demonstrated in full-color illustrations with simple instructions.	"El Tren," p. T66, CD1:37. "El Tren" is an example of folk music from South America.
Vocabulary, pp. 51–52 Assessment, pp. 51–52 Art Across the Curriculum Resource Book, pp. 151–156 Technique Tips Flip Chart, p. 26 Lesson Plans Book, p. 27	Overhead Transparency #26, *Various Fish* and *Thunderbird Shield* Artist Profile Book, pp. 33, 71 Large Print, *The Hunt of the Unicorn*…	1. *Armadillo Rodeo* (1995) by Jan Brett is highly detailed with textures and patterning and unique borders that exemplify visual texture. 2. *Look! Look! Look!* (1988) by Tana Hoban will help students notice texture and develop their sense of observation through the photographs of familiar objects in this book.	"Pueblo Corn Grinding Song," p. T128, CD3:39. "Pueblo Corn Grinding Song" is an example of Native American music.
Vocabulary, pp. 53–54 Assessment, pp. 53–54 Art Across the Curriculum Resource Book, pp. 157–162 Technique Tips Flip Chart, p. 27 Lesson Plans Book, p. 28	Overhead Transparency #27, *Louis XV as a Child* and *Buddha* Artist Profile Book, pp. 14, 41 Large Prints, *Henry VIII* and *The Hunt of the Unicorn*…	1. *The Lion's Whiskers* (1995) by Nancy Raines Day has collages representing a variety of textured papers and materials composing the pages of this Ethiopian folktale. 2. *Home in the Sky* (1984) by Jeannie Baker will help students grasp the concept of texture by exploring the 3-D quality pages of this original picture book.	"Gugie," from *Sonata for Violin and Continuo,* by Archangelo Corelli, p. T103, CD3:13. "Gigue" is an example of music written during the Baroque period, which lasted from about 1600 to 1750.
Vocabulary, pp. 55–56 Assessment, pp. 55–56 Art Across the Curriculum Resource Book, pp. 163–168 Technique Tips Flip Chart, p. 28 Lesson Plans Book, p. 29	#28, Overhead Transparency *Water Lilies* and *The Telegram, Detention Room, Ellis Island* Artist Profile Book, pp. 34, 51 Large Print, *The Hunt of the Unicorn*…	1. *Swimmey* (1963) by Leo Lionni has watercolor prints showing symmetry, patterns, and balance used in printmaking illustrations. 2. *Printing* (1994) by Ruth Thomson discusses basic printing methods by using large, instructive photographs to demonstrate the creative process of a final project.	"Cortege," by Lili Boulanger, p. T359I, CD9:10. "Cortege" is an example of French music by an early twentieth-century composer whose musical style was similar to Impressionism in painting.
Vocabulary, pp. 57–58 Assessment, pp. 57–58 Art Across the Curriculum Resource Book, pp. 169–174 Technique Tips Flip Chart, p. 29 Lesson Plans Book, p. 30	Overhead Transparency #29, *Double Wedding Ring Quilt* and *Floor Covering Detail* Artist Profile Book, pp. 3, 72 Large Print, *Henry VIII*	1. *Rechenka's Eggs* (1988) by Patricia Polacco has lively text and patterns decorating the minds of viewers in this enchanting folktale filled with contrasting designs. 2. *Koshi and His Magic* (1996) by Maya Angelou has detailed photographs that capture the textures, patterns, sights, and sounds of a West African community while describing a young boy's attempt to weave a kente cloth.	"Grasshoppers Three," by Henry Newbolt, adapted by Ruth Boshkoff, p. T173, CD4:39. "Grasshoppers Three" is an example of bluegrass music.
Vocabulary, pp. 59–60 Assessment, pp. 59–60 Art Across the Curriculum Resource Book, pp. 175–180 Technique Tips Flip Chart, p. 30 Lesson Plans Book, p. 31	Overhead Transparency #30, *Purple Robe and Anemones* and *Parasol* Artist Profile Book, pp. 31, 73 Large Print, *The Hunt of the Unicorn*…	1. *Patterns–Math Counts* (1995) by Henry Pluckrose presents the idea of patterns in large, colorful photographs. 2. *Children of Clay: A Family of Pueblo Potters* (1992) by Rina Swentzell shows that the rhythm of patterns can be expanded upon by learning about the tradition of creating pottery in a family from Santa Clara Pueblo.	"Who Built the Ark?" p. T332, CD8:34. "Who Built the Ark?" is an example of alternating phrases (questions and answers) in music.
	Artsource Performing Arts Audio/Video Resource Package: *Voice/Dance* (videocassette, audiocassette)		

*Music references are from **Share the Music,** Macmillan/McGraw-Hill School Publishers

LESSON PLANNER

Objectives

After completing this lesson, students will be able to:

- identify how texture in an artwork affects the look of color. *Aesthetic Perception*
- plan and create a collage using texture. *Creative Expression*
- use the four steps of art criticism to evaluate their own collages. *Art Criticism*
- compare the use of texture by artists from Peru and Brazil. *Art History and Culture*

Program Resources

- **Overhead:** Both the *Feather Headdress* and the *Shirt Section* are available on overhead 25.
- **Large Prints:** *Henry VIII* by Hans Holbein the Younger and *The Hunt of the Unicorn, II, The Unicorn Dips His Horn into the Stream to Rid It of Poison*
- **Technique Tips Flip Chart,** page 25
- **Vocabulary Book** pages 49–50
- **Art Manipulative Kit:** fabric swatches
- **Artist Profiles Book:** Artists unknown pages 69 and 70
- **Art Across the Curriculum Book** pages 145–150
- **Multimedia Workshop CD-ROM**
- **National Geographic Picture Atlas of the World CD-ROM**
- **Animals Through History Time Line**
- **Assessment Book** pages 49–50

Multiple Intelligences

Verbal/Linguistic Students can use descriptive words to describe textures.

Vocabulary

texture *textura* an element of art that refers to how things feel to the touch or look as if they might feel

FOCUS

Time: About 10 minutes

Activating Prior Knowledge

"Picture someone wearing black socks and shiny black shoes. How does the black of the shoes look different from the black of the socks?"

"Imagínense a alguien usando medias negras y zapatos negros brillantes. ¿En qué se diferencia el negro de los zapatos del negro de las medias?"

- Discuss students' responses to the question. Talk about how the different textures of the shoes and the socks affect the look of the color.

Texture

Artists create texture in their artwork to show how objects might feel if you touched them.

Artist unknown. (Brazil). *Feather Headdress.* Early twentieth century. Reeds, palm-leaf spines, cotton cord, and macaw feathers. $23\frac{1}{4} \times 30\frac{3}{4}$ inches. Courtesy of the Smithsonian National Museum of the American Indian, NY. Collected by Frances Gow-Smith. Photo by David Heald.

Look at the artworks on these pages. The feather headdress from Brazil was made in the early 1900s. It was part of a costume worn in a special ceremony. The colorful shirt was woven in Peru about 1,000 years earlier. Texture is an important element in both works of art. What do you think they would feel like if you could touch them?

ART Background

About the Artists

The specific identities of the artists who created *Feather Headdress* and *Shirt Section* are unknown. *Shirt Section* was woven by an ancient Peruvian artist.

- Have students view the **National Geographic Picture Atlas of the World CD-ROM** to learn more about South American culture.

About Subject Matter* The *Feather Headdress* and the *Shirt Section* are both useful iconographic artworks.

About the Media The *Feather Headdress* is made from a variety of feathers. The *Shirt Section* is made with alpaca wool and cotton. Alpaca is a fine, silky wool from a domesticated South American animal called the alpaca, which is closely related to the llama.

Artist unknown. Coastal Huari (Peru). *Shirt Section.* c. A.D. 600–1000. Alpaca wool and cotton. 21 × 12⅞ inches. The Metropolitan Museum of Art, The Michael C. Rockefeller Memorial Collection, bequest of Nelson A. Rockefeller, 1979, New York, New York.

Study the textures of both works of art.

☑ Look at the yellow-orange areas in both pieces. How do the different textures change the way the color looks?

☑ How do the orange areas in the headdress look different from the orange areas in the shirt?

☑ If you could touch the red in each artwork, in what way would they feel different?

Lesson 1

137

SEEING LIKE AN ARTIST

Look around your classroom. Find objects that are smooth or rough.

Introducing the Art

"Let's take a look at the two artworks."
"Vamos a observar las dos obras de arte."

• **Describe:** Have students describe the subject matter in each artwork. (Both are iconographic.)

• **COMPARE AND CONTRAST** Have students make a list of the similarities and differences in the two artworks. (Both artworks are functional, utilize warm colors, and incorporate real textures. The *Feather Headdress* was designed to wear on the head, has overlapping objects that create a sense of depth, and has regular rhythm in its design. The *Shirt Section* was created to cover the trunk of the body, does not have areas of overlap, and is designed in a random rhythm.)

• Share and discuss information about the lives, work, and times of the artists from **Art Background** and the **Artist Profiles Book.**

• Have students answer the questions about texture on page 137. Discuss the **Animals Through History Time Line**, highlighting information on the the dates of this lesson's artwork. (See **Perception Hints** below.)

FOR THE ART SPECIALIST

Use the **Overhead** and the **Large Prints** *Henry VIII* and *The Hunt of the Unicorn* to demonstrate how artists create texture in their artwork to show how objects might feel if you touched them.

Perception Hints

Smooth *Feather Headdress.* The feathers look smooth in texture.

Rough *Shirt Section.* The entire surface of the woven design looks rough.

Bumpy *Feather Headdress.* The woven headband at the center appears to be bumpy in texture.

Color *Shirt Section* and *Feather Headdress.* The orange color of the feathers in the headdress looks bright. The orange color of the geometric shapes in the *Shirt Section* looks dull. Generally, the orange and red areas look brighter on the smooth surface of the *Feather Headdress* and duller on the rougher textures of the *Shirt Section.*

TEACH

Time: About 30 minutes

Practice

Materials

- found objects of the same color but of different textures

Alternate Materials: liquid tempera paints

"How do different textures change the look of a color?"

"¿Cómo cambian el aspecto de un color las diferentes texturas?"

- Discuss the definition of *texture* on page 138.
- Have students identify and describe a variety of textures.
- Have students follow the directions on page 138 for contrasting textures and the appearance of color. Ask them to answer the Decide question by discussing their responses with a partner.

Create PROBLEM SOLVING

Materials

- 9- × 12-inch stiff paper or cardboard
- assorted fabrics and paper of varied textures
- scissors
- glue

Safety! For safety issues about glue and other information about safety in the art classroom, see page T22.

Alternate Materials: textures cut from magazines

"Let's use a variety of textures to make a collage."

"Vamos a usar una variedad de texturas para hacer un collaje."

- Use simple shapes such as coins, bottle caps, buttons, sticks, straws, or screws.
- Use various textured fabrics such as those found in the **Art Manipulative Kit.**
- See page 25 in the **Technique Tips Flip Chart** for visual examples of techniques.
- Distribute materials and have students follow the directions on page 139.
- Students can paint the entire surface of their collages one color to emphasize texture.

FOR THE ART SPECIALIST

Compare the feather headdress with the headdresses of the American Plains tribes.

Using Texture

Texture is the way the surface of an object feels or *looks* as if it would feel if you could touch it. You saw examples of different textures in the artwork on pages 136–137.

Every surface has a texture. You can feel the texture of an object by touching it.

Furry, bumpy, smooth, and *rough* are just a few of the words that describe texture. Look at the objects below. What words would you use to describe how each object might feel if you touched it?

furry   bumpy   smooth   rough

Textures can also change the way *colors* look. For example, red looks different on a carpet than it does on a shiny new bicycle.

Practice

Compare and contrast the way a color looks on different objects. Use found objects.

1. Find two objects that are about the same color but have different textures. One of the objects should have a rough or bumpy texture. The other object should be smooth.

2. What words describe the texture of each? How does texture affect the look of the color?

Decide What differences do you see in the way the colors look?

Activities in ART Across the Curriculum Book

Reading/Language Arts List words that describe the textures of objects in the classroom, and then make a rubbing of an object with texture. (page 145)

Math Identify shapes in the pattern on the Peruvian shirt, and then create your own shirt showing shapes and textures. (page 146)

Science Learn more about feathers like the ones seen in the *Feather Headdress.* (page 147)

Social Studies Understand how tools are related to different occupations, first thinking about the artists who made the feather headdress. (page 148)

The Arts Describe how you could act out certain textures. (page 149)

Technology Use the *Multimedia Workshop* CD-ROM to create a design filled with patterns that look like textures. (page 150)

Sean Cunningham. Age 8. *The Night in the Mountains.* Felt, woven fabric, white cardboard, a feather, and burlap on black posterboard.

What materials did this student artist use to create a mixed-media collage?

Create

What textures could you use in a collage? Create a mixed-media collage.

1. Think about interesting textures. Collect as many materials as you can that have related colors but different textures.

2. Cut some of your texture samples into simple shapes—such as circles and triangles—of different sizes.

3. Arrange the shapes in different ways. Cut some of your samples, if necessary, to improve your design. Select the best arrangement, filling your entire cardboard with texture. Glue the pieces into place.

Describe Describe the textures of the materials you used.

Analyze How do the different textures change the look of the color?

Interpret Think of words to describe the mood of the collage.

Decide If you could make another multimedia texture collage, what would you do differently?

Lesson 1

139

Discovery Use the artwork as a springboard to discover different textures found in the furnishings of students' homes.

Identity Use the artwork as visual examples to identify how different textures *feel* to the touch and how colors *look* on different textures.

Celebrations Use the artwork to discuss the role that costumes play in special occasions, such as ceremonies and holidays.

ESL students may not have the vocabulary to describe texture. As you are introducing texture, use objects in the classroom to demonstrate what textures the words actually describe. You may wish to involve all students in this introduction by inviting volunteers to find objects in the classroom and pass them around for all students to touch.

CLOSE

Time: About 5 minutes

"How does the texture of material change the look of a color?"

"¿Cómo la textura del material cambia el aspecto de un color?"

Review

Use the **Large Prints** *Henry VIII* and *The Hunt of the Unicorn* to have students compare the use of texture in the print to its use in the works in this lesson.

Art Criticism

Have students answer the four art criticism questions—Describe, Analyze, Interpret, and Decide—orally or in writing. After their collages are dry, discuss how the color is affected by different textures in their artwork.

Assess

Use the **Assessment Book** pages 49–50 as a formal assessment for this lesson.

Evaluation Criteria

• Can the student explain how texture in an artwork affects the look of color?

• Can the student incorporate a variety of textured materials in a creative collage?

• Can the student use the four steps of art criticism to evaluate his or her own work?

• Can the student compare the use of texture by artists from Peru and Brazil?

Reteaching • • • • • • • • • • •

Textures Have students look through the book to find three different works of art that illustrate textures. Ask them to list the title of each work and describe how each of the textures might feel to the touch.

Perception Hints for Student Art

The student used felt, woven fabric, white cardboard circles, a feather, and burlap on black posterboard.

Tactile Texture

Artists may use a variety of tactile textures in their work.

Artist unknown. Absaroke (United States). *Thunderbird Shield.*
c. 1830. Buffalo hide shield with inner cover decorated with
paintings and feathers. Courtesy of the Smithsonian National
Museum of the American Indian, NY. Collected by W. Wildschut.
Photo by David Heald.

Look at the works of art on these pages.
Thunderbird Shield was made more than 100
years before the appliqué. The artist created it to
wear when hunting or fighting and in special
ceremonies. *Various Fish* is a fabric **appliqué**
designed and stitched by Ayako Miyawaki. Both artists
used a number of tactile textures in their work.

140   Unit **5**

LESSON PLANNER

Objectives
After completing this lesson, students will be
able to:
• identify how artists use tactile texture in a
  work of art. *Aesthetic Perception*
• plan and stitch a fabric appliqué using tactile
  texture. *Creative Expression*
• use the four steps of art criticism to evaluate
  their own appliqués. *Art Criticism*
• compare the uses of artwork in Native
  American and Japanese cultures. *Art
  History and Culture*

Program Resources
• **Overhead:** Both the Miyawaki and
  Thunderbird Shield are available on
  overhead 26.
• **Large Print:** *The Hunt of the Unicorn, II,
  The Unicorn Dips His Horn into the Stream to
  Rid It of Poison*
• **Technique Tips Flip Chart,** page 26
• **Vocabulary Book** pages 51–52
• **Art Manipulative Kit:** music audiotapes
• **Artist Profiles Book:** Miyawaki page 33
  and Artist unknown page 71
• **Art Across the Curriculum Book** pages
  151–156
• **Multimedia Workshop CD-ROM**
• **Assessment Book** pages 51–52

Multiple Intelligences
Body/Kinesthetic Students can
comprehend tactile textures as they touch
and feel various surfaces.

Vocabulary
appliqué *aplicación* an art form in which
cutout fabric decorations are fastened to a
larger surface to create a new design

tactile texture *textura táctil* the element of
art that refers to how things actually feel
when you touch them

architect *arquitecto* a person who plans and
designs buildings, cities, and bridges

interior designer *diseñador de interiores* an
artist who designs the insides of buildings and
selects their furnishings, such as carpeting,
furniture, and drapes

ART Background

About the Artists
Ayako Miyawaki (ä ē kō mē yä wä kē, Japanese, 1905–   ) began to make appliqué
works after the end of World War II. Using the fabric from old clothes and rags, she
created her own designs based on objects she observed in nature.

Thunderbird Shield (c. 1830) was created by a member of the Absaroke (Crow) group. The
artist's identity is unknown.

About Subject Matter* *Various Fish* by Miyawaki and the *Thunderbird Shield* are
iconographic.

About the Media *Various Fish* is appliqué. Miyawaki used brightly colored fabrics with
Japanese designs. Sometimes she dyed worn fabric into the vivid colors she liked.

Thunderbird Shield is an artwork made of buffalo hide and feathers.

Ayako Miyawaki. (Japanese). *Various Fish*. 1967. 13 × 11¾ inches. Cotton collage on burlap. The National Museum of Women in the Arts, Washington, DC. Gift of the artist.

Study both artworks to find tactile textures.

✓ Locate the smooth fabrics and the smooth-looking animal skin.

✓ Find the bumpy lines and dots made with string. How would they feel if you could touch them?

✓ Which artwork was made to look at and which was made for a particular function?

SEEING LIKE AN ARTIST

Look through the artwork in this book. Find a work of art that includes real textures.

Lesson 2   **141**

About Art History* *Various Fish* is a fabric appliqué, a popular art form in Japan for many centuries. It characterizes the Japanese appreciation of life and nature.

The *Thunderbird Shield* is characteristic of the highly symbolic art of the Plains people. The war shield was the most sacred and valuable possession of the Plains people. Because their only function was decorative, these shields survive today.

Cultural Perspectives Miyawaki's appliqué was created in postwar Japan when America's influence affected a variety of political, social, and economic reforms that changed Japanese society. For the first time, women were allowed to vote and own property.

The *Thunderbird Shield* was created in the nineteenth century, a time when the Plains people lived in small, nomadic bands that followed the migrating bison, animals that provided meat, bones for tools, and skins for clothing and shelter.

*See **More About** pages 206–227 for more about art history and subject matter.

Time: About 10 minutes

Activating Prior Knowledge

"Imagine walking outside in your bare feet. Why might some textures hurt your feet when you walk on them?"
"Imagínense caminando descalzos afuera. ¿Por qué algunas texturas pudieran hacerles daño a sus pies cuando caminan sobre ellas?"

• Discuss students' responses to the questions and the differences between touching bumpy or rough textures and smooth or silky textures.

Introducing the Art

"Let's take a close look at the two artworks."
"Vamos a observar detalladamente las dos obras de arte."

• **Describe:** Have students describe the subject matter in each artwork. (Both are iconographic.)

• **COMPARE AND CONTRAST** Have students make a list of the similarities and differences in the two artworks. (Both pieces include images found in nature, incorporate found materials, and contain objects stitched in place. Miyawaki's appliqué is made entirely with fibers, is intended to be displayed on the wall, and has a rectangular format. The *Thunderbird Shield* includes painted areas, is functional as well as decorative, and has a circular format.)

• Share and discuss information about the lives, work, and times of the artists from **Art Background** and the **Artist Profiles Book.**

• Have students answer the questions about tactile texture on page 141.
(See **Perception Hints** below.)

FOR THE ART SPECIALIST

Use the **Overhead** and the **Large Print** *The Hunt of the Unicorn* to demonstrate how artists use a variety of tactile textures in their work.

Perception Hints

Smooth textures from nature *Thunderbird Shield*. The shield is made with smooth feathers and a smooth-looking animal skin.

Bumpy stitches *Various Fish*. The lines and dots stitched on the fish look as if they would feel rough or bumpy to the touch.

Artwork to hang *Various Fish*.

Functional artwork *Thunderbird Shield*.

TEACH

Time: About two 30-minute periods

Practice

"Find the different tactile textures in your clothing."
"Encuentren las diferentes texturas táctiles en su ropa."

- Discuss students' responses to the question.
- Ask students to use adjectives to describe various textures.
- Have students follow the directions on page 142 for identifying and describing tactile textures. Ask them to answer the Decide question on a sheet of paper.

Create PROBLEM SOLVING
Materials

- assorted pieces of colorful felt or other fabric
- burlap
- yarn
- tapestry needles
- glue
- scissors
- sketch paper
- pencils
- markers
- tape
- music audiotapes from the **Art Manipulative Kit**

Safety! For safety issues about needles and other information about safety in the art classroom, see page T22.

Alternate Materials: wallpaper

"Let's use different fabrics and stitches to create an appliqué."
"Vamos a usar diferentes telas y puntadas para hacer una aplicación."

- Place a small amount of glue in the middle of each shape and attach it to the burlap.
- See page 26 in the **Technique Tips Flip Chart** for visual examples of techniques.
- Distribute materials and have students follow the directions on page 143.
- Review procedures for creating the running stitch and the satin stitch. Use this to add a decorative border around the edge of each shape.
- Listen to the music audiotapes while students create.

FOR THE ART SPECIALIST

Have the students add found objects to their appliqués to make them even more representative of themselves.

Using Tactile Texture

Tactile texture is the way the surface of an object *actually* feels when you touch it. It is an important element in many forms of art. Tactile textures are often the first things noticed in sculptures, jewelry, and weavings. Textured papers and fabrics make the surface of a drawing more interesting. Materials such as feathers and sand in a painting call attention to the rich variety of textures in our world.

Some artists use appliqué to create tactile texture. **Appliqué** is an art form in which cutout fabrics are attached to a larger surface.

Architects use tactile textures such as wood, brick, glass, and stone in designing buildings.

 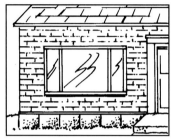

Interior designers use tactile textures in furniture, carpets, and curtains to decorate the inside of a building. What textures are on the outside of the building where you live? What textures do you have in your bedroom or kitchen?

Practice

Look carefully at tactile textures in your clothing.

1. Find different textures in your clothing.
2. Describe how each texture feels when you touch it.

Decide What words come to mind when you touch each object?

Activities in ART Across the Curriculum Book

Reading/Language Arts Describe something you were proud of. (page 151)
Math Estimate measurement of cloth to cover objects in the classroom. (page 152)
Science Identify textures of objects in the classroom and outside, then identify whether texture is for a purpose or decoration. (page 153)
Social Studies Understand how artists use materials from their environments in their artwork. (page 154)
The Arts Create a celebration dance. (page 155)
Technology Use the *Multimedia Workshop* CD-ROM to create a design that looks like an appliqué. (page 156)

Tawny Kern. Age 8. *All About Me*. Burlap and marker.

What does this appliqué banner tell you about the student artist?

Create

What symbol would you choose to represent yourself? Design and stitch an appliqué banner.

1. Think about symbols that represent you. Make several sketches.

2. Choose your best sketch as a model. Cut out shapes from colorful fabric. Arrange them onto a piece of burlap.

3. Attach shapes using glue. Stitch around the edges of each shape and add details with marker.

Lesson 2

Describe Name the different materials and tactile textures in your artwork. Describe how the textures feel when you touch them.

Analyze How did you organize the shapes on your banner?

Interpret How do the shapes in the banner represent you?

Decide What do you like best about your artwork?

143

Discovery Use Miyawaki's piece as a springboard to discuss different bodies of water and the objects found in each.

Cultures Use the works of art as visual examples of how nature is a source of inspiration for artists from different cultures.

Patterns Use the artwork as a springboard to discuss patterns such as tactile opposites such as *smooth* and *rough*.

ESL

You may wish to use this lesson to focus on vocabulary development for all your students. Create a list to describe the textures of clothing mentioned in the Practice portion of the student book. Then, make a corresponding list of descriptive words relating to that texture. Encourage ESL students to use the chart when describing their appliqué banner.

CLOSE

Time: About 5 minutes

"What kinds of textures can artists use in their work?"
"¿Qué tipos de texturas pueden usar los artistas en sus obras?"

Review
Display the students' banners and have them compare the textures with each others' and with the works in this lesson.

Art Criticism
Have students answer the four art criticism questions—Describe, Analyze, Interpret, and Decide—orally or in writing. Discuss the use of tactile textures in their fabric appliqués.

Assess
Use the **Assessment Book** pages 51–52 as a formal assessment for this lesson.

Evaluation Criteria
• Can the student identify and describe tactile textures in a work of art?
• Can the student incorporate a variety of textures in a creative fabric appliqué?
• Can the student use the four steps of art criticism to evaluate his or her own work?
• Can the student compare the uses of artwork in Native American and Japanese cultures?

Reteaching • • • • • • • • • • •

Tactile textures Make a paper appliqué. Create tactile textures by manipulating the paper—for instance, fold, pierce, crinkle, or curl it.

Perception Hints for Student Art
This student artist probably likes to sing and likes flowers.

LESSON PLANNER

Objectives

After completing this lesson, students will be able to:

- identify the difference between tactile texture and visual texture. *Aesthetic Perception*
- plan and create a still-life drawing with visual texture. *Creative Expression*
- use the four steps of art criticism to evaluate their own drawings. *Art Criticism*
- compare works by artists from different cultures and how they use visual textures in their artwork. *Art History and Culture*

Program Resources

- **Overhead:** Both the Rigaud and the Flack are available on overhead 27.
- **Large Prints:** *Henry VIII* by Hans Holbein the Younger and *The Hunt of the Unicorn, II, The Unicorn Dips His Horn into the Stream to Rid It of Poison*
- **Technique Tips Flip Chart,** page 27
- **Vocabulary Book** pages 53–54
- **Art Manipulative Kit:** flash cards
- **Artist Profiles Book:** Rigaud page 41 and Flack page 14
- **Art Across the Curriculum Book** pages 157–162
- **Multimedia Workshop CD-ROM**
- **National Geographic Picture Atlas of the World CD-ROM**
- **National Museum of Women in the Arts Collection:** cards
- **Assessment Book** pages 53–54

Multiple Intelligences

Visual/Spatial Students can understand visual textures through looking.

Vocabulary

visual texture *textura visual* the illusion of a three-dimensional surface based on the memory of how things feel

highlights *claros* small areas of white used to show the very brightest spots on an object

---

Visual Texture

Artists can create visual texture in their work.

Audrey Flack (American). *Buddha.* 1975. Airbrushed acrylic over polymer emulsion on canvas. 70 × 96 inches. Purchase: Contemporary Art Society and Tax Funds, The Saint Louis Art Museum, St. Louis, Missouri.

Study the paintings on these pages. Artist Audrey Flack's *Buddha* is a still-life painting that looks as real as a photograph. See how she makes the beads appear to shine. The portrait of King Louis XV was painted by Hyacinthe Rigaud 260 years earlier. He is best known for painting people in the royal court in France. Notice how he has created the visual texture of fur.

ART Background

About the Artists

Hyacinthe Rigaud (ē ä sant' rē gō, French, 1659–1743) was one of the most successful portrait painters during the reign of Louis XIV. He was almost exclusively a court artist because of the success of a portrait he painted of the king's brother.

Audrey Flack (ô' drē flak, American, 1931–   ) paints a photo-realistic picture. Her still-life compositions are filled with contemporary objects, as well as images from the old masters. After she has assembled a still life, she takes a slide of it with her camera, projects the photograph onto a canvas, and then paints over the image with an airbrush.

- Use the cards from the **National Museum of Women in the Arts Collection** to identify other portrait painters.

About Subject Matter* The Rigaud painting is a portrait, and the Flack painting is a still life.

Hyacinthe Rigaud. (French).
Portrait of Louis XV as a Child. 1715.
Oil on canvas. 1.89 × 1.35 meters.
Giraudon/Art Resource, New York,
New York.

Look closely at both paintings to find visual textures.

- ✓ Find the textures that look smooth.
- ✓ Where are the furry-looking textures?
- ✓ Find the bumpy textures and shiny objects.

SEEING LIKE
AN ARTIST

Find the shiniest object
in your classroom.
What makes it look so
shiny?

Lesson **3**   **145**

About the Media Rigaud's *Louis XV as a Child* is an oil painting. The Flack is an acrylic painting.

About Art History* Rigaud's painting was created during a time when French palaces were decorated to glorify the power and grandeur of the king.

Flack's painting was created in the 1970s, when photo-realism flourished in the American art world. Artists who painted in this style usually specialized in one subject.

Cultural Perspectives Rigaud's *Louis XV as a Child* was created in France during the last year of Louis XIV's life. His love of power led him into endless wars.

Flack's painting was created in 1975, when Americans were preparing for the Bicentennial, the 200th anniversary of the nation's independence, in 1976.

*See **More About** pages 206–227 for more about art history and subject matter.

FOCUS

Time: About 10 minutes

Activating Prior Knowledge

"Suppose that you are looking at a photograph of yourself. Can you actually feel the different textures of your hair and clothes? How?"

"Vamos a suponer que están viendo una fotografía de ustedes. ¿Pueden en realidad sentir las diferentes texturas de sus cabellos y de su ropa? ¿Cómo?"

- Discuss students' answers. Point out that, even though a photograph feels smooth, textures can be identified because of previous experience.

Introducing the Art

"Let's take a close look at the two paintings."

"Vamos a observar detalladamente las dos pinturas."

- **Describe:** Have students describe the subject matter in each painting. (Rigaud: portrait; Flack: still life)
- **COMPARE AND CONTRAST** Have students make a list of the similarities and differences in the two paintings. (Both paintings are indoor scenes, show depth, and are realistic in style. Rigaud's painting includes a person, emphasizes a single subject, and illustrates a variety of visual textures. Flack's painting does not include any people, emphasizes a variety of objects, and illustrates shiny texture only.)
- Share and discuss information about the lives, work, and times of the artists from **Art Background** and the **Artist Profiles Book.**
- Have students answer the questions about visual texture on page 145. (See **Perception Hints** below.)

FOR THE ART SPECIALIST

Use the **Overhead** and the **Large Prints** *Henry VIII* and *The Hunt of the Unicorn* to demonstrate how artists can create visual texture in their work.

Perception Hints

Smooth textures *Flack.* The red glass bottle and the green ribbon have smooth textures.

Shiny textures *Flack.* The cherub figurine and the strands of pearls have textures that are bumpy and shiny.

Furry textures *Rigaud.* The white ermine robe has a furry texture.

TEACH

Time: About two 30-minute periods

Practice

Materials

- one sheet of 9- × 12-inch paper
- pencils
- textured objects

Alternate Materials: crayons

"How can you create visual texture of an actual object?"
"¿Cómo pueden crear la textura visual de un objeto real?"

- Discuss ways to create visual textures by making a rubbing. Use the flash cards from the **Art Manipulative Kit** to further discuss visual texture.

- Distribute materials and have students follow the directions on page 146 for illustrating visual texture. Ask them to answer the Decide question on the back of their paper.

Create PROBLEM SOLVING

Materials

- 12- × 18-inch construction paper
- 9- × 12-inch aluminum foil
- oil pastels
- glue
- scissors
- shiny still-life objects

Alternate Materials: colored pencils

Safety! For safety issues regarding oil pastels and other information about safety in the art classroom, see page T22.

"Let's use foil and oil pastels to draw a still life that shows shiny texture."
"Vamos a usar estaño y pinturas pasteles al óleo para dibujar una naturaleza muerta que muestre una textura brillante."

- Have students discuss the importance of light in visual texture that is shiny.

- Review ways to blend oil pastels in **More About Technique Tips** on page 197.

- See page 27 in the **Technique Tips Flip Chart** for visual examples of techniques.

- Distribute materials. After students have set up a still life, turn out the lights so that only natural light is reflected on the objects.

- Have students follow the directions on page 147.

FOR THE ART SPECIALIST

Have students use charcoal to add another visual texture to their still lifes.

Using Visual Texture

Visual texture is texture you see with your eyes.

Rub the surface of the pictures below with your fingers. You cannot actually feel the different textures. You feel the smoothness of the paper instead.

If you have felt these textures before, you probably remember how they feel. Your eyes "see" the textures even though you cannot actually feel them. This is called visual texture.

Artists show shiny surfaces by using highlights. **Highlights** are small areas of white used to show the very brightest spots on an object.

Practice

Make a rubbing of a texture to illustrate visual texture. Use pencil.

1. Find an example of texture in your classroom.

2. Place a piece of paper on top of the object. Use the side of a pencil to rub the surface of the paper to create visual texture.

Decide What lines, shapes, or values help you see the texture of the object on your paper?

Activities in
ART Across the Curriculum Book

Reading/Language Arts Write a short story about what might happen next in the painting *Louis XV as a Child*. (page 157)

Math Learn about Roman numerals, as seen in the title *Louis XV as a Child*. (page 158)

Science Understand the difference between reflection and refraction. (page 159)

Social Studies Describe how rules and laws are made in the United States. (page 160)

The Arts Learn how musical texture can describe a particular scene. (page 161)

Technology Use the *Multimedia Workshop* CD-ROM to create a still life with a variety of visual textures. (page 162)

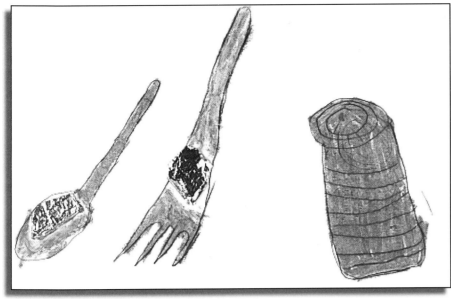

Trina Clemens. Age 8. *Shiny*. Mixed-media.

How did this student artist show visual texture?

Create

What shiny objects can you think of? Draw a still life of shiny objects showing their visual textures.

1. Think about shiny objects of different shapes and sizes. Work in small groups to collect and arrange them into a still life.

2. Draw the still life you arranged. Make the shapes large.

3. Look for the brightest parts. Glue pieces of aluminum foil onto the shapes that you drew to show where the brightest parts are.

4. Color the rest of the shapes with oil pastels.

Describe What objects did you use for your still life?

Analyze How did you use shiny visual texture in your drawing?

Interpret What is the mood or feeling of this drawing? How would the feeling change if you took out the highlights and shadows?

Decide If you could do this artwork over again, what would you do differently?

Lesson 3 147

Discovery Use Rigaud's painting as a springboard to discover how facial expressions and assorted objects communicate information about the person in a portrait.

Identify Use Flack's painting to have students identify objects that are functional and objects that are decorative.

Connections Use Rigaud's painting to discuss portraiture as a career in the visual arts.

ESL

The group still-life project is an especially supportive way for ESL students to feel that they are a productive part of the class. Prepare all children to appreciate each individual's strengths and weaknesses, especially as these pertain to language development. ESL students can learn a great deal from peers, but only if the relationship is based on trust and supportive interaction.

CLOSE

Time: About 5 minutes

"How do artists use visual texture to create a sense of touch in their paintings?"

"¿Cómo los artistas usan la textura visual para crear una sensación táctil en sus pinturas?"

Review

Use the **Large Prints** *Henry VIII* and *The Hunt of the Unicorn* to have students compare visual texture in the print to its use in the works in this lesson. Use the **National Geographic Picture Atlas of the World CD–ROM** to learn more about the cultures of this lesson's artists.

Art Criticism

Have students answer the four art criticism questions—Describe, Analyze, Interpret, and Decide—orally or in writing. Discuss the use of visual texture in their drawings.

Assess

Use the **Assessment Book** pages 53–54 as a formal assessment for this lesson.

Evaluation Criteria

- Can the student describe the difference between tactile texture and visual texture by comparing the works of Flack and Rigaud?
- Can the student create visual texture in a unique still life?
- Can the student use the four steps of art criticism to evaluate his or her own work?
- Can the student compare works by artists from different cultures and how they use visual textures in their artwork?

Reteaching • • • • • • • • • •

Visual texture Have students look through their textbooks to find five different works of art that illustrate visual texture. Ask them to list the title of each work and describe the textures found in each.

Perception Hints for Student Art

This student artist shows visual texture by adding foil where she saw highlights.

UNIT 5
LESSON 4

LESSON PLANNER

Objectives

After completing this lesson, students will be able to:

- discover how artists use random rhythm in a work of art. *Aesthetic Perception*
- plan and create a print using random rhythm. *Creative Expression*
- use the four steps of art criticism to evaluate their own prints. *Art Criticism*
- describe how the artworks of Monet and Walter are similar or different. *Art History and Culture*

Program Resources

- **Overhead:** Both the Monet and the Walter are available on overhead 28.
- **Large Print:** *The Hunt of the Unicorn, II, The Unicorn Dips his Horn into the Stream to Rid It of Poison*
- **Technique Tips Flip Chart,** page 28
- **Vocabulary Book** pages 55–56
- **Art Manipulative Kit:** music audiotapes
- **Artist Profiles Book:** Monet page 34 and Walter page 51
- **Art Across the Curriculum Book** pages 163–168
- **Multimedia Workshop CD-ROM**
- **National Geographic Picture Atlas of the World CD-ROM**
- **National Museum of Women in the Arts Collection:** prints
- **Assessment Book** pages 55–56

Multiple Intelligences
Musical/Rhythmic Students can relate the random rhythm in art to that used in a song they like.

Vocabulary

motif *motivo* a shape or an object that is repeated

random rhythm *ritmo aleatorio* visual rhythm in which a motif is repeated in no apparent order, with no regular spaces

visual rhythm *ritmo visual* rhythm created by the repetition of shapes, colors, or lines

regular rhythm *ritmo regular* visual rhythm that is created by repeating the same motif with equal amounts of space in between

---

Random Rhythm

Artists use random rhythm to create a feeling of movement in their work.

Oscar Claude Monet. (French). *Water Lilies.* 1905. Oil on canvas. $35\frac{1}{4} \times 39\frac{1}{2}$ inches. Museum of Fine Arts, Gift of Jackson Holmes, Boston, Massachusetts.

Compare the paintings on these pages. Claude Monet painted water lilies growing in his garden. Martha Walter painted a scene showing people from other countries who had just arrived in the United States around 1922. Both artists used random rhythms in the design of their work.

ART Background

About the Artists

Claude Monet (klōd mō nā′, French, 1840–1926) was one of the first artists to take his canvases outside. He realized that colors of a subject changed as the day progressed. He worked on many canvases at a time, recording the subject at different times of the day.

- Have students use the **National Geographic Picture Atlas of the World CD-ROM** to learn more about France.

Martha Walter (mär thə wôl′ tər, American, 1875–1976) was born in Philadelphia. She studied at the Pennsylvania Academy of Fine Arts where she was introduced to impressionism. By 1912, she had become famous for her beach scenes. Walter painted into her 90s.

About Subject Matter* *Water Lilies* is a landscape, and *The Telegram, Detention Room, Ellis Island* is a genre painting. Find other genre paintings in prints from the **National Museum of Women in the Arts Collection.**

Martha Walter. (American). *The Telegram, Detention Room, Ellis Island.* 1922. Oil on panel. 14 × 18 inches. The National Museum of Women in the Arts, Washington, DC. Gift of Jacques S. Zinman.

Study each painting to find the following elements of rhythm.

☑ Which work has colors that are repeated?

☑ Find the shapes that are repeated.

☑ How are textures used in each artwork?

SEEING LIKE AN ARTIST

Look around the room. Find objects that are repeated.

Lesson **4**   **149**

About the Media *Water Lilies* and *The Telegram, Detention Room, Ellis Island* are both oil paintings. Oil is a slow-drying medium that comes in lush colors.

About Art History* Monet's painting was done during the Impressionist movement when artists departed from tradition and illustrated changes in light and color.

Walter was an American Impressionist. She focused on capturing impressions of a moment.

Cultural Perspectives Monet painted during a time when French artists wanted freedom from the old styles and strict rules for creating artwork.

Walter dropped out of art school in Paris because she felt it restricted her ideas too much. She then set up her own art studio in France. She was joined by many other young American women artists who were studying art abroad.

*See **More About** pages 206–227 for more about art history and subject matter.

Activating Prior Knowledge

"Think about leaves falling from a tree. Do they fall from the tree or land on the ground in any particular order?"

"Piensen acerca de las hojas que caen de un árbol. ¿Caen desde el árbol o caen encima de la tierra en cualquier orden?"

• Discuss students' responses and how the leaves fall and land at random.

Introducing the Art

"Let's take a close look at the two paintings."

"Vamos a observar detalladamente las dos pinturas."

• **Describe:** Have students describe the subject matter in each painting. (Monet: landscape; Walter: genre)

• **COMPARE AND CONTRAST** Have students make a list of the similarities and differences in the two paintings. (Both paintings have oval shapes, create an illusion of depth by using overlapping shapes, and create a feeling of movement through random rhythm. Monet's painting illustrates recognizable objects, is an outdoor scene, and has large areas of negative space. Walter's painting is an indoor scene, emphasizes color rather than objects, and has small areas of negative space.)

• Share and discuss information about the lives, work, and times of the artists from **Art Background** and the **Artist Profiles Book.**

• Have students answer the questions about random rhythm on page 149.

(See **Perception Hints** below.)

FOR THE ART SPECIALIST

Use the **Overhead** and the **Large Print** *The Hunt of the Unicorn* to demonstrate the use random rhythm to create a feeling of movement in their work.

Perception Hints

Repeated colors *Monet.* Rhythm is created by the frequent repetition of the green of the lily pads and the pink of the flowers. *Walter.* Red, blue, black, and white are repeated.

Repeated shapes *Monet.* The free-form shapes in the leaves and flowers are repeated. *Walter.* The free-form shapes of the people and the geometric columns are repeated.

Textures *Monet* and *Walter.* In each work, the textures are repeated at irregular intervals, creating random rhythm.

TEACH

Time: About two 30-minute periods

Practice

Materials
- 6- × 9-inch colored construction paper • scissors
- 9- × 12-inch construction paper of another color

Alternate Materials: liquid tempera paints

"How can you create random rhythm with cut-paper shapes?"

"¿Cómo pueden crear ritmo aleatorio con figuras de papel cortadas?"

- Discuss the definition of *random rhythm* on page 150.
- Have students follow the directions on page 150 for illustrating random rhythm. Ask them to answer the Decide questions with a partner.

Create PROBLEM SOLVING

Materials
- 12- × 18-inch colored construction paper
- liquid tempera paints • grapefruit spoons
- containers of water • flat brushes
- potatoes • paper plates • pencils
- paper towels • sketch paper • newspaper

Alternate Materials: modeling clay

"Let's print a variety of shapes to create random rhythm."

"Vamos a estampar una variedad de figuras para crear ritmo aleatorio."

- Review ways to create random rhythm.
- Review procedures for stamp printing in **More About Technique Tips** on page 201.
- See page 28 in the **Technique Tips Flip Chart** for visual examples of techniques.
- Cut the potatoes in half for the students.
- Use grapefruit spoons or paper clips to cut away the potato.
- Brush paint onto the carved potato. The stamp can be used several times before adding paint again to create different values.
- Have students follow the directions on page 151 while listening to the music audiotapes from the **Art Manipulative Kit.**

FOR THE ART SPECIALIST

Hang craft paper in the classroom on which all students can stamp their designs using random rhythm.

Using Rhythm

We hear rhythm when sounds such as water dripping and hands clapping are repeated over and over. Rhythm can also be seen. Several children walking in line is an example of rhythm that can be seen. In artwork, shapes are repeated to create rhythm.

Visual rhythm is the feeling of movement created when artists repeat colors, shapes, lines, and textures. Your eyes move along their artwork, following the parts that are repeated. Each shape or object that is repeated is called a **motif**. In *Water Lilies,* the lily is a motif.

Random rhythm is created when a motif is repeated but in no particular order. For example, if you dropped a handful of crayons onto the floor, they would land pointing in all directions. This would show random rhythm.

Crayons lined up in their box are in a particular order. This shows **regular rhythm**.

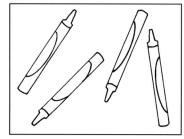 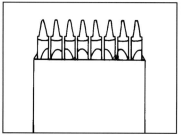

Practice

Demonstrate random rhythm. Use colored paper.

1. Cut a sheet of colored paper into many small pieces of the same shape.

2. Sprinkle the pieces on a large piece of colored paper. Try this several times.

Decide What is the motif in each design? In what order did the shapes land? Is the space between them always the same?

Activities in ART Across the Curriculum Book

Reading/Language Arts Write a poem about a flower. (page 163)

Math Understand how rhythm and patterns allow predictions to be made. (page 164)

Science Learn about the needs and environments that different plants need in order to grow, looking at Claude Monet's water lilies as an example. (page 165)

Social Studies Work with a group of classmates to list some concerns about the environment. (page 166)

The Arts Understand how rhythm and motifs are used in music, in comparison to works of art. (page 167)

Technology Use the *Multimedia Workshop* CD-ROM to create a design with random rhythm. (page 168)

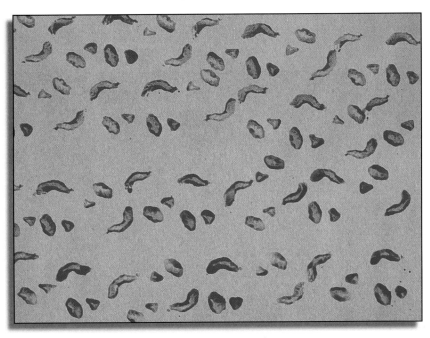

Sonnie Kroen. Age 8. *Kitchen Wallpaper.* Tempera paint.

How did this student artist create random rhythm?

Create

How can you use random rhythm to make wrapping paper? Design wrapping paper using random rhythm.

1. Think about a motif for your design. Make several sketches and choose your favorite.

2. Make a stamp of your design using half of a potato and a grapefruit spoon. Use random rhythm to print your motif on paper.

Describe What is your motif?

Analyze How did you create random rhythm? Can you clap out the rhythm of the motif with your hands?

Interpret Is the rhythm you used more like the one in Monet's painting or Walter's? How can you tell?

Decide Were you successful in creating a regular rhythm?

Lesson **4**   **151**

Patterns Use Monet's painting to discuss patterns of shapes and colors.

Relationships Use both paintings to discuss relationships between the plants' and the immigrants' needs.

Change Use Monet's painting to talk about how changing daylight affects the artist's work.

ESL

When conducting the introduction to rhythm in art, you should use as many real-life examples as possible. For example, clap a rhythm, ask students to place their hands on their hearts to feel the rhythm, and point to the repeating water lilies and ovals in the artwork as you describe motif. You may wish to demonstrate dropping crayons to demonstrate random rhythm and lining them up in a box to demonstrate regular rhythm.

CLOSE

Time: About 5 minutes

"How can you recognize random rhythm in a work of art?"
"¿Cómo pueden reconocer el ritmo aleatorio en una obra de arte?"

Review

Display the students' stamp prints and compare random rhythm in the prints to its use in the works in this lesson.

Art Criticism

Have students answer the four art criticism questions—Describe, Analyze, Interpret, and Decide—orally or in writing. Discuss the use of random rhythm in their artwork after the paint has dried.

Assess

Use the **Assessment Book** pages 55–56 as a formal assessment for this lesson.

Evaluation Criteria

• Can the student describe how artists use random rhythm in a work of art?

• Can the student create random rhythm in a print expressive of his or her own individuality?

• Can the student use the four steps of art criticism to evaluate his or her own work?

• Can the student tell how artworks of Monet and Walter are similar and different?

Reteaching • • • • • • • • • • •

Random rhythm Have students look outside to find five examples of random rhythm in nature. Ask them to list the examples, identify the motif, and describe the random rhythm that is seen in each.

Perception Hints for Student Art

This student artist used the same stamp motif in no particular order.

LESSON PLANNER

Objectives

After completing this lesson, students will be able to:

- describe how regular rhythm is used by artists to create a feeling of movement. *Aesthetic Perception*
- plan and create a quilt using regular rhythm. *Creative Expression*
- use the four steps of art criticism to evaluate their own artwork. *Art Criticism*
- compare and contrast an American quilt and a Turkish floor design. *Art History and Culture*

Program Resources

- **Overhead:** Both the Byler and *Floor Covering Detail* are available on overhead 29.
- **Large Print:** *Henry VIII* by Hans Holbein the Younger
- **Technique Tips Flip Chart,** page 29
- **Vocabulary Book** pages 57–58
- **Art Manipulative Kit:** dragonfly's eye
- **Artist Profiles Book:** Byler page 3 and Artist unknown page 72
- **Art Across the Curriculum Book** pages 169–174
- **Multimedia Workshop CD-ROM**
- **National Museum of Women in the Arts Collection:** cards
- **Assessment Book** pages 57–58

Multiple Intelligences

Logical/Mathematical Students can explore regular rhythm by using repeated abstract patterns.

Vocabulary

regular rhythm *ritmo regular* visual rhythm achieved through repeating identical motifs that are separated by the same intervals of space

motif *motivo* a shape or an object that is repeated

Regular Rhythm

Artists use regular rhythm to create a feeling of movement and order in their artwork.

Mrs. Andy G. Byler. (American). *Double Wedding Ring Quilt*. c. 1930–1940. Cotton, wool, linen, and rayon. 84 × 66⅙ inches. From the permanent collection of the Museum of American Folk Art, New York, New York. Gift of Mrs. Andy G. Byler.

Look at the textile art on these pages. The *Double Wedding Ring Quilt* was made by sewing colorful scraps of cloth together with decorative stitches. The Ottoman floor covering was woven in the late 1500s, 350 years before the quilt. Regular rhythm was used in the design of both pieces.

ART Background

About the Artists

Mrs. Andy G. Byler (än' dē bī lər, American) created the *Double Wedding Ring Quilt* from a mass-produced kit. In 1932, the *Double Wedding Ring Quilt* kit sold for $3.95. The *Double Wedding Ring Quilt* was one of the most popular patterns in the Depression era.

- Use the cards from the **National Museum of Women in the Arts Collection** to identify other artists who created an artwork for a functional purpose.

The specific identity of the artist who created *Floor Covering Detail* is unknown. The work is an example of the large naturalistic designs of leaves and flowers characteristic of Turkish court carpets.

About Subject Matter* The *Double Wedding Ring Quilt* is a nonobjective design, and *Floor Covering Detail* is a floral design.

Artist unknown.
(Turkish). *Floor Covering* (Detail). Second half of sixteenth century. 16 feet 1 inch × 8 feet 9½ inches. Velvet. Photograph © 1996 Detroit Institute of Arts, Gift of Edsel B. Ford, Detroit, Michigan.

Examine both textiles to find examples of regular rhythm.

✓ Find the shapes that are repeated over and over again. About how much space is between them?

✓ Which colors are repeated?

✓ Find negative or empty spaces that have been repeated. Find negative spaces that are about the same size and shape.

Lesson 5   153

SEEING LIKE AN ARTIST

Look at clothes and other fabrics in your classroom. Find repeated shapes, lines, colors, or textures in them that are spaced evenly apart.

About the Media The *Double Wedding Ring Quilt* is made from cotton fabric, and *Floor Covering Detail* is made of velvet.

About Art History* The *Double Wedding Ring Quilt* was created in the 1930s during the Ragtime and Jazz era of American music.

Bursa, the former Ottoman capital, was the possible manufacturing center of Turkish Ottoman rugs. These rugs were made only during the late sixteenth and seventeenth centuries.

Cultural Perspectives The *Double Wedding Ring Quilt* was created during the Great Depression when vast numbers of unemployed Americans lived in "towns" of tents.

The *Floor Covering Detail* was created during a period of extravagance, when the Ottoman Empire reached its height under Sultan Suleiman I.

*See **More About** pages 206–227 for more about art history and subject matter.

FOCUS

Time: About 10 minutes

Activating Prior Knowledge

"Imagine that you can hear a clock tick. Clap hands to the rhythm it makes. How would you describe the rhythm?"

"Imagínense que pueden oir el tictac de un reloj. Aplaudan al ritmo que hace. ¿Cómo describirían el ritmo?"

• Discuss students' responses and how a sound repeated at regular intervals creates a regular rhythm.

Introducing the Art

"Let's take a close look at the two artworks."

"Vamos a observar detalladamente las dos obras de arte."

• **Describe:** Have students describe the subject matter in each artwork. (Byler: nonobjective; *Floor Covering Detail:* floral design)

• **COMPARE AND CONTRAST** Have students make a list of the similarities and differences in the two artworks. (Both pieces are made from natural fibers, are functional, and repeat motifs in a regular pattern. The quilt has geometric shapes, uses many colors, and was made to be used on the bed. The carpet has free-form shapes, uses three colors only, and was made to be placed on the floor.)

• Share and discuss information about the lives, work, and times of the artists from **Art Background** and the **Artist Profiles Book.**

• Have students answer the questions about regular rhythm on page 153. (See **Perception Hints** below.)

 FOR THE ART SPECIALIST

Use the **Overhead** and the dragonfly's eye from the **Art Manipulative Kit** to demonstrate how artists use regular rhythm to create a feeling of movement and order in their artwork.

Perception Hints

Shapes and space *Floor Covering.* There are equal amounts of space between the ring shapes. *Double Wedding Ring Quilt.* Black negative spaces are also repeated in equal amounts throughout the quilt between the ring shapes.

Repeated colors In *Floor Covering,* the colors red, white, and blue are repeated and are placed evenly throughout the piece.

TEACH

Time: About 30 minutes

Practice

Materials

- 9- × 12-inch paper folded into six boxes
- pencils or markers

Alternate Materials: liquid tempera paints

"How can you illustrate regular rhythm?"

"¿Cómo pueden ilustrar el ritmo regular?"

- Discuss how to create regular rhythm with shapes.
- Distribute materials and have students follow the directions on page 154 for illustrating regular rhythm. Ask them to answer the Decide questions on the back.

Create PROBLEM SOLVING

Materials

- 6- × 6-inch tagboard
- 12- × 18-inch colored construction paper
- scissors
- glue
- pencils
- sketch paper

Alternate Materials: cardboard relief prints

"Let's repeat paper shapes to create regular rhythm in a quilt."

"Vamos a repetir las figuras de papel para crear el ritmo regular en una colcha."

- Have students brainstorm a variety of objects seen in nature.
- Review the definition of *regular rhythm*.

 See page 29 in the **Technique Tips Flip Chart** for visual examples of techniques.

- Distribute materials and have students follow the directions on page 155.

FOR THE ART SPECIALIST

Give a more in-depth look at the art from the Ottoman Empire. Compare and contrast repetition used in a variety of media.

Using Regular Rhythm

Regular rhythm is visual rhythm that is created by repeating the same motif with equal amounts of space in between. Regular rhythm is used to arrange things in an orderly way. Boxes and cans are usually placed in neat rows on shelves in grocery stores. This makes it easier to find what you are looking for. Parking spaces are arranged in regular rhythms, too. What would happen if people parked their cars wherever they wanted?

Artists sometimes use regular rhythm in their work, as well. Regular rhythm helps to organize motifs. A **motif** is a shape or an object that is repeated. For example, architects use regular rhythm to arrange windows in tall buildings.

Look at the drawing below. Name the motif. Why is it an example of regular rhythm?

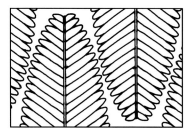

Practice

Illustrate regular rhythm. Use pencil or a marker in one color.

1. Fold a sheet of paper into six equal boxes. In the middle of the first box, draw a large geometric shape. Or you can write large and print a letter of the alphabet.

2. Draw exactly the same motif in each of the other boxes to create regular rhythm. Put equal amounts of space in between each letter or shape.

Decide Does the motif look the same in each box? Are there equal amounts of space between each one?

Activities in ART Across the Curriculum Book

Reading/Language Arts Use an encyclopedia to find information about different topics, such as the Turkish Ottoman Dynasty. (page 169)

Math Determine how much material is needed for a quilt maker and a rug maker by solving word problems. (page 170)

Science Learn more about the materials that make up the artworks. (page 171)

Social Studies Describe things that you would put into a time capsule. (page 172)

The Arts Create a march, recognizing how marches show regular rhythm with a regular beat and equal spacing between rows. (page 173)

Technology Use the *Multimedia Workshop* CD-ROM to create a design with regular rhythm. (page 174)

Fidel Gomez. Age 8. Construction paper.

What could you add to this student artist's design so that the design would still show regular rhythm?

Create

What objects would you choose to design a quilt? Design a quilt to illustrate regular rhythm.

1. Think about objects like those you see in nature. Select a few and make a rough sketch of each. Choose one as a motif.

2. Draw an outline of the object on stiff paper and cut it out. On colored paper, trace your motif six times. Cut out the shapes.

3. Fold a large sheet of paper into six boxes. Open it up. Glue a shape into each box. Remember to use equal amounts of space between the shapes.

4. Use colored scraps to add details to your motif in every other box.

Describe What object did you use for your motif? What colors did you repeat?

Analyze How did you create regular rhythm?

Interpret Explain what this motif means to you. Did repeating the motif change its meaning or the feeling of it? In what ways?

Decide If you could redo this collage, what parts would you change?

Lesson 5 155

Change Use the *Double Wedding Ring Quilt* as a springboard to discuss quilting bees as a means for early American women to socialize and communicate.

Origins Use the artworks as examples of the origins of crafts that are still being done today.

Traditions Use the *Double Wedding Ring Quilt* to discuss traditions within students' own cultures.

ESL students may feel shy or hesitant to answer the interpretive question about their artwork. You may wish to phrase the question as an either/or choice so that the vocabulary needed to answer the question is contained in the question itself.

CLOSE

Time: About 5 minutes

"What makes regular rhythm different from random rhythm?"

"¿En qué se diferencia el ritmo regular del ritmo aleatorio?"

 Review
Use the **Large Print** *Henry VIII* to have students identify the motif and compare the use of regular rhythm to the works in this lesson.

Art Criticism
Have students answer the four art criticism questions—Describe, Analyze, Interpret, and Decide—orally or in writing. Discuss the use of regular rhythm in their collages.

Assess
Use the **Assessment Book** pages 57–58 as a formal assessment for this lesson.

Evaluation Criteria
• Can the student describe regular rhythm as used by the artists?
• Can the student illustrate regular rhythm in an interesting quilt?
• Can the student use the four steps of art criticism to evaluate his or her own work?
• Can the student compare and contrast rhythm in the American quilt and the Turkish floor design?

Reteaching • • • • • • • • • • • •

Regular rhythm Have students look through the book to find five different works of art that illustrate regular rhythm. Ask them to list the titles and describe how regular rhythm is used in each.

Perception Hints for Student Art

A possible answer might be that an animal could be added to the quilt design beside the first and third trees in the first row and the second tree in the second row.

LESSON PLANNER

Objectives

After completing this lesson, students will be able to:

- identify techniques used by artists for creating alternating rhythm. *Aesthetic Perception*
- plan and create a collaborative mural using alternating rhythm. *Creative Expression*
- use the four steps of art criticism to evaluate their own prints. *Art Criticism*
- compare the use of alternating rhythm in the two artworks. *Art History and Culture*

Program Resources

- **Overhead:** Both the Matisse and *Parasol* are available on overhead 30.
- **Large Print:** *The Hunt of the Unicorn, II, The Unicorn Dips His Horn into the Stream to Rid It of Poison*
- **Technique Tips Flip Chart,** page 30
- **Vocabulary Book** pages 59–60
- **Art Manipulative Kit:** flash cards
- **Artist Profiles Book:** Matisse page 31 and Artist unknown page 73
- **Art Across the Curriculum** pages 175–180
- **Multimedia Workshop CD-ROM**
- **National Geographic Picture Atlas of the World CD-ROM**
- **Assessment Book** pages 59–60

Multiple Intelligences

Interpersonal Students can explore alternating rhythm as they work with a partner.

Vocabulary

alternating rhythm *ritmo alterno* a visual rhythm set up by repeating motifs but changing position or content of motifs or spaces between them

FOCUS

Time: About 10 minutes

Activating Prior Knowledge

"Imagine that you are playing a game of checkers. How are the squares arranged on the game board? How are the checker pieces placed on the board?"

"Imagínense que están jugando damas o ajedrez. ¿Cómo están ordenados los cuadros en el tablero? ¿Cómo están ordenadas las piezas en el tablero?"

Alternating Rhythm

Artists use alternating rhythm in their artwork to create movement and interest.

Henri Matisse. (French). *Purple Robe and Anemones.* 1937. Oil on canvas. 73.1 × 60.3 cm. The Baltimore Museum of Art: The Cone Collection, formed by Dr. Claribel Cone and Miss Etta Cone of Baltimore, Maryland. © 1998 Succession H. Matisse, Paris/Artists Rights Society (ARS), New York.

Look at the artwork on these pages. *Purple Robe and Anemones* was painted by Henri Matisse. The deerhide *Parasol* was decorated with quills and beads. It was created in the early 1900s in the eastern Sioux style. Both artists have used alternating rhythm to design their artwork.

ART Background

About the Artists

Henri Matisse (än rē' mä tēs, French, 1869-1954) first studied law but turned to art at the age of 21. His paintings are filled with bright colors and patterns. He became bedridden at the age of 73 and used this time to create a new form of art, "drawing with scissors."

*Use the **National Geographic Picture Atlas of the World CD-ROM** to learn more about France.

The Teton Lakota *Parasol* was created by the Sioux. The work is representative of their use of traditional materials, such as quills, beads, and deer hide, to create objects influenced by European styles.

About Subject Matter* Matisse's painting is a portrait and *Parasol* is a floral design.

About the Media Matisse uses oils. *Parasol* is decorated with quills, which are the hard, hollow stems in feathers.

Artist unknown. Teton Lakota. (United States). *Parasol.*
Buckskin, quilled and beaded. $25\frac{1}{4} \times 23$ inches. Courtesy of the
Smithsonian National Museum of the American Indian, NY.
George H. Bingenheimer Collection. Photo by David Heald.

Search for the alternating rhythms in both works
  of art.

- ☑ Find the motifs in each artwork. Which has more than
  one motif?

- ☑ In which piece is the alternating rhythm harder to find?

- ☑ Find the artwork in which the motifs take turns
  repeating.

- ☑ Which rhythm seems faster to you? Which seems
  calmer? What other words describe the way these
  rhythms feel?

Lesson 6

SEEING LIKE
AN ARTIST
Look at the designs in
the clothes your
classmates are
wearing. Find
examples of
alternating rhythm.

157

About Art History* Matisse's painting is a direct outgrowth of Fauvism. The Fauves, or
"wild beasts," used exaggerated and vibrant color to express feelings in their paintings.
After the movement died out, only Matisse, a leading member of this group, continued to
explore the use of pure color and to reduce objects to their simplest shapes and forms.

Parasol was created sometime during the late nineteenth century when beadwork was
added to quillwork as a major form of decoration.

Cultural Perspectives Matisse's painting was created shortly before the oubreak of
World War II, when Europe was experiencing political and social problems such as
economic depression, unemployment, and the threat of communism.

The Sioux *Parasol* was created during a time when Native Americans were driven onto
reservations and an English-speaking and Christian lifestyle was imposed on them.

***See More About** pages 206–227 for more about art history and subject matter.

- Discuss how the colored squares on the game
  board and checker pieces are arranged
  alternately.

Introducing the Art

"Let's take a close look at the two artworks."

"Vamos a observar detalladamente las dos obras de arte."

- **Describe:** Have students describe the subject
  matter in each artwork. (Matisse: portrait; *Parasol:*
  functional)

- **COMPARE AND CONTRAST** Have students make
  a list of the similarities and differences in the
  two artworks. (Both pieces use floral designs, have
  free-form shapes, and incorporate alternating rhythm
  throughout. Matisse's painting is two-dimensional and
  creates subtle alternating rhythm. The *Parasol* is three-
  dimensional, has empty negative spaces, and creates
  alternating rhythm by adding a second motif that is
  repeated every other time.)

- Share and discuss information about the lives,
  work, and times of the artists from **Art
  Background** and the **Artist Profiles Book.**

- Have students answer the questions about
  alternating rhythm on page 157.
  (See **Perception Hints** below.)

⚙ **FOR THE ART SPECIALIST**

Use the **Overhead** and the **Large Print**
The Hunt of the Unicorn to demonstrate
how artists use alternating rhythm in
their artwork to create movement and
interest.

Perception Hints

Motifs *Matisse.* The motif is colorful lines. *Parasol.* The
motif is flowers.

Alternating rhythm *Matisse.* The alternating rhythm
created by the lines is hard to find.

Repeating motifs *Parasol.* The floral motifs take turns
repeating to create alternating rhythm. *Matisse.* The stripes
take turns repeating. The Matisse work seems faster, and
the *Parasol* seems slower. *Energetic* and *peaceful* are other
words that can be used to describe the movement in each.

Time: About two 30-minute periods

Practice

Alternate Materials: pencils and paper

"How can you role-play alternating rhythm?"

"¿Cómo pueden hacer el papel de ritmo alterno?"

- Discuss and review the different ways of creating alternating rhythm on page 158.
- Have students follow the directions on page 158 for creating alternating rhythm. Their rhythms can be created either frozen or moving. Ask them to answer the Decide question in their groups.

Create PROBLEM SOLVING

Materials
- cardboard
- toothpicks
- yarn and glue
- sheets of 18- × 24-inch colored paper
- pencils
- scissors
- markers
- paintbrushes
- palettes
- paper towels
- liquid tempera paints
- sketch paper
- containers of water
- newspaper

Alternate Materials: cut potato prints

"Let's use alternating rhythm to print a self-portrait mural with a partner."

"Vamos a usar ritmo alterno para estampar un mural de un autorretrato con un compañero."

- Review the different ways to create alternating rhythm.
- Review procedures for printing in **More About Technique Tips** on page 202.
- See page 30 in the **Technique Tips Flip Chart** for visual examples of techniques.
- Distribute materials and have students follow the directions on page 159 collaboratively.
- Have students use toothpicks to press the yarn into the glue. They should wait until the glue is dry and paint only the yarn on their stamp.

Safety! For safety issues about glue and paint, and other information about safety in the art classroom, see page T22.

FOR THE ART SPECIALIST

Have students experiment with different rhythms and discover the different effects from each one.

Using Alternating Rhythm

Alternating rhythm is a visual rhythm that can be created in different ways. It can be created by using two repeated motifs that alternate within a line. The motifs can also repeat in every other line.

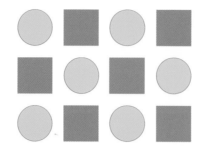

Another way to create rhythm is to use one motif and change its position to make a different alternating rhythm.

Practice

Role-play alternating rhythm in small groups.

1. Use your imagination to create an alternating rhythm with your group. Simple shapes will work best.

2. Try different ways to create alternating rhythm.

Decide What kinds of alternating rhythm did you show?

Activities in
ART Across the Curriculum Book

Reading/Language Arts Identify types of media as informative, entertainment, or persuasive, noting how communication has changed over the years. (page 175)

Math Learn how even and odd numbers can create alternating rhythms. (page 176)

Science Learn how to make a spider web. (page 177)

Social Studies Understand how jobs are assigned and carried out. (page 178)

The Arts Present an echo reading to the class with a partner illustrating alternating rhythm by using two different voices and locations. (page 179)

Technology Use the *Multimedia Workshop* CD-ROM to create a design with alternating rhythm. (page 180)

Teresa Diaz. Age 8. Tempera.

How did this student artist create alternating rhythm?

Create

How can you use alternating rhythm to show action figures? Design a mural featuring alternating rhythm.

1. Think about how you would look doing your favorite action activity. Make several sketches. Choose your best one.

2. Draw a self-portrait action outline, filling a piece of cardboard. Glue pieces of yarn around the outer edges and all other important lines.

3. Choose a partner and print a small mural using alternating rhythm.

Describe How did you create your action figure print? List the steps you used to create your mural.

Analyze How did you and your partner create alternating rhythm?

Interpret What action did you want your figures to show? Do they?

Decide What did you like best about making this mural?

Lesson 6

159

THEME Connections

Culture Use Matisse's painting as a springboard to discuss France.
Patterns Use *Parasol* to identify the patterns used in both artworks.
Discovery Use *Parasol* as a springboard to discover how objects can be both functional and decorative.

ESL

ESL students will benefit from working with a supportive peer to create a mural of alternating rhythm. You may wish to teach all of your students strategies for active listening and questioning that facilitate communication between people.

CLOSE
Time: About 5 minutes

"How do artists create alternating rhythm?"
"¿Cómo crean los artistas ritmo alterno?"

Review
Display the students' murals and have them compare the use of alternating rhythm to the works in this lesson.

Art Criticism Art TEKS: 3.1B, 3.4A
Have students answer the four art criticism questions—Describe, Analyze, Interpret, and Decide—orally or in writing. After the ink has dried, discuss the use of alternating rhythm in their artwork.

Assess
Use the **Assessment Book** pages 59–60 as a formal assessment for this lesson.

Evaluation Criteria
• Can the student identify techniques used by artists for creating alternating rhythm?
• Can the student illustrate alternating rhythm in a creative, collaborative-printed mural?
• Can the student use the four steps of art criticism to evaluate his or her own work?
• Can the student compare the use of alternating rhythm in the two artworks?

Reteaching • • • • • • • • • • •

Alternating rhythm Have students look through the book to find five different works of art that illustrate alternating rhythm. Ask them to list the title and describe how alternating rhythm was created in each.

Perception Hints for Student Art

This student artist created alternating rhythm by alternating two motifs.

LESSON PLANNER

Objectives

After completing this lesson, students will be able to:

- create and respond to vocal and percussion sound qualities in a range of textures and rhythms. *Aesthetic Perception*
- express individual interpretations of these sounds using creative movement. *Creative Expression*
- use the four steps of art criticism to evaluate their own responses to sound and movement. *Art Criticism*
- demonstrate knowledge about improvisational work and choreography. *Art History and Culture*

Program Resources

Artsource Performing Arts Audio/Video Resource Package

Voice/Dance performed by Bobby McFerrin and Tandy Beal. Videocassette Running Time: 8:05. Audiocassette Running Time: 3:00.

FOCUS

Time: About 10 minutes

Activating Prior Knowledge

"Think about the different sounds of voices. What kinds of sounds can we make with our voices?"

"Piensen acerca de los diferentes sonidos de las voces. ¿Qué tipos de sonidos podemos hacer con nuestras voces?"

- Discuss students' answers and talk about the importance of the voice as a means of self-expression through words, sounds and song.

Introducing the Art

"Look at the two performers in the picture."

"Observen a los dos actores en la pintura."

- Discuss the photograph and information on page 160. Share information from **Art Background** about the artists, improvisation, and choreography. If you have the *Artsource* videocassette, have students view the *Voice/Dance* performance.
- Call out several types of sounds: sighing, clicking, shushing, humming, sneezing, laughing, groaning, puffing, etc. Have the class respond. Using your voice, make short patterns of sound the class will echo.

Texture and Rhythm in Music and Dance

"Voice/Dance": Tandy Beal and Bobby McFerrin.

have you ever done your own dance to music? You made up the movements as you went along. That's what a dancer and a musician do. One person sets out an idea and the other responds. They bounce ideas back and forth. In the picture, a musician is using his voice to respond to a dancer's moves. Together they create rhythm with movements and sounds.

ART Background

About the Artists

Tandy Beal and Bobby McFerrin met in 1975 when he was playing the piano for dance classes at the University of Utah. Bobby and Tandy were performing in many of the same places, but never at the same time. Finally, in London, Tandy was able to catch the end of Bobby's show. Backstage afterwards, a plan was set in motion for a collaboration that resulted in their improvisation known as *Voice/Dance*.

About Subject Matter Improvisational work is challenging; it requires a great deal of trust, alertness, and the ability of each participant to respond fully to the other in the present moment. The "players" in improvisational work do not necessarily repeat moves; rather, they respond again and again in new ways to similar challenges.

Make up movement in response to sounds.

Materials

✓ a drum or other musical instrument

1. Stand with your back to a drummer. He or she will beat a series of sounds with silences in between. When the drum is hit, respond with a quick, strong movement. Move in a different way each time.

2. Respond quickly to the sound. Move the moment you hear it. Move in a way that shows the rhythm or quality of the sound.

3. Next, experiment with sounds of the voice. These sounds could be yawning, coughing, sneezing, shushing, sighing, and whispering. Make a movement that catches the feeling and rhythm of the sound.

Describe Tell how you responded to the sounds.
Analyze Explain how you expressed rhythm.
Interpret What kinds of feelings or moods did you create?
Decide Which did you like better—making the sounds or the movements? Which was easier? Why?

Extra Credit

Work with a partner. Take turns creating the sounds and responding in movements. Perform for others.

Music and Dance 161

Cultural Perspectives Tandy Beal states, "Some of the best moments of artistry have to do with playing." Choreographers take a great deal of time to brainstorm ideas and play with them to see what works and what doesn't. Even when they get a clear idea, they may change it when they see how their dancers respond and look. For choreographers and dancers, the stage is like a dance canvas where the artist arranges and rearranges dancers and movement until the result is satisfying.

TEACH

Time: Two 30-minute periods

Materials
• a drum or other musical instrument

"We're going to experiment with sound and movement."
"Vamos a experimentar con el sonido y el movimiento."

• Tell students to respond quickly to each sound by using a movement that captures the rhythm or quality of the sound.

• Have students form a circle around one student chosen to play a drum. Tell them to face their backs to the drummer, so as not to anticipate the beats.

• Have a drummer beat a short sequence of sounds alternated with silences. Have students respond with quick, strong movements.

• Next, have students respond to a variety of vocal sounds, such as yawning, coughing, and so on.

• Form students into three groups, responding to sounds simultaneously to create aural and visual textures.

CLOSE

Time: About 5 minutes

"Now that you have had a chance to experiment with vocal and percussion sounds, think about other types of sounds you could interpret."
"Ahora que han tenido la oportunidad de experimentar con sonidos vocales y de percusión, piensen en otros tipos de sonidos que pudieran interpretar."

Assess
Have students answer the four art criticism questions on page 161—Describe, Analyze, Interpret, and Decide—orally or in writing.

Evaluation Criteria
• Can the student create and respond appropriately to a range of textures and rhythms in the qualities of sound?

• Can the student demonstrate an ability to interpret sound stimuli with improvised movement?

• Can the student use the four steps of art criticism to evaluate his or her performance?

• Can the student demonstrate knowledge about improvisation and choreography?

UNIT 5

Reviewing Unit Concepts

"Artists use tactile and visual texture and random, regular, and alternating rhythm to create texture and rhythm in works of art."

"Los artistas usan textura táctil y visual y ritmo aleatorio, regular y alterno para crear textura y ritmo en las obras de arte."

• Review the techniques artists use to create texture and rhythm on pages 162 and 163. Have them identify examples found in their environment. Art TEKS: 3.1A

Examining the Artwork

"Let's look closely at the work of art." Art TEKS: 3.1B, 3.4B
"Vamos a observar detalladamente la obra de arte."

• Have students study Tommye Scanlin's *Blackeyed Susans* and answer the questions on page 163. (See **Perception Hints** below.)

Student Portfolio

Have students review all the artwork they have created in this unit and select the pieces they wish to keep in their portfolios.

Art Criticism Activity

Have students select an artwork from this unit and study it using the four steps of art criticism. (See pages 206–209 for more information about Art Criticism.) Have students work alone or in pairs and present their findings orally or in writing.

Perception Hints

Visual texture This artwork looks as if it would be somewhat rough to the touch.

Rhythm
Visual rhythm The repetition of the leaves and the petals on the flower and the repetition of the colors of the leaves and petals give the weaving a feeling of movement.
Random rhythm The placement of the leaves in no particular order creates random rhythm.
Regular rhythm The repeating placement of the petals in order creates regular rhythm.

Wrapping Up Unit 5
Texture and Rhythm
Reviewing Main Ideas

The lessons and activities in this unit cover the techniques that artists use to create texture and rhythm.

1. **Texture** is the way the surface of an object feels or *looks* as if it would feel if you could touch it.
   • **Tactile texture** is the way the surface of an object *actually feels* when it is touched. *Appliqué* is an art form which creates tactile texture, by attaching cutout fabrics to a larger surface.

   • **Visual texture** is texture you see with your eyes.
2. **Visual rhythm** is the feeling of movement created by artists repeating colors, shapes, lines, and textures.

Tommye Scanlin. (American). *Blackeyed Susans.* Tapestry. 63 × 37 inches. Courtesy of Tommye Scanlin.

ART Background
Art TEKS: 3.4B

About the Artist
Tommye Scanlin (tom' ē scan' lin, American, 1947–   ) graduated from the University of Georgia with a major in art. Her areas of concentration were drawing, painting, and printmaking. After teaching high school for two years, she began weaving, and this has been her focus since then.

About Subject Matter* Scanlin likes to make pictures with her loom. Tapestry is a special way of doing this. Sometimes, she adds paint to her weavings.

About the Media Wool and natural fibers are used in Scanlin's weavings.

- **Random rhythm** is created when a motif is repeated in no particular order.
- **Regular rhythm** is created by repeating a motif with equal amounts of space in between.
3. **Alternating rhythm** is created by changing a motif every other time it appears or by taking turns repeating more than one motif.

Summing Up

Look at the weaving *Blackeyed Susans* by Tommye Scanlin. The artist used some of the techniques you learned about in this unit to create texture and rhythm.

- What kind of texture does the weaving have?
- What kind of rhythm do you see in the leaves and in the petals of the flowers?

By using techniques to create texture and rhythm, artists can create works of art that show how things feel and move.

Careers in Art
Weaver

Tommye Scanlin is a weaver who lives in Georgia. Weaving probably began when people twisted twigs and reeds together to make huts. Today, many artists, like Tommye Scanlin, use a loom and a variety of textured fibers to weave their own cloth. Many weavers study this craft in college. Scanlin taught herself how to weave by reading books. She creates her tapestry weavings on her own harness loom. She is a member of the Southern Highland Handicraft Guild. This is a group of craftspeople who sell their work in guild shops, hold exhibits, and bring people together to share ideas about handicrafts.

Tommye Scanlin, weaver

163

Learning About Careers in Art

A *pictorial tapestry* weaver, such as Tommye Scanlin, initially creates a preparatory drawing or design known as a *cartoon*. Drawn on paper the size of the tapestry to be woven, the cartoon is placed behind the warp (vertical threads) and traced with a marker. The weaver completes the tapestry using the cartoon as a model.

- Ask the students to list woven objects they might have in their own homes.
- Discuss various functions of a pictorial weaving.
- Encourage interested students to find out more about a career as a weaver. Have them share their findings with the class.

A Final Thought

"Art transfigures while it transfixes—it is art that molds, remakes and preserves."

—Andre Malraux

About Art History* People have been weaving for thousands of years. The first weavings were of baskets made with grasses. It is estimated that textile weaving began around 2500 B.C.

Cultural Perspectives The Industrial Revolution in Europe during the 1700s and early 1800s brought the greatest improvement in weaving machinery. The first power loom was invented in 1785 by Edmund Cartwright.

*See **More About** pages 206–227 for more about art history and subject matter.

UNIT 6

UNIT OVERVIEW

This unit will cover the principles of harmony, variety, and unity. Harmony stresses the similarities of separate but related parts. Variety is concerned with difference or contrast. Unity allows the viewer to see a combination of elements, principles, and media as a whole.

Harmony is a way of emphasizing what different parts of a work of art have in common. Harmony is covered in Lessons 1 and 3.

Variety, the idea that different elements are needed to make a work of art interesting, is covered in Lessons 2 and 3.

Unity, the "invisible glue" that makes different parts look as if they belong together, is covered in Lessons 4–6.

Introducing Unit Concepts

"Artists use harmony and variety to create unity in all kinds of art."

"Los artistas usan armonía y variedad para crear unidad en todos los tipos de arte."

Harmony
• Have students suggest words that come to mind when you say the word *harmony*, e.g. *getting along, music*.

Variety
• Ask students to list a variety of games they like to play. Have them compare their answers with a partner. Encourage them to share their similarities and differences with the class.

Unity
• Have the students name vegetables that can be used to make a salad. List them on the chalkboard. Ask them to describe how they are different (variety). Have them identify what they have in common (harmony). Discuss how these differences and similarities come together to create a salad unity.

An Introduction to
Harmony, Variety, and Unity

Artists create harmony, variety, and unity in their artwork.

Frederic Remington. (American). *Mountain Man*, 1903. Bronze. The Carleton Collection.

 **ART** *Background*

About the Artist
Frederic Remington (fred' rik rem' ing tən, American, 1861–1909) is famous for his realistic portrayal of the American West, a subject that was the focus of his life's work. First recognized in 1885, when American interest was directed to the West, a great demand for his work resulted. He made numerous trips out West throughout his life drawing, painting, illustrating, sculpting, and writing the drama of the land and its people.

About Subject Matter* The *Mountain Man* is a portrait depicting the character of man in America's western frontier.

About the Media Remington had no formal training as a sculptor. He would create his work quickly in plasticine, a commercial wax, and then send the model off to be cast in bronze. The first sculpture he ever made, *The Bronco Buster*, was considered to be a masterpiece.

Artists use **harmony** to make works of art look pleasing or peaceful.

- Where do you see shapes in *Mountain Man* that are similar?
- Which textures do you see more than once?

Some artists use **variety** to create interest.

- Describe at least two different textures you see.
- Describe some of these objects you see.

Harmony and variety create a feeling of **unity** in artwork.

- What unifies the sculpture?

Artist Profile

Frederic Remington
1861–1909

Self-Portrait on a Horse.

Frederic Remington was born in Canton, New York, on October 1, 1861. As a young boy, he loved to draw Native Americans, cowboys, soldiers, and horses. When he was 19 years old, he left college and traveled west. He spent four years as a cowboy and a rancher and sketched everything he saw. His artwork focuses on the American West.

Frederic Remington and other artists use harmony and variety to help them create unity in their artwork. In this unit you will learn and practice techniques for creating harmony and variety and learn how harmony and variety create a feeling of unity. You will study:

- Harmony
- Variety
- Unity

165

About Art History* Remington drew horses so realistically that he was credited for being the first American to give character to the horse in art. Horses had previously been drawn in a static, or hobbyhorse, position.

Cultural Perspectives Remington created the *Mountain Man* at a time when an era in American history was coming to an end. Buffalo, which had once roamed the prairies, had disappeared. The Native Americans, forced onto reservations by the U.S. government, had depended on the buffalo for food, clothing, and shelter and were now relegated to depend on the government for these needs. The once-barren grasslands were being settled by farmers, who created fertile farmland.

*See **More About** pages 206–227 for more about art history and subject matter.

You may wish to introduce the unit by showing the **Video** *Meet Leo Lionni*. Then, discuss his life and how he feels about the importance of the arts.

Examining the Artwork

"Let's look closely at the sculpture."
"Vamos a observar detalladamente la escultura."

- Have the students look at Remington's sculpture *Mountain Man*. Ask them to describe what they see.
- Have students answer the questions on page 165 pertaining to harmony, variety, and unity in Remington's sculpture.
  (See **Perception Hints** below.)

Artist Profile

Share with students information about the artist, including his self-portrait.

Encourage students to use their **Art Journals** to practice art concepts and record ideas from lesson to lesson.

About Music

Harmony in music refers to different pitches played or sung at the same time to produce chords. Have students take turns playing three-note chords, for example, every other note on the piano (C-E-G). Then, have them play notes that are adjacent (C-D-E) and observe the inharmonious effect.

Unity and variety give each composition its identity and character. Have students sing a song, or listen to an orchestral selection, and identify what seems to create unity and variety (repeated and contrasting melodies, rhythm patterns, and speed).

Perception Hints

Harmony The main shape of the man and horse together is similar to the shape of the rock. The rough texture of the horse's mane is repeated in the blanket and the rock.

Variety The man's helmet and rifle have a smooth texture, while the man's hair, the horse's tail, and the rock have a rough texture. The mountain man is holding, or wearing, a rifle, tin cup, leather whip, reins, and small leather satchel.

Unity The bronze medium and color of the *Mountain Man* unifies the sculpture.

UNIT 6 Planning Guide

Lesson	Lesson Title	Suggested Pacing	Create Activities	Materials	
1	Harmony	75 minutes	Build a clay slab container designed with a texture to show harmony.	white or red clay 18- x 24-inch muslin rolling pin or thick dowel sticks 4- x 4-inch tagboard templates textured objects for stamping containers of slip and water 8- x 8-inch cardboard covered with muslin masking tape paper clips wooden slats paintbrushes	
2	Variety	75 minutes	Make a weaving with a variety of colors and textures.	9- x 12-inch pieces of cardboard string (about 12 feet per student) a variety of fabrics and natural fibers rulers or straightedges tape scissors pencils	
3	Harmony and Variety	75 minutes	Create a paper mosaic to show harmony and variety.	12- x 18-inch black construction paper dustless chalk warm and cool colored construction paper scissors glue clay tile from **Art Manipulative Kit**	
4	Unity	75 minutes	Design a dream room that illustrates unity.	12- x 18-inch white construction paper crayons sketch paper watercolor paints pencils brushes paper towels containers of water tape flash cards from **Art Manipulative Kit**	
5	Unity, Repetition, and Grouping	75 minutes	Create a crayon engraving showing unity.	9- x 12-inch white construction paper washable black ink and liquid soap crayons sketch paper paintbrushes palettes large paper clips pencils containers of water newspaper audiotapes from **Art** paper towels **Manipulative Kit**	
6	Unity in Handmade Books	75 minutes	Show unity in a book about the author.	9- x 12-inch white construction paper, crayons, and/or markers staplers 9- x 12-inch colored construction paper fabric swatches from **Art Manipulative Kit**	
Artsource Lesson	Harmony, Variety, and Unity in Theater	45 minutes	Use the body and voice to express information about science and nature.	poems and stories recordings of music	

Test preparation activities using the Large Prints *A Dash for the Timber* and *Illuminated Page with Louis IX and Queen Blanche of Castile* can be found on pages 28–31 of the Test Preparation Book.

Program Resources (Books)	Art Resources	Literature Resources	*Music Resources
Vocabulary, pp. 61–62 Assessment, pp. 61–62 Art Across the Curriculum Resource Book, pp. 181–186 Technique Tips Flip Chart, p. 31 Lesson Plans Book, p. 32 Home Connection, pp. 15 and 16	Overhead Transparency #31, *Jar* and *Pottery Vessels* Artist Profile Book, pp. 28, 74 Large Print, *Louis IX and Queen Blanche of Castile*	**1.** *The Hidden Jungle* (1992) by Simon Henwood informs of ways to overlap by following the illustrations in this fun and vibrant jungle tale. **2.** *The Stinky Cheeseman and Other Fairly Stupid Tales* (1992) by Jon Scieszka has a uniquely absurd collection of hilarious fairy tales using expressive designs of text.	"In the Good Old Summertime" (Barbershop Quartet), by George Evans and Ron Shields, p. T304, CD7:32. "In the Good Old Summertime" is an example of harmony in music.
Vocabulary, pp. 63–64 Assessment, pp. 63–64 Art Across the Curriculum Resource Book, pp. 187–192 Technique Tips Flip Chart, p. 32 Lesson Plans Book, p. 33	Overhead Transparency #32, *Child's Beaded Shirt* and *Pictorial Weaving* Artist Profile Book, pp. 22, 75 Large Prints, *Dash for the Timber* and *Louis IX and Queen Blanche of Castile*	**1.** *Dots, Spots, Speckles, and Stripes* (1987) by Tana Hoban has brilliant photographs from the environment reinforcing the concepts of variety found in numerous subjects. **2.** *Cubs and Colts and Calves and Kittens* (1991) by Alan Fowler portrays variety in animals by noticing differences in this strongly attractive photographic collection of baby animals.	"Hopi Lullaby," p. T128, CD3:38. "Hopi Lullaby" is an example of Native American music.
Vocabulary, pp. 65–66 Assessment, pp. 65–66 Art Across the Curriculum Resource Book, pp. 193–198 Technique Tips Flip Chart, p. 33 Lesson Plans Book, p. 34	Overhead Transparency #33, *Ishtar Gate* and *Ravenna Mosaic* Artist Profile Book, pp. 76, 77 Large Prints, *Dash for the Timber* and *Louis IX and Queen Blanche of Castile*	**1.** *Ashanti to Zulu: African Traditions* (1976) by Margaret Musgrove is a Caldecott-winning book that explains the traditions and customs of 26 African tribes and uses numerous patterns and examples of variety and contrast. **2.** *Rechenka's Eggs* (1988) by Patricia Polacco has lively text and patterns in this enchanting folktale filled with contrasting designs.	"Los mariachis," p. T165, CD4:25. "Los mariachis" shows both unity and variety through its form, which has a returning "A" section alternating with a contrasting "B" section, "C" section, etc. This is also known as "rondo" form.
Vocabulary, pp. 67–68 Assessment, pp. 67–68 Art Across the Curriculum Resource Book, pp. 199–204 Technique Tips Flip Chart, p. 34 Lesson Plans Book, p. 35	Overhead Transparency #34, *Bedroom (cubiculum nocturnum)* and *Duncan House Bedroom* Artist Profile Book, pp. 78, 79 Large Prints, *Dash for the Timber* and *Louis IX and Queen Blanche of Castile*	**1.** *Ox-Cart Man* (1979) by Donald Hall uses low-intensity colors that are united harmoniously to depict the daily life of an early nineteenth-century New England family in folk-art style paintings. **2.** *Christmas at Long Pond* (1992) by William T. George uses soft, subtle colors to harmoniously create the mood and setting of this visually refreshing picture book.	"Allegro vivace," from Sonata No. 8 for Violin and Piano, by Ludwig van Beethoven, p. T356, CD9:5. Beethoven's Sonata No. 8 for Violin and Piano is an example of music written in the 1800s.
Vocabulary, pp. 69–70 Assessment, pp. 69–70 Art Across the Curriculum Resource Book, pp. 205–210 Technique Tips Flip Chart, p. 35 Lesson Plans Book, p. 36	Overhead Transparency #35, *Woman in Blue* and *Ancestral Spirit Dance Series* Artist Profile Book, pp. 8, 31 Large Prints, *Dash for the Timber* and *Louis IX and Queen Blanche of Castile*	**1.** *Ashanti to Zulu: African Traditions* (1976) by Margaret Musgrove explains the traditions and customs of 26 African tribes and uses numerous patterns of balance and harmony. **2.** *I Am an Artist* (1992) by Pat Lowery Collins is an excellent book for referring to the lesson concept that art is everywhere around us, be it in lines, colors, shapes, or textures.	"Salamanca Market," by Mary Goetze, p. T152, CD4:19. "Salamanca Market" is a song about a market in Hobart, Tasmania, an island off the coast of Australia. It can be sung as a canon, or round.
Vocabulary, pp. 71–72 Assessment, pp. 71–72 Art Across the Curriculum Resource Book, pp. 211–216 Technique Tips Flip Chart, p. 36 Lesson Plans Book, p. 37	Overhead Transparency #36, *Cover of Armenian Gospel Book* and *Book Cover* Artist Profile Book, pp. 17, 80 Large Prints, *Dash for the Timber* and *Louis IX and Queen Blanche of Castile* Artsource Performing Arts Audio/Video Resource Package: *On the Day You Were Born* (videocassette)	**1.** *My Painted House, My Friendly Chicken, and Me* (1996) by Maya Angelou has photography unified with the expressions and textures in the many faces of a Ndebele culture in South Africa. **2.** *The Stinky Cheeseman and Other Fairly Stupid Tales* (1992) by Jon Scieszka uses expressive designs of text to enhance and bond with the originality of this book.	"African Postal Workers," p. T175, CD4:40. This music was created by African postal workers from the University of Ghana. One worker clinking scissors to the beat provides unity, while a whistler and two workers stamping ink pads and letters provides variety.

*Music references are from ***Share the Music,*** Macmillan/McGraw-Hill School Publishers

LESSON PLANNER

Objectives

After completing this lesson, students will be able to:

- identify how artists create harmony with related colors, similar shapes, and repetition. *Aesthetic Perception*
- plan and create a clay slab container that illustrates harmony. *Creative Expression*
- use the four steps of art criticism to evaluate their own pottery. *Art Criticism*
- compare works by Nancy Youngblood Lugo and Japanese artists. *Art History and Culture*

Program Resources

- **Overhead:** Both the Lugo and the *Jar* are available on overhead 31.
- **Large Prints:** *Illuminated Page with Louis IX and Queen Blanche of Castile*
- **Technique Tips Flip Chart,** page 31
- **Vocabulary Book** pages 61–62
- **Artist Profiles Book:** Artist unknown page 74 and Lugo page 28
- **Art Across the Curriculum Book** pages 181–186
- **Multimedia Workshop CD-ROM**
- **National Museum of Women in the Arts Collection:** cards
- **Assessment Book** pages 61–62

Multiple Intelligences

Intrapersonal Students can recognize that harmony can give a work of art a peaceful feeling.

Vocabulary

harmony *armonía* the quality of unity in a design that is created by stressing similarities in its related parts

FOCUS

Time: About 10 minutes

Activating Prior Knowledge

"Think about getting dressed in the morning. Why do you choose clothes with colors that go well together?"

"Piensen cuando se visten en las mañanas. ¿Por qué escogen la ropa con colores que combinan?"

- Discuss students' responses to the question and how related colors give a feeling of harmony.

Harmony

Artists create harmony to make a work of art look pleasing or peaceful.

Artist unknown. (Japan). Middle Jomon period. *Jar.* c. 3000–2000 B.C. Earthenware clay with applied, incised, and cord-marked decoration. $27\frac{1}{2}$ inches. The Metropolitan Museum of Art, New York, New York. The Harry G. C. Packard Collection of Asian Art, Gift of Harry G. C. Packard and Purchase, Fletcher, Rogers, Harris Brisbane, Dick and Louis V. Bell Funds, Joseph Pulitzer Bequest and the Annenberg Fund, Inc. Gift 1975.

Compare the ceramic containers shown on these pages. The *Jar* was created in Japan more than 4,000 years ago. The *Pottery Vessels* were crafted by Nancy Youngblood Lugo in the 1990s. All the containers were made with clay. Both works contain repeated lines and textures that create harmony.

ART Background

About the Artists

Nancy Youngblood Lugo (nan' sē yung' blud lu go, American, 1955–) was born in Fort Lewis, Washington. Her mother is Native American. Lugo studied at the San Francisco Art Institute on a scholarship. She began to incorporate seashell motifs in her work after a visit to St. Martin's Island in the Caribbean.

- Use the **National Museum of Women in the Arts Collection** cards to find other examples of pottery made by women artists.

The *Jar* is characteristic of the low-fired pottery that was made with the coiling method. Typically, these pots were decorated with reliefs or impressions of a cord pattern.

About Subject Matter* The *Jar* and two of the containers in *Pottery Vessels* are nonobjective. The container on the left has seashells as the subject.

Nancy Youngblood Lugo. Pueblo (United States). *Pottery Vessels.* c. 1980–1985. Pottery. $4\frac{1}{2} \times 6$ inches in diameter. Courtesy Nancy Youngblood Lugo, © Jerry Jacka Photography.

Look closely at each ceramic piece to find examples of visual harmony.

- ✓ Look for shapes that are repeated.
- ✓ Find the textures that are repeated.
- ✓ Locate one of the **motifs** in each piece.
- ✓ Where do you see lines that are repeated?

SEEING LIKE AN ARTIST

Find a work of art in this book that seems peaceful to you. Which shapes, lines, or colors are repeated in it?

Lesson 1 167

About the Media Lugo's pots are made with clay found around Santa Clara. The *Jar* is also made with clay.

About Art History* Lugo is one of the well-known potters from the Tafoya family. Southwest potters have been using the same clay and methods for centuries.

The *Jar* was created in Japan sometime between 3000–2000 B.C. The earliest artifacts found in Japan are pottery vessels, stone and bone tools, wooden bowls, and figurines.

Cultural Perspectives Lugo incorporates traditional Southwest Native American styles into her work, and manages to make each piece distinctly hers. All show the natural, rich colors of the earth.

The *Jar* was created sometime during the mid-Jomon period in Japan. Similarities with early cultures of Northeast Asia and even America are often cited.

*See **More About** pages 206–227 for more about art history and subject matter.

Introducing the Art

"Let's take a close look at the ceramic containers."
"Vamos a observar detalladamente los recipientes de cerámica."

- **Describe:** Have students describe the subject matter in each clay pot. (Lugo: nonobjective and seashells; *Jar:* nonobjective)
- **COMPARE AND CONTRAST** Have students make a list of the similarities and differences in the two clay vessels. (They are all three-dimensional, have areas of relief, and repeat such elements as texture and shape. Lugo's *Pottery Vessels* are in the form of spheres, are glazed, and illustrate regular rhythm. The *Jar* is in the form of a cylinder, is not glazed, and illustrates alternating rhythm.)
- Share and discuss information about the lives, work, and times of the artists from **Art Background** and the **Artist Profiles Book.**
- Have students answer the questions about harmony on page 167.
(See **Perception Hints** below.)

FOR THE ART SPECIALIST

Use the **Overhead** and the **Large Print** *Louis IX and Queen Blanche of Castile* to demonstrate how artists create harmony to make a work of art look pleasing or peaceful.

Perception Hints

Shapes *Lugo.* The ceramic pot has free-form shell shapes.
Textures *Lugo* and *Jar.* The bumpy textures are repeated in Lugo's two pots and the rough, rope texture is repeated in the jar.
Motifs *Lugo* and *Jar.* The seashells surrounding the opening of Lugo's pot is a motif. The incised, curved line at the top of the jar is also a motif.
Lines *Jar.* The horizontal lines are repeated over and over.

TEACH

Time: About two 30-minute periods

Practice

Materials
- 9- × 12-inch paper folded into three sections
- pencils and markers

Alternate Materials: crayons

"How can you illustrate the three ways to create harmony?"

"¿Cómo pueden ilustrar las tres formas para crear armonía?"

- Discuss the definition of *harmony* and three techniques for creating it on page 168.
- Distribute materials. Have students follow directions on page 168 for illustrating harmony.
- Ask students to answer the Decide questions on the back of their papers.

Create PROBLEM SOLVING

Materials
- white or red clay, about the size of a baseball (three per student)
- 18- × 24-inch muslin
- rolling pin or thick dowel sticks
- 4- × 4-inch tagboard templates
- textured objects for stamping
- containers of slip and water
- 8- × 8-inch cardboard covered with muslin
- masking tape
- paper clips
- slats
- paintbrushes

Alternate Materials: oil clay

"Let's repeat textures to create harmony in a clay slab container."

"Vamos a repetir las texturas para crear armonía en un recipiente con una plancha de arcilla."

- Review procedures for working with clay in **More About Technique Tips** on page 205.
- Cover tabletops with muslin and tape down.
- See page 31 in the **Technique Tips Flip Chart** for visual examples of techniques.
- Distribute materials and have students follow the directions on page 169. Have them construct their containers on the cardboard base covered with muslin.

FOR THE ART SPECIALIST

Have the students use watercolor to add color to their containers.

Using Harmony

Harmony is the peaceful look made when related elements of art are put together. Visual artists create harmony in many ways.

Harmony can be created with **colors** that are related on the color wheel.

Harmony can be created with similar **shapes**.

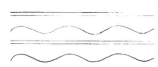

Harmony can be created with **repeated** lines, colors, shapes, textures, and objects.

Practice

Create harmony with color, shape, and repetition. Use markers or crayons.

1. Fold a sheet of paper into three parts. In the first part, draw a simple shape. Color it with three related colors.

2. In the second part, draw a geometric shape. Repeat the shape in different sizes until this part is filled.

3. In the last part, draw rows of repeating lines and shapes.

Decide Which part looks the most peaceful to you? Why?

Activities in
ART Across the Curriculum Book

Reading/Language Arts Learn the difference between fiction books and nonfiction books. (page 181)

Math Identify patterns in sets of alternating geometric shapes and numbers. (page 182)

Science Study different kinds of shells found in nature. (page 183)

Social Studies Understand the importance of compromise to create harmony between people. (page 184)

The Arts Compare harmony in art to harmony in music, then create sounds that show harmony. (page 185)

Technology Use the *Multimedia Workshop* CD-ROM to design a pot or container using harmony. (page 186)

*Readiness

What could be kept in this student artist's clay container?
Molly McCloskey. Age 8. *Star*. Clay.

Create

What would you keep in a clay container?
Build a clay slab container designed with
a texture to show harmony.

1. Think about textures you could add to your container. Gather objects that you could use to create texture.

2. Roll out a large slab of clay. Look at the textures each object makes on clay. Choose one.

3. Cut out a square from stiff paper, lay it on the clay, and cut around it. This will be your base.

4. Press your objects into the remaining clay slab until it is covered with texture. Trace the paper square and cut out four more pieces for the container's sides. Use proper joining techniques to assemble your container.

Describe What object did you use to create your textures?

Analyze Which elements did you repeat?

Interpret What does the texture you made remind you of?

Decide Does the container show harmony? Is there anything you would like to add or change to make it look more pleasing?

Lesson 1 169

THEME Connections

Discovery Use the artworks to discover how nature plays a significant role in the development (clay), decoration (shell motif), and completion (fire) of ceramic forms.

Connections Use the artworks as visual examples of art that is both decorative and functional.

Traditions Use Lugo's *Pottery Vessels* as a springboard to discuss the Native American tradition of making pottery.

ESL

ESL students may have difficulty following oral directions without some visual support. Consider modeling with the whole class the steps in building a clay slab container. To review, sketch the steps on the chalkboard before asking students to complete the activity.

CLOSE
Time: About 5 minutes

"What could you do to create harmony in your next work of art?"
"¿Qué podrían hacer para crear armonía en su próxima obra de arte?"

Review
Have students compare harmony in their artworks to the works in this lesson.

Art Criticism
Have students answer the four art criticism questions—Describe, Analyze, Interpret, and Decide—orally or in writing. Discuss the repetition of texture to create harmony in their clay containers.

Assess
Use the **Assessment Book** pages 61–62 as a formal assessment for this lesson.

Evaluation Criteria
• Can the student identify the three techniques for creating harmony?
• Can the student repeat textures to create harmony in a clay slab container?
• Can the student use the four steps of art criticism to evaluate his or her own work?
• Can the student verbally compare the two artworks?

Reteaching ● ● ● ● ● ● ● ● ● ●

Harmony Have students look through the book to find three different works of art that illustrate harmony. Ask them to list the title and identify the technique used to create harmony in each.

Perception Hints for Student Art

The answers to the question will vary. Reasonable answers might be jewelry, pencils, or coins.

Variety

Artists use variety to create interest in their artwork.

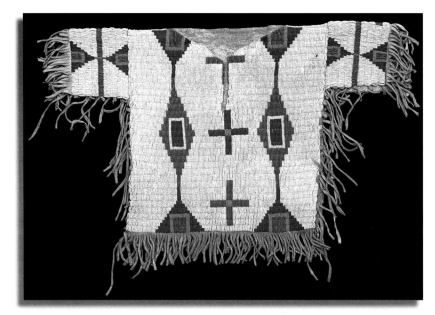

Artist unknown. Northern Cheyenne or Teton Dakota (United States). *Child's Beaded Shirt.* c. 1865. Buffalo hide, glass seed beads. 33.5 × 58.5 cm. Courtesy of the Dallas Museum of Art, Textile Purchase Fund.

Look at the **textile art** on these pages. A Central Plains woman made the *Child's Beaded Shirt* around 1865. It is decorated with a variety of textures, colors, and materials. The Navajo artist Isabel John created *Pictorial Tapestry* more than 100 years later with a variety of shapes and colors. Both artists used variety in their designs to create interest.

LESSON PLANNER

Objectives

After completing this lesson, students will be able to:

- identify the use of variety to create interest in a work of art. *Aesthetic Perception*
- create a weaving using a variety of colors and textures. *Creative Expression*
- use the four steps of art criticism to evaluate their own weavings. *Art Criticism*
- describe textiles used by artists from two Native American cultures and explain why each culture might have used the chosen materials. *Art History and Culture*

Program Resources

- **Overhead:** Both the John and *Child's Beaded Shirt* are available on overhead 32.
- **Large Prints:** *A Dash for the Timber* by Frederic S. Remington and *Illuminated Page with Louis IX and Queen Blanche of Castile*
- **Technique Tips Flip Chart,** page 32
- **Vocabulary Book** pages 63–64
- **Art Manipulative Kit:** fabric swatches
- **Artist Profiles Book:** Artist unknown page 75 and John page 22
- **Art Across the Curriculum Book** pages 187–192
- **Multimedia Workshop CD-ROM**
- **Assessment Book** pages 63–64

Multiple Intelligences
Visual/Spatial Students can learn about variety by creating various visual images.

Vocabulary
variety *variedad* different lines, shapes, colors, and textures used to make a work of art interesting

FOCUS

Time: About 10 minutes

Activating Prior Knowledge

"Think about eating a slice of bread. What if you had to eat a plain slice of bread every day? What would make it taste better? What would make it more fun to eat?"

"Piensen acerca de comerse una rebanada de pan. ¿Qué pasaría si tuvieran que comer una rebanada de pan diariamente? ¿Qué la haría saber mejor? ¿Qué la haría más divertida para comer?"

- Discuss students' responses to the question and how variety creates interest.

ART Background

About the Artists

Isabel John (iz' ə bel jän, American) is a weaver who shears sheep and spins and dyes her own wool to use in her pictorial tapestries. She weaves by hand on an upright loom.

The *Child's Beaded Shirt* is representative of the beadwork done by the Plains Native American women. Based on earlier quill work designs, the beadwork patterns are not only decorative but have symbolic and spiritual meanings.

About Subject Matter* John's weaving is a genre scene, and the *Child's Beaded Shirt* is iconographic.

About the Media John made her weaving with sheep's wool that was dyed naturally.

Instead of using needle and thread, the unknown artist attached the beads to this shirt with sinew, the tendon that connects muscle to bone in an animal's body.

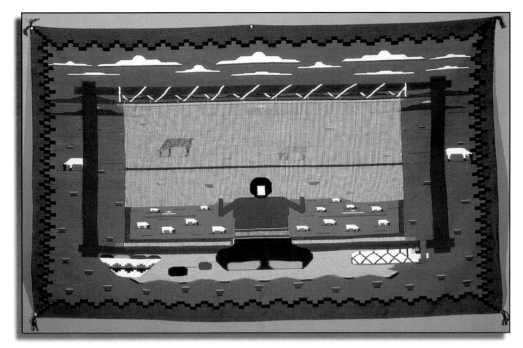

Isabel John. Navajo (United States). *Pictorial Tapestry*. Mid 1980s. Wool, commercial, and natural dyes. $44 \times 77\frac{1}{2}$ inches. Collection of the Birmingham Museum of Art, Birmingham, Alabama. Museum purchase in memory of Richard Kenneth McRae, with funds from family and friends.

Study both works of art to find examples of variety.

- ☑ Find different geometric and free-form shapes in the same artwork.
- ☑ Find shapes of different sizes in each piece.
- ☑ Locate places where you see different textures.
- ☑ Which work of art seems to have more variety?

SEEING LIKE AN ARTIST

Choose an element of art such as line, color, shape, or texture. How many different varieties can you find in your classroom?

Lesson **2**

171

Art History* A fairly recent development in Navajo weaving, the landscape pictorial became popular in the 1970s, just a short time before Isabel John created *Pictorial Weaving*. These weavings portray scenes from everyday life on the Navajo Reservation.

After European traders introduced glass beads into the central plains area of the United States at the end of the eighteenth century, Native American artists began using beads in place of quills as the major form of decoration.

Cultural Perspectives A nomadic people, the Navajo adopted many elements of older Pueblo cultures. Navajos are the largest Native American group in the United States. The *Child's Beaded Shirt* was created in the second half of the nineteenth century, when horses gave the Plains people more mobility. They became nomadic in order to follow migrating buffalo, which provided them with meat, bones for tools, and skins for clothing and shelter.

See **More About pages 206–227 for more about art history and subject matter.

Introducing the Art

"Let's take a close look at the two artworks."
"Vamos a observar detalladamente las dos obras de arte."

- **Describe:** Have students describe the subject matter in each textile. (John: landscape; *Child's Beaded Shirt:* iconographic)
- **COMPARE AND CONTRAST** Have students make a list of the similarities and differences in the two textiles. (Both textiles include the stepped pyramid pattern; have formal balance; and use primarily red, white, and blue. John's weaving was created for display, incorporates only wool, and has geometric and free-form shapes. The *Child's Beaded Shirt* was created to be worn, incorporates a variety of materials, and has only geometric shapes.)
- Share and discuss information about the lives, works, and times of the artists from **Art Background** and the **Artist Profiles Book.**
- Have students answer questions about variety on page 171. (See **Perception Hints** below.)

 FOR THE ART SPECIALIST

Use the **Overhead** and the **Large Prints** *A Dash for the Timber* and *Louis IX and Queen Blanche of Castile* to demonstrate how artists use variety to create interest in their artwork.

Perception Hints

Shapes *John* and *Child's Beaded Shirt.* There are free-form cloud shapes near the top of the weaving. The large red diamonds on either side of the middle of the shirt are geometric shapes.
Different sizes *John.* The clouds and sheep are different sizes.
Textures *Child's Beaded Shirt.* The beads look like they have a bumpy texture, and the buffalo hide fringe looks smooth.
More variety John's *Pictorial Weaving* has more variety.

TEACH

Time: About two 30-minute periods

Practice

Materials
- 9- × 12-inch paper
- pencils or crayons

Alternate Materials: oil pastels

"How can you illustrate variety in a design?"
"¿Cómo pueden ilustrar la variedad en un diseño?"

- Discuss the definition of *variety* and different ways that variety can be achieved on page 172.
- Distribute materials and have students follow the directions on page 172 for illustrating variety. Ask them to write answers to the Decide questions on the back of their work.

Create PROBLEM SOLVING

Materials
- 9- × 12-inch pieces of cardboard
- rulers, pencils, and scissors
- tape
- string (about 12 feet per student)
- a variety of fabrics and natural fibers

Alternate Materials: paper weaving

"Let's use a variety of colors and textures in a weaving."
"Vamos a usar una variedad de colores y texturas en un tejido."

- After notching the cardboard, string the warp by starting at the top left notch. Bring the string down to the bottom left notch, pull it behind this notch, and then bring it back up again to the next notch. Keep going until the cardboard is completely strung with an uneven number of threads.
- Begin weaving by leaving 1 inch of fabric sticking out. Be sure to leave loops of the weaving fabric on the side so that the warp won't be pulled too tight.

warp

weft

- See page 32 in the **Technique Tips Flip Chart** for visual examples of techniques.
- Distribute materials and have students follow the directions on page 173.

⚙ FOR THE ART SPECIALIST

Have the students draw a pattern and then weave it.

Using Variety

Variety is using different lines, shapes, colors, and textures to make a work of art interesting.

Too much of the same color, line, or shape in an artwork can be boring, but adding something different or unexpected can break up the repetition. Using a variety of colors or lines can give people more to think about.

See if you can tell what has been changed to add variety to each of the designs below.

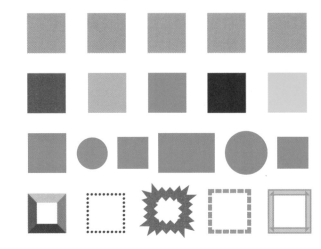

Practice

Create a design that has variety. Use pencil and one other medium, if you like.

1. Draw a geometric or free-form shape on your paper with a pencil. Repeat the shape, the same size, until your paper is filled.

2. Add a different element to your design to create variety. For example, you might add different colors, lines, or textures.

Decide What did you do to add variety to your design? Did the variety make the design more interesting?

Activities in ART Across the Curriculum Book

Reading/Language Arts Use synonyms to create variety in writing. (page 187)

Math Solve a variety of problems relating to the subject depicted in *Pictorial Weaving*. (page 188)

Science Study the characteristics of objects made of woven cloth. (page 189)

Social Studies Evaluate different types of clothing and reasons to wear each one. (page 190)

The Arts Present an interpretation of a story using a variety of voices to describe the different characters. (page 191)

Technology Use the *Multimedia Workshop* CD-ROM to design a tapestry using a variety of lines. (page 192)

*Readiness

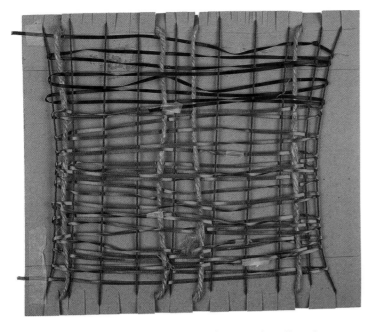

Aaron Romaro. Age 8. *Varied Lines*. Yarn, ribbon, and cardboard.

What textures did this student artist use in his weaving?

Create

What different ways can you use a weaving? Make a weaving with a variety of colors and textures.

1. Think about how you will use your weaving. Select a variety of ribbons, natural fibers, and yarn for your weaving.

2. Cut out a piece of cardboard, and notch it on the top and the bottom. Then, string the warp thread on it.

3. Weave your fibers to create variety.

Describe What colors and textures did you use in your weaving?

Analyze Which colors and textures did you repeat? Where did you create variety?

Interpret How would the interest of your weaving change if you had used only one color and one texture?

Decide If you could add other colors and textures, what would you choose?

Lesson 2   **173**

THEME Connections

Discovery Use the *Child's Beaded Shirt* as a springboard to discover how different colors and shapes are symbolic and communicate meanings.

Communities Use the artwork as a springboard to discuss various aspects and traditions of Native American communities.

Connections Connect John's weaving to the landscape in the western region of the United States.

ESL

During the Seeing Like an Artist activity, pair an ESL student with a fluent English-speaking peer to see how many different varieties of line, color, shape, or texture they can find in the classroom. Encourage pairs to share with other classmates to maximize the opportunities for ESL students to engage in discussions.

"What can artists do to create variety in their work?"
"¿Qué hacen los artistas para crear variedad en su trabajo?"

 ART MANIPULATIVES **Review** Use the fabric swatches from the **Art Manipulative Kit** to review variety of colors and textures.

Art Criticism

Have students answer the four art criticism questions—Describe, Analyze, Interpret, and Decide—orally or in writing. Discuss the use of variety in their weavings.

Assess
Use the **Assessment Book** pages 63–64 as a formal assessment for this lesson.

Evaluation Criteria

• Can the student identify the use of variety to create interest in a work of art?

• Can the student incorporate a variety of colors and textures in a weaving in a unique and creative way?

• Can the student use the four steps of art criticism to evaluate his or her own work?

• Can the student describe the textiles of the two Native American artists and explain how they might have used them?

Reteaching ● ● ● ● ● ● ● ● ● ● ● ●

Variety Have the students look outside to find three examples of variety. Ask them to list the areas and describe how variety is created in each.

Perception Hints for Student Art

The student artist used yarn and ribbon in his weaving.

Harmony and Variety

Artists create harmony with similar shapes, lines, or textures. They introduce variety by changing some of these elements.

Artist unknown. (Babylonia). *Ishtar Gate.* c. 605–562 B.C. State Museum, Berlin, Germany. Erich Lessing/Art Resource, NY.

Look at the mosaics on these pages. *Ishtar Gate* was designed and created in Babylonia about 2,500 years ago. The other work of art is a small part of a large mosaic in a church. Both mosaics have harmony and variety.

174   Unit **6**

UNIT 6   LESSON 3

LESSON PLANNER

Objectives
After completing this lesson, students will be able to:
- identify harmony and variety used by artists in a work of art. *Aesthetic Perception*
- create a paper mosaic using harmony and variety. *Creative Expression*
- use the four steps of art criticism to evaluate their own work. *Art Criticism*
- compare mosaics from Babylonia to the mosaic from Italy. *Art History and Culture*

Program Resources
- **Overhead:** Both *Ishtar Gate* and detail from *First Bishop of Ravenna Apse Mosaic* are available on overhead 33.
- **Large Prints:** *A Dash for the Timber* by Frederic S. Remington and *Illuminated Page with Louis IX and Queen Blanche of Castile*
- **Technique Tips Flip Chart,** page 33
- **Vocabulary Book** pages 65–66
- **Art Manipulative Kit:** clay tile
- **Artist Profiles Book:** Artists unknown pages 76 and 77
- **Art Across the Curriculum Book** pages 193–198
- **Multimedia Workshop CD-ROM**
- **Animals Through History Time Line**
- **Assessment Book** pages 65–66

Multiple Intelligences
Logical/Mathematical Students can understand harmony by analyzing likenesses and differences.

Vocabulary
mosaic *mosaico* a picture or design made with inlaid bits of colored stone, glass, or tile

harmony *armonía* the use of similar shapes or related colors throughout a design

variety *variedad* the use of different materials, lines, shapes, colors, or textures in a design

---

ART Background

About the Artists
Ishtar Gate was originally one of the main entrances to the city of Babylon. The brilliantly glazed gate portrays the figures of the dragon of Marduk and the bull of Adad.

The *Ravenna Mosaic* is in St. Apollinaris church in the port of Classe outside Ravenna, Italy. The church was consecrated in A.D. 549. The detail is part of a beautiful mosaic in the front part of the church.

About Subject Matter* *Ishtar Gate* and the detail of *First Bishop of Ravenna Apse Mosaic* are both iconographic murals.

About the Media *Ishtar Gate* is made out of turquoise and gold-colored glazed bricks and topped with notches. The *Ravenna Mosaic* is made of colored glass set in cement. Gold leaf is applied to the back of the pieces of glass.

Artist unknown. (Italy). *Ravenna Apse Mosaic (Detail)*. A.D. 549. The Church of Saint Apollinaris, Ravenna, Italy. Scala/Art Resource, New York.

Study each mosaic to find the following examples of harmony and variety.

☑ Find colors that are related to each other.

☑ Locate the shapes that are repeated all over.

☑ Find geometric shapes next to free-form shapes.

☑ Locate colors that are different from each other.

Lesson 3

175

SEEING LIKE AN ARTIST

Look through this book and find an artwork that shows harmony and variety together in the same piece.

About Art History* Mosaic art is made by placing small, colored pieces of glass or stone side by side in wet cement. A mosaic artist uses the small pieces of glass or stone to create broken lines that outline shapes.

It is suggested that each brick in *Ishtar Gate* might have been molded and enameled separately.

Cultural Perspectives *Ishtar Gate* was created in 575 B.C., during a time when Babylonia rose to power once again. The empire was ruled by King Nebuchadnezzar, who built the famous walls and hanging gardens of Babylon, one of the seven wonders of the world.

Ravenna, Italy, possesses many monuments and artifacts of the First Golden Age (A.D. 526–726).

• Use the **Animals Through History Time Line** to compare the use of animals during different periods of time.

*See **More About** pages 206–227 for more about art history and subject matter.

FOCUS

Time: About 10 minutes

Activating Prior Knowledge

"Think about how your favorite room at home is decorated. What colors are the walls? What different textures or shapes make the room interesting?"

"Piensen acerca de cómo están decoradas sus habitaciones en sus casas. ¿Qué colores tienen las paredes? ¿Qué texturas o figuras diferentes hacen interesante la habitación?"

• Discuss students' answers.

Introducing the Art

"Let's take a close look at the two mosaics."

"Vamos a observar detalladamente los dos mosaicos."

• **COMPARE AND CONTRAST** Have students make a list of the similarities and differences in the two mosaics. (Both have a dark background, depict mythological figures, and are realistic. They also have formal balance and limited colors. The *Ishtar Gate* illustrates flat space, and the *Ravenna* appears rounded.)

• Share information about the lives, work and times of the artists from **Art Background** and the **Artist Profiles Book.**

• Have students answer questions on page 175. (See **Perception Hints** below.)

⟲ **FOR THE ART SPECIALIST**

Use the **Overhead** and the **Large Prints** *A Dash for the Timber* and *Louis IX and Queen Blanche of Castile* to demonstrate how artists create harmony with similar shapes, lines, or textures, and how they can change elements to create variety.

Perception Hints

Related colors *Ishtar Gate.* Various related blues are found throughout, and the tan animals relate to the band along the bottom. *First Bishop of Ravenna.* Brown is related to the border, the houses, and the tree trunks, and green is related to the ground and the trees.

Shapes *Ishtar Gate* and *First Bishop of Ravenna.* Both have repeated rectangular bricks and horses.

Geometric and free-form shapes *Ishtar Gate.* Borders have geometric shapes placed near free-form animal figures. *First Bishop of Ravenna.* The border is geometric, and the sheep are free-form.

Color contrast *Ishtar Gate.* The warm color of the animals and decorative border contrasts with the cool-colored background. *First Bishop of Ravenna.* White contrasts with the dark green background.

LESSON 3 **175**

TEACH

Time: About two 30-minute periods

Practice

Materials

- 9- × 12-inch construction paper in related colors
- 9- × 12-inch black paper
- pencils

Alternate Materials: magazine pages

"How can you show harmony and variety in a paper mosaic?"

"¿Cómo pueden mostrar armonía y variedad en un mosaico de papel?"

- Discuss the definition of *harmony* on page 176.
- Distribute materials and allow students to select two pieces of paper that are related colors and another black piece.
- Have students follow the directions on page 176 for illustrating harmony. Ask students to answer the Decide question orally.

Create PROBLEM SOLVING

Materials

- 12- × 18-inch black construction paper
- dustless chalk
- warm- and cool-colored construction paper
- scissors and glue
- clay tile from the **Art Manipulative Kit**

 For safety issues about glue and chalk and other information about safety in the art classroom, see page T22.

Alternate Materials: painted background pieces

"Let's show harmony and variety in a paper mosaic."

"Vamos a mostrar armonía y variedad en un mosaico de papel."

- Have students think about animal shapes.
- Show students the clay tile and discuss the way the mosaics in the lesson were made.
- Review ways to create harmony and variety.

See page 33 in the **Technique Tips Flip Chart** for visual examples of techniques.

- Distribute materials and have students follow the directions on page 177.

FOR THE ART SPECIALIST

Add texture to the paper mosaics by using wallpaper samples.

Using Harmony and Variety in Mosaics

A **mosaic** is a picture made by setting small pieces of colored tile, glass, or stone side by side.

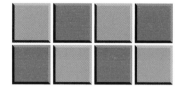

Harmony can be created in mosaics by using similar shapes throughout the design. This sometimes creates a feeling of peacefulness.

Variety can also be found in mosaics through the use of different materials, such as glass, marble, tile, stone, gold, and shell. Using a variety of lines, shapes, colors, and textures also adds interest.

The art of mosaic is still used today to decorate religious and public buildings.

Practice

Illustrate harmony in a paper mosaic. Use construction paper.

Decide How did you create harmony?

1. Draw the large outline of an object on a sheet of paper.

2. Choose construction paper in two related colors. Tear the paper into strips. Tear the strips into rectangles and triangles to make tiles.

3. Lay the pieces on the drawing until it is filled. Leave small spaces between the pieces.

Activities in
ART Across the Curriculum Book

Reading/Language Arts Identify sentences as fact or opinion, after noting how facts and opinions could be examples of harmony and variety. (page 193)

Math Learn how to measure the area of a rectangle to solve problems, comparing the creation of a mosaic to laying tile for walls or floors. (page 194)

Science Study a weather calendar to answer questions. (page 195)

Social Studies Learn about another large structure created by the Babylonians, and compare it to others. (page 196)

The Arts Use variety in movement to show particular feelings. (page 197)

Technology Use the *Multimedia Workshop* CD-ROM to create harmony and variety in a mosaic design. (page 198)

How did this student artist create variety and harmony in an animal mosaic?

Jack Maloy. Age 8. *Owl.* Cut paper.

Create

What animal shape would make an interesting mosaic? Create a paper mosaic to show harmony and variety.

1. Think about the shapes of different animals. Choose one and draw its shape with chalk on black paper.

2. Make mosaic pieces by cutting colored paper into strips. Cut the strips into the shapes you want to use. Fill the outline with warm colors and a variety of small shapes. Glue them down.

3. Next, cut small pieces of cool-colored construction paper. Glue them onto the background areas around your animal.

Describe What colors did you use for your mosaic? Describe the shapes of the mosaic pieces.

Analyze Did you create variety? Did you create harmony?

Interpret Where would be the best place in town to hang your class's mosaics? Explain.

Decide How did you balance harmony and variety in your mosaic?

Lesson 3   177

THEME Connections

Patterns Use both artworks as examples of patterns used as visual communication.

Cultures Use the artworks as visual examples of art created for public spaces cross culturally.

Traditions Discuss how *Ishtar Gate* was created by the Babylonians to convey a feeling of power to visitors entering the temple.

ESL

ESL students will benefit from working with a supportive English-speaking peer for the Practice activity. Encourage ESL students to ask questions when they do not understand and to ask their partners to help them understand the vocabulary from the lesson.

CLOSE

Time: About 5 minutes

"What parts of a mosaic create harmony? What parts can add variety?"

"¿Qué partes de un mosaico crean armonía? ¿Qué partes pueden agregar variedad?"

LARGE PRINT **Review**

Use the **Large Prints** *A Dash for the Timber* and *Louis IX and Queen Blanche of Castile* to have students compare the use of harmony and variety to the works in this lesson.

Art Criticism

Have students answer the four art criticism questions—Describe, Analyze, Interpret, and Decide—orally or in writing. Discuss the use of harmony and variety in their paper mosaics.

Assess

Use the **Assessment Book** pages 65–66 as a formal assessment for this lesson.

Evaluation Criteria

• Can the student identify and demonstrate harmony and variety in a work of art?

• Can the student create harmony and variety in a unique paper mosaic?

• Can the student use the four steps of art criticism to evaluate his or her own work?

• Can the student compare the two mosaics in this lesson?

Reteaching • • • • • • • • • • • • •

Harmony and variety Have students look through the book to find two different works of art that have harmony and variety. Ask them to list the title of each work and describe how harmony and variety are created in each.

Perception Hints for Student Art

This student artist created harmony by using similar shapes that are repeated. He created variety by using different colors.

U NIT 6
LESSON 4

LESSON PLANNER

Objectives

After completing this lesson, students will be able to:

• identify techniques used by artists to create a feeling of unity. *Aesthetic Perception*

• plan and create a crayon-resist drawing that illustrates unity. *Creative Expression*

• use the four steps of art criticism to evaluate their wax-resist drawings. *Art Criticism*

• compare and contrast early American and Roman rooms. *Art History and Culture*

Program Resources

• **Overhead:** Both the Duncan House Bedroom and *Bedroom (cubiculum nocturnum)* are available on overhead 34.

• **Large Prints:** *A Dash for the Timber* by Frederic S. Remington and *Illuminated Page with Louis IX and Queen Blanche of Castile*

• **Technique Tips Flip Chart,** page 34

• **Vocabulary Book** pages 67–68

• **Art Manipulative Kit:** flash cards

• **Artist Profiles Book:** Artists unknown pages 78 and 79

• **Art Across the Curriculum Book** pages 199–204

• **Multimedia Workshop CD-ROM**

• **Assessment Book** pages 67–68

Multiple Intelligences
Verbal/Linguistic Students can understand unity as they learn vocabulary and explanations.

Vocabulary

unity *unidad* the quality of wholeness or oneness that is achieved through the effective use of elements and principles of art

harmony *armonía* the use of similar shapes or related colors throughout a design

variety *variedad* the use of different materials, lines, shapes, colors, or textures in a design

simplicity *simplicidad* created by the use of one color, texture, or shape in a work of art

---

Unity

Artists balance harmony and variety to create unity in a work of art.

Artist unknown. (United States). *Duncan House Bedroom.* c. 1805. Bed-sitting room. Haverhill, Massachusetts. The Metropolitan Museum of Art, New York, New York.

Look at the rooms on these pages. The *Duncan House Bedroom* was designed in 1805 for a private home in Massachusetts. *Bedroom (cubiculum nocturnum)* is a Roman burial chamber. It was built and decorated more than 2,000 years ago. Both rooms were designed and decorated to create a feeling of unity. The variety of materials and objects is balanced by the harmony of colors and shapes.

178

ART Background

About the Artists

Duncan Phyfe (dung' kən fīf, American, 1768–1854) was an American furniture designer. Influenced by English neoclassical and Regency styles, he produced furniture with elegant proportions and slender lines. The four-poster bed, from the workshop of Duncan Phyfe, was made by many different craftsmen.

The paintings of the *Bedroom (cubiculum nocturnum)* make up the greatest collection of Roman paintings outside of Italy. These paintings are from a villa that was buried by the eruption of Mt. Vesuvius in A.D. 79. The paintings survived intact.

About Subject Matter* Both the *Duncan House Bedroom* and the *Bedroom (cubiculum nocturnum)* are examples of interior architecture and furnishings.

About the Media The *Duncan House Bedroom* is decorated with a variety of fabrics and materials. The walls of the *Bedroom (cubiculum nocturnum)* are covered with frescoes, which are paintings on wet plaster.

Artist unknown. (Roman). *Bedroom (cubiculum nocturnum).*
40–30 B.C. Fresco on lime plaster. 8 feet 8½ inches × 19 feet 1⅞ inches × 10 feet 11½ inches.
The Metropolitan Museum of Art, New York,
New York. Rogers Fund, 1903. Photograph by Shecter Lee.

Study both rooms to find examples of unity.

- ☑ Find related shapes. Where are they repeated?

- ☑ Find the two main colors in each room. Where do you see them repeated?

- ☑ Do you see a variety of textures? Describe them.

- ☑ Locate objects that are repeated.

- ☑ Does one room seem to have more variety than the other? Does one have more harmony? How can you tell?

Lesson 4   **179**

SEEING LIKE
AN ARTIST

Look around your classroom. List examples of harmony in the room. Then, list examples of variety. Which list is the longest?

About Art History* The Federal period extended from the end of the American Revolution to 1840. The work of Duncan Phyfe, used to decorate the *Duncan House Bedroom,* typifies Federal furniture.

The *Bedroom (cubiculum nocturnum)* was built during the first century B.C. By this time, the Romans used concrete to create sculpted decoration for embellishment.

Cultural Perspectives The *Duncan House Bedroom* was designed in America during the time when the nation was expanding to the Southeast and West, and new states were being added to the union.

The *Bedroom (cubiculum nocturnum)* was built at the time when the Roman Republic had become an empire and Rome ruled much of the known Western world.

*See **More About** pages 206–227 for more about art history and subject matter.

FOCUS

Time: About 10 minutes

Activating Prior Knowledge

"Suppose you are eating out with your family at a fancy restaurant. Describe how the place settings are arranged."
"Vamos a suponer que están comiendo en un restaurante. Describan cómo colocan los servicios de mesa."

- Discuss students' responses. Students may point out that various objects are similar in shape; that repeated colors connect the different objects.

Introducing the Art

"Let's take a close look at the two rooms."
"Vamos a observar detalladamente las dos habitaciones."

- **COMPARE AND CONTRAST** Have students make a list of the similarities and differences in the two rooms. (Both interiors show approximate symmetry, and have decorative molding. The *Bedroom* has a flat ceiling and several pieces of furniture. The *Cubiculum* has a vaulted area in the ceiling and pictorial images covering the walls.)

- Share and discuss information about the lives, work, and times of the artists from **Art Background** and the **Artist Profiles Book.**

- Have students answer questions about unity on page 179. (See **Perception Hints** below.)

FOR THE ART SPECIALIST

Use the **Overhead** and the **Large Prints** *A Dash for the Timber* and *Louis IX and Queen Blanche of Castile* to demonstrate how artists balance harmony and variety to create unity in a work of art.

Perception Hints

Shapes *Cubiculum.* The bench and stool are similar shapes. *Bedroom.* The carpet pattern and the scallops on the curtains and canopy.
Colors *Cubiculum.* Red and blue. *Bedroom.* Red and white.
Textures *Bedroom.* There are a variety of shiny and smooth textures on the bedspread, canopy, and curtains.
Objects *Bedroom.* Statues on fireplace.
Variety and harmony *Bedroom* and *Cubiculum.* The *Bedroom* seems to have more variety than the *Cubiculum* because of the various textures, patterns, and materials. The *Cubiculum* seems to have more harmony than the bedroom because of the rectangular-shaped panels that are repeated on the walls.

TEACH

Time: About two 30-minute periods

Practice

Materials

- 9- × 12-inch paper
- colored pencils

Alternate Materials: crayons

"How can you illustrate unity in a design?"

"¿Cómo se pueden ilustrar unidad en un diseño?"

- Discuss definitions of *harmony* and *variety* and discuss how they create unity in a work of art.
- Distribute materials and have students follow the directions on page 180 for illustrating unity. Ask them to answer the Decide question on the back of the drawing.

Create PROBLEM SOLVING

Materials

- 12- × 18-inch white construction paper
- crayons   • sketch paper and pencils
- watercolor paints and brushes   • tape
- containers of water   • paper towels
- flash cards from the **Art Manipulative Kit**

Alternate Materials: oil pastels and liquid tempera

"Let's use harmony and variety to create unity in a crayon-resist drawing."

"Vamos a usar armonía y variedad para crear unidad en un dibujo resistente al creyón."

- Have students brainstorm ideas for their dream room. Use the flash cards to discuss harmony and unity in color and texture.
- Review techniques for creating unity and warm and cool colors.
- Review techniques for using watercolors in **More About Technique Tips** on page 200.
- See page 34 in the **Technique Tips Flip Chart** for visual examples of techniques.
- Distribute materials and have students follow the directions on page 181.
- Remind the students to cover the paper heavily with crayon.

FOR THE ART SPECIALIST

Have students draw a floor plan of their room and construct them in shoe boxes.

Using Unity

Unity is the "invisible glue" that makes different parts look as if they belong together. It helps you see a work of art as a whole instead of as separate parts. Artists have different ways of creating unity. One way is to balance harmony and variety. This gives them equal weight.

Harmony is created by using similar shapes or related colors to give a work the feeling of oneness or belonging.

Variety is created by using different lines, shapes, colors, and textures to give a work the feeling of oneness or belonging.

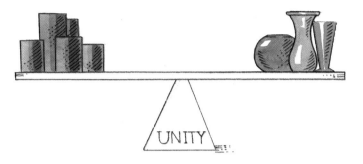

Simplicity is another way to create unity. Sometimes artists make everything in a work one color, texture, or shape to create simplicity.

Practice

Create and color a design that illustrates unity. Use colored pencils.

Decide How did you create unity in your design?

1. Draw a variety of geometric and free-form shapes to create a design.

2. Color the shapes with warm colors.

3. Choose a cool color to fill the spaces between and around the shapes.

Activities in ART Across the Curriculum Book

Reading/Language Arts Understand how unity is used in speeches to inform, persuade, and entertain. (page 199)

Math Study and identify how a variety of shapes helped to create unity in *Bedroom* (*cubiculum nocturnum*). (page 200)

Science Learn how animals sleep differently from people. (page 201)

Social Studies Determine why a person might sleep in a place other than a bed. (page 202)

The Arts Imagine how you prepare for rest, then role-play your bedtime routine. (page 203)

Technology Use the *Multimedia Workshop* CD-ROM to design a room using harmony and variety to create unity. (page 204)

*Readiness

Yori Lai. Age 8. Crayon.

What is the center of interest in this student artist's dream room?

Create

What would be the perfect room for you? Design a dream room that illustrates unity.

1. Think about what your dream room would look like. Make several sketches of it. Choose one and draw it with crayon.

2. Create harmony in your drawing by repeating colors that are related. Use a contrasting color to create a center of interest.

3. To create unity, cover the whole paper with one color of watercolor.

Describe What objects did you draw in your room? What colors did you use?

Analyze Where did you create harmony in the room? Where did you add variety? How did you give your drawing a feeling of unity?

Interpret Does your drawing look like your dream room? Explain.

Decide What do you like best about this room?

Lesson **4**   **181**

THEME Connections

Diversity Use the artwork to discuss the differences in the rooms.
Culture Use the artwork as a springboard to discuss the two cultures.
Connections Compare and contrast the bedroom in one artwork to your dream bedroom.

ESL

When conducting the introduction of unity, show the text examples that answer the questions you have posed. Point to the examples that a student suggests as answers to the question and paraphrase the student's response. ESL students will increase their comprehension from the visual support and the language repetition.

CLOSE

Time: About 5 minutes

"What happened to the watercolor painted on crayon?"
"¿Qué le pasó a la acuarela pintada sobre creyón?"

Review
Have students compare the ways in which a feeling of unity is created in their artworks and in the works of this lesson.

Art Criticism
Have students answer the four art criticism questions—Describe, Analyze, Interpret, and Decide—orally or in writing. After the paint has dried in their drawings, discuss their use of the techniques for creating unity.

 Assess
Use the **Assessment Book** pages 67–68 as a formal assessment for this lesson.

Evaluation Criteria
• Can the student describe and demonstrate at least two ways to create unity in a work of art?
• Can the student use harmony and variety to create unity in a crayon-resist drawing?
• Can the student use the four steps of art criticism to evaluate his or her own work?
• Can the student compare and contrast the Early American and Roman bedrooms?

Reteaching ● ● ● ● ● ● ● ● ● ●

Unity Have students look through the book to find five different works of art that illustrate unity. Ask them to list the title of each work and describe the techniques used that create a feeling of unity in each.

Perception Hints for Student Art

The television is the center of interest in the student artist's drawing.

UNIT 6 LESSON 5

LESSON PLANNER

Objectives

After completing this lesson, students will be able to:

- identify how repetition and grouping create a feeling of unity. *Aesthetic Perception*
- plan and create a crayon engraving that shows unity. *Creative Expression*
- use the four steps of art criticism to evaluate their own engravings. *Art Criticism*
- compare the cultures of both artists. *Art History and Culture*

Program Resources

- **Overhead:** Both the Matisse and the Davis are available on overhead 35.
- **Large Prints:** *A Dash for the Timber* by Frederic S. Remington and *Illuminated Page with Louis IX and Queen Blanche of Castile*
- **Technique Tips Flip Chart,** page 35
- **Vocabulary Book** pages 69–70
- **Art Manipulative Kit:** music audiotapes
- **Artist Profiles Book:** Davis page 8 and Matisse page 31
- **Art Across the Curriculum Book** pages 205–210
- **Multimedia Workshop CD-ROM**
- **National Geographic Picture Atlas of the World CD-ROM**
- **Assessment Book** pages 69–70

Multiple Intelligences

Interpersonal Students can make the connection of groupings that create unity in art and groupings that create unity in relationships with others.

Vocabulary

repetition *repetición* a technique for creating rhythm and unity in which a motif or single element appears again and again

unity *unidad* the quality of wholeness or oneness that is achieved through the effective use of the elements and principles of art

---

Unity, Repetition, and Grouping

Artists use repetition and grouping to create unity in a work of art.

Willis Bing Davis. (American). *Ancestral Spirit Dance Series.* 1990. Oil pastel. 60 × 40 inches. Courtesy of Willis Bing Davis.

Look at the paintings on these pages. Henri Matisse painted *Woman in Blue* in France. About 50 years later, Willis Bing Davis painted *Ancestral Spirit Dance Series*, an abstract design based on memories of African dancers. Both artists have created unity to give their work a feeling of wholeness.

182

Unit **6**

ART Background

About the Artists

Henri Matisse (än rē′ mä tēs, French, 1869–1954) first studied law but turned to art at the age of 21. His paintings are filled with bright colors and patterns.He spent the last 15 years of his life in a wheelchair, creating artwork from paper cutouts.

*Use the **National Geographic Picture Atlas of the World CD-ROM** to learn more about French culture.

Willis "Bing " Davis (bing dā vəs, American, 1937–) has two loves—athletics and the arts. He attended DePauw University on a sports scholarship and earned a degree in art education. Davis has pioneered such projects as the national "Artists in the Schools."

About Subject Matter* The Matisse painting is a portrait, and Davis's piece is symbolic.

About the Media The Matisse is an oil painting. The Davis is created with oil pastels.

Henri Matisse. (French). *Woman in Blue.* 1937. Oil on canvas. 36½ × 29 inches. Philadelphia Museum of Art, Philadelphia, Pennsylvania. Gift of Mrs. John Wintersteen/© 1998 Succession H. Matisse, Paris/Artists Rights Society (ARS), New York.

Study both artworks to find examples of unity.

✓ Where do you see geometric shapes combined with wild zigzag lines?

✓ Name the colors in each work. How many are there in each?

✓ Locate the thin lines repeated throughout *Woman in Blue.*

Lesson 5

183

SEEING LIKE AN ARTIST

Look outdoors. Find objects in nature that are surrounded by a single color.

About Art History Matisse's painting is a direct outgrowth of Fauvism. The Fauves used exaggerated and vibrant color to express feelings. After the movement died out, only Matisse continued to explore the use of pure color and to reduce objects to their simplest shapes and forms.

Davis's style is a combination of both his African and African American backgrounds. A fellowship led him to Nigeria, where he explored the customs and the heritage of his ancestors. An understanding of his background is incorporated into his art.

Cultural Perspectives Matisse's painting was created shortly before the outbreak of World War II, when Europe was experiencing political and social problems.

Davis uses African patterns, motifs, and color to help him express his images of the African American experience. He has devoted his efforts to create artworks that span the two cultures.

*See **More About** pages 206–227 for more about art history and subject matter.

FOCUS

Time: About 10 minutes

Activating Prior Knowledge

"Imagine that you are looking into a fishbowl. What are some different objects that you see? How does the bowl give a feeling of unity to all these different objects?"

"Imagínense que están viendo una pecera. ¿Cuáles son algunos de los diferentes objetos que ven? ¿Cómo la pecera da la sensación de unidad a todos estos diferentes objetos?"

• Discuss students' answers to the questions and the fact that the fishbowl brings objects close together in a small area.

Introducing the Art

"Let's take a close look at the two paintings."

"Vamos a observar detalladamente las dos pinturas."

• **COMPARE AND CONTRAST** Have students make a list of the similarities and differences in the two paintings. (Both paintings have lines engraved into the paint and repeat limited colors. Matisse's shows shallow space, has bright colors, and repeats lines throughout the painting. The Davis painting shows flat space, has contrasting colors, and repeats lines in a contained space.)

• Share and discuss information about the lives, work, and times of the artists from **Art Background** and the **Artist Profiles Book.**

• Have students answer questions about unity on page 183. (See **Perception Hints** below.)

FOR THE ART SPECIALIST

Use the **Overhead** and the **Large Prints** *A Dash for the Timber* and *Louis IX and Queen Blanche of Castile* to demonstrate how artists use repetition and grouping to create unity.

Perception Hints

Geometric shapes and zigzag lines The Davis has triangles and squiggly lines.

Colors *Matisse.* Colors are limited to the primary colors, black, and white. *Davis.* Black background; white, pink, and light blue across the center with darker shades of these colors on the top and bottom.

Thin lines *Matisse.* Thin, crisscrossed lines are found throughout the background.

TEACH

Time: About two 30-minute periods

Practice

Materials

- 9- × 12-inch paper
- pencils and crayons

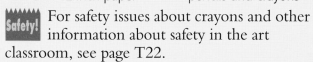**Safety!** For safety issues about crayons and other information about safety in the art classroom, see page T22.

Alternate Materials: markers

"How can you illustrate unity?"

"¿Cómo pueden ilustrar la unidad?"

- Discuss ways to create unity through repetition on page 184.
- Distribute materials and have students follow the directions on page 184 for illustrating unity. Ask them to answer the Decide question on the back of their papers.

Create PROBLEM SOLVING

Materials

- 9- × 12-inch white construction paper
- crayons and large paper clips • sketch paper
- washable black ink and liquid soap • pencils
- paintbrushes and palettes • paper towels
- containers of water • newspaper
- audiotapes from the **Art Manipulative Kit**

Alternate Materials: oil pastels

"Let's show unity in a crayon engraving."

"Vamos a mostrar unidad en un grabado a creyón."

- Discuss techniques for using repetition and grouping to create unity.
- Thin ink with a few drops of liquid soap.
- See page 35 in the **Technique Tips Flip Chart** for visual examples of techniques.
- Distribute materials and have students follow the first step of the directions on page 185.
- While the ink is drying, have students brainstorm a variety of reptiles and insects. Then, have students complete steps 2 and 3. Students can either scratch in, or engrave, the background or the design.
- Play audiotapes while students are creating.

⭐ FOR THE ART SPECIALIST

Have students try other objects besides paper clips to create different engraving patterns.

---

184 Unit 6

Using Unity

Unity is the feeling of wholeness in a work of art. You have already seen how harmony and variety can create unity in a work of art.

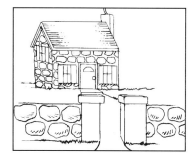

Repetition is another way artists show that different parts of a work belong together. An architect, for example, might repeat the colors and textures found in the environment on the outside of the house.

Seashells arranged on a beach are a good example of unity. They are usually different shapes and sizes, but the sand in the background unifies them.

Practice

Illustrate unity. Use pencil and crayon.

1. Draw a large free-form shape. Fill it with a variety of smaller geometric shapes.

2. Use pencil to darken the spaces between the geometric shapes. Use crayon to color the whole area outside the free-form shape one color.

Decide How did you create unity in your design?

184 Unit 6

Activities in

ART Across the Curriculum Book

Reading/Language Arts Write a story about the character depicted in *Woman in Blue*. (page 205) *

Math Understand how math uses unity, repetition, and grouping to solve problems. (page 206)

Science Learn about objects that move. (page 207)

Social Studies Determine whether statements about America and its people show unity or separateness. (page 208)

The Arts Create a dance with repetition, grouping dance steps into beginning, middle, and end. (page 209)

Technology Use the *Multimedia Workshop* CD-ROM to draw an object that shows unity through repeated lines, colors, and grouping. (page 210)

*Readiness

How does this student artist show unity in her design?

Toni Thompson. Age 8. *Kingdom.* Crayon and school acrylics.

Create

How can you use creatures to show unity? Create a crayon engraving.

1. Think about insects and reptiles with interesting shapes. Use crayons to cover a sheet of paper with many different colors. Then, paint the whole surface with thinned black ink until you can't see the color.

2. While the ink is drying, sketch a few real or imaginary reptiles and insects on scratch paper. Choose some to draw.

3. Engrave the creatures in different shapes and sizes by scratching lines and line patterns in the black background with the pointed end of a paper clip. This is called **crayon engraving.** Add detail and texture.

Describe What creatures did you draw? What colors did you use? Describe your lines.

Analyze How did you create unity in your engraving? What happened when you engraved your lines?

Interpret How would the mood of your picture change if you had not covered the surface with black ink?

Decide Can you think of another theme to use for this art project?

Lesson 5

185

THEME Connections

Cultures Use the two paintings to discuss the diverse cultures.
Energy Use Davis's painting to discuss how an illustrated artwork can create a sense of energy.
Relationships Matisse's use of color can inspire discussion of students' perceptions about the relationship between moods and feelings.

ESL

ESL students may feel hesitant about answering the interpretive question concerning their artwork. You may wish to phrase the questions as an either/or choice so that the vocabulary needed to answer the question is contained in the question itself.

CLOSE
Time: About 5 minutes

"How can you show unity in a crayon engraving?"
"¿Cómo pueden mostrar unidad en un grabado hecho con creyón?"

Review
Have students identify and compare techniques used for creating unity in the print and in the other works of art in this book.

Art Criticism
Have students answer the four art criticism questions—Describe, Analyze, Interpret, and Decide—orally or in writing. Discuss the use of techniques to create unity in their artwork.

Assess
Use the **Assessment Book** pages 69–70 as a formal assessment for this lesson.

Evaluation Criteria
- Can the student identify how repetition and grouping create a feeling of unity?
- Can the student create a feeling of unity in an engraving?
- Can the student use the four steps of art criticism to evaluate his or her own work?
- Can the student compare the cultures of the two artists?

Reteaching • • • • • • • • • •

Unity Have students look through the book to find three different works of art that illustrate repetition and proximity to create a feeling of unity. Ask them to list the title of each work and describe how a feeling of unity was created.

Perception Hints for Student Art
The black ink unifies the student artist's artwork.

Unity in Handmade Books

Artists unify pages when they make
books and their covers.

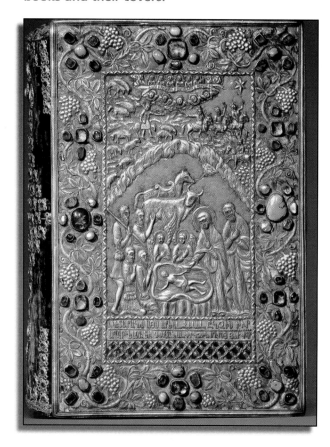

Artist unknown. (Armenia).
Cover of Armenian Book.
Thirteenth century. Carved and
hammered silver, gilded and
enameled, and set with jewels,
rubricated vellum. $10\frac{1}{4} \times 7\frac{3}{8}$
inches. The Metropolitan
Museum of Art, New York, New
York. Gift of Mrs. Edward S.
Harkness, 1916.

Look at the book covers on these pages.
The *Cover of Armenian Book* is made from
precious metal and decorated with a variety of
gemstones. Kathryn Gough created *Book Cover* in
the 1990s. She painted make-believe gemstones and
precious metal. The covers unify the pages of these
books. Unity is also an important part of the designs
on the covers.

UNIT 6 — LESSON 6

LESSON PLANNER

Objectives

After completing this lesson, students will be
able to:

- identify how books can create unity.
  Aesthetic Perception
- create an illustrated autobiographical book.
  Creative Expression
- use the four steps of art criticism to evaluate
  their own books. *Art Criticism*
- compare works by artists from different
  cultures. *Art History and Culture*

Program Resources

- **Overhead:** Both the Gough and *Armenian
  Book* are available on overhead 36.
- **Large Prints:** *A Dash for the Timber* by
  Frederic S. Remington and *Illuminated Page
  with Louis IX and Queen Blanche of Castile*
- **Technique Tips Flip Chart,** page 36
- **Vocabulary Book** pages 71–72
- **Art Manipulative Kit:** fabric swatches
- **Artist Profiles Book:** Artist unknown
  page 80 and Gough page 17
- **Art Across the Curriculum Book** pages
  211–216
- **Multimedia Workshop CD-ROM**
- **National Museum of Women in the
  Arts Collection:** prints
- **Assessment Book** pages 71–72

Multiple Intelligences
Body/Kinesthetic Students use fine
motor skills to create books.

Vocabulary
bookmaking *encuadernación* the art of
designing, printing, and binding books

FOCUS

Time: About 10 minutes

Activating Prior Knowledge

"Imagine yourself looking through a family photo album.
How does the album create unity?"

*"Imagínense que están viendo un álbum familiar. ¿Cómo crea
unidad el álbum?"*

- Discuss students' responses and how the
  album cover helps to unify the pages and
  photos within.

ART Background

About the Artists
Christianity became the official religion of Armenia during the fourth century. Armenian
artists used scenes from the Gospel and images of Christianity to decorate their churches
and to illustrate their manuscripts.

Kathryn Gough (kath' rin gof, American, 1968–   ) grew up in a family of artists. Her
father, Alan Gough, is a well-known artist who paints landscapes in a naturalistic style. Her
mother works in watercolors, and her brother is a photographer. As a child, Gough
designed fanciful sets for her marionettes and hand puppets.

- Use the **National Museum of Women in the Arts Collection** prints to compare other
  works of art created around the same time period.

About Subject Matter* The *Armenian Book Cover* is a narrative, and Gough's *Book
Cover* is nonobjective.

Kathryn Gough. (American). *Book Cover*, 1995. Oil on paper. 5 × 6 inches. Hudak private collection.

Study both book covers to find examples of unity.

- ✓ Find shapes that are similar.
- ✓ Where do you see the same motif repeated?
- ✓ Name the colors in each. How many are there?
- ✓ Where do you see a variety of shapes grouped closely together?
- ✓ Locate the negative spaces painted or dyed one color.
- ✓ Find shapes and colors that are inside a larger shape.

SEEING LIKE AN ARTIST
Look at books in your classroom. What clues on the covers hint at what is inside?

About the Media The *Armenian Gospel Book Cover* is made with hammered gold, paint, and gemstones. Gough's *Book Cover* is an oil painting.

About Art History* Existing illustrated Armenian manuscripts date from the ninth to the seventeenth centuries. They are based on early Christian and Byzantine art.

Gough's *Book Cover* was created in the 1990s, at the time of the rap era in American music and the revival of musicals from earlier times.

Cultural Perspectives Gough's *Book Cover* was created in the United States at a time when the Cold War between the former Soviet Union and the United States was coming to an end.

*See **More About** *pages 206–227 for more about art history and subject matter.*

Introducing the Art

"Let's take a close look at the two book covers."
"Vamos a observar detalladamente las dos cubiertas del libro."

- **COMPARE AND CONTRAST** Have students make a list of the similarities and differences in the two book covers. (Both covers repeat a motif, utilize metallic gold areas throughout, and show approximate symmetry. The *Armenian Gospel Book* cover incorporates real gemstones, has areas of relief, and illustrates depth. Gough's book cover simulates gemstones, is flat, and illustrates flat space.)
- Share and discuss information about the lives, work, and times of the artists from **Art Background** and the **Artist Profiles Book.**
- Have students answer questions about unity on page 187. (See **Perception Hints** below.)

FOR THE ART SPECIALIST

Use the **Overhead** and the **Large Prints** *A Dash for the Timber* and *Louis IX and Queen Blanche of Castile* to demonstrate how artists unify pages when they make books and their covers.

Perception Hints

Similar shapes *Gough.* Rectangular shapes are repeated throughout.
Repeated motifs *Armenian Gospel Book.* The grape and leaf motifs are repeated in the border.
Colors *Armenian Gospel Book.* Blue, green, and gold are repeated throughout. *Gough.* Reds, blues, and greens are repeated throughout.
Grouping *Armenian Gospel Book.* The figures in the center of the cover are grouped closely together. *Gough.* The four designs that surround the center circle are tightly grouped.
Negative spaces *Armenian Gospel Book.* The negative space in the center area is filled with the color blue. The negative space in the border is filled with the color green.
Unity *Gough.* Circles and half moon shapes colored blue, green, and red are contained within the larger circle in the center of the cover.

TEACH

Time: About two 30-minute periods

Practice

Materials
- 6- × 9-inch drawing paper
- 12- × 18-inch colored construction paper

Alternate Materials: tagboard or posterboard

"How can a book create unity for your artwork?"
"¿Cómo puede crear unidad un libro en sus obras de arte?"

- Discuss how a cover is a unifying element on page 188.
- Distribute materials and have students follow the directions on page 188 for showing unity.
- Staple the cover onto the pages. Ask students to answer the Decide question orally.

Create PROBLEM SOLVING

Materials
- 9- × 12-inch white construction paper
- crayons and/or markers   • staplers
- 9- × 12-inch colored construction paper
- fabric swatches from the **Art Manipulative Kit**

Safety! For safety issues about crayons and markers and other information about safety in the art classroom, see page T22.

Alternate Materials: yarn and tapestry needles for binding

"Let's create unity in a book about yourself."
"Vamos a crear unidad en un libro acerca de ustedes mismos."

- See page 36 in the **Technique Tips Flip Chart** for visual examples of techniques.
- Distribute drawing materials and have students follow the directions on page 189.
- Use fabric swatches to discuss colors and textures that would make good book covers.
- When the drawings are finished, demonstrate binding procedures using yarn and tapestry needles as an alternative to stapling. Punch holes along the folded side of the book and then use the yarn and a needle to "sew" the book together.

FOR THE ART SPECIALIST

Have the students use a variety of ways to unite their pages.

Using Bookmaking to Show Unity

Bookmaking is the art of binding or tying pages together inside a cover. It is an example of **unity,** or wholeness. A cover design unifies the contents of a book by holding the pages together.

Artists have been making books by hand for thousands of years. They create books in many different ways using a variety of materials.

Practice

Create an alphabet book for a kindergarten class. Use crayon.

Decide How did you unify the drawings?

1. Each student can illustrate a letter, adding objects that begin with the letter.

2. Place all the letters inside a folded paper to make a book.

3. Add a title and decorate the cover.

Activities in
ART Across the Curriculum Book

Reading/Language Arts Learn about the different parts of a book, like *Book Cover* in the art lesson. (page 211)

Math Study a bar graph of books checked out from a library. (page 212)

Science Learn how books were created in the past without machines, like in the *Cover of Armenian Book*. (page 213)

Social Studies Understand how inventions have changed our lives. (page 214)

The Arts Name songs that you know to answer questions. (page 215)

Technology Use the *Multimedia Workshop* CD-ROM to design a book for a young child. (page 216)

How did this student artist create unity?

Leanne Jewel. Age 8. Markers.

Create

What are the most important things about you? Show unity in a book about yourself.

1. Think about things you like to do and things that are important to you.

2. Put two sheets of paper together and fold them in half to make the pages of a book. Draw pictures that tell about you.

3. Fold a sheet of paper in half to make a cover. Write your name and the title of your book. Then, illustrate the front. Slide your pages inside and staple.

Describe What things describe you?

Analyze How did you create unity in your book?

Interpret Why did you choose the title?

Decide If you could redo some of the pages, which ones would you change? Why?

Lesson 6   **189**

THEME Connections

Systems Use the artworks as a springboard to discuss different systems used for communication.

Connections Use the artworks as visual examples of how objects can be functional as well as decorative.

Discover Use the artworks as a springboard to discover when the first books were made.

ESL

ESL students may have difficulty following oral directions without some kind of visual support. Consider modeling the steps with the whole class. To review, sketch the steps on the chalkboard before asking students to complete the activity.

CLOSE

Time: About 5 minutes

"What created unity in the books?"
"¿Qué creó unidad en los libros?"

Review
Have students identify and compare various techniques for creating a sense of unity in their artwork and in the works of this lesson.

Art Criticism
Have students answer the four art criticism questions—Describe, Analyze, Interpret, and Decide—orally or in writing. Discuss the use of unity in their books after they are bound.

Assess
Use the **Assessment Book** pages 71–72 as a formal assessment for this lesson.

Evaluation Criteria
• Can the student identify how a book creates unity?
• Can the student create an illustrated autobiographical book?
• Can the student use the four steps of art criticism to evaluate his or her book?
• Can the student compare works by artists from different cultures?

Reteaching • • • • • • • • • • •

Unity Have students identify and describe four different kinds of books that unify the bound pages.

Perception Hints for Student Art

This student artist created unity by adding a book cover.

UNIT 6

LESSON PLANNER

Objectives
After completing this lesson, students will be able to:

- create harmony, variety, and unity in the creation of movements and sounds related to natural forces. *Aesthetic Perception*
- express individual and group interpretations of such natural forces as the spinning earth and pulling gravity. *Creative Expression*
- use the four steps of art criticism to evaluate their own performances. *Art Criticism*
- relate information about *In the Heart of the Beast Puppet and Mask Theatre* and their production of *On the Day You Were Born. Art History and Culture*

Program Resources
Artsource Performing Arts Audio/Video Resource Package
On the Day You Were Born performed by In the Heart of the Beast Puppet and Mask Theatre; Sandy Spieler and Debra Frasier. Videocassette Running Time: 8:30.

FOCUS

Time: About 10 minutes

Activating Prior Knowledge
"Think about natural events that happen on the earth, such as the sun rising. What are some other natural events?"

"Piensen acerca de los eventos naturales que ocurren en la Tierra tal como la salida del sol. ¿Cuáles son otros eventos naturales?"

- Discuss how the book *On The Day You Were Born* is a celebration of natural events.

Introducing the Art
"Look at the picture of a scene from the play. Describe it."

"Observen la pintura de una escena de la obra. Describan lo."

- Discuss the information on page 190. Share facts from **Art Background.** If you have the *Artsource* videocassette, have students view it.

- Warm up by having the class form a big circle. Ask one student to go into the center and begin a simple, repetitive movement. One at a time, others join in, each adding a movement that relates to those that have gone before, so that the whole creates harmony, variety, and unity. Coach them to use their whole bodies and different levels in the space. After 5–8 students have participated, begin a new cycle.

Harmony, Variety, and Unity in Theater

In the Heart of the Beast Puppet and Mask Theatre: *On the Day You Were Born.*

*O*n the Day You Were Born is a book by Debra Frasier. It tells about events in nature that happen on the day a child enters the world. A play based on the book uses puppets, paintings, poems, and music to celebrate nature. The play welcomes each new member of the human family into the world.

ART Background

About the Artists
The *In the Heart of the Beast Puppet and Mask Theatre*, of Minneapolis, Minnesota, is known for its imaginative productions featuring puppets of all sizes and styles, from epic totems to tabletop proportions. Provocative and strikingly beautiful, these puppets are all built by hand from recycled materials.

Cultural Perspectives The idea for the production of *On the Day You Were Born* began when author/illustrator Debra Frasier asked Sandy Spieler and *In the Heart of the Beast* to create something to celebrate the publication of her book. The theater had wanted to do a play about the natural wonders of the world, and Frasier's book was perfect in both theme and visual style.

What To Do

Use your body and voice to express information about science and nature.

Materials
- ✔ poems and stories
- ✔ recordings of music

1. List some natural events.

2. Take each event and add an action word to it. Example: spinning Earth.

3. Work in a small group. Choose one event to explore through sound and movement. Think of different ways to show each event. You can combine dance, music, poems, and stories.

4. Think of an exciting way to begin. Next, plan some actions with sounds of talking or music to go with them. Then, decide on the end. Use harmony and variety to create balance in your scene.

5. Perform your scene for the class.

Describe Tell how your group thought up ideas and made decisions.

Analyze Explain how you used harmony, variety, and unity to dramatize your idea.

Interpret What is the mood of your scene?

Decide Do you think you succeeded in creating movements and sounds to express your ideas?

Extra Credit

Select another natural event. Use the same sound and motion techniques to work out a new scene. Work alone or with a partner. Perform your scene for others.

Theater 191

About Subject Matter Spieler worked in close collaboration with Frasier in the creative process of bringing the book off the page and onto the stage. She began by storyboarding the book into sections: a prologue, an invocation, the revelation of wonders, and finally the birth and welcome song. They then constructed tagboard models of the show's three large boxes, which open to reveal the text and action of the story.

TEACH
Time: About 30 minutes

Materials
- poems and stories
- recordings of music

"We're going to work in groups using movement and sound to illustrate several of the natural forces that govern the earth."

"Vamos a trabajar en grupos usando movimientos y sonidos para ilustrar algunas de las fuerzas naturales que goviernan la Tierra."

- Have students brainstorm natural events, and encourage students to suggest an action word for each.

- Have students form groups. Have each group select a topic to explore through sound and movement and then brainstorm ideas that communicate the topic.

- Have each group choose a way to begin. Then direct them to work on middle sections that show several types of actions accompanied by vocal sounds. Allow them to combine poems, stories, dance, and music.

- Finally, direct each group to find a position or scene as their ending. Explain that in theater this is called a "tableau."

CLOSE
Time: About 5 minutes

"What did you learn about using harmony, variety, and movement in theater?"

"¿Qué aprendieron acerca de usar la armonía, la variedad y el movimiento en el teatro?"

Assess
Have students answer the four art criticism questions on page 191—Describe, Analyze, Interpret, and Decide—orally or in writing.

Evaluation Criteria
- Can the student incorporate harmony, variety, and unity in his or her work?
- Can the student demonstrate an ability to get the essence of each natural force across?
- Can the student use the four steps of art criticism to evaluate his or her performance?
- Can the student relate information about the players and the performance?

UNIT 6

Reviewing Unit Concepts

"Artists use harmony and variety to create unity in works of art."

"Los artistas usan la armonía y la variedad para crear unidad en las obras de arte."

• Review ways that artists can create harmony, variety, and unity on pages 192 and 193. Have the students write down the different ways and list examples found in their environment.

Examining the Artwork

"Let's look closely at the work of art."

"Vamos a observar detalladamente la obra de arte."

• Have students look at Rodin's *The Thinker* and answer questions about the sculpture on page 193. (See **Perception Hints** below.)

Student Portfolio

Have students review all the artwork they have created in this unit and select the pieces they wish to keep in their portfolios.

Art Criticism Activity

Have students select an artwork from this unit and study it using the four steps of art criticism. (See pages 206–209 for more information about Art Criticism.) Have students work alone or in pairs and present their findings orally or in writing.

Perception Hints

Harmony Diagonal lines are repeated in the back, arms, legs, and neck.
Variety The texture of the skin is smooth and slightly bumpy, while the texture of the rock is rough.
Unity The overall bronze color of the sculpture creates a feeling of unity in the piece.

Harmony, Variety, and Unity

Reviewing Main Ideas

The lessons and activities in this unit cover the techniques that artists use to create harmony, variety, and unity.

1. **Harmony** is the peaceful look made when related elements of art are put together. Harmony can be created by using related colors, shapes, and repetition of elements.

2. **Variety** is created when different lines, shapes, colors, and textures are used to make a work of art interesting.
   • *Repetition* is one way artists create unity.
   • *Bookmaking,* binding pages together inside a cover, also creates unity.

3. *Mosaics* are pictures made by setting small pieces of colored tile, glass, or stone side by side. Harmony can be created in mosaics by using similar shapes. Variety can be created by using different materials.

4. **Unity** is a feeling of oneness in a work of art. Unity can be created by balancing harmony and variety.

Auguste Rodin. *The Thinker,* 1880. Bronze. $51\frac{1}{4} \times 55\frac{1}{4}$ inches. The Rodin Museum, Philadelphia: Gift of Jules E. Mastbaum.

ART Background

About the Artist
Auguste Rodin (ō gūst rō dan, French, 1840–1917). His early career as an artist was unsuccessful. In the 1870s, a trip to Italy became a turning point for him as a sculptor. Inspired by the work he saw by Michelangelo, Rodin felt liberated from the strict rules of academic art. He is credited for single-handedly bringing sculpture back to the center of public attention through his expressive and naturalistic portrayal of the human figure.

About Subject Matter* *The Thinker* is a portrait. Using live models, Rodin modeled the body in motion as a means of expressing emotion.

About the Media Rodin sculpted his figures in clay. A mold was made of the original model and then cast in bronze.

Summing Up

The *Thinker* is a sculpture by Auguste Rodin. In this sculpture, Rodin used the principles of harmony, variety, and unity covered in this unit.

- Which lines do you see more than once in this sculpture?
- How many different kinds of textures can you find in this sculpture?
- What color is the sculpture?

Harmony, variety, and unity are important principles in art. By using techniques to create harmony, variety, and unity, artists can create a work of art that is pleasing, interesting, and has a feeling of oneness.

Let's Visit a Museum

The Philadelphia Museum of Art was established in Philadelphia, Pennsylvania, in 1875. There are over 300,000 objects in the museum's collection. The Asian collection has artwork dating from 500 B.C. to the present. The European collections have sculpture, stained glass, and paintings. The American collections have paintings, furniture, silver, and Pennsylvania German art. In addition, the museum offers many programs for people of all ages. These include school tours, workshops, and performances for families.

The Philadelphia Museum of Art

193

Learning About Museums

Visitors to the Philadelphia Museum of Art feel as if they are taking a walk through time. Due to the vision of Fiske Kimbell, the museum's architectural historian, curators were sent to all parts of the world to find architectural interiors that were well preserved. As museum-goers move from gallery to gallery, they pass through an Indian temple, a Chinese palace hall, and a Japanese teahouse.

- Make a list of names and addresses of various museums throughout the United States. (See pages T30–T33.) Ask student teams to write a letter to the museum of their choice requesting information about the institution. Have students share the literature with the class.

  TIMELINE For more information about this and other museums, see pages T13, T30–T33, and the back of the **Animals Through History Time Line.**

- The World Wide Web address for the museum is as follows: http://www.pma.libertynet.org/

About Art History* *The Thinker* was created during a time in Europe when the human figure was idealized in sculptures. Contrary to this conventional style, Rodin sculpted his figures with extreme naturalism and was accused of having cast a live model.

Cultural Perspectives Rodin sculpted *The Thinker* during the same time the French people donated the *Statue of Liberty* to America. This monument, which embodied the Greek ideals of the human figure, was felt to symbolize characteristics necessary in a national symbol. Rodin, however, abolished these ideals and found a new means of interpreting the human figure.

*See **More About** pages 206–227 for more about art history and subject matter.

A Final Thought

"Art is a technique of communication. The image is the most complete technique of all communication."—Claes Oldenburg

TECHNIQUE TIPS

OVERVIEW

The purpose of the technique tips is to provide additional information, beyond what is on the student pages, about the proper and possible uses for the media. Learning the proper techniques and using materials safely will add to students' confidence and enthusiasm for art. (For more about Safety in the Art Classroom, see page T22.) These pages can help your students combine imagination with media to create art.

Drawing (pages 194–198)
Pencil

• Blending to Create Values
Most third-grade students should be ready to begin shading to create the illusion of form in their drawings. (For example, they should be able to recognize shadows.) **Blending** is a technique of shading in which the student holds the pencil on its side between the thumb and other fingers and shades with the side of the lead.

- Primary grade pencils with a medium-soft lead are ideal for shading.
- To create darker values, students should use the side of the pencil lead, press harder, and shade over areas more than once.
- To create lighter values, the students should press lightly, and shade over the area less.
- Gradations from dark to light can be created by smearing a shaded area into an area not yet shaded with a paper stump made of a tightly rolled paper towel.

Colored Pencil

- When blending colors with colored pencils, it is important to color the lighter color before the darker one. A color can easily be darkened, but it is almost impossible to lighten a color.
- To create shadows, blend complementary colors. This will create browns and darker colors.

Technique Tips

Pencil

With the side of your pencil lead, press harder and shade over areas more than once for darker values. With a pencil, you can add form to your objects by shading.

Colored Pencil

You can blend colors with colored pencils. Color with the lighter color first. Gently color over it with the darker color until you have the effect you want.

Shadows or darker values can be created by blending complementary colors.

More About...
Technique Tips

Crayon

Crayons can be used to make thin lines or thick lines. You can use both ends of the crayon.

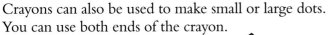

Crayons can also be used to make small or large dots. You can use both ends of the crayon.

Use either the side of the point or the side of the whole crayon to color large spaces.

You can also blend different colors to create the hues you want. Color with the lighter color first. Gently color over it with the darker color until you have the effect you want.

More About...Technique Tips   **195**

Crayon

- Thin lines and small dots can be created with the sharpened end of the crayon.
- Thick lines and large dots can be made with the flat end.
- Large areas can be colored in with the side of an unwrapped crayon.
- As with colored pencils, when blending, it is important to color the lightest color first. It is easy to darken a color. It is almost impossible to lighten one.
- Students may become concerned over broken crayons. Reassure them that these pieces are still useful for drawing and coloring in areas.

TECHNIQUE TIPS

(continued)

Marker

- To avoid damage and achieve better control, the students should not press hard on the marker tip.
- A conical-tipped marker can be used to make thin lines and dots. The side of the tip can be used to make wider lines and color in areas.
- Remind the students to always replace the cap to prevent drying.

More About...

Technique Tips

Marker

Marker can be used to make either sketches or finished drawings. Use the point of a marker to make thin lines and small dots.

The side of the tip makes thick lines.

Always replace the cap so the marker doesn't dry out.

More About...Technique Tips

More About...
Technique Tips

Oil Pastels

Oil pastels can be used like crayons. When you press down hard with oil pastels, your pictures will look painted. Oil pastels are soft and can break easily. These pieces are still usable. Oil pastels can be messy. Wash your hands with soap and water after using them.

Colors can be mixed or blended by smearing them together with your finger or a tissue.

You can also use oil pastels to color over other media, such as tempera or crayon. Then, you can scratch through this covering to create a design.

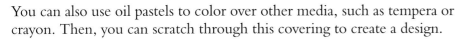

Oil Pastels

Oil pastels are pigments that are mixed with oil and compressed into sticks. They are used like crayons.

- By pressing with gentle force and coloring over an area several times, students can create the effect of paint.
- Students can create lines by drawing with the tip.
- Large spaces can be colored with the tip or the side.
- Textures can be created by making marks such as dots and lines. Textures can also be made by layering colors and scratching through with a paper clip straightened at one end.
- Colors can be mixed or blended by smearing them with a paper towel wrapped around a finger.
- Oil pastels break easily. Reassure the students that these pieces can still be used like new ones.
- If oil pastels become dirty from use, instruct students to mark with them on a paper towel until the colors are clean again.

Colored Chalk

Colored chalks are used to make colorful, soft designs.

- The tip of the chalk is used much like an oil pastel to make lines.
- To fill a space or shape with solid color, use gentle force and color over an area more than once.
- Colors can be mixed or blended by smearing them together with a paper towel wrapped around a finger.
- Colored chalks break easily. Reassure the students that these pieces can still be used like new ones.
- Colored chalks become dirty from use. Instruct the students to mark with them on a paper towel until the colors are clean.

More About...

Technique Tips

Colored Chalk

Colored chalks can be used to make colorful, soft designs. Because they are soft, colored chalks break easily. These pieces are still usable.

You can make bolder colors by coloring over an area more than once.

You can also blend colors by using your finger and a soft tissue.

More About...
Technique Tips

Tempera

1. Fill water containers halfway. Dip your brush in water. Wipe your brush on the inside edge of the container. Then, blot it on a paper towel to get rid of extra water. Remember to clean your brush before using a new color.

2. Always mix colors on a palette. Put some of each color that you want to mix on the palette. Add the darker color a little at a time to the lighter color.

3. To create lighter values, mix a little of the color or hue into white. To darken a value, add a tiny amount of black until you have the value you want.

4. Use a thin, pointed brush to paint thin lines and details. For thick lines or large areas, press firmly on the tip or use a wide brush.

5. Wash your brushes when you are done. Reshape the bristles. Store brushes with the bristles up.

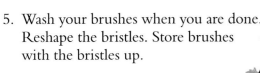

More About...Technique Tips   **199**

Painting (pages 199-200)
Tempera

For best results, it is recommended that quality liquid tempera paint be used.

Emphasize the following with students:

1. To remove excess water from the brush, gently wipe the end of the brush on the inside edge of the container. Discourage the students from tapping brushes on the rim of the can. This will prevent paint splatters.
2. Mix paints on a palette. Paper plates work well and reduce cleanup.
3. Always mix the darker color into the lighter color a little at a time until the desired color is reached. This reduces wasted paint.
4. Use a wide brush for large spaces.
5. Use a thin brush to paint details.

Watercolors

Below are some tips for using and controlling watercolors.

- Thick lines can be created by gently pressing down on the brush.
- Thin lines can be created by lightly touching the paper's surface with the tip of the brush.
- To create textures such as stipple (dots) or lines, demonstrate these techniques.
  1. Wet a round, soft-bristled watercolor brush.
  2. Carefully squeeze excess water from the bristles.
  3. Gently divide the bristles into spikes.
  4. Carefully touch the moistened paint cake with the bristle tips so that some paint is absorbed by the bristles.
  5. Lightly touch the paper with the separated bristles. Gentle taps create irregular dots. Gentle, upward strokes create irregular lines.
  6. When finished, rinse, clean, and reshape the brush.
- To create lighter values, the hue should be thinned with water using these steps:
  1. Use a watery brush.
  2. Thin the hue on the palette with water.
  3. Brush water over an already painted area.
  4. Blot the wet, painted area with a paper towel.
- To create darker values, add drops of black to the hue on the palette, *one at a time,* until the desired value is achieved.

Wash

Painting or sponging water onto the paper prior to painting will create soft lines, soft-edged shapes, and softer colors. The water should be allowed to soak into the paper before painting.

- To create sharp, clear lines and shapes, students should paint on dry paper with a damp brush.
- To create a fuzzy look, students should paint on dry paper with a dry brush and very little paint.

More About...
Technique Tips
Watercolor

1. Fill water containers halfway. Dip your brush in water. Wipe your brush on the inside edge of the container. Then, blot it on a paper towel to get rid of extra water. With your brush, add a drop of water to each watercolor cake and stir. Remember to clean your brush whenever you change colors.

2. Always mix colors on a palette. Put some of each color that you want to mix on the palette. Add the darker color a little at a time to the lighter color.

3. To create lighter values, add more water. To darken a hue, add a tiny amount of black until you get the value you want.

4. Use a thin, pointed brush to paint thin lines and details. For thick lines or large areas, press firmly on the tip or use a wide brush.

5. For a softer look, tape your paper to the table with masking tape. Use a wide brush to add water to the paper, working in rows from top to bottom. Let the water soak in a little. Painting on wet paper will create a soft or fuzzy look. For sharper forms or edges, paint on dry paper. Use only a little water in your brush.

6. Wash your brushes when you are done. Reshape the bristles. Store brushes with the bristles up.

More About...

Technique Tips

Printmaking: Making Stamps

Various ways of making stamps for printmaking are listed below. You can cut either a positive or negative shape into most of these objects.

- Cut sponges into shapes.

- Draw or sculpt a design on a flat piece of modeling clay. Use a pencil, a clay tool, the tip of a paperclip, or another object.

- The following procedure can be used to make sponge prints:
  1. If students wish to cut a sponge into a specific shape, use thin sponges. Draw the shape on the sponge with a marker and use scissors to cut it out.
  2. Dispense colors onto individual palettes, or spread out on a surface large enough to avoid mixing. Lightly press the sponge into the paint, being careful not to get too much paint on it. Lift the sponge and lightly press it into place on the paper. The sponge should be thoroughly rinsed between colors.

- Oil-based modeling clay can also be used to make a stamp. This is done by drawing or sculpting a design on a flat piece of modeling clay. There are a variety of tools manufactured for carving clay. Some classroom items that will work just as well include plastic eating utensils, craft sticks, and paper clips. The straightened end of a paper clip can be used to draw in the clay. The rounded end can be used as a gouge to carve clay away. To create a raised stamp, simply add pieces of clay to the bottom of the clay stamp.

TECHNIQUE TIPS

(continued)

More About Making Prints

- Below is the procedure for using a brayer, which is a soft roller, to make prints.

  1. Pour a small amount of water-based printing ink or paint onto a flat, solid surface. Roll the brayer in the ink or paint until there is an even coating on the surface and brayer.

  2. Roll the brayer over the top of the stamp. The ink should cover the paper evenly without getting into the grooves of the design.

  3. Apply the stamp carefully to the paper, rubbing the back of the paper with the side of the fist.

  4. Peel the paper and stamp apart.

  5. Reink the stamp as needed if you wish to make more than one print.

  6. When finished, wash the brayer, surface, and stamp.

- Another method for making prints calls for a paintbrush to apply the ink or paint. This method works better than the brayer with a raised stamp that the brayer would flatten out. Brush the ink or paint onto the stamping surface. Then follow the steps above, ending with thoroughly cleaning the brush.

Technique Tips

Printmaking: Printing Stamps

1. Put a small amount of water-based printing ink or some paint onto a flat, solid surface. Roll a soft roller, called a brayer, back and forth in the ink until there is an even coating of paint on both the surface and the brayer.

2. Roll the brayer over the top of your stamp. The ink should cover the stamp evenly without going into the grooves of your design.

3. Apply your stamp carefully to your paper. You can rub the back of the paper with the side of your fist to make sure all parts of the stamp get printed. Then, peel the paper and stamp apart and check your print. If you wish to make several prints of your design, you should ink your stamp again as needed.

4. When you are finished, wash the brayer, surface, and stamp.

More About...
Technique Tips

Collage

In a collage, objects or pieces of paper, fabric, or other materials are attached to a surface to create a work of art. When planning your collage, consider such things as:

- Size of shapes and spaces
- Placement of shapes and spaces
- Color schemes
- Textures

Remember that the empty (negative) spaces are also part of your design. Plan a collage as you would plan a painting or drawing. Decide what shapes and objects you want to use. Arrange them on the paper. When you have made an arrangement you like, glue your shapes and objects to the paper.

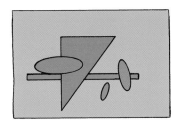 

More About...Technique Tips   **203**

Collage
Using Scissors

- It is important to teach the students safety when using scissors. They should always cut away from their bodies. Of course they should never point their scissors at others, spin them on the table, or walk around the room with them.
- There are scissors specially made to spring open for students who are physically challenged. Many scissors on the market today can be used with the right or left hand. If these are not available, keep a supply of "lefty" scissors for students who need them.
- To cut thick yarn or fabric, encourage students to work with a partner. While one cuts, the other can stretch the yarn or fabric. This makes cutting easier and encourages cooperation.

Arranging a Design

A collage is a work of art in which bits and pieces of paper, fabric, and other materials are glued onto a surface to create a **composition.**

- Provide a variety of textured and colored papers, yarns, fabrics, and found objects. Hard-to-cut materials can be precut.
- When using paper, students may choose to tear and/or cut the shapes.
- Encourage them to arrange the design first, paying as much attention to the negative spaces as the positive ones.
- Glue only after the final colors, shapes, and textures have been chosen and arranged.

Using Glue

Below are some tips to share with students to prevent waste, mess, and wrinkling of paper:

1. To attach two pieces of paper or fabric, use only a few drops of glue and smooth them with the tip of the bottle.
2. When finished, students should wipe the bottle clean with a paper towel, close the top, and store upright.

Technique Tips

Papier-Mâché—Strip Method

The strip method of papier-mâché ("mashed paper") uses paper combined with paste. Often, papier-mâché is molded over a form that helps it keep its shape while it's drying.

1. Create a supporting form, if needed. Forms can be made from clay, wadded-up newspaper, cardboard boxes and tubes, balloons, wire, or other materials. Masking tape can be used to hold the form together.

2. Tear paper into strips. Either dip the strips into a thick mixture of paste or rub paste on the strips with your fingers. Use wide strips to cover wide forms. Use thin strips or small pieces to cover a small shape.

3. Apply five or six layers of strips. Lay each layer in a different direction. For example, lay the first layer vertically and the second horizontally. Smooth over all rough edges with your fingers. If you are going to leave the form in place, two or three layers of strips should be enough.

4. When it is dry, you can paint your sculpture.

More About...Technique Tips

TECHNIQUE TIPS

(continued)

Papier-Mâché

Papier-mâché is a French term that means "mashed paper." It refers to sculpting methods that use paper and liquid paste. The wet paper and paste material is molded over supporting structures such as wadded dry paper or crumpled foil. The molded paper dries to a hard finish.

- Below are three common papier-mâché solutions:

  1. Mix one part white glue to one part water by adding one half the amount of water to a glue bottle that is half full. Close the lid. Shake vigorously. Add second half of the water. Close the lid and shake until mixed.

  2. Make a creamy mixture of wheat paste and water. To mix wheat paste, wear a dust mask and pour dry paste into a large mixing bowl. Add water and stir until the mixture is creamy. Mash lumps with a spoon or your hands.

  3. Use liquid starch.

More About...
Technique Tips

Clay

1. Pinch and pull clay into the desired shape.

2. To join two pieces of clay together:
   - *score,* or scratch, both pieces so they will stick together.
   - attach the pieces with some *slip,* which is watery clay
   - *squeeze* the two pieces together
   - *smooth* the edges

3. To carve a design out of clay, scratch or dig out your design with a paper clip or other tools.

4. To roll a slab of clay, press a ball of clay into a flat shape on a cloth-covered board. Place one 1/4" slat on each side of the clay. Use a roller to press the slab into an even thickness. With a straightened paper clip, trim the slab into the desired shape.

5. Wrap unfinished sculptures in plastic to keep them moist until you are finished.

Sculpting
Working with Clay

To help prevent earth clay from drying and cracking, students should not overhandle the clay. Keep damp paper towels nearby for students to keep their hands moist.

- The following steps are for modeling a person or animal from clay:
  1. Roll the piece of clay into an oval-shaped form. Describe this to the students as a "potato" shape.
  2. Pinch a head shape on one end.
  3. Pinch and pull out arms and legs.
  4. Leave some, but not too much, clay for the body.
  5. Squeeze the head, arms, legs, and body into the desired shapes.

Joining Clay

Clay is joined by using **slip,** a creamy mixture of clay and water. Slip can be made by putting a few dry pieces of clay in a container and covering them with water. When the clay dissolves, stir to achieve a creamy consistency. Joining clay also requires a scoring tool such as a straightened paper clip. The steps below are called the four *S's*—score, slip, smooth, and squeeze.

1. **Score** the two pieces to be joined.
2. Apply **slip** to one of the surfaces.
3. **Smooth** the seam.
4. **Squeeze** the two surfaces together.

Carving Clay

There are a variety of tools manufactured for carving clay. Some classroom items that will work just as well are plastic eating utensils, craft sticks, and paper clips. The straightened end of a paper clip can be used to draw in the clay. The rounded end can be used as a gouge to carve clay away.

OVERVIEW

Art Criticism is an organized system for looking at and talking about art. You can criticize art without being an expert on art. All that is needed are eyes to see and a brain to think about what is seen. The purpose of art criticism is to get the viewer involved in a perception process that delays judgment until all aspects of the visual image have been studied.

Learning art criticism will give each viewer the confidence to discuss a work of art without worrying what other people might think. The more a viewer interacts with a work of art, the better the chances are that the viewer will be involved in an aesthetic experience.

Describe

During this step, the viewer lists all the obvious things in the work. During this step, you must be objective. You do not *know* from looking at *Victorian Parlor II* that you see a room that is used by two people. All you can say is that you see a room with furniture.

Questions to Discuss

Ask the students to list and describe every object they see in the painting. (See **Perception Hints** below.)

Perception Hints

- There is a green rug with a design. There is a round, brown pedestal table, with a lace doily, and a large vase filled with flowers.
- On each side of the table is a black chair. Each chair has doilies to protect the head and arm areas. There is a brown footstool at the foot of each chair. There is a basket of yarn on the floor.
- On the left against the wall, there is a small, square table with a doily under a lamp. There is a book on a shelf under the tabletop. On the right is a bookcase with glass doors. There are books in the bookcase. There are three pitchers on top of the bookcase. The wall behind the chairs is gray. There are two framed paintings on the wall.

Horace Pippin. (American). *Victorian Parlor II.* 1945. Oil on canvas. $25\frac{1}{4} \times 30$ inches. The Metropolitan Museum of Art, New York, Arthur H. Heam Fund, 1958.

ART Background

About the Artist

Born to a poor mother in Pennsylvania, Horace Pippin (1888-1946) worked in a feed store, coal yard, hotel, and factory. In his free time, he sketched in pencil and crayon. At school, he drew all his spelling words—and then had to stay after school to do the lesson again, the "right" way.

When World War I began, Pippin joined the army and was sent to France in 1917. After a bullet partially paralyzed his right arm, he was sent home, but he could no longer draw well. In time, he married a widow and gained some control over his arm, which never completely healed.

In 1937, an art collector noticed one of Pippin's paintings in a shoemaker's shop in Pennsylvania. A year later, his work hung in New York's Museum of Modern Art. The exhibit was titled "Masters of Popular Painting." Pippin's great talent was finally recognized, and soon all museums wanted a "Pippin."

More About...
Art Criticism

DESCRIBE

Make a list of everything you see in this painting.

ANALYZE

How has the artist used line, shape, color, value, space, and texture?

How has the artist used rhythm, balance, emphasis, variety, and harmony to organize this painting?

Analyze

Questions to Discuss

Analyze

Questions to Discuss
- Describe the elements of art you see.
- How has the artist used the principles of design?

Perception Hints

Line There are horizontal lines where the floor meets the wall, on the wall, and in the rug.

Shape The tabletops, the bookcase, the lamp, the doilies, and the picture frames are geometric. The chairs, the vase, the flowers and leaves, and the pitchers are free-form shapes.

Color The rug has bright red flowers and bright green background. The same bright red is on the pitchers, some books, and one flower. The bottom of the lamp matches the rug. The top of the lamp is light yellow. The tables, the bookcase, and the picture frames are dull brown. The two chairs are flat black. The colors of the books match the colors in the flowers.

Value The darkest areas are the two chairs and the center table. The lightest areas are the doilies and the wall.

Texture Most of the textures in the painting are smooth. The rug has a rough texture.

Space There is very little overlapping to show depth. The space between the foreground and the wall in the background is very shallow.

Rhythm There is rhythm in the design on the rug. There is rhythm in the repetition of pairs of objects, the repetition of doilies, and in the lace designs of the doilies. There is rhythm in the repetition of red colors.

Balance The painting has formal balance, but it is not symmetrical. Things match, but not perfectly.

Emphasis The area of emphasis is the center with the table and vase that are larger than the other objects, and the two black matching chairs.

The Four Steps of Art Criticism

The process of art criticism is like playing detective. Each viewer must assume that the artist has a secret message inside the work. Art criticism is a four-step system that will help the viewer collect clues to deduce the hidden message. The four steps are **Describe, Analyze, Interpret,** and **Decide** or judgment.

Each step answers a question.

1. "What do I see?" (Describe)
2. "How is the work organized?" (Analyze)
3. "What is the artist saying to me?" (Interpret)
4. "What do I think about this work?" (Decide)

Interpret

During interpretation, the student will make inferences about the message in the work of art. This step needs to go beyond narration to a statement about meaning, to a generalization about life. This can be the most difficult step because it requires the viewer to dare to be different.

Each interpretation can be different because each is based upon the feelings and life experiences of the viewer. No person has done or seen exactly the same things as the next person. The viewer may see ideas in a work of art that were never dreamed of by the artist. This is not wrong. It simply means that the work is so powerful that it has special meanings for everybody. Interpretation is a time to guess, but all guesses must be based upon the facts collected during the first two steps.

Questions to Discuss

- What is the artist trying to tell us about this room? *(This is a living room from a time before electricity. There are no cords for the lamp. It is a kerosene lamp. The doilies also date this. There is no evidence of modern technology.)*

- Who lives here? What are they like? *(Answers will vary about the people. The most common guess is that a woman uses the chair on the right because of the basket of yarn, and her husband probably uses the left one. He has turned his chair toward the light so that he can see the book he is going to read while she knits. They may be elderly because there is no sign of children. They are very neat people. They like things arranged in balance. The large bouquet of flowers tells us that they love to garden.)*

- What does the rest of the house look like? *(The rest of the house is also very clean. The kitchen is big with a wood-burning stove and a big kitchen table. The dining room is seldom used. The bedroom has two twin beds, two dressers, one night table between the beds, and is probably arranged using formal balance.)*

Horace Pippin. (American). *Victorian Parlor II.* 1945. Oil on canvas. $25\frac{1}{4} \times$ 30 inches. The Metropolitan Museum of Art, New York, Arthur H. Heam Fund, 1958.

ART Background

About the Media
Pippin began his career by burning designs into wood with a hot poker, but he preferred working with oils on canvas.

About the Technique
For most of his life, Pippin painted in a small room in his home lit by one shadeless bulb. He sometimes worked for seventeen hours straight, painting the images in his mind with carefully chosen colors.

More About...
Art Criticism

INTERPRET

What is the artist telling you about the people who live in this room?

DECIDE

Have you ever seen another work of art that looks like this painting?

Is it successful because it is realistic?

Is it successful because it is well-organized?

Is it successful because you have strong feelings when you study it?

Decide

If the viewers were mature adults, knowledgeable about art, they could make a judgment about the quality of the work. Was this the artist's best work? Is this good art? These are the questions a professional critic would answer. The critic may also use aesthetic theories to defend his or her judgment. The students are not ready to make these kinds of decisions. They have not seen enough art to judge the quality of these pieces. On top of that, the artworks in this book have all been chosen because they are all examples of excellent art. But there are aesthetic decisions they can make.

Questions to Discuss
- Have you ever seen any works of art that look like this? (Answers will vary)
- Have you seen any works in this book that look similar to the style of this artist? (Faith Ringgold's *Tar Beach* and Joseph Jean–Gilleo's *Haitian Landscape*)
- Can you find any work of art that shows rooms that make you wonder about the people like this one did? (*Duncan House Bedroom*)
- Is this successful because it is realistic, because it is well organized, or because it makes you have strong feelings when you study it? (*Well organized, probably, but answers may vary*)

Aesthetic Theories
There are three common theories about aesthetic perception.

Imitationalism/Realism A work of art is good because the objects in it are realistically portrayed. The subject matter is clear and easily recognized.

Formalism/Composition A work of art is good because the artist has organized the elements using the principles successfully.

Emotionalism/Feelings A work of art is successful because it strongly affects the feelings of the viewer.

More About...
Aesthetic Perception

OVERVIEW

Aesthetic perception encourages children to make choices rather than give "right" answers. The perception of works of art happens in a "moment of transaction" in which the viewer/perceiver/ learner is totally engaged in the moment. By understanding the process, the perceiver gives the work validity. This encourages students to tap into their own files, to see or hear something with new eyes and ears, and finally, to realize that art is all around them.

Works of art created by masters or professional artists is central to exciting aesthetic perception experiences. Teachers can help to bridge the gap between the work of art and perceiver through designed activities that enable students to more fully understand key features of the work of art. Insight, commitment, knowledge, and love of the arts make teachers the cornerstones of aesthetic perception.

Journal writing is an integral part of aesthetic perception. It is an ongoing record of what a student does, notices, and thinks. Journals track the evolution of thoughts and experiences over time. Through this recorded journey, the student has the ability to go back, to reflect on where one has been and where one is going. Writing down thoughts, reactions, perceptions, new information and questions intensifies and makes more real each student's life experiences. We encourage both teachers and students to keep ongoing journals to reflect their aesthetic perception experiences on the work of art.

More About...
Aesthetics

LOOK

Horace Pippin. (American). *Victorian Parlor II.* 1945. Oil on canvas. $25\frac{1}{4} \times$ 30 inches. The Metropolitan Museum of Art, New York, Arthur H. Heam Fund, 1958.

ART Background

About Aesthetic Perception

Aesthetics has been defined as the branch of philosophy that focuses on the nature of beauty, the nature and value of art, and the inquiry processes and human responses associated with those topics. During the mid-1960s, the issue of arts education took on new importance. The shock of Sputnik sparked an educational reform movement, which led to the establishment of the arts and humanities endowments by the U.S. government. As a part of that, a 25-year history in the exploration of aesthetic perception has shown that to give youngsters an understanding of all the arts and the positive values they represent, the feelings and sensibilities of the viewer (perceiver) rather than solely those of the creator of the work of art, become the keystone of current aesthetic perception practice.

More About...
Aesthetics

LOOK AGAIN

Look at the work of art.

What sounds are in this work of art?

What smells are in this work of art?

If you could take parts away from the work of art, what would they be and why?

What happened just before and just after in this work of art?

Questions to Discuss

As students step back from their work and consider its impact, they should decide what are public questions and what are private questions in their journal writing or discussion groups. Whether or not they choose to share all of their work, these decisions should be made regularly and will serve to inform their continuing and changing thinking about the work of art.

Look

- What do you see?
- What do you hear?
- What do you smell?

Look Again

- Does the work of art give you any surprises?
- What do you think is beyond the edge of the painting?

More About...Aesthetics   211

Questions to Discuss

Look Inside

- What is happening in this work of art?
- What is this work of art about?
- If you were in this work of art, what would you be doing?
- What is your favorite part of this work of art?
- What is most important in this work of art?
- What happened just before and just after in this work of art?

Look Outside

- What have you learned about the work of art?
- What does the artist want you to know or think about in this work of art?
- How do you feel about the work of art; what does it make you feel?
- What will you remember about this work of art?
- If you could take images or elements away from the work, what would they be and why?
- Has this work of art changed my thinking?

Things to Do

- Draw yourself into this work of art.
- Draw what you can't see in this work of art.
- Act out or show the story in the work of art.
- Collect images that are similar to the qualities, colors, or ideas in this work of art and assemble a collage in response to it.
- Write a journal entry explaining what changes you would make in this work of art to make it more like your own experience.
- Role-play an interview with the artists about how the work of art was made.

Horace Pippin. (American). *Victorian Parlor II.* 1945. Oil on canvas. $25\frac{1}{4} \times 30$ inches. The Metropolitan Museum of Art, New York, Arthur H. Heam Fund, 1958.

LOOK INSIDE

Look at the work of art.

Describe the rest of this house. How many rooms are there and what is in each room?

Tell or write a story about this work of art with a beginning, a middle, and an end.

How would it feel to sit in one of those chairs?

More About...Aesthetics

ART Background

About Art History

Pippin expressed his experiences through folk art: simple designs and colors used to communicate complex ideas. He took a few art classes late in his life but decided that art could not be taught. On his own, he mastered color and design.

About the Artwork

Pippin first painted his experiences during the war. Then he returned to his childhood and the everyday lives of African Americans during that time. His work included portraits, still lifes, Bible scenes, and scenes from his heritage, such as *John Brown Going to His Hanging.*

More About...
Aesthetics

LOOK OUTSIDE

Look at the work of art.

How is this like or different from your own life?

How would you change this work of art to be more like your life? What would the changes be? What would the artwork look like?

What does the artist want you to know or think about in this work of art?

Describe the people who visit this house.

What does the outside of this house look like? What kind of neighborhood is it in?

What will you remember about this work?

More About...Aesthetics   **213**

About Aesthetic Perception

Third graders like to know what is important about the work of art. They also like to know what was important to the artist. They like to analyze and reinterpret material. They are fascinated with information and questions and descriptions.

There are some guiding principles in the development of appropriate aesthetic perception at this level. These guiding principles can profoundly influence teaching practice.

1. All aesthetic perception actively involves the learner.
2. All aesthetic perception involves reflection.
3. The works of art have substance, their tools and a working vocabulary are vital to empower the learner.
4. Aesthetic perception is a process, based upon examination of the artist's choices and the choices in response made by the learner.
5. All responses are valid. Right and wrong are irrelevant issues when viewing works of art.
6. All works of art relate to each other, and each relates to all other areas of life.

More About...
Art History

OVERVIEW

Art history is the record of art from the past to the present. Studying it is like looking into a treasure chest of humankind's past. Through close examination of these pages, students will learn more about famous artworks and where they originated.

Understanding Art History

Begin helping your students to learn about the meaning of art history by doing the following:

Art History Is a Story

• Explain that art history is a record of art from past to present—it is the story of art.

TIMELINE Show the students the **Animals Through History Time Line.** Show the visual story of how artists long ago up to the present created images of animals. Have them indicate the oldest image on the time line (the cave art). Explain that by looking at art from the past, we learn what the people who lived before us were like—their feelings and beliefs, clothes, food, houses, and even how they viewed animals.

An Art Historian's Job

• Explain that an art historian investigates who, what, when, where, and how art was created. They are like detectives. They search for clues and evidence so that they can tell the most complete and accurate story about art. Have students name detectives they know about (Sherlock Holmes, Encyclopedia Brown, Colombo,). Tell them that when looking at these images, they need to have a "detective" mind-set.

More About...
Art History

Artist unknown.
Three Cows and One Horse.
15,000–13,000 B.C. France.

Artist unknown.
Statues from Abu Temple.
2700–2000 B.C. Iraq.

Artist unknown.
Tutankhamen Mask (side view).
c. 1340 B.C. Egypt.

Artist unknown.
Adena Effigy Figure.
1000–300 B.C. United States.

Artist unknown.
Chuang.
1100 B.C. China.

214

More About...Art History

214

Artist unknown.
Colossal Head.
1500–300 B.C. Mexico.

Artist unknown.
Woman Playing Harp.
(Detail from vase.) c. 490 B.C.

Artist unknown.
Parthenon.
448–432 B.C. Greece.

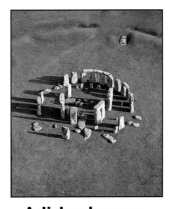

Artist unknown.
Stonehenge.
1800–1400 B.C. England.

More About...Art History 215

Art History Coming Alive

- Art history comes alive for students when they role-play the life of an artist or put on a short performance about an artwork. Have students work in pairs to do research on an artist using the **Artist Profiles Book,** the **National Museum of Women in the Arts Collection,** or some computer or library resource materials to find out some facts about an artist's life. (Example: birth and death dates, home country, interests, influences, style of art used, etc.) After researching the topic, have student write a simple story and act it out. A television interview format may be used with one student acting as the host and the other acting as the guest star.

Introducing the Art

- Discuss with students the organization of pages 214-221 (the dates at the top of each two pages, the chronological order of the artwork presented).

Below are some ideas to help you guide your students in using these pages.

- Help students read the artist's name under each artwork. Some artists are unknown. Explain to students that the unknown artists' names have been lost over time. Sometimes art historians can discover who created an unknown work.
- Have students read the country label under each artwork. Have students indicate on what continent each artwork is located. Ask students to share interesting facts they know about each country.
- Have students read the date under each artwork. Point out that sometimes there is a span of years rather than one specific year. This is because art historians are not sure exactly when the art was made. Have them indicate the oldest image on each page. Draw a line on the chalkboard and plot some or all of the art.

Special Note: Point out the green stain at the top of the *Mona Lisa,* a painting by Leonardo da Vinci, found on page 218. Explain that the painting was damaged during a restoration process undertaken by the museum. While photographs of this well-known artwork are often altered to remove the stain, the original painting which hangs in the Louvre in Paris, France, is as it appears on page 218.

Questions to Discuss

Based on Bloom's taxonomic categories, guide your students through discussion asking some or all of these questions.

- **Knowledge: What?**
1. Who created this artwork?
2. When was this artwork created?
3. Where was this object found?
4. Have you ever seen an object like this? Where?
5. What is the artwork's title?
6. If you could speak to the artist, what would you ask?

- **Comprehension: What and Why?**
1. Compare the artworks of a similar time period on the page. How are they alike and different?
2. Is this object useful? How is it used?
3. Is this an artwork you would like to own? Explain.
4. What interests you most about this artwork?
5. What is the major theme of this artwork?

- **Application: How, When, and in What Order?**
1. In what countries would this art be used?
2. What type of materials were used to create this art?
3. Explain how this object could have a different use today.
4. Demonstrate how the artwork was created.

- **Synthesis: What, How, and to What Extent?**
1. Create a plan to make this artwork more valued.
2. Devise a marking plan to sell this artwork.
3. How many titles can you think of for this artwork? Name them.
4. Name a person you would like to give this artwork to as a gift. Why?
5. Suppose the self-portrait by Rembrandt is having a conversation with the Close self-portrait. What would they say to each other? What would you ask them?

Artist unknown.
Shiva as Lord of the Dance.
1000. India.

Artist unknown.
Ravenna Apse Mosaic. (Detail).
A.D.100. Italy.

Artist unknown.
The Pantheon.
A.D. 118–125. Italy.

Artist unknown.
Hagia Sophia.
A.D. 532–537. Turkey.

Artist unknown.
The Great Stupa (at Sanchi).
200–100 B.C. India.

216

More About...Art History

Artist unknown.
Page from *The Book of Lindisfarne*.
Late 600s. England.

Artist unknown.
*Pagoda of the Temple
of the Six Banyan Trees.*
A.D. 537. China.

Artist unknown.
Stupa (at Borobudur).
800. Indonesia.

Artist unknown.
Great Mosque
(at Samarra).
648–852. Iraq.

More About...Art History   **217**

- **Analysis: What and How?**
1. Name all the paintings on these pages. How are they similar?
2. What are the main elements in this artwork?
3. Name all the architecture on these pages. What do they have in common? How are they different?
4. Name all the sculpture on these pages. How are they alike? How are they different?

- **Perception: Which, Where, and to What Extent?**
1. Name the artist that made a moving sculpture. (Calder)
2. Find an object built by an American President. (Jefferson's Monticello)
3. Find an artwork made out of fabric. (Bayeux Tapestry)
4. Which artwork comes from Mexico? (Colossal Head)
5. Find a mysterious artwork from England. (Stonehenge)
6. Find a famous Greek building. (Parthenon)
7. Name the artist that created a dancer. (Degas)
8. Find the most famous painting in the world. (Mona Lisa)
9. Find an artwork with primary colors. (Broadway Boogie Woogie)
10. Find an image with water in it. (The Great Wave)

- **Evaluation: What and Where? How and Why? To What Extent and Why?**
1. What artwork is the most interesting to you? How and why did you make your choice?
2. Explain in detail an artwork's unique qualities.
3. If someone were to give you this artwork, what would you do with it?
4. Rank your five favorite artworks from these pages and tell why they are your favorites.
5. How have you learned to see in new ways?

Rembrandt van Rijn.
Self-Portrait.
1660. The Netherlands.

Leonardo da Vinci.
Mona Lisa.
1503–1505. Italy.

Artist unknown.
Bayon Temple at Angkor Thom.
1100s–1200s. Cambodia.

Artist unknown.
Shrine Head. (Yorub).
1100–1300. Nigeria.

Torii Kiyotada.
Actor of the Ichikawa Clan.
1710–1740. Japan.

Artist unknown.
Chartres Cathedral.
1145–1220. France.

Thomas Jefferson.
Monticello.
1770–1784. United States.

Artist unknown.
Bayeux Tapestry. (Detail).
1070–1080. England.

Artist unknown.
Anasazi culture petroglyphs.
United States.

Artist unknown.
Taj Mahal.
1632–1648. India.

More About...Art History

219

More About...
Art History

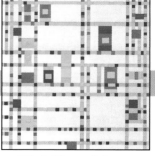

Piet Mondrian.
Broadway Boogie-Woogie.
1941. The Netherlands.

Claude Monet.
Impression, Sunrise.
1872. France.

Edgar Degas.
Little Dancer of Fourteen.
1880–1881. France.

Katsushika Hokusai.
The Great Wave off Kanagawa.
1831–1833. Japan.

Pablo Picasso.
Gertrude Stein.
1906. Spain.

Chuck Close.
Self-Portrait.
1987. United States.

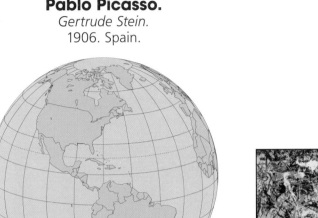

Jackson Pollock.
Convergence.
1952. United States.

Maria Martínez.
Black on Black Pot.
1920. United States.

Alexander Calder.
Untitled Mobile.
1959. United States.

More About...Art History

221

OVERVIEW

In art, *subject* means something an artist has depicted or represented in an artwork. For example, the subject matter of Vincent van Gogh's painting of a vase of flowers is called a still life. Some subject matter, like the objects in van Gogh's still life, are easy to identify. Others are more difficult because the artwork may be symbolic or nonobjective. Artists create artworks on a variety of subjects: the natural world, literature, religion, the constructed world, history, and so on. These pages deal with several of the most common subject-matter topics—people, objects, everyday life, stories, things outside, colors and shapes, and things that have a deeper meaning.

How to Use These Pages

Talk with students about each subject-matter topic description below. Encourage them to look for examples of different subject matter in the lessons. By helping them to look at each subject in greater detail and by asking thoughtful questions, your students will begin to develop an understanding for difference among subject matter in art.

Still Life

Artists create artworks that show a variety of objects. Traditional still lifes are bowls, vases, bottles, pitchers, fruit, flowers, food on a table, and/or musical instruments, among other things, that are artfully arranged.

Question: What are the objects in this still life?

Artists create art **about many subjects.** *Subject matter* **refers to the content of an artist's artwork. For example, the subject of a painting can be a vase of flowers or a self-portrait. This subject matter is easy to identify. The subject matter becomes more difficult to understand when the artwork stands for something beyond itself. Look at the artwork on these pages. Notice the different words used to identify different kinds of subject matter.**

Still Life

Odilon Redon. *Bouquet of Flowers.* 1905. Pastel on paper. $31\frac{5}{8} \times 25\frac{1}{4}$ inches. Metropolitan Museum of Art, New York, Gift of Mrs. George B. Post, 1956.

More About...Subject Matter

More About...
Subject Matter

Landscape

Thomas Hart Benton. (American). *July Hay.* 1943.
Oil and egg tempera on composition board. 38 × 26¾ inches.
Metropolitan Museum of Art, New York, George A. Heam Fund,
© 1998. T. H. Benton and R. P. Benton Testamentary Trusts/
Licensed by VAGA, New York, NY.

Things Outside

This area includes the natural world—plants, animals, or a landscape. The suffix "scape" means "a view of . . . ." For example, "cityscape" means buildings and city life seen in an artwork or "seascape," a scene of the sea.

Question: What are some of the things in this painting that make it a landscape?

Genre

In art, the term *genre* is used to indicate subjects that have to do with ordinary people engaged in everyday activities.

Question: What everyday activity is this girl doing?

Jean-Honoré Fragonard. (French). *A Young Girl Reading.*
c. 1776. National Gallery of Art,
Mellon Collection, Washington, D.C.

More About...
Subject Matter

Nonobjective

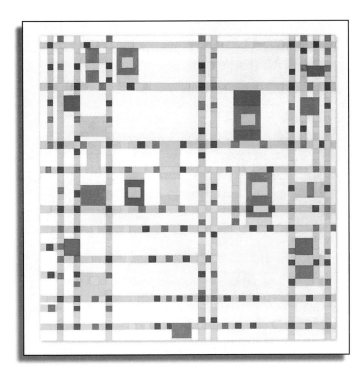

Piet Mondrian. (Dutch). *Broadway Boogie-Woogie.* 1942–43.
Oil on canvas. 50 × 50 inches. The Museum of Modern Art,
New York. Given anonymously. Photograph © 1998
The Museum of Modern Art, New York.

Nonobjective
Sometimes artwork is nonobjective. It does not have an identifiable subject matter—no familiar subjects are shown. People respond to the way the artwork has been organized and designed. Nonobjective art focuses specifically on the elements and principles of art: line, shape, color, and so on.

Question: The artwork does not use a subject we can identify. What are some of the lines, shapes, and colors you see in this picture?

Portrait

This category includes portraits, self-portraits, and group portraits. Portraits are one of the oldest subjects in art history. Artists try to present both an accurate depiction and also other aspects of a person's character in a portrait.

Question: This artist has done a self-portrait. What do you think he is telling us about himself?

Symbols

Sometimes artworks contain symbols—visual signs of something invisible. For example, a dove can be a symbol of peace, or an hourglass may represent the passing of time. Symbols represent a broader idea or sometimes have a secret meaning.

Questions: This painting contains flags. What are flags symbols of? Do you recognize any of the flags in the painting?

More About...
Subject Matter

Self-Portrait

Gerard Dou. (Dutch). *Self-Portrait.* Oil on wood. $19\frac{1}{4} \times 15\frac{3}{8}$ inches. Metropolitan Museum of Art, New York, Bequest of Benjamin Altman, 1913.

Symbols

Childe Hassam. (American). *Avenue of the Allies, Great Britain.* 1918. Oil on canvas. $36 \times 28\frac{3}{8}$ inches. Metropolitan Museum of Art, New York, Bequest of Miss Adelaide Milton de Groot (1876–1967) 1967.

More About...
Subject Matter

A Story Shown as Symbols

Artist unknown. (English). *The Five Senses: Hearing.* (Detail).
c. 1650–1675. White satin embroidered in petit
point and enriched with seed pearls and coral.
Metropolitan Museum of Art, New York.

Stories
A story is an account of some incident from a real person's life, an historic event, or from a myth, legend, or other symbolic literature.

Question: This antique, needle-crafted artwork tells a story about one of the five senses. Which sense does it depict?

More About...
Drawing

More About Drawing Still Lifes

OVERVIEW

Objective

After completing this lesson, students recognize that still lifes are made of lines and shapes.

Creative Expression

Set up a still life similar to the one in the photo.

- Find the horizontal lines on the edges of the table. *(There are two horizontal lines on the front edge of the table. The one on the top and the one on the bottom combine to make a thick horizontal line.)*

- Find the vertical lines on the edges of the table legs. *(Two parallel vertical lines combine to create one thick vertical line that is each leg of the table.)*

- During the drawing activity, use a trash can from the room to point out that the width of the ellipse changes as the viewpoint changes.

More About...
Still-Life Drawing

Everything you see is filled with lines and shapes you already know how to draw.

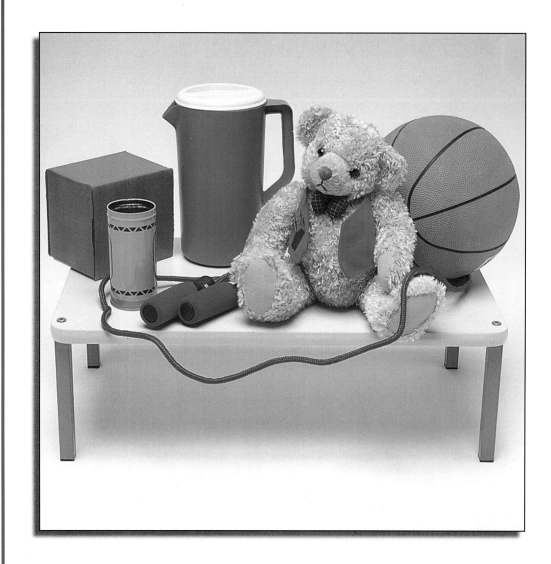

More About...Still-Life Drawing

ART *Background*

The objective of these lessons is to improve and increase perception skills. Accompanying each photograph will be a set of statements and questions to help the students observe and perceive specific concepts such as lines, shapes, and forms. Students are given perception readiness activities that involve searching the photograph and classroom for specific shapes and lines. Following this will be a drawing activity in which the students can practice and apply what they have perceived and learned. The students are learning through observing, questioning, thinking, and decision making. By asking questions and guiding the students visually through the photographs and their classroom, the teacher will be an integral part of these lessons. Whenever possible, objects similar to those in the photograph should be set up in the room for the perception activities and drawing practices. Discourage drawing from the photograph.

More About...
Still-Life Drawing

LOOK

Look carefully at the photograph of the still life.

- Find the square around the front edge of the red box.
- Find the circle that makes the edge of the basketball.
- Find the free-form shape that outlines the teddy bear.
- Find the horizontal lines on the front edge of the table.
- Find the diagonal lines on the edges of the sides of the table.
- Find the vertical lines on the edges of the four table legs. Notice that the back legs of the table appear shorter.

PRACTICE

Look for a table in your classroom. Find lines like the ones you see in the photograph. Practice drawing the table in your room.

More About...Still-Life Drawing   **229**

More About...
Drawing

More About Drawing People
OVERVIEW

Objective

After completing this lesson, students will be able to improve their perception of the shapes and forms of people.

Questions to Discuss

• How are the walking person's arms and legs bending? *(at the elbow and knees)*

• Where does the sitting person's body bend? *(at the waist)*

• How is the shape of the person's head that's facing you different from the profile of the people facing sideways? *(The person's head facing us is like an oval. The profile is a free-form. The back of the head is a curve that curves down and in toward the neck. The edge face is like a line that curves in and out forming the forehead, nose, lips, chin, and jaw. Note that the shape of eyes in a profile is different from a frontal view. The eyes in a profile are more triangular and are back away from the front edge near the top of the nose. In the frontal view, the eyelids are an ellipse enclosing a sphere.)*

Approach the drawing activity carefully. Some children may be sensitive about being drawn by others.

230

People are made of free-form shapes. These shapes change depending upon what position a person is in.

More About...
Drawing People

LOOK

Look at the three people in the photograph. Notice the shape and size of heads, necks, torsos, arms, legs, hands, and feet. These are free-form shapes.

- How are the walking person's arms and legs bending?
- Where does the sitting person's body bend?
- The standing person's feet are pointing toward you. These are like vertical ovals.
- How is the shape of the person's head that's facing you different from the profile of the people facing sideways?

PRACTICE

Look at the people in your classroom. Can you find the same shapes in their heads as you see in the picture? Practice drawing a person facing you. Try to draw vertical oval shapes to make their feet look like they are pointing toward you.

More About...
Drawing

More About Drawing Landscapes
OVERVIEW

Objective

After completing this lesson, students will be able to improve their perception of the lines and shapes in landscape drawing.

Questions to Discuss

If possible, take the students outdoors to compare the photograph with the real outside environment.

- Where is the foreground? *(In art, the foreground is near the bottom of the page. Objects in the foreground appear larger and can extend from the bottom of the page to the top.)*

- Where is the background? *(The background is located near the top.)*

- What are two things that overlap in this landscape? *(Overlapping helps create the illusion of depth. Objects in the foreground overlap those in the background.)*

Guide the students through the overlapping drawing exercise. Using different colors for the shapes, the students may wish to practice this exercise with colored pencils or markers.

1. Have students draw a simple shape as suggested in the student text. Shade it in to make it look solid.

2. Begin drawing a second shape at an edge of the shape in front.

3. Draw the second shape until the pencil point bumps into the front shape in another spot. This will make the solid shape appear in front.

232

More About...
Drawing Landscapes

When you look at a landscape, you can see that some things are in front of or behind other things.

More About...
Drawing Landscapes

LOOK

Look at the landscape with the horses.

- Find the horse in the **foreground,** the front of the picture.
- Find the horse in the **background,** the back of the picture.

The one in the foreground is larger because it is closer. Things that are far away appear smaller. You cannot see part of the horse in the background because the tree and the other horse are in front of it, or **overlap** it.

PRACTICE

Practice overlapping. Draw a large square in front of a small circle. First, draw the large square. Place your pencil point on an edge of the square. Begin drawing part of a small circle. Stop your pencil when you bump back into the square.

Look around your classroom for objects that overlap. Practice drawing them.

Visual Index: Artworks Arranged in Time Order

Artist unknown
Jar
3000–2000 B.C.
page 166

Artist unknown
Portrait of a Boy
Second century
page 118

Artist unknown
Winged Genie
883–859 B.C.
page 93

Artist unknown
*Ravenna Apse
Mosaic (Detail)*
A.D. 549
page 175

Artist unknown
Ishtar Gate
c. 605–562 B.C.
page 174

Artist unknown
Shirt Section
c. A.D. 600–1000
page 137

Artist unknown
*Bedroom (cubiculum
nocturnum)*
40–30 B.C.
page 178

Artist unknown
*Hats: Birds and
Geometric Patterns*
700–1000
page 50

Visual Index

Artist unknown
Jar
Twelfth century
page 107

Artist unknown
*Cover of Armenian
Book*
Thirteenth century
page 186

Artist unknown
Mihrab
1354
page 29

Lorenzo Ghiberti
*The Meeting of
Solomon and Sheba:
The Gates of Paradise*
1425–1452
page 92

Artist unknown
*Sleeveless Shirt
(two cats)*
c. 1438–1532
page 76

Wang Chao
*The Three Stars of
Happiness, Wealth,
and Longevity*
c. 1500
page 21

Visual Index

Artist unknown
Covered Jar
1522–1566
page 67

John Singleton Copley
Daniel Crommelin Verplanck
1771
page 36

Artist unknown
Floor Covering Detail
Second half of sixteenth century
page 153

Artist unknown
Symmetrical View of a Totem Pole
Nineteenth century
page 114

Hyacinthe Rigaud
Louis XV as a Child
1715
page 145

Artist unknown
Symmetrical View of a Totem Pole
Nineteenth century
page 115

Rachel Ruysch
Roses, Convolvulus, Poppies and Other Flowers in an Urn on a Stone Ledge
c. 1745
page 24

Artist unknown
Yam Mask
Nineteenth century
page 110

Visual Index

Artist unknown
Duncan House Bedroom
1805
page 178

Artist unknown
Child's Beaded Shirt
c. 1865
page 170

Artist unknown
Thunderbird Shield
c. 1830
page 140

Artist unknown
Double Saddlebag
1875
page 28

Artist unknown
Parasol
Mid-nineteenth century
page 157

Artist unknown
Washington's Headquarters
c. 1876
page 81

Albert Edward Edensaw
Dancing Headdress Frontlet
1860–1870
page 111

Edgar Degas
Waiting
c. 1882
page 123

Visual Index

Claude Monet
Bridge over a Pool of Water Lilies
1899
page 17

Wassily Kandinsky
Improvisation No. 27
1912
page 20

Artist unknown
Feather Headdress
Early twentieth century
page 136

Allen E. Cole
Silas Johnson
1920s
page 37

Artist unknown
Necklace
Twentieth century
page 96

Martha Walter
The Telegram, Detention Room, Ellis Island
1922
page 149

Claude Monet
Water Lilies
1905
page 148

Joseph Henry Sharp
Sunset Dance-Ceremony to the Evening Sun
1924
page 33

Visual Index

Paul Klee
Rotes Haus
1929
page 62

Berenice Abbott
Nos. 4, 6, & 8 Fifth Avenue
1936
page 32

Mrs. Andy G. Byler
Double Wedding Ring Quilt
1930–1940
page 152

Henri Matisse
Purple Robe and Anemones
1937
page 156

Shirley Russell
Boys' Day
1935
page 46

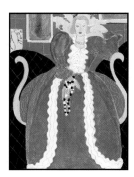

Henri Matisse
Woman in Blue
1937
page 183

Emily Carr
Sky
1935
page 59

Man Ray
La Fortune
1938
page 54

Visual Index

Yves Tanguy
Indefinite Divisibility
1942
page 58

Fernand Léger
The Walking Flower
1951
page 88

Horace Pippin
Victorian Parlor II
1945
page 106

Hughie Lee-Smith
The Piper
1953
page 80

Philip Evergood
Her World
1948
page 119

Allan Houser
Apache Crown Dance
1953
page 126

Calvin Jones
Brilliant as the Sun Upon the World
c. 1950
page 55

Charles Burchfield
Orion in December
1959
page 16

Visual Index

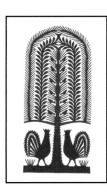

Stanistawa Bakula
Tree of Life
1962
page 77

Audrey Flack
Buddha
1975
page 144

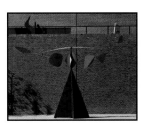

Alexander Calder
The Spinner
1966
page 89

Nancy Youngblood Lugo
Pottery Vessels
c. 1980–1985
page 167

Ayako Miyawaki
Various Fish
1967
page 141

Rosalind Ragans
Firebirds
1983
page 63

Isabel John
Pictorial Tapestry
Mid 1980s
page 171

Joseph Jean-Gilles
Haitian Landscape
1973
page 84

Visual Index

Yvonne Jacquette
Tokyo Street with Pachinko Parlor II
1985

William T. Wiley
Remedial Archaeology and the Like
1986

Faith Ringgold
Tar Beach
1988

Idelle Weber
Pistia Kew
1989

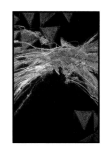

Bing Davis
Ancestral Spirit Dance Series
1990

Janet Fish
Arcanum
1990

Sylvia Plimack Mangold
The Locust Trees with Maple
1990

Jane Freilicher
The Sun Breaks Through
1991

Visual Index

Iris Sandkühler
*Tuxedo Studs
and Cufflinks*
1994
page 97

Kathryn Gough
Book Cover
1995
page 187

Glossary

alternating rhythm
(ôl tər nā´ ting rîth´ əm), **noun**

When one motif is repeated after a second, different motif.

architecture
(är´ kə tek´ chûr), **noun**

The art of designing and planning buildings for people.

appliqué
(ap´ li kā´), **noun**

An art form in which cutout fabrics are attached onto a larger surface.

background
(bak´ ground´), **noun**

The area of the picture that seems farthest from the viewer.

approximate symmetry
(ə prok´ sə mit sim´ i trē), **noun**

When both sides of a design are *almost* exactly the same. Approximate symmetry is a type of formal balance.

batik
(bə tēk´), **noun**

A way to design fabric using hot wax and dyes.

architect
(är´ kə tekt), **noun**

An artist who plans and designs buildings.

bookmaking
(bu̇k mā´ king), **noun**

The art of binding or tying pages together inside a cover.

244

Glossary

Glossary

center of interest
(sen´ tər əv in´ trist), **noun**

The area of an artwork that a viewer immediately looks at first.

central axis
(sen´ trəl ak´ sis), **noun**

An imaginary line dividing a work of art in half.

color spectrum
(kul´ ər spek´ trəm), **noun**

The range of colors that come from light.

color wheel
(kul´ ər hwēl´), **noun**

A design for organizing colors that shows the spectrum bent into a circle.

complex geometric shape
(kom´ pleks jē´ ə met´ rik shāp), **noun**

A shape made by combining simple geometric shapes such as triangles, squares, and rectangles.

contrast
(kon´ trast), **noun (verb)**

A difference between two things in a work of art.

cool colors
(kül´ kul´ ərz), **noun**

Spectral colors that give a feeling of coolness. Green, blue, and violet are cool colors.

culture
(kul´ chər), **noun**

Another word for *custom.*

curved
(kûrvd), **adj.**

Lines that bend and change direction slowly.

depth
(depth), **noun**

The appearance of distance on a flat surface.

Glossary   **245**

Glossary

diagonal
(dī ag´ ə nəl), **adj. (noun)**

Lines that are slanted.

diamond
(dī´ mənd), **noun**

emphasis
(em´ fə sis), **noun**

The way an artist makes
something in a work of art
stand out.

exaggerate
(eg zaj´ ə rāt), **verb**

To make much larger than actual
size.

foreground
(fôr´ ground´), **noun**

The area of the picture that
seems closest to the viewer.

form
(fôrm), **noun**

A three-dimensional object.
Forms can be measured in three
ways: height, width, and depth.

formal balance
(fôr´ məl bal´ əns), **noun**

A way of organizing a design so
that equal or very similar
elements are placed on opposite
sides of an imaginary, central
dividing line.

free-form (shape)
(frē´ fôrm´), **noun**

A shape that is uneven and not
regular; a shape that is not
geometric.

freestanding
(frē´ stan´ ding), **noun (adj.)**

A three-dimensional sculpture
that has empty, negative space all
around.

geometric (shape)
(jē´ ə met´ rik), **noun (adj.)**

A math shape, such as a circle,
triangle, rectangle, or square.

Glossary

guidelines
(gīd´ līnz´), **noun**

Lines that help an artist place things in a work of art.

harmony
(här´ mə nē), **noun**

The peaceful look made when related elements of art are put together.

hexagon
(hek´ sə gon), **noun**

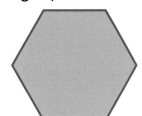

highlight
(hī´ līt´), **noun**

A small area of white used to show the very brightest spot on an object.

horizontal
(hôr´ ə zon´ təl), **adj.**

Lines that are straight across from side to side.

hue
(hū), **noun**

Another word for *color.*

interior designer
(in tîr´ ē ər di zī´ nər), **noun**

An artist who decorates the insides of buildings using furnishings, such as carpeting, furniture, and drapes.

intermediate color
(in´ tər mē´ dē it kul´ ər), **noun**

A color made by mixing a primary color and a secondary color.

jeweler
(jü´ ə lər), **noun**

An artist who designs and makes jewelry.

jewelry
(jü´ əl rē), **noun**

Three-dimensional art that is made for people to wear.

Glossary

line

(līn), **noun**

A mark drawn by a tool such as a pencil, pen, or paintbrush as it moves across a surface.

line variety

(līn və rī´ ə tē), **noun**

Short or long, thick or thin, rough or smooth, and broken or solid lines.

mask

(mask), **noun**

Three-dimensional art form of a sculpted face.

mosaic

(mō zā´ ik), **noun**

A picture made by setting small pieces of colored tile, glass, or stone side by side.

motif

(mō tēf´), **noun**

A shape or object that is repeated.

negative space

(neg´ ə tiv spās´), **noun**

The empty area around shapes and objects in an artwork.

octagon

(ok´ tə gon), **noun**

overlap

(ō´ vər lap´), **verb (noun)**

When one object covers part of a second object.

parallelogram

(pâr´ ə lel´ ə gram), **noun**

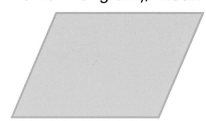

Glossary

pentagon
(pen´ tə gon), **noun**

portrait
(pôr´ trit), **noun**

A picture of a person.

positive space
(poz´ i tiv spās´), **noun**

The area that shapes and objects fill in a work of art.

primary color
(prī´ mer ē kul´ ər), **noun**

One of the three basic colors: red, yellow, and blue. Primary colors cannot be made by mixing other colors.

random rhythm
(ran´ dəm rith´ əm), **noun**

When a motif is repeated in no particular order.

regular rhythm
(reg´ yə lər rith´ əm), **noun**

Visual rhythm that is created by repeating the same motif with equal amounts of space in between.

relief sculpture
(ri lēf´ skulp´ chər), **noun**

Artwork in which forms stand out from a flat surface.

repetition
(rep´ i tish´ ən), **noun**

When an artist repeats lines, colors, or textures.

sculpture
(skulp´ chər), **noun**

A kind of art that is three-dimensional.

secondary color
(sek´ ən der´ ē kul´ ər), **noun**

A color made by mixing two primary colors.

Glossary

shade

(shād), **noun**

Any dark value of a color.

shape

(shāp), **noun**

A flat, two-dimensional area. Shapes can be measured by length and width.

simplicity

(sim plis´ i tē), **noun**

A method of creating unity by using only one color, shape, or texture in a work of art.

spectral color

(spek´ trəl kul´ ər), **noun**

One of the six colors of the rainbow. Red, orange, yellow, green, blue, and violet are spectral colors.

symmetry

(sim´ i trē), **noun**

A type of formal balance when both halves of a design are identical, mirror images of each other.

tactile texture

(tak´ təl teks´ chər), **noun**

The way the surface of an object actually feels when you touch it.

texture

(teks´ chər), **noun**

The way the surface of an object feels or looks as if it would feel.

three-dimensional

(thrē´ di men´ shə nəl), **adj. (noun)**

Forms that can be measured by height, width, and depth.

tint

(tint), **noun**

Any light value of a color.

trapezoid

(trap´ ə zoid), **noun**

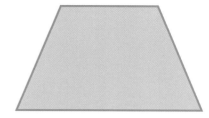

Glossary

two-dimensional
(tü´ di men´ shə nəl), **adj.**
(noun)

Shapes that are flat and can be measured by length and width.

unity
(ū´ ni tē), **noun**

The feeling of wholeness in a work of art.

value
(val´ ū), **noun**

The lightness or darkness of a color.

variety
(və rī´ ə tē), **noun**

The use of different lines, shapes, colors, and textures to make a work of art interesting.

vertical
(vûr´ tə kəl), **adj.**

Lines that move straight up and down.

visual rhythm
(vizh´ ü əl rith´ əm), **noun**

The feeling of movement created by artists repeating colors, shapes, lines, and textures.

visual texture
(vizh´ ü əl təks´ chər), **noun**

Texture you see with your eyes but cannot feel with your hands.

warm colors
(wôrm´ kul´ ərz), **noun**

Spectral colors that give a feeling of warmth. Yellow, orange, and red are warm colors.

zigzag
(zig´ zag´), **noun (adj.)**

Diagonal lines that connect.

Index

Index

Index

Index

Index

Professional Development for Art Education

Table of Contents

The Elementary Art Curriculum

Rosalind Ragans Ph.D., Associate Professor Emerita, Georgia Southern University

Art education is for all students. It provides learning opportunities for the artistically talented few, as well as the many students who may never produce art outside the classroom.

A strong elementary visual arts curriculum teaches students that they can communicate a variety of ideas and emotions in many different ways. It teaches students to use both verbal and nonverbal methods to express abstract ideas and emotions and to trust their creative intelligence. In art education, students will learn that some problems have many different solutions, and they will not be afraid to use divergent thinking strategies. They will learn concepts and techniques that will give them control of the visual images they produce.

A strong elementary art curriculum will enable students to expand their perceptive, interpretive, and analytical abilities. They will learn to find meaning in visual images, and they will learn to identify aesthetic qualities in a variety of artworks and in the environment. They will learn the language of visual art so that they have a precise vocabulary of visual symbols with which to express their ideas. They will begin to develop the ability to make aesthetic judgments.

In a strong elementary art curriculum, students will become sensitive to and understand the broad cultural foundation upon which their own culture is based. The visual arts have always been an integral component in the history of humanity, and through the study of art history, students will develop a better understanding of beliefs and ideas that are different from their own.

The four components of a quality art program are Aesthetic Perception, Art Criticism, Art History and Culture, and Art Production and Creative Expression.

AESTHETIC PERCEPTION

Aesthetics is a branch of philosophy. In visual art, aesthetics becomes the study of the nature of beauty and art. Aesthetics is concerned with the Big Question: "What is art?" In the past, *aesthetics* was defined as the study of beauty because the creation of beauty was thought to be the purpose of art. Today, in our more complex society, the purpose of art has also become more complicated. Some aestheticians still believe that the purpose of art is to create beauty, or beautifully organized arrangements of the elements of art. Some believe that art must imitate reality. Others think of art as a strong means to communicate ideas and emotions.

Aesthetic concepts are the core of the *Art Connections* curriculum. They are the framework upon which all aspects of art learning are constructed. The **More About Aesthetics** section in the *Student* and *Teacher Editions* offers

concrete methods for introducing students to aesthetics.

ART CRITICISM

Works of art are the focus of every lesson. Art criticism is the sequential process used in this text to guide students through the procedures needed to learn from these works. Art criticism enables students to learn from works of art that have been created by artists from many cultures and time periods. Art criticism also provides a procedure that students can use to objectively study their own art products.

The four-step process of art criticism will help students expand their perceptive, analytical, interpretive, and aesthetic valuing abilities. The sequential steps of art criticism are similar to those used in the scientific method. During the first two steps, *Describe* and *Analyze,* students are asked to collect data objectively. During the third step, *Interpret,* students speculate about the

> " Art education is for all students. It provides learning opportunities for the artistically talented few, as well as the many students who may never produce art outside the classroom. "

meaning of the work based on the data collected: they make a hypothesis about the idea, emotion, or mood expressed by the artist. During the fourth step, *Decide* or aesthetic judgment, the students offer their conclusions about the work of art.

Art criticism will help students study a work of art noticing subject, composition, and meaning before making an aesthetic judgment. Too often, beginners look at a work of art briefly and immediately make a value judgment. The sequential procedures in art criticism force the students to postpone judgment while becoming immersed in the image. It forces them to have a fully funded visual experience before drawing conclusions about a work.

Detailed lessons in the **More About Art Criticism** sections of *Art Connections* will help teachers and students practice and apply art criticism procedures.

ART HISTORY AND CULTURE

Art Connections is not an art history text, but any study of art should begin with learning something about the history of world art and the people who created it. Information about art history related to the featured work of art in each lesson is provided for the students throughout the text. The **More About Art History Around the World** section provides an

overview of the meaning of art history. Additional information is provided for the teacher in each text, and in ancillary materials such as the *Artist Profiles* books, the *Animals Through History Time Line,* and on the backs of the *Large Prints.*

ART PRODUCTION AND CREATIVE EXPRESSION

Each lesson includes an art production activity identified as **Practice** and **Create** in the *Student Editions.* This is the place for each student to creatively explore the lesson concept. Hands-on activities are often the most enjoyable aspect of art learning. The student integrates and internalizes the verbal and visual concepts of the lesson during the creative manipulation of art materials. While every component in the art program is equally important, every component does not need equal time. Art Production requires the longest amount of time.

Do not skip the self-assessment section of the lesson. Most students would be embarrassed to offer subjective statements about their own work or the work of classmates. The four steps of art criticism offer an objective procedure for thinking about the concepts and technical procedures used during the creation of art.

CURRICULUM INTEGRATION

Art Connections provides a strong art curriculum that makes connections to all the arts and to all areas of the curriculum. The *Art Across the Curriculum* book at each grade level provides specific activities to connect each lesson to Reading/Language Arts, Mathematics, Science, Social Studies, Technology, and the Arts.

Elementary art programs enrich the entire curriculum in so many ways. In art, unlike so many other subjects, students have a natural opportunity to demonstrate their multiple intelligences every day. In art, students practice problem solving and critical thinking, they learn about history and culture through art, and they learn to more effectively use their senses to explore the world. All of these enrich other areas of the curriculum and help students establish habits of mind that will last a lifetime.

A Sampling of Art Magazines Resources for Teachers	
American Artist	Arts and Activities
Art Education	Arts Education Policy
Art to Zoo	Review
ARTnews	Crayola Kids
ARTnews	Scholastic Art
for Students	School Arts

Classroom Management and Motivation Strategies for Teaching Elementary Art

Bunyan Morris, Demonstration Art Teacher, Marvin Pittman Laboratory School, Georgia Southern University

While motivating students to express themselves visually through creative means, the elementary art teacher is challenged with the task of maintaining proper classroom management. The purpose of this article is to provide some practical methods of motivating creative thought and action under the guidance of successful classroom management. Combine these methods with your own to give students the best learning experience possible.

Be Prepared. Begin the lesson excited and ready. Students will pick up on your mood the moment they walk into the room. If you set the tone at the beginning and grasp immediate control, it will be much easier to keep it throughout the lesson. It is important to have art prints and demonstration materials ready and in place for the initial focus. Practice an activity before demonstrating it if it is the first time that it has been taught. Something might happen that could not be foreseen. Prepare for the best and worst. Also, it might be a good idea to practice if it is a concept or an activity that has not been taught in a long time. Even classroom veterans forget things.

Focus. For the initial focus of the lesson, gather the students into a group on the floor, in chairs, or on benches in an area of the room that is ready for discussion and demonstration. By gathering the students into a compact group, it is easier to make eye contact and to keep the attention of all learners. If there is no room for a separate demonstration and discussion spot, gather the tables or desks into a closer group so that no one is "out of reach."

Introduce the Art. Always introduce a lesson with a work of art that relates to what the students will be learning. Students get excited playing detective. Finding clues and ideas in a painting or sculpture allows them to make their own interpretations and assessments about art. They will in turn learn to apply this to their own work. The students don't have to know that this activity has a lofty term called *art criticism* to gain from its purpose. Encouraging them to ask questions and share ideas about a master work will give the students motivation and fresh ideas to take into the Create portion of the lesson.

Moving to Art Production. Always control the manner in which the students move to the create area from the demonstration/discussion center. Release the students in a manner that will keep order but not quell their enthusiasm about the lesson. Use positive reinforcement by

complimenting those who are sitting quietly, and send them first. It will not take long for the others to catch on. After time most of the students will become conditioned to this expectation. Even if they've been involved in a lively discussion, they will automatically become settled as this transitional period approaches.

Classroom Design. Not only should the students be orderly, but the classroom must also be organized and conducive to the movement of the teacher and students. The create stations should have enough space between them for the teacher to reach every student. There should be enough space in traffic areas for student movement. Children need easy access to supply shelves, to sinks, and to move from one create station to another unencumbered. The supplies should be organized on labeled shelves so that the students will return them to their proper places. If the teacher keeps the room and supplies organized, hopefully the students will.

> **" Always introduce a lesson with a work of art that relates to what the students will be learning. "**

As well as keeping the room and supplies organized, the rest of the room should be visually pleasing. Display student art with master prints. This builds self-esteem. When possible, display every child's work. Make learning centers organized and interesting. Keep interesting objects about the room for visual reference. These objects might include plants, pottery, old bottles, discarded sports equipment, old toys, or anything that might capture the attention and interest of your students. Use these objects in still lifes and as objects of visual reference for lines, shapes, and other elements and principles of art.

When moving about the room assisting students, it is important to keep the senses alive and be aware of what is happening with the other students. See and hear what they think you can't.

Closing the Lesson. Normally one should try to close the class with a review of the lesson's objectives. This should be short and interesting. This is also the time to reward the students for good behavior. The art teacher must set the criteria for earning the award. Do not give the award if it is not earned. Of course, the students must be aware of the opportunity to earn an award ahead of time.

One method that works is to award the students with a "Super Behavior Card." This is simply a colorful card that can be given to the class to take back to their classroom teacher for having good behavior during art. This requires the cooperation of the classroom teacher to award the students in some manner for collecting a certain number of Super Behavior Cards. Awards might include a popcorn party or extra time at recess. If the classroom teacher is unwilling, you will have to provide the award in your class. Awarding of the Super Behavior Card can be coordinated with cleanup at the end of the period. Choose one student at the table who cleans up most thoroughly and gets quietest first to carry the Super Behavior Card back to the classroom teacher. The students at each table will work together trying to earn the Super Behavior Card.

Hopefully, these ideas and suggestions will reduce the challenge of maintaining classroom control and motivating students. The individual teacher must decide what works best for each situation. All of the motivation and management techniques here have been tried and have been proven to work. They may not work for everyone, but combined with one's individual strategies, they will increase the probability of success in the art classroom.

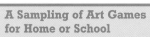

A Sampling of Art Games for Home or School

Art Lotto: National Gallery of Art Safari Limited, Miami, FL
ARTDECK Aristoplay, Ann Arbor, MI, 1-800-634-7738
The Fine Art Game Piatnik, Wiener Spielkartenfabrik, Ferd. PIATNIK & Söhne
Where Art Thou? WJ Fantasy, Inc., Bridgeport, CT 1-800-ABC-PLAY

Meeting National and State Standards for Art Education

Nan Yoshida, Former Art Supervisor, Los Angeles Unified School District, California

Art Connections has been carefully designed to help educators meet the standards of state and national art curriculum guidelines.

The *National Standards for Arts Education* are part of Goals 2000, the overarching plan for improving American education, called for by the President. Approved by the United States Congress in 1994, the Standards describe what every young American student should know and be able to do in the arts.

In addition to *National Standards,* individual states have curriculum documents that set forth guidelines and requirements in subject areas. For example, both the *Visual and Performing Arts Framework for California Public Schools, Kindergarten through Grade Twelve* © 1996 and the *Texas Essential Knowledge and Skills for Art* © 1997 discuss four components of visual arts education common to most other state guidelines.

Placing the *National Standards* side by side with the *California Framework* and *Texas Essential Knowledge and Skills,* one can readily see that the documents match in their expectations of what students should know and be able to do in the visual arts.

Art Connections has been developed with these national and state expectations in mind. Every lesson in the program is designed to address the components of art education in Aesthetic Perception, Art History and Culture, Creative Expression, and Art Criticism.

Aesthetic Perception (Artistic Perception)
Each lesson begins with **Activating Prior Knowledge,** which asks students to recall and visualize an image from personal experience that will help them take a purposeful look at the artwork.
Introducing the Art focuses students' attention on specific attributes of the artwork, design elements and principles, underlying structures, and functions. As students answer the questions about the painting or sculpture, they develop critical *looking* skills.
Seeing Like an Artist directs students to extend their artistic perception to their environment and objects in the environment. The transition is made to use keen visual and tactile perception of formal art objects in everyday life (lifelong learning).

Art History and Culture (Cultural Context)
In *Art Connections,* the range of world art is broad as students are exposed to a variety of types and styles of art from many cultures and historical periods. Students study art from Africa; Asia; Australia; Europe; and North, Central, and South America. They learn about the role of the artist in societies. They develop appreciation for paintings, drawings, prints, photographs,

sculptures, textiles, and architecture. They relate to folk, decorative, functional, and formal arts.

While information about the artwork and the artist is necessarily brief in the *Student Edition,* teachers are encouraged to use the **Art Background** section of the *Teacher Edition* and the *Artist Profiles* books to provide students with enriching information about the artist, the period of art history, and cultural perspectives.

Creative Expression (Art Production)
Creative expression is fundamental to every art lesson. The **Practice** activity provides a structure for students to apply lesson concepts in meaningful practice. In the **Create** activity, students refine their new knowledge and skills by producing an original artwork based on their personal vision. The lessons throughout the program introduce a variety of art media and techniques.

Art Criticism (Aesthetic Valuing)
Reflection and self-assessment are inherent in the art-making process. Upon completion of the **Create** activity, students evaluate their own work using the four steps of art criticism: Describe, Analyze, Interpret, Decide. These four steps of art criticism are a method for making an informed critique of others' artwork, as well.

Arts Integration
In addition to the high priority placed on teaching the visual arts as a unique discipline, both the National Standards and the California Framework recommend the appropriate integration or interrelation of the visual arts with the other arts disciplines of music, dance, and theater. Toward this goal, every unit in *Art Connections* culminates with a lesson integrating one of these performing arts.

Curriculum Integration
Furthermore, the *Teacher Edition* has an **Art Across the Curriculum** section that references activities in the *Art Across the Curriculum* books. These activities were developed to relate the visual arts concepts to concepts and experiences in other areas of the curriculum. Every lesson has a connection to reading/language arts, math, science, social studies, technology, and the arts. Thematic connections, technology, and special needs are also addressed.

The lessons in the *Art Connections* program are thoughtfully prepared to assist teachers in meeting the visual arts requirements of the National Standards, the California Framework, the Texas Essential Knowledge and Skills for Art, and most other state guidelines for art education.

National Standards for Arts Education © 1994
1. Understand and apply media, techniques, and processes.
2. Use knowledge of structures and functions.
3. Choose and evaluate a range of subject matter, symbols, and ideas.
4. Understand the visual arts in relation to history and cultures.
5. Reflect upon and assess the characteristics and merits of their work and the work of others.
6. Make connections between the visual arts and other disciplines.

California Framework © 1996
Artistic Perception
Goal 1. Students use their senses to perceive works of art, objects in nature, events, and the environment.
Goal 2. Students identify visual structures and functions of art using the language of the visual arts.
Creative Expression
Goal 3. Students develop knowledge of and artistic skills in a variety of visual arts media and technical processes.
Goal 4. Students create original artworks based on personal experiences or responses.
Goal 5. Students develop skills in the visual arts and appreciation for using the visual arts in lifelong learning.
Historical and Cultural Context
Goal 6. Students explore the role of the visual arts in culture and human history.
Goal 7. Students investigate major themes . . . and styles of the visual arts throughout the world.
Aesthetic Valuing
Goal 8. Students derive meaning from artworks through analysis, interpretation, and judgment.

Texas Essential Knowledge and Skills for Art © 1997
A. Perception: Awareness of and sensitivity to surroundings are important to understanding the structure of natural and human-made objects and to applying that understanding to the creative process. Students recognize this visual information as a source for creating original works of art.
B. Creative Expression/Performance: Visual expression is a unique means of communication which is vitally important throughout the world. Students recognize that visual communication challenges the imagination, fosters reflective thinking, encourages disciplined effort, involves problem-solving, and develops self-confidence.
C. Historical/Cultural Heritage: Art is a visual record of history and diverse cultures. Students understand and appreciate different historical periods, cultures, and artistic styles and develop respect for the traditions and contributions of diverse societies.
D. Response/Evaluation: Evaluation skills are developed by responding to and analyzing the artworks of self and others. Students engage in a critical thinking process while learning to make judicious decisions about art and lifelong consumer choices.

Art and Cross Curricular Connections

Tina Farrell, Director of Visual and Performing Arts,
Clear Creek Independent School District, Texas

The study and production of artwork enhances learning in all areas of the curriculum. When teachers and students connect art to their other subjects, learning occurs in the natural and interrelated way that it exists in the real world. We know from experience that learning is most meaningful when it is interconnected—not isolated. Therefore, making the natural connections that exist within each discipline of study and art enhances total understanding and brings meaning to fragmented information.

Below are just a few of the ways that art education can impact the study of other subjects.

> **" When teachers and students connect art to their other subjects, learning occurs in the natural and interrelated way that it exists in the real world. "**

Reading/Language Arts. In the viewing and analysis of a work of art, students develop oral and written communication skills. Teachers can enhance the language process by writing art terms and concepts on the board, having students generate lists of adjectives and adverbs to describe artworks, encouraging reflective inquiry into art, having students read about art and artists, and having students use works of art as stimuli for all forms of writing.

Mathematics. Mathematics concepts are enhanced through art. When math concepts are presented or expressed in a visual or manipulative manner, students can more easily grasp them. The comparison and development of shapes and forms, visual-spatial relationships, measurement, proportion, estimation, and grids and graphs, for example, all are best explained through art.

Science. In the art-making process, children learn that multiple ways to solve problems exist. They learn to discover, imagine, try new materials and techniques, experiment, develop and test hypotheses, and observe and record visual data. These are many of the skills, objectives, and habits of mind taught in science.

Social Studies. The history of the world is reflected in the functional and aesthetic works of art produced by the peoples of the world. Children can gain great insights about near and distant cultures through the study of art, artifacts, and architecture.

The Arts. The arts all complement each other in the skills, elements, principles, and beliefs

that are emphasized in each discipline. Each area presents a unique way to express ideas and transform emotions into song, dance, interactions, words, and images. Visual artists research, develop rough drafts (sketches), plan, develop ideas, produce completed visual ideas, and sign and title their works. These are the processes that authors, writers, dancers, composers, actors, and poets also employ.

Life Skills. In art, children develop craftsmanship, self-discipline, dedication to a task, skills for working both individually and cooperatively, and pride in one's work. These skills are necessary for success in any area of their lives.

Critical Thinking Skills. Studying the visual arts develops higher-level thinking skills as students analyze, compare, interpret, synthesize, and make inferences and judgments about works of art.

Art is a great integrating subject because art, first and foremost, is a form of human communication. Art is one of the first forms of communication for children. Children often express complex ideas through visual symbols that represent their beginning language system. Art is a vehicle for children to learn about the world around them and to organize the information in a comprehensive format. As young children draw, they take textures, shapes, and colors from a complex world and form them into coherent visual images. This visual cognition, a powerful way for children to process information, is the basis for learning in and through art.

A Sampling of Art Program Resources for Schools

The California Arts Project 415-499-5893 (http://www.ucop.edu/tcap/aeol.html)

Crayola Dream-makers Binney & Smith, Easton, PA 800-CRAYOLA

Getty Education Institute for the Arts Los Angeles, CA 800-223-3431 (http://www.artsednet.getty.edu)

Institute for Arts Education San Diego, CA 619-260-1594

Original Works Yours Stillwater, NY 800-421-0020

Polaroid Education Program Portfolio 2000 Cambridge, MA 800-343-5000

Start with the Arts Very Special Arts John F. Kennedy Center for the Performing Arts, Washington, D.C. 800-933-8721

Safe Use of Art Materials

Mary Ann Boykin, Director, The Art School for Children and Young Adults, University of Houston–Clear Lake, Texas

Elementary art teachers are responsible for the safety of their students. To ensure safety in art class, teachers need to be aware of safety issues that can affect the well-being of the children they teach, as well as themselves. Specific safety standards have been established by the Center for Safety in the Arts, and these guidelines should be diligently followed in order to assure that neither the children nor their teachers are injured by the use of unsafe art materials.

Elementary teachers should do two things to prevent problems. The first is to keep all toxic and hazardous substances out of the classroom. The second is to know how to use the materials safely because any materials can become hazardous when used inappropriately.

TOXIC SUBSTANCES

A toxic substance is defined by the Center for Occupational Hazards as "a poison which can damage your body's organ systems when you are over exposed to it." This harm can be immediate or can be the result of repeated exposure over periods of time. Toxic substances can enter the body in three ways:
1) absorption through the skin;
2) inhalation through the nose or mouth;
3) ingestion through eating or drinking in the area where toxic materials are being used.
It is up to the teacher to make sure toxic substances do not enter the classroom and that all materials are used safely to avoid problems.

Pregnant women and those who are nursing infants must be especially careful to prevent exposure to toxic substances. All of the dangers to the fetus or infant have not been clearly defined, but enough information has been discerned to issue a clear warning to this population. Fumes, sprays, dusts, and powders present a real hazard to the fetus, can be transferred to the infant through the mother's milk, and can be carried home to the infant or young child through dusts and residue picked up by clothing and hair. The safe path is to completely avoid exposure to any toxin by carefully reading labels and applying common sense to the situation. For example, if you plan to mix powdered tempera paint or work with chalks or clay, the safe method would include use of a respirator mask, which would prevent inhalation of these substances.

CHILDREN AND SAFE ART MATERIALS

Preschool and elementary children are particularly vulnerable to unsafe art materials for a variety of reasons. Their lower body weight allows a toxic substance to be more concentrated in their bodies. Recent headlines regarding lead

poisoning in young children point out this fact. In addition, because children have a more rapid metabolism than adults, toxic substances are more quickly absorbed into their bodies.

> **❝ Preschool and elementary children are particularly vulnerable to unsafe art materials for a variety of reasons. ❞**

Children also tend to have more hand-to-mouth contact than adults, which allows accidental as well as purposeful ingestion of toxic materials. Furthermore, children are easily distracted from safety warnings regarding materials as they become involved in the art process. The tendency of children to have cuts and scratches also allows for ready entry of toxins into their bodies.

WHAT THE LABELS MEAN

Since 1990 our government has required the labeling of all hazardous materials. Any product labeled as hazardous is totally inappropriate for the elementary school. Safe art materials carry the statement that the material "Conforms to ASTMD-4236." A simple "nontoxic" statement on a product is not adequate.

The Arts and Crafts Materials Institute developed a voluntary program to provide a safe standard for materials used by children. Products bearing the labels AP (Approved Product) or CP (Certified Product) have actually been tested by toxicologists in major universities and have been deemed safe for children to use. The HL (Health Label) on art products indicates that these products are appropriate to use with children 12 years old or older under the supervision of an art teacher. Products with HL labels are not safe for elementary children.

SAFE ART MATERIALS

The following are guidelines for choosing and using basic art materials in a safe manner.

Drawing Materials
Markers
- Use only water-soluble AP- or CP-designated markers. Permanent markers are extremely dangerous and can cause lung and liver damage if inhaled. Never use permanent markers in the elementary classroom.
- The use of scented markers is also discouraged. This teaches children to sniff or smell materials.

Chalks
Use only dustless chalk. Most chalks are better used outside for sidewalk art. The amount of dust created in a classroom by twenty children wiping and blowing chalk can be irritating to those who suffer from allergies, asthma, and other respiratory problems.

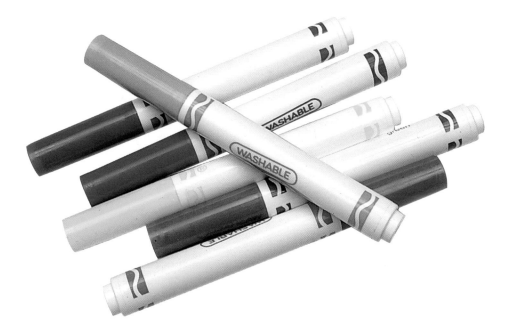

- Use absolutely no permanent markers or solvent-based materials in the art room. If a material stains the clothes or hands and does not clean up with simple soap and water, it is not appropriate or safe for young children to use.
- Use plastic containers for washing brushes; glass is dangerous in the hands of young children.
- Paper cutters should not be used by elementary children. The paper cutter should be kept out of the students' reach, and left in a locked position always with the blade turned to the wall or out of reach.
- Do not use commercial dyes with children; use vegetable or natural dyes (flowers, teas, nut shells, onion skins).
- Do not allow children in the room where a kiln is firing; both the heat and the fumes are dangerous.

Crayons
Use oil pastels; the colors are richer and the satisfaction is greater! Crayons should also bear the AP or CP label to ensure that no lead is present in these materials.

Painting Materials
- Use only liquid tempera and/or watercolor paints. If you must use powdered tempera paints, mix these outside and have the paints ready before children enter the classroom. Avoid inhaling the powders of tempera colors.
- Do not use any spray paints or fixatives. These are extremely dangerous.

Printmaking Materials
- Use only water-soluble printer's inks. Do not use any solvent-based inks.
- Use pencils to carve into unused Styrofoam meat trays for a printing block. Do not use mat knives or other sharp instruments.

Collage Materials
Scissors
Sharp scissors should not be used by young children; blunt points are safe. Fourth and fifth graders may use rounded points with teacher supervision.

Glue and Paste
Use only school paste or white glue for adhering papers. Do not use rubber cement unless it bears the AP or CP label. Do not use any solvent-based glues.

Sculpture and Three-Dimensional Materials
Clay
- Use premixed, moist clay for sculpture and pottery. Do not allow students to take home any unfired clay.
- Remind children to wash their hands thoroughly after using clay. The residual dust can be harmful and irritating if inhaled.
- Paint clay pieces with tempera or watercolor paints.

Glazes
Do not use glazes. Some have the approved labels, but they are not recommended for elementary use.

Carving Tools
Use pencils, craft sticks, or other blunt tools to carve clay. Soapstone should not be used for carving in a closed environment.

Papier-Mâché
Read labels carefully on pastes used for papier-mâché because some pastes contain pesticides or preservatives that are extremely harmful.

Stitchery, Weaving, and Fiber Materials
- Use blunt plastic needles and loosely woven fabrics such as burlap for stitchery. Blunt metal tapestry needles are safe if supervised.
- Young children will have trouble cutting fabric and yarns with their scissors. Precut some lengths of yarn prior to introducing the task.

GENERAL SAFETY PRECAUTIONS FOR ART
- Read the labels on all materials used in the art room. Look carefully for the AP/CP labels. If these are not present, be suspicious. Imported art materials should be looked upon with extreme caution. In this case, "buying American" is the safe path. Other countries have not developed the rigid safety codes adopted by the United States.
- Do not accept or use old art materials that may have been left in the school or donated by some well-meaning adult. If the materials do not bear the current safety codes, toss them out!
- Allow no food or drink in the room where art activities are being conducted. Dust and even fibers float freely in the air and can readily contaminate food.
- Practice cleanliness. Have children wash their hands thoroughly with soap after using art materials.

References
Babin, A., Editor, *Art Hazards News,* Vol. 17, No. 5, 1994.
Babin, A, Peltz, P.A., Rossol, M. "Children's Art Supplies Can Be Toxic." New York: Center for Safety in the Arts, 1992.
McCann, Michael. *Artist Beware.* New York: Watson-Guptill Publications, 1979.
McCann, Michael, "Hazards in the Arts." New York: Center for Safety in the Arts, 1989.
Qualley, Charles A. *Safety in the Art Room.* Massachusetts: Davis Publications, Inc., 1986.

For further information:

Center for Safety in the Arts
5 Beekman Street, Suite 820
New York, New York 10038

(212) 227-6220

Art Assessments

Assessment in art can be problematic for a variety of reasons. Many educators are reluctant to evaluate a student's creative expression in a work of art as good or bad. Because there are often no right or wrong answers, students and their parents could challenge a teacher's subjective opinion of a work if it were reflected in a letter grade. Furthermore, many teachers without a strong art background do not feel qualified to grade student artwork. In addition, teachers do not want to discourage creative expression by giving a low grade or an undeserved grade. People also often feel that talented students have the advantage in art class and that students should not be evaluated on how talented they are, but rather on how much effort they put into their work and how much progress they make.

All of these assessment troubles stem from a focus on art production in the art classroom, rather than a reflection of art history and culture, aesthetics, or art criticism. A broader focus in the art classroom and a variety of assessment options may help in more effective art assessment.

Assessment of Lesson Objectives
Instead of subjective opinions of whether or not one likes a student's artwork, students can be evaluated on whether or not they met the art lesson objectives or demonstrated the knowledge and skills introduced in the lesson. In a quality art program, there are objectives for aesthetic perception, art history, and art criticism, as well as for demonstrating understanding of the elements and principles of art in art production.

In *Art Connections,* every lesson has four clear, measurable objectives. At the end of each lesson, in the **Evaluation Criteria,** teachers are provided questions to consider for each objective as they evaluate students.

Art Production: Evaluating Student Artwork
Art teachers frequently evaluate student artwork on the basis of how well it reflects the elements and principles of art that are being stressed in the lesson and how well the student met the criteria for the artwork. Some teachers make up rubrics or standards for the artwork beforehand and tell students how their work will be evaluated at the time it is assigned. Some teachers use written or mental checklists of their standards as they look at student artwork. Some teachers use this evaluation as an opportunity to discuss the work with the student and find out whether the student thought he or she met the objectives for artwork.

In *Art Connections,* teachers can also use the **Assessment Masters** in the *Assessment Book* to get an idea of whether a student understands the element or principle of art for the lesson.

Art Criticism and Aesthetic Perception: Self- and Peer-Assessment
The four-step process of art criticism (Describe, Analyze, Interpret, Decide) provides a procedure that students can use to objectively study their own art products, as well as the works of others. The sequential steps of art criticism are similar to those used in the scientific method. During the first two steps, Describe and Analyze, students are asked to collect data objectively. During the third step, Interpret, students speculate about the meaning of the work based on the data collected: they make a hypothesis about the idea, emotion, or mood expressed by the artist. During the fourth step, Decide, the students offer their aesthetic judgment about the work of art. The sequential procedures in art criticism force the students to postpone judgment while becoming immersed in the image. It forces them to have a fully funded visual experience before drawing conclusions about a work.

> 66 Art educators could claim to have inspired the growing use of portfolio assessment in other subject areas. 99

Art Connections includes art criticism questions for every Practice and Create activity. These questions appear in the *Student Edition* in grades 3–5 and in the *Teacher Edition* in grades K–2. Additionally, the **Seeing Like an Artist** feature in every lesson of the *Student Edition* provides students with an opportunity to evaluate their developing aesthetic perception.

Art History and Culture
Art is a visual record of history and diverse cultures. The goals for elementary art education are that students understand and appreciate different historical periods, cultures, and artistic styles and develop respect for the traditions and contributions of diverse societies.

In *Art Connections* every lesson introduces fine art from a particular culture, time, and style. In the **Introducing the Art** strategies, teachers are encouraged to compare, contrast, and share the **Art Background** information as well as the information provided in the *Artist Profiles* to help students develop an understanding of the visual arts in relation to history and cultures. Through discussion and elements in their own artwork, teachers can evaluate students' awareness in this area.

Portfolio Assessment
Art educators could claim to have inspired the growing use of portfolio assessment in other subject areas. Many art teachers collect the best examples of a student's work and look at the progress over time. They display it and discuss it

with students and parents. Student art journals with ideas, drawings, and sketches also provide an opportunity for portfolio assessment.

In *Art Connections,* students are encouraged to keep their best work in a *Student Portfolio* and to maintain an **Art Journal.** Reminders of these types of portfolio assessments appear in the *Teacher Edition.*

Performance Assessment
Unlike other subject areas, art education has a long tradition of performance assessment. In art class students make things to demonstrate what they can do. In quality art programs, teachers use performance descriptions for not only art production, but art criticism, art history and culture, and aesthetic perception to aid them in evaluating student demonstrations of their knowledge and skills in art.

In *Art Connections,* every work of art a student produces can be considered for performance assessment of the lesson concept. Performance assessments can also involve discussions about the artworks to introduce the lesson concept and art criticism questions. The exercises in the *Vocabulary Book* also help teachers to get an idea of how well students understand the art vocabulary of the lesson; they can be using this vocabulary, the language of art, in their discussions about their own and others' artwork.

Art not only enables teachers to evaluate student knowledge and skills in art each year, but it also provides a wonderful opportunity to assess a student's growth and development over time. Students and parents are often reluctant to discard artwork and fondly review it from time to time to see how children's ideas and skills have changed. Schools often keep an example of student artwork in a student's portfolio from year to year. Student artwork can also be evaluated by professionals to assess a student's emotional and mental health.

A thoughtful and fair art assessment program enables teachers to really see how much their students are capable of accomplishing.

References

Armstrong, Carmen. L. *Designing Assessment in Art.* Reston, VA: The National Art Education Association. 1994.

Into the Portfolio Process: A Handbook for Student Assessment. California Art Education Association, Butte County Office of Education. 1995.

Rudner, Lawrence M. and Carol Boston. *A Look at Performance Assessment for Art Education.* Reston, VA: The National Art Education Association. 1994.

Art and Multiple Intelligences

Gloria McCoy, K–12 Art Supervisor, Spring Branch Independent School District, Texas

In the last twenty years, a group of researchers and educators headed by Dr. Howard Gardner, co-director of Project Zero at Harvard Graduate School of Education and Adjunct Professor of Neurology at the Boston University School of Medicine, have come to the conclusion that there are many ways of knowing and solving the same problem. Others such as Thomas Armstrong and David Lazear have written extensively on the subject and have developed practical applications of the theory of multiple intelligences in the classroom. The multiple intelligences theory has direct and indirect connections to art education.

The theory of multiple intelligences addresses the issue of intelligence quotients. At the beginning of the twentieth century, IQ tests were developed and quickly gained popularity as a "radar detector" of genius. These tests, designed on a curved scale, were touted to be able to sort people by their intelligence. Unfortunately, these tests have been shown to be unreliable when measuring *success* in the world outside the classroom. In one study, for example, more than a third of highly successful people scored low on IQ tests. Men and women throughout history, such as Thomas Edison and Albert Einstein, who were not very successful in school have made great contributions to our world. Leonardo da Vinci, one of the finest minds and artists of all time, grieved at the end of his life that he had not lived up to his potential because of his poor spelling, penmanship, and other language skills.

Gardner realized that IQ tests often tested only those skills that were used in schools, such as reading and math. As a consequence, many areas of the human ways of knowing and learning were omitted. Gardner defined intelligence as the *ability to solve problems* or fashion products that are of consequence in a particular cultural setting.

In the development of his theory, Gardner identified at least seven different intelligences. All of us have each of these intelligences to some degree; however, the degree may depend on how fully we have developed them. Some of them such as music develop early in life, while others such as math may develop later. There are indicators that children may repress some intelligences if they are not valued or developed in early childhood. Each of the intelligences can stand on its own, but most of the time they work together with other intelligences to solve problems.

Following are examples of Gardner's intelligences and how they are expressed in the art classroom.

Visual/Spatial intelligence most often comes to mind in the visual arts. It relies on the sense of sight and visualization, as well as creating internal mental images and finding one's way in space. Pilots, artists, and mechanical engineers are a few of those who rely on this intelligence.

In *Art Connections,* the **Create** activity in each lesson includes use of this intelligence. Many students who have a real strength in this area have an opportunity to use it in the art room.

Body/Kinesthetic is related to physical movement, handling objects skillfully, and the wisdom of the body, including the part of the brain that controls motion—the motor cortex. Some of those who use this intelligence are surgeons, craftspeople, athletes, and mechanics.

In *Art Connections* there is a natural link to both the **Practice** and the **Create** activities as students cut, draw, paint, and otherwise manipulate materials and tools. Students will use this intelligence in every lesson.

> **“ Unlike many other subjects that depend on one intelligence, art education provides an opportunity for students to use all of their intelligences to solve problems. ”**

Verbal/Linguistic is the intelligence that relates to words and language, both written and spoken, and dominates most of our educational systems. Lawyers, poets, storytellers, and journalists are a few of the groups who rely heavily on this intelligence.

This intelligence is also a natural part of every art lesson, whether the students are reading, listening to information, expressing opinions, or dialoguing with others.

Interpersonal is the intelligence based on person-to-person relationships and communication, as well as empathy skills. Careers in this area include therapists, social workers, politicians, and pastors.

This intelligence could be used frequently in art lessons as works of art are discussed in groups. Art discussions allow all students an opportunity to participate and often encourage even the most shy student. Structured cooperative learning also supports this intelligence.

Intrapersonal intelligence relates to our understanding of ourselves, reflections on what we've done and why, our inner state of being, thinking about thinking or metacognition, and our awareness of spiritual realities. Counselors, theologians, and even self-employed businesspeople might depend on this intelligence in day-to-day work.

The connection of intrapersonal intelligence to art is a natural as students are asked to express their feelings or thoughts through the creation of artwork or reflect on the process afterward. The **Art Journal** suggestions in *Art Connections* are also intended to support this intelligence.

Logical/Mathematical is the intelligence that is sometimes called "scientific thinking" because it deals with inductive and deductive thinking and reasoning, numbers, and recognition of abstract patterns. Scientists, accountants, and computer programmers are dependent on this intelligence.

In art, students use logical/mathematical intelligence when they look for abstract patterns, use deductive reasoning to determine the meaning of a work of art, use grids and measurements in drawing, or use geometric shapes to create designs.

Musical/Rhythmic intelligence is based on tonal patterns and their recognition. It includes a variety of environmental sounds, as well as the sensitivity to rhythm and beats. Musicians, band directors, and dancers depend on this intelligence.

Rhythm is a principle of art and is part of the artmaking process. In addition, *Art Connections* includes audiotapes of classical music to play during the Create process to enhance creative thinking. **Music Connections** appear in the *Teacher Edition.* In addition, The ARTSOURCE Lessons at the end of each unit focus on connecting visual art to music, dance, and theater.

Unlike many other subjects that depend on one intelligence, art education provides an opportunity for students to use all of their intelligences to solve problems. Often students succeed in art class when they have trouble in other areas.

One of the most profound findings of multiple intelligence is something that art educators have known for years. When students employ a variety of ways to solve a problem, they can all come up with successful solutions. There is no one right answer, but many.

References

Armstrong, Thomas. *Multiple Intelligences in the Classroom.* Virginia: Association for Supervision and Curriculum Development, 1994.

Armstrong, Thomas. *Seven Kinds of Smart: Identifying and Developing Your Many Intelligences.* New York: Plume/Penguin, 1993.

Gardner, Howard. *Multiple Intelligences: The Theory in Practice. A Reader.* Basic Books/ Harper Collins, 1993.

Lazear, David. *Seven Ways of Knowing: Teaching for Multiple Intelligences.* Illinois: Skylight Publishing, 1991.

About Aesthetic Perception

Richard W. Burrows, Executive Director, Institute for Arts Education, San Diego, California

The Association of Institutes for Aesthetic Education promotes and fosters aesthetic education principles and practices through professional and institutional development. The Association provides policy and program leadership to the arts and education field at the national, state, and local levels.

Aesthetics has been defined as the branch of philosophy that focuses on the nature of beauty, the nature and value of art, and the inquiry processes and human responses associated with those topics.

Aesthetic perception can be most simply defined as an educational approach designed to enhance understanding of artistic expression. Aesthetic perception requires two primary elements to exist: the work of art and a viewer to perceive it. An aesthetic perception approach to viewing works of art is predicated on the belief that the arts can be studied in an active, experiential way. The focus is on developing skills of perception by using works of art as a "textbook" or a focus for study. The instruction delivered by the teachers is in partnership with the work of art.

Aesthetic perception provides opportunities to heighten perception and understanding through direct encounters with a broad spectrum of artworks. Students and teachers become actively involved with the artwork: observing, listening to and discussing works of art, and exploring their perceptions of these works through participatory activities. The focus is on developing skills of perception through greater understanding of art forms, of how artists make aesthetic choices, and of how these understandings relate to other aspects of life.

Misconceptions About Aesthetic Perception

As aesthetic perception approaches have become more widely used, a number of misconceptions have developed about the purpose of aesthetic perception education in the understanding of works of art.

Multidisciplinary Versus Interdisciplinary

The purpose of aesthetic perception is not to explore the commonalities among works of art. Each work of art must be studied separately first; connections should be made after an in-depth understanding of that particular work. Every work of art has a separate intention and different meaning. If aesthetic perception is to develop a thinking- or meaning-based understanding of the work of art, then activities must reflect that point of view.

You Cannot Teach What You Do Not Like

A strong "personal" negative reaction to a work of art does not invalidate it as an object for study for students.

Arts Integration

While arts experiences must integrate with all other areas of the curriculum, it is important to understand the separate language that the arts have and acknowledge the connections with other cross-curriculum areas as they arise.

> ❝ Aesthetic perception requires two primary elements to exist: the work of art and a viewer to perceive it. ❞

The Therapeutic Value of Aesthetic Perception

Very often students and teachers will comment on the therapeutic value of aesthetic perception. . . it seems separate from the actual art-making processes. This is often a side effect of active engagement in artistic creation and perception. It is not the purpose of aesthetic perception, which should be seen as an alternative way of viewing the work of art and the world in which it lives.

Using Aesthetic Perception

Below are some guidelines for using an aesthetic perception approach to education.

Deciding What to Teach

It would not be appropriate to teach the same elements over and over in connection with each work of art. Instead, knowledge of all of the elements within a given art discipline should provide the background knowledge for making

a decision about what aesthetic perception experiences to design. These decisions should be based on the most predominant elements in the work of art—the responses and the backgrounds of the students across time.

Creating a Safe Space and Adopting a Critical Stance

It is important to create a working and learning environment with both students and teachers in which they feel comfortable taking risks and trying out new ideas. This does not mean, however, that everything that occurs in aesthetic perception has to be met with uncritical approval. Instead, experiences can be structured so that participants receive feedback on their aesthetic choices and are given an opportunity to revise and improve their solutions to problems.

Documenting the Experience

Various types of documentation serve as a way of recording the aesthetic perception events as they occur or are revisited. This documentation should include written observations, interviews, journals, and student projects. It is important in any case to record this work in order to be able to see the "habits of mind" that reveal themselves in this complex and rich way of thinking and knowing.

Aesthetic perception is a long-term undertaking and requires a patient conviction that the arts and aesthetic perception should be a part of the learning experience of young people. It requires flexibility, stamina, ingenuity, and perseverance. The rewards are astronomical in terms of student response, content understanding, and classroom relationships.

It Takes a Village: The Community as a Resource for Art Materials

Willis Bing Davis, Art Department Chair, Central State University, Ohio

Ingenuity, resourcefulness, and creative survival have always been a close friend to most successful art and classroom teachers when it comes to providing meaningful arts experiences for students. We are known as collectors who never (almost never) throw anything away. Some art and classroom teachers will need to acquire the skill of always being on the lookout for resources, materials, and supplies that can supplement art materials in the classroom. It can be a lot of fun; plus, it stimulates the imagination and creative impulse. This is also a great way to build bridges and advocates for arts education.

Think of all the things you use in the art room. How many can be found locally? Any safe, usable materials or supplies that can be found free or reduced in price leaves more of the art budget to buy the things that have to be purchased. There are different forms of searching for inexpensive to free materials for art activities. The following are a few tried and proven ways to acquire materials, supplies, and resources that can be used for art and other educational activities.

Materials in the School Building
- Leftover wood or metal from a shop class
- Empty milk and food containers from the food-service area
- Cardboard tubes from the food service, rest room, or copy machine
- Scrap paper from copy machines

Annual Open House Night Resources
Open house is a great time to post a small list of hand tools needed for the art program. You would be surprised how many extra hammers, pliers, screwdrivers, bent forks, and so on are lying around garages and basements.

Many parents also work at places that have by-products that could supplement the art materials in the art program.

Local Business Material Sources
- *Wood.* Lumberyards are usually willing to let teachers collect boxes of scrap wood for art production. Some lumberyards will even let you leave a box with your school name on it.
- *Wallpaper.* Ask for discontinued wallpaper design sample books from paint stores.
- *Paper.* Large quantities of damaged paper may be available from local paper or paper distribution companies.

Community Resources
- Many communities participate in the popular "Take-a-Child-to-Work" programs that allow children to see and experience where their parents work. Almost every school also has a Career Day when many professional individuals visit schools to talk to students about potential careers. Both programs put schools, students, or teachers into direct contact with local businesses. Both groups are already open to helping schools and would welcome other, more direct ways to contribute to positive educational experiences.

> " Any safe, usable materials or supplies that can be found free or reduced in price leaves more of the art budget to buy the things that have to be purchased. "

- Teachers may find that companies with national headquarters in their communities often have a strong commitment to those communities and their educational systems. Teachers can assist these companies in reaching their community commitment goals by suggesting ways that they can assist the school art program. Local businesses may want to sponsor the visit of a local artist or donate materials.
- Many local service organizations have an interest and commitment to youth and the arts. They often go begging for art and cultural events and activities to which they can contribute. Find out what they want to contribute and help them reach their goal, be it providing scholarships to talented art students, funding an exhibit, hosting an art reception, donating materials and supplies, framing student artworks for the hallways, sponsoring a local or major art field trip, and so on.

Artist Resources
- Local and regional emerging artists live in every community and can make meaningful contributions to the school art program. Artists from the community or region offer a "realness" to the program from knowing and living in the area.
- Some artists do a good job at demonstrating, some do a good slide-lecture, some are more effective in large groups or small groups, some do great critique sessions, and some may be better mentoring one-on-one. Each individual teacher or school district can develop an annotated artist directory listing the artists' strong points for reference.
- Most communities also have one or more local arts groups or arts organizations that can assist schools in identifying and securing the services of local artists. A local arts group may be willing to do a series of Member Art Demos over the course of the year in your school.
- Another great source of local and regional artists can be found in the colleges and universities in your area. It is a win-win situation because the college and university art program can show your students some of the quality art teachers they may be working with in the future. This a great source of judges for student competitions.

Art Agencies at Local and State Levels: While everyone is aware of the existence of the National Endowment for the Arts in Washington, D.C., many may not be aware that there are state arts agencies and many community-based Arts Councils that can be an important resource for your art program.

Find ways to let everyone in the community help your art program to be the best it can be because remember, **it takes a village.**

A Sampling of Art Supplies Resources

J. L. Hammett Co. Braintree, MA
  800-333-4600
Nasco Arts & Crafts Modesto, CA
  800-558-9595
Sax Arts & Crafts New Berlin, WI
  800-558-6696
United Art and Education Supply Co., Inc. Fort Wayne, IN 800-322-3247

The Importance of Cultural Diversity Through Art in the Elementary Classroom

Jane Rhoades Hudak, Ph.D., Professor of Art, Georgia Southern University

James Banks, noted multicultural expert, says: "By the year 2050 the average United States resident will trace his or her ancestry to Africa, Asia, Latin America, the Pacific Islands, Arabia, and almost anywhere but Europe. Today in New York State 40 percent of the elementary and secondary pupils belong to ethnic minorities. By the year 2000 this figure will be 50 percent." With this in mind, the following is an overview of the benefits of a culturally diverse art program.

Culture is learned. People acquire information about the world and how to deal with it as members of a society. Individuals do not learn about their culture by themselves. Children learn about the art of their own culture and other cultures through family and friends, through the mass media, and through the Internet. The information learned this way is often valuable, but it cannot be relied upon to always give adequate and correct information. Schools are often the most effective place for giving students the opportunity to learn about the art of their culture and other cultures.

Our view of the nature of the world and our place in it is expressed and communicated culturally. Every society has institutions that teach culture—family and school are two of the best examples in our society. All societies have religions, which are bodies of cultural knowledge and practices. We also have rituals for birth and death. All cultures have objects that are used for everyday living. We express our world views through dance, drama, music, and art. We decorate our world and our bodies. We paint our faces and the walls of our houses. We make music with instruments and our voices. All this activity is shaped by our participation in a cultural tradition.

A quality elementary art program provides a wonderful opportunity for teachers to expose students to a variety of cultures as well as their own and to help them to become culturally aware. Following are several of the areas such a program can enhance.

Art Promotes Intracultural Understanding

Through a culturally diverse art program, students begin to understand the role and function that art and artists play in society. Through learning about the art of other cultures, they have the opportunity to identify similarities and differences between their culture and others. They learn that art reflects the religion, politics, economics, and other aspects of a culture.

Through a quality art program, students can address issues of ethnocentrism, bias, stereotyping, prejudice, discrimination, and racism. Students can learn that no one racial, cultural, or national group is superior to another and that no one group's art is better than another.

Art Teaches Self-Esteem Through Diversity

Through a quality art program, students learn to recognize, acknowledge, and celebrate racial and cultural diversity through art within their own society. A good program helps promote the enhancement and affirmation of their self-esteem and encourages pride in one's own heritage. Personal expression is encouraged, and the result is often a statement in visual form that is both inventive and filled with personal meaning.

> " A quality elementary art program provides a wonderful opportunity for teachers to expose students to a variety of cultures as well as their own and to help them to become culturally aware. "

Art Teaches Effective Communication

When a quality art program is implemented, students are encouraged to increase their visual literacy skills. Students begin to understand that artists transmit information that cannot be disclosed through other modes of communication. Students learn visual literacy by looking, understanding, talking, writing, and making images. They learn that each society has its own way of communicating through images. Through a culturally sensitive art program, students will be able to discuss and compare art from other societies. Students learn to visually communicate by creating images that convey knowledge, create new knowledge, shape opinions, disclose the depths of human emotion, and impart the most profound values found universally throughout the world.

Art Teaches About the Past

Through a quality art program, students develop a sensitivity and understanding of the history of humankind. For many periods in history, it is only through visual remains or material culture that societies' cultures can be pieced together. A study of art history reveals varied world views, concepts, symbols, styles, feelings, and perceptions. Experiences that students have with these art objects from the past teach them respect for others, challenge their minds, and stimulate not only the intellect but also the imagination.

Art Teaches Critical Thinking

A culturally sensitive art program encourages a variety of critical thinking skills. When students are faced with looking at art from other cultures, they make critical judgments and develop their own opinions. Students are asked to identify and recall information; to organize selected facts and ideas; to use particular facts, rules, and principles; to be able to figure out component parts or to classify; and to combine ideas and form a new whole.

Art Teaches Perceptual Sensitivity and Aesthetic Awareness

As a result of a quality art program, students develop a keen sense of awareness and an appreciation for beauty. They learn that each culture has its own criteria for beauty. Art experiences help cultivate an aesthetic sensitivity and respect for the natural and human-made environment around the world. Art classes are the only place in the school curriculum where students learn about what constitutes quality visual design—about harmony, order, organization, and specific design qualities (such as balance, movement, and unity).

Art Teaches Creativity

When a culturally sensitive art program is implemented, creativity in all students is stimulated and nurtured. Students learn to solve problems creatively. They learn that every society has some form of creative expression. Students learn that artists in other cultures have expressed their creativity in a wide range of ways as a magician, myth maker, teacher, propagandist, shaman, and catalyst of social change. In some societies, no one special person is called an artist—everyone in the culture makes "art" objects.

Teachers can help prevent students from having a simplistic view of other cultures and help them understand the cultural context of how and why artworks are created. *Art Connections* has been carefully constructed so that students will be exposed to artwork that represents a wide variety of cultures. Questions and strategies are designed to help teachers put art in a cultural context for students. The **Art Background** feature in this *Teacher Edition* and the *Artist Profiles* book provides additional information about the artwork and the artists.

As a teacher in the school, you are a cultural transmitter. A quality art education program taught by a culturally sensitive teacher benefits every student. When educators teach in a systematic, meaningful way, students acquire knowledge about art and cultures that will benefit them throughout their lives.

Museum Education

Marilyn JS Goodman, Director of Education, Solomon R. Guggenheim Museum

Museums are truly magnificent places. In recent years, these bastions of culture have taken tremendous strides toward making their collections accessible to a broader audience. Museum educators are usually eager to share new information and ideas and are delighted to assist school educators with programs and materials that can easily be incorporated into the classroom. Museums contain a wealth of treasures that offer extraordinary resources for teachers and their students, and which will undoubtedly enrich the overall classroom experience.

Getting acquainted with museums in your region can be a real eye-opener. Museums collect objects that document human achievement, both in our own and in other cultures. A local historical society or farm museum might contain an array of clothing and tools that can bring history to life. A science museum may offer interactive exhibits about phenomena in the natural or physical sciences, or maybe about sensory perception, new technologies, or space exploration. A children's museum will offer hands-on displays specially designed to motivate young children to learn by doing. And art museums contain a visually stunning smorgasbord of works that reflect the diversity of human thought and experiences.

Museums do not supplant classroom instruction. They enhance and reinforce what is taught by providing honest-to-goodness raw materials in the form of objects, artifacts, and exhibits. They give students the chance to see and sometimes handle the real thing. It's one thing, for example, to talk about Egypt's role in the history of civilization. It's another thing entirely to see the wrappings on a cat mummy, discover hieroglyphs on a sarcophagus, or be overwhelmed by the power and grandeur of large stone sculptures of kings and queens.

When students have the chance to look at portraits, still lifes, landscapes, genre scenes, furniture, clothing, and artifacts, they learn more than by just seeing a picture of a person, place, or thing. They learn how to "read" a culture. But perhaps more importantly, they learn to develop their own processes of investigation and critical inquiry. What was this person's life really like? What can one learn about the class structure of this society? What can we tell about craftspeople, available materials, or the objects this society held dear? How does the clothing tell us about the climate of the region? What can we learn about the geography, topography, and vegetation? What did people eat? How did they spend leisure

time? What were their religious beliefs? Is there any evidence of trade and communication with other regions? What scientific inventions were present at the time? Can one tell if they communicated through language or by writing? As children are naturally curious, objects will motivate them to think, research, and learn.

A visit to a museum will make the curriculum come alive as a class begins to explore objects and learn about their meanings. Museum objects give us information in a way that's very different from reading texts. Students must think critically to determine both the questions and answers for themselves. A first-hand, visual investigation of an object's style, material, subject matter, and physical characteristics offers preliminary clues to deciphering its meaning. When the exploration is combined with other knowledge—such as the geography and natural resources of a region; the historical context; the social, political, and economic structure of a culture; or even advances in science and technology—students can be engaged in a type of learning that is truly multidisciplinary, and which may lead them into other areas. Moreover, methods for gathering information go far beyond what one sees.

> **" Museums contain a wealth of treasures that offer extraordinary resources for teachers and their students, and which will undoubtedly enrich the overall classroom experience. "**

Exploring objects and works of art allows students to use a multiplicity of senses combining intellect with intuition. The opportunity for experiential, emotional, and intellectual learning is always present.

Museum objects present different historical and cultural perspectives. One can gather information about a person, a culture, a belief system, values, and the way people lived in the past. Museum visits encourage students to see things from broader global and intellectual points of view, developing respect for the work, lives, and points of view of others. Students are encouraged to respond in a variety of ways and on different levels. Most importantly, students are invited to formulate and express their ideas and then discuss them with others.

To learn about museum resources, teachers can contact the education department of museums in their region. If teachers explain the level of their students, the subjects they are studying, and which specific aspects of the

curriculum they would like to supplement, the museum's education department can help to tailor the resources to the classroom. In addition to guided tours and workshops, the museum education department may offer materials for loan including slides, pamphlets, posters, postcards, kits, and other printed materials. Some museums have teacher resource rooms filled with books, films, videos, CD-ROMS, and computer databases geared to educators. There will always be trained staff to answer questions or to help teachers develop a complete learning unit that can integrate museum objects with classroom studies.

Using museums is an excellent way to enrich and enliven the classroom experience. Educators can take the first step by learning all they can about the rich and diverse resources available to them and their students.

A Sampling of Fine Art CD-ROM Resources

A Is for Art, C Is for Cezanne, Philadelphia Museum of Art
Art Gallery, Microscoft
ArtRageous, Softkey
Le Louvre: The Palace and Its Paintings, Montparnasse Multimedia
The Louvre Museum: Museums of the World for Kids, Voyager
Painters Painting, Voyager
A Passion for Art: Renoir, Cezanne, Matisse, and Dr. Barnes Corbis Publishing
With Open Eyes: Images from the Art Institute of Chicago, Voyager

United States Museum Resources

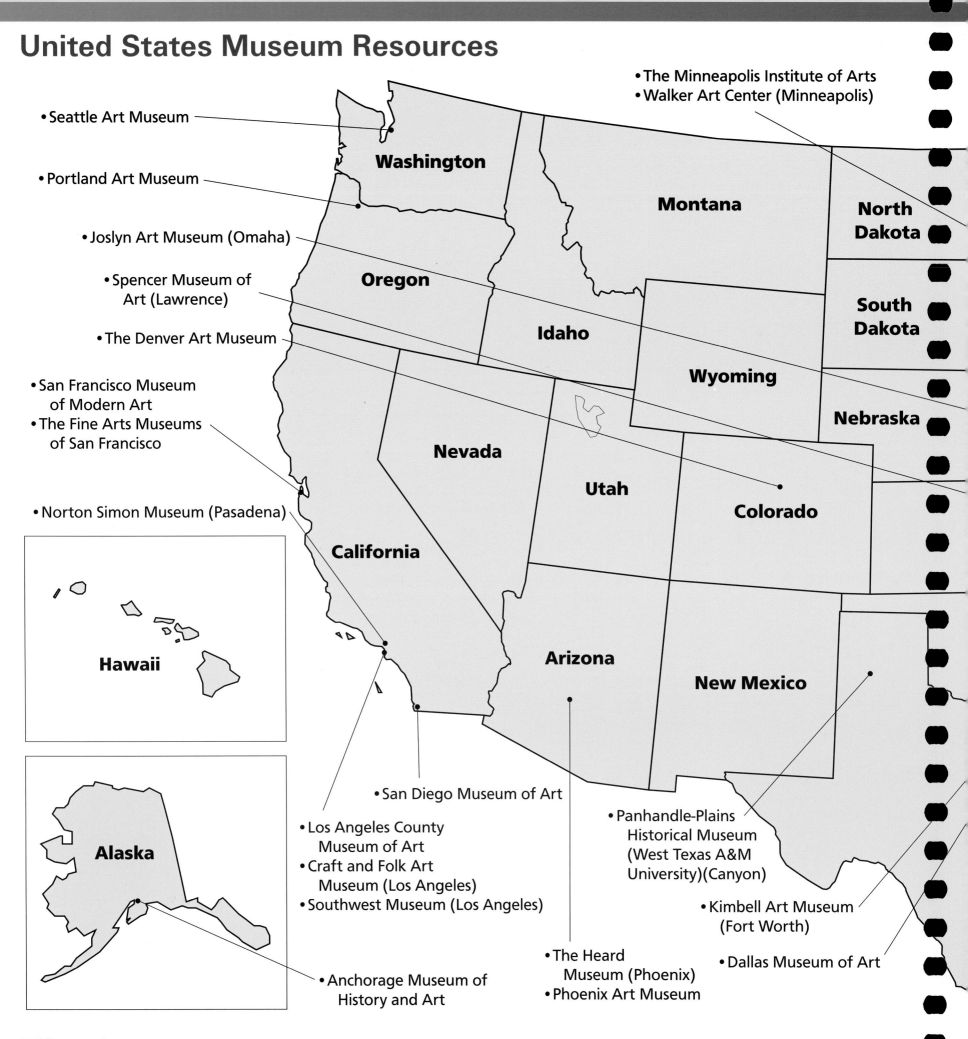

- Seattle Art Museum
- Portland Art Museum
- Joslyn Art Museum (Omaha)
- Spencer Museum of Art (Lawrence)
- The Denver Art Museum
- San Francisco Museum of Modern Art
- The Fine Arts Museums of San Francisco
- Norton Simon Museum (Pasadena)
- The Minneapolis Institute of Arts
- Walker Art Center (Minneapolis)

Washington

Montana

North Dakota

Oregon

Idaho

South Dakota

Wyoming

Nebraska

Nevada

Utah

Colorado

California

Arizona

New Mexico

Hawaii

Alaska

- San Diego Museum of Art
- Los Angeles County Museum of Art
- Craft and Folk Art Museum (Los Angeles)
- Southwest Museum (Los Angeles)
- Anchorage Museum of History and Art
- Panhandle-Plains Historical Museum (West Texas A&M University)(Canyon)
- Kimbell Art Museum (Fort Worth)
- The Heard Museum (Phoenix)
- Phoenix Art Museum
- Dallas Museum of Art

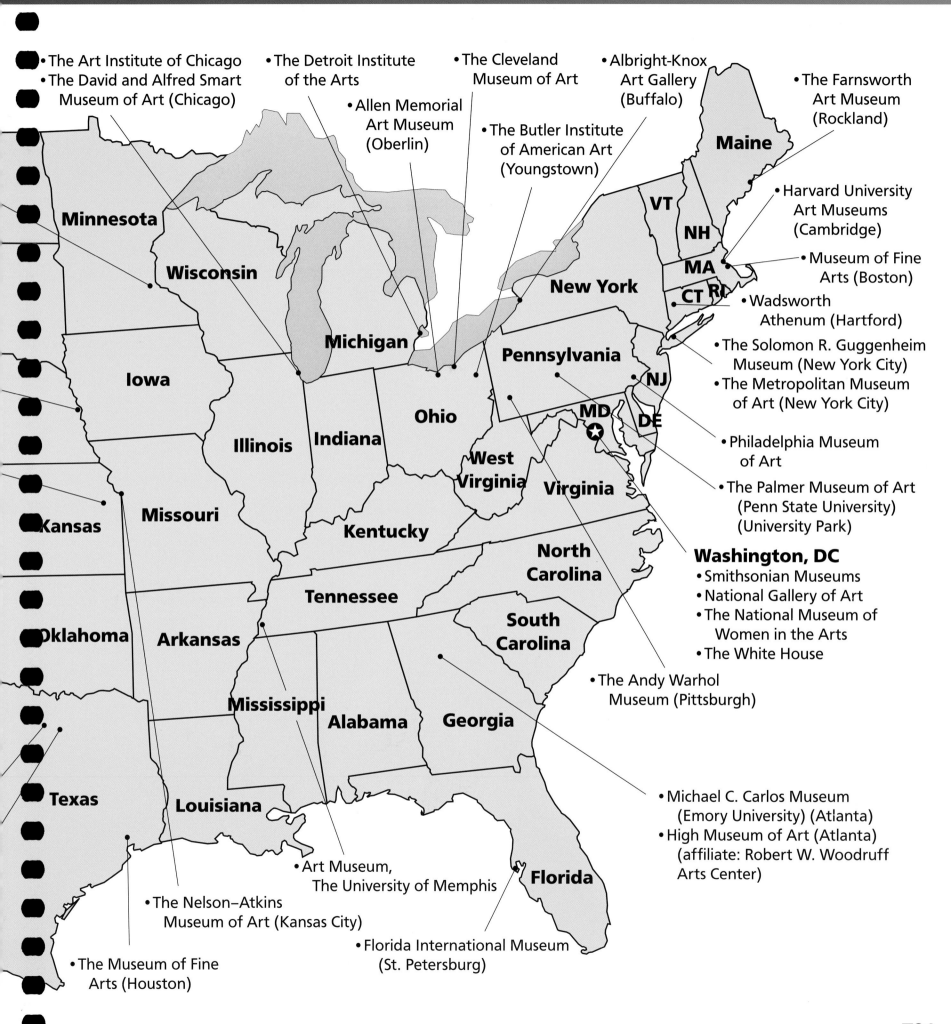

• The Art Institute of Chicago
• The David and Alfred Smart
  Museum of Art (Chicago)

• The Detroit Institute
  of the Arts

• The Cleveland
  Museum of Art

• Albright-Knox
  Art Gallery
  (Buffalo)

• The Farnsworth
  Art Museum
  (Rockland)

• Allen Memorial
  Art Museum
  (Oberlin)

• The Butler Institute
  of American Art
  (Youngstown)

Maine

VT

NH

• Harvard University
  Art Museums
  (Cambridge)

MA

CT RI

• Museum of Fine
  Arts (Boston)

Minnesota

Wisconsin

Michigan

New York

• Wadsworth
  Athenum (Hartford)

• The Solomon R. Guggenheim
  Museum (New York City)

Iowa

Pennsylvania

NJ

• The Metropolitan Museum
  of Art (New York City)

Ohio

MD

DE

• Philadelphia Museum
  of Art

Illinois

Indiana

West
Virginia

Virginia

• The Palmer Museum of Art
  (Penn State University)
  (University Park)

Kansas

Missouri

Kentucky

North
Carolina

Washington, DC
• Smithsonian Museums
• National Gallery of Art
• The National Museum of
  Women in the Arts
• The White House

Oklahoma

Arkansas

Tennessee

South
Carolina

• The Andy Warhol
  Museum (Pittsburgh)

Mississippi

Alabama

Georgia

• Michael C. Carlos Museum
  (Emory University) (Atlanta)
• High Museum of Art (Atlanta)
  (affiliate: Robert W. Woodruff
  Arts Center)

Texas

Louisiana

Florida

• Art Museum,
  The University of Memphis

• The Nelson–Atkins
  Museum of Art (Kansas City)

• Florida International Museum
  (St. Petersburg)

• The Museum of Fine
  Arts (Houston)

T31

UNITED STATES MUSEUM RESOURCES

SRA is not responsible for the content of these Websites, which may contain content and images which may be inappropriate for student use.

Allen Memorial Art Museum
Oberlin College
Oberlin, OH 44074
Phone: (216) 775-8665
URL: (WWW address): http://www.oberlin.edu/wwwmap/allen_art.html
Site description: Ohio's Oberlin College is the host of this site. The on-line collection includes ancient to modern, Africa to America.

Andy Warhol Museum, The
117 Sandusky St.
Pittsburgh, PA 15212
Phone: (412) 237-8300
URL: (WWW address): http://www.clpgh.org/warhol/
Site description: The pop art inventer is featured in this Pittsburgh institution. Many of Warhol's most famous images are included, such as Jackie Kennedy. Tour info, calendars, and all other museum offerings.

Boston Museum of Fine Arts
465 Huntington Ave.
Boston, MA 02115
Phone: (617) 267-9300
URL: (WWW address): http://www.mfa.org
Site description: The highlight of the site is the museum's on-line exhibit of 19th century American artist Winslow Homer.

Butler Institute of American Art
524 Wick Ave.
Youngstown, OH 44502
Phone: (330) 743-1711
URL: (WWW address): http://www.butlerart.com
Site description: This museum in Youngstown, Ohio was the first U.S. museum built exclusively for housing American art. Works of Winslow Homer, Mary Cassatt, and Thomas Hart Benton are included.

Cleveland Museum of Art
11150 East Blvd.
Cleveland, OH 44106
Phone: (216) 421-7340
URL: (WWW address): http://www.clemusart.com/
Site description: This site contains images of its collection from ancient Egypt to the present. A selection of education links is accessible.

Farnsworth Art Museum
352 Main Street, Box 466
Rockland, ME 04841
Phone: (207) 596-6457
URL: (WWW address): http://www.midcoast.com/~farnsworth/
Site description: Images from Andrew Wyeth's personal collection in addition to the museum's own can be viewed at this site.

Florida International Museum (Treasures of the Czars)
100 Second St. North
St. Petersburg, FL 33701
Phone: (813) 824-6734
URL: (WWW address): http://www.sptimes.com/treasures/
Site description: A new museum, opened in 1995, the site displays examples from its premier exhibit.

Fine Arts Museums of San Francisco
Golden Gate Park
San Francisco, CA 94118
Phone: (415) 750-3600
URL: (WWW address): http://www.famsf.org/
Site description: This site has the largest searchable art image base in the world—65,000!

Harvard University Art Museums
32 Quincy St.
Cambridge, MA 02138
Phone: (617) 495-9400
URL: (WWW address): http://www.fas.harvard.edu/~artmuseums/
Site description: The Fogg Art Museum, the Busch-Reisinger Museum, and the Arthur M. Sackler Museum, all located in Cambridge, MA, are accessed at this virtual address.

High Museum (Woodruff Arts Center)
1280 Peachtree St. N. E.
Atlanta, GA 30309
Phone: (404) 848-4711
URL: (WWW address): http://www.high.org/
Site description: Contains information on educational programs, teacher resources, and outreach programs.

Los Angeles County Museum of Art
5905 Wilshire Blvd.
Los Angeles, CA 90036
Phone: (213) 857-6000
URL: (WWW address): http://www.lacma.org/
Site description: A complete listing of museum education resources is included in the site. Images of current and past exhibitions and samples of the permanent collection can be viewed.

Los Angeles Craft and Folk Art Museum
5800 Wilshire Blvd.
Los Angeles, CA
Phone: (213) 937-5544
URL: (WWW address): http://www.lam.mus.ca.us/~cafam/
Site description: This museum celebrates contemporary craft, international folk art, and design from around the world. Includes information on educational outreach, year-round exhibitions, and its permanent collection.

Memphis, University of, Egyptian Artifacts Exhibit
The University of Memphis Campus
Memphis, TN 38152
Phone: (901) 678-2224
URL: (WWW address): http://www.memst.edu/egypt/main.html
Site description: Visitor can take a brief "Tour of Egypt" and view a 4000-year-old loaf of bread from the mortuary temple of Mentuhotep II at Dein al Behari in Western Thebes.

Michael C. Carlos Museum (Emory University)
571 S. King St.
Atlanta, GA 30322
Phone: (404) 727-4282
URL: (WWW address): http://www.emory.edu/CARLOS/
Site description: Described as "the best virtual tour of a museum outside of the Louvre." It includes a video.

Minneapolis Institute of Arts
2400 Third Ave.
S. Minneapolis, MN 55404
Phone: (612) 870-3000
URL: (WWW address): http://www.arts MIA.org
Site description: The museum offers information about its collections, exhibits, and programs. Includes images ranging from African Art to 20th century post-modern.

Norton Simon Museum
411 W. Colorado Blvd.
Pasadena, CA 91105
Phone: (818) 449-6840
URL: (WWW address): http://www.citycent.com/ccc/Pasadena/nsmuseum.html
Site description: Images include works of Rembrandt, Goya, and Picasso, along with some examples of South Asian sculpture and Impressionist art.

Palmer Museum of Art, The (Penn State University)
Curtin Road
University Park, PA 16802-2507
Phone: (814) 865-7672
URL: (WWW address): http://www.cac.psu.edu/~mtd120/palmer/
Site description: This site contains painting images and includes a link to an art class via computer. Considered an example of an excellent Internet site plan and design.

Panhandle-Plains Museum (West Texas A&M University)
2401 Fourth Ave.
Canyon, TX 79015
Phone: (806) 656-2244
URL: (WWW address): http://www.webtex.com/webtex/museum
Site description: Images of cowboys, Native Americans, gunfighters, and ranchers out of the Old West. The site is dedicated to the preservation of the northwest Texas heritage.

Phoenix Art Museum
1625 N. Central Ave.
Phoenix, AZ 85004
Phone: (602) 257-1880
URL: (WWW address): http://www.azcentral.com/community/phx art/home.html
Site description: Site includes an on-line museum map pointing to areas with art images that can be viewed.

Portland Art Museum
1219 S. W. Park Ave.
Portland, OR 97205
Phone: (503) 226-2811
URL: (WWW address): http://www.pam.org/pam/
Site description: A rotating on-line tour of the collection of this encyclopedic art museum.

San Diego Museum of Art
1450 El Prado-Balboa Park
San Diego, CA 92112
Phone: (619) 232-7931
URL: (WWW address): http://www.sddt.com/sdma.html/
Site description: This site includes works from the Far East, South Asia, Europe, and the U.S. Numerous links to art resources on the Web.

Smart Museum of Art
5550 S. Greenwood Ave.
Chicago, IL 60637
Phone: (773) 702-0200
URL: (WWW address): http://csmaclab-www.uchicago.edu/Smart Museum
Site description: Located at the University of Chicago, this museum has an on-line catalog, a virtual tour, news, and a summary of its collection. Includes a video of kids giving talks about art.

Southwest Museum
234 Museum Dr.
Los Angeles, CA 90065
Phone: (213) 221-2164
URL: (WWW address): http://www.annex.com/southwest/museum.htm
Site description: Site of a collection related to native cultures of the Americas. Includes images of Prehispanic, Spanish Colonial, Latino, and Western American art and artifacts.

Spencer Museum of Arts
University of Kansas
Lawrence, KS 66045
Phone: (913) 864-4710
URL: (WWW address): http://www.ukans.edu/~sma/prints.html
Site description: The University's print collection is available at this site. Contains detailed information about prints.

INTERNET ART RESOURCES

American Memory
URL: (WWW address): http://rsb.loc.gov/amhome.htm
Site description: Hosted by the Library of Congress this site includes collections of art and items relating to American culture and history.

ArtsEdNet
URL: (WWW address): http://www.artsednet.getty.edu/
Site description: Art educators resource sponsored by the Getty Center for Education in the Arts. Contains images, lesson plans, Web gateways, and a search engine.

Native American Fine Arts Movement
URL: (WWW address): http://www.heard.org/EDU/NAFAMRG/full.html
Site description: A resource guide for the Native American Fine Arts Movement.

Eyes on Art
URL: (WWW address): http://www.kn.pacbell.com/wired/art/art.html
Site description: A variety of study guides and art activities for students and teachers.

Art Education Resources
URL: (WWW address): http://www.umass.edu/education/links/art.html
Site description: Well-constructed link to many, many art education resources.

ArtResources (Ferguson-Taylor Group)
URL: (WWW address): http://www.ftgi.com
Site description: A basic art search engine. Gateway to Internet ArtResources.

Crayola
URL: (WWW address): http://www.crayola.com
Site description: Contains education links and art resources.

Kennedy Center for Education In the Arts
URL: (WWW address): http://www.artsedge.kennedy-center.org/
Site description: Lesson plans, curriculum resources, and on-line communication tool for the art teacher. Site contains a catalog of arts education materials and a search capability.

Internet ArtResources
URL: (WWW address): http://www.artresources.com/
Site description: This site is a powerful link to over 1100 museums, galleries, and institutions. It can serve as a starting point for a virtual trip to almost anywhere.

Library of Congress
URL: (WWW address): http://www.loc.gov
Site description: Contains list of databases.

The Incredible Art Department
URL: (WWW address): http://www.in.net/~kenroar/
Site description: Lesson plans, careers, art news, art images, and more.

Museum Resource Guides
URL: (WWW address): http://www.ucmp.berkeley.edu/subway/musreguide.html
Site description: This site is a valuable navigation aid. A valuable tool to acquire Internet educational resources.

World Wide Arts Resources
URL: (WWW address): http://wwar.com
Site description: A complete listing of arts resources worldwide.

VIRTUAL MUSEUMS (Collections)

Dale Chihuly
URL: (WWW address): http://www.chihuly.com
Site description: The works in glass of America's first National Living Treasure are here.

Diego Rivera Museum, The
URL: (WWW address): http://www.diegorivera.com/diego_home_eng.html
Site description: A virtual museum devoted to the works of Mexican artist Diego Rivera.

Erte Museum – Art Deco
URL: (WWW address): http://www.webcom.com/ajarts/erte.html
Site description: The artist famous for his role in the Art Deco style is represented here. Images of his costume designs are included here.

Korean American Museum of Art and Cultural Center (KOMA) (CA)
URL: (WWW address): http://koma.org/
Site description: This virtual museum offers information and images of Korean art, including historical background.

Leonardo da Vinci Museum
URL: (WWW address): http://www.leonardo.net/main.html/
Site description: Voted one of the top ten sites on the Web. Images of paintings, drawings, and a historical perspective are included.

Mesa Arts Center – Galeria Mesa (Arizona)
URL: (WWW address): http://aztec.asu.edu/AandE/mac5.html
Site description: Images of the most current rotating exhibits are accessible.

New York Museums Home Page
URL: (WWW address): http://www.museumsny.com
Site description: Museums New York provides a tour of various exhibits happening in the city and profiles the work of famous New York artists.

World of Escher
URL: (WWW address): http://lonestar.texas.net/~escher/gallery/
Site description: Individual works by M. C. Escher can be accessed. Browse, study, and become more familiar with Escher's life and some of his best creations.

WebMuseum, Paris
URL: (WWW address): http://sunsite.unc.edu/wm/
Site description: From Paris! A vast collection of images and art resources from museums the world over.

World Art Treasures
URL: (WWW address): http://sgwww.epfl.ch/BERGER/index.html
Site description: Collection of paintings, sculptures and decorative art, representing all movements and periods. A variety of useful links.

Elements and Principles of Art Scope and Sequence

SRA Art Connections	Level K						Level 1						Level 2						Level 3					
Elements of Art	U1	U2	U3	U4	U5	U6	U1	U2	U3	U4	U5	U6	U1	U2	U3	U4	U5	U6	U1	U2	U3	U4	U5	U6
Color			1–6						1–6						1–6					1–6				
Form				2–6						1–6				1–3, 6							4–6			
Line	1–6						1–6						1–4						1–2					
Shape		1–6							1–6	6			5–6	1						3–6				
Space				1						2, 5					4–5							1–3		
Texture					1–6						1–4						4–6						1–3	
Value															2–4					1				

Principles of Art	U1	U2	U3	U4	U5	U6	U1	U2	U3	U4	U5	U6	U1	U2	U3	U4	U5	U6	U1	U2	U3	U4	U5	U6
Balance					1–2							3			1–3, 6					1–4				
Emphasis											1–2					5				5–6				
Harmony																	1, 4–6						1, 3–4	
Movement and Rhythm					3–6					5–6					1–6							4–6		
Proportion																								
Unity						6						4–6					4–6							4–6
Variety																	2–3, 5–6							2–4

★Numbers indicate lesson numbers within given unit.

Elements of Art

Elements of Art	Level 4 U1	U2	U3	U4	U5	U6	Level 5 U1	U2	U3	U4	U5	U6	Level 6§ Introducing Art	Level 7§ Exploring Art	Level 8§ Understanding Art
Color			1–6					1–4, 6					Chapters 1-2, 5-7, 9-10, 12	Chapters 4, 6-13	Chapters 1, 3, 12-16
Form				1–6					4–6				Chapters 1, 4-5, 7, 9-10	Chapters 4, 6-9, 11-12	Chapters 1, 3, 5, 9, 12, 15, 16
Line	1–6						1, 4						Chapters 1, 4-5, 7, 9-11, 14	Chapters 4, 6-12, 14	Chapters 1-3, 5, 9-14, 16-17
Shape		1–2					2						Chapters 1-2, 6, 8, 10	Chapters 4, 6-12	Chapters 1, 3-4, 6-7, 9, 11-13, 15-17
Space					1–4				1–2		4–6		Chapters 1, 5-7, 10	Chapters 4, 6-9, 11-12	Chapters 1, 3-5, 8, 11
Texture					5–6				3–6				Chapters 1, 4, 7-9, 12	Chapters 4, 6-9, 11-14	Chapters 1, 3, 5, 9-12, 14-17
Value		2, 5–6					3–6						Chapters 1-2, 4, 10	Chapters 4, 6-9, 11-12, 14	Chapters 1-3, 11, 14-16

Principles of Art

Principles of Art	Level 4 U1	U2	U3	U4	U5	U6	Level 5 U1	U2	U3	U4	U5	U6	Introducing Art	Exploring Art	Understanding Art
Balance					1–3						1–3		Chapters 2, 12	Chapters 5, 7-9, 11, 14, 15	Chapters 1, 4, 6-8, 10-11, 13
Emphasis					5							1–2	Chapters 2, 4	Chapters 5, 7-9, 11	Chapters 1, 13, 16
Harmony					4							4–5	Chapters 2, 10	Chapters 5, 7-9, 11, 15	Chapters 4, 6, 8, 15-17
Movement and Rhythm		3–6						5–6					Chapters 2, 6, 9, 11-13	Chapters 5, 7-11	Chapters 1-3, 8-9, 12, 16
Proportion										1–6			Chapters 2, 4	Chapters 5, 7-9, 11, 14	Chapters 4, 11
Unity					6							5–6	Chapters 2, 14	Chapters 5, 7-9, 11	Chapters 6, 16-17
Variety					5							3, 5	Chapters 2, 9-10, 13	Chapters 5, 7-9, 11, 15	Chapters 1, 17

§Available from **Glencoe/McGraw-Hill, secondary division of McGraw-Hill.**

Media Scope and Sequence

SRA Art Connections	Level K						Level 1						Level 2						Level 3					
Media	U1	U2	U3	U4	U5	U6	U1	U2	U3	U4	U5	U6	U1	U2	U3	U4	U5	U6	U1	U2	U3	U4	U5	U6
Collage	4–5	2	2–3	1	1	1, 6		1, 6	2, 5		1	1,4	5	4		6	1	1–3	4	6		6	1, 5	3
Drawing	2, 6	1, 3–5	1, 4–5	3	2	1, 3, 6	1, 4–6	1–2, 4–5	1, 4–5	6	2, 4	3, 5–6	2–3	4–5	5–6	1–2, 5	2		1–2, 5–6	1, 4–6	2–5	1–2, 5–6	2–5	3–4, 6
Fiber Arts	4			4, 6							5	2					4–5						2	2
Mixed Media			4, 5	5	3	1		5		5		1	2–3	5	5	2, 5–6	6	4, 6		3, 6	6		1, 3 6	4–5
Painting	1, 3	3, 6	4–6	5		2, 4–5	2–4	2–3, 5	1, 3, 6	5–6	4	4	2–4	5	2–5	2, 5	2, 3	4, 6	2–3	1, 2, 5–6	2	2, 4		4–5
Photography																								
Printmaking						5	3				6				1	3–4					1		4, 6	
Three-Dimensional Forms				2–6	3, 5		5			1–5	3		1, 6	1–3, 6			3, 6	5–6		3–4	4–6	2–3		1

★ Numbers indicate lesson numbers within given unit.

Media	Level 4						Level 5						Level 6§ Introducing Art	Level 7§ Exploring Art	Level 8§ Understanding Art
	U1	U2	U3	U4	U5	U6	U1	U2	U3	U4	U5	U6			
Collage		1, 4	2–3				1, 6	3–4	3	2	3		Chapters 3, 7-8, 12-14	Chapters 1-2, 7, 11	Chapters 6, 8, 10, 16
Drawing	1–6	1–2, 5–6	1, 3	5	1–3	1–3, 6	2–5	2	1–2, 4–5	1, 3–4	2, 4–6	2–3, 5	Chapters 1-14	Chapters 1-8, 11, 14	Chapters 1-17
Fiber Arts					5							1–2	Chapters 4, 12, 13	Chapter 13	Chapters 8, 13
Mixed Media				4, 6	1, 6	4–6	1			5	3	4–6	Chapters 3-9, 12-13	Chapters 1, 3, 7	Chapters 2, 8, 12, 14
Painting	6	2, 5	2, 4–6	4	1, 3, 6	2, 4	2	1–2, 5–6		5	2, 5	4	Chapters 1-10, 12-14	Chapters 3-8, 10-11, 15	Chapters 1-5, 7-9, 12-15, 17
Photography				4			6						Chapter 11	Chapter 15	Chapter 11
Printmaking		3									1		Chapters 3, 6, 7	Chapters 3, 9	Chapters 2, 13, 16-17
Three-Dimensional Forms				1–5		4–6			6	5–6		4–6	Chapters 1-5, 7-13	Chapters 3-5, 12-15	Chapters 5-7, 9-12, 14, 17

§Available from **Glencoe/McGraw-Hill, secondary division of McGraw-Hill.**

PROGRAM GLOSSARY

A

Abstract art Twentieth-century art containing shapes that simplify shapes of real objects to emphasize form instead of subject matter.

Abstract Expressionism Painting style developed after World War II in New York City that stressed elements and principles of art as subject matter and emotion rather than planned design. Abstract Expressionism is also called action painting because artists applied paint freely to huge canvases.

active lines Lines that show action and add energy to a work of art. Diagonal, zigzag, and curved lines are active lines.

additive sculpture A type of sculpture to which something is added. The sculpture may be relief or freestanding.

alternate rhythm (alternating rhythm) When one motif is repeated after a second, different motif.

analogous color scheme A color scheme using colors that are side by side on the color wheel.

analogous colors Colors that are side by side on the color wheel.

ant's view Viewers feel they are looking up toward an object or figure.

appliqué Art made by attaching fabric shapes onto a fabric background by gluing or sewing.

approximate symmetry When both sides of a design are almost exactly the same. Approximate symmetry is a type of formal balance.

architect A person who plans and designs buildings, cities, and bridges.

architecture The art of designing and planning the construction of buildings, cities, and bridges.

armature A framework for supporting material used in sculpting.

art form A type of art.

assemblage A technique in which an artist collects found materials and assembles them into a three-dimensional work of art. A work of art in which a variety of objects are assembled to create one complete piece.

asymmetry Another name for informal balance. Asymmetry is a way of organizing parts of a design so that unlike objects have equal visual weight.

B

background The part of the picture plane that seems to be farthest from the viewer.

balance The principle of design that deals with visual weight in a work of art.

Baroque Artistic style that emphasized movement, strong value contrast, and variety. It developed after the Reformation in the seventeenth century. Artists used movement of forms and figures toward the viewer, dramatic lighting effects, contrast between dark and light, ornamentation, and curved lines to express energy and strong emotions.

batik A way to design fabric using wax and dyes.

bird's-eye view Viewers feel they are looking down on a scene.

black ▬▬▬

blind contour A type of drawing done by looking at the object being drawn and not at the paper.

blue ▬▬▬

body proportions Ratios of one part of the body to another.

bookmaking The art of binding or tying pages together inside a cover.

bright color A pure spectral color.

broken (line) A line interrupted by space.

brown ▬▬▬

building Places where we live, work, meet, and play.

Byzantine Artistic style that developed around the city of Constantinople (now Istanbul, Turkey) in the eastern Roman Empire. The style blended Roman, Greek, and Oriental art. It featured very rich colors and figures that were flat and stiff. These works blended Greek, Roman, and Asian styles and usually had a religious theme.

C

carving Cutting away of a hard material like wood or marble to create a three-dimensional work of art.

center of interest Area of an artwork that a viewer immediately looks at first.

central axis An imaginary vertical line that splits a work of art in half. The central axis is used in formal balance.

circle A shape where all points are equidistant from the center.

Classical Referring to the art of ancient Greece and Rome. The Greeks created art based on the ideals of perfect proportion and logic instead of emotion. The Romans adapted Greek art and spread it throughout the civilized world.

close-up Viewers feel they are right next to the object or are a part of the action in a picture.

collage Bits and pieces of things glued onto paper.

Color-Field Painting Twentieth-century style of painting using flat areas of color for the pure sensation of color. Artists creating color-field paintings are not trying to express emotion or use a precise design.

color intensity The brightness or dullness of a color.

color scheme A plan for organizing the colors used in an artwork.

color spectrum Range of colors that come from light.

color wheel A design for organizing colors that shows the spectrum bent into a circle.

complementary color Colors that are opposite each other on the color wheel.

complementary color scheme A color scheme that uses complementary colors.

complex geometric shape A shape made by combining simple geometric shapes such as triangles, squares, and rectangles.

contour The edge or surface ridges of an object or figure.

contour drawing A drawing in which only contour lines are used.

contour lines Lines that show the edges and surface ridges of an object.

contrast A difference created when elements are placed next to each other in a work of art.

cool color A color that seems to move away from the viewer and suggests coolness. Green, blue, and violet are cool colors.

cool hues Blue, green, and violet. Another name for *cool colors*.

cross-hatching A shading technique in which two or more sets of parallel lines cross each other.

Cubism Twentieth-century art movement that emphasizes structure and design. Three-dimensional objects are pictured from many different points of view at the same time.

culture How a group of people thinks, believes, and acts.

curved A line that bends and changes direction slowly.

D

Dadaists Early twentieth-century artists using fantastic and strange objects as subject matter.

darker Having more black in a color.

deckle A framed screen used for papermaking.

depth The appearance of distance on a flat surface.

de Stijl Dutch for "the style." A painting style developed by Mondrian in Holland in the early twentieth century that uses only vertical and horizontal lines; black, white, and gray; and the three primary colors.

diagonal (line) A slanted line.

diamond A four-sided shape made by combining two triangles.

difference The state of being not the same.

dimension Measurement in height, width, or depth.

direct observation Technique when artists study an object from various viewpoints, looking closely at the important details, and recording those details in their drawings.

distortion Stretching an object or figure out of normal shape so that it does not appear real. Distortion is used to communicate ideas or feelings.

dominant element The element that is noticed first in a work of art.

dull color A low-intensity color that has been subdued by the addition of its complement, brown, gray, etc.

E

emphasis The principle of design that makes one part of the artwork stand out more than the other parts.

emphasize To make something look important.

environmental art Art that is created to be part of a landscape.

even balance Both halves are equal. Left side and right side are the same.

exaggerate Make much larger than actual size.

exaggeration Increasing or enlarging an object or a figure or one of its parts to communicate ideas or feelings.

Expressionism Twentieth-century art movement in which artists tried to communicate their strong emotional feelings and which stressed personal feelings rather than composition.

F

fabric Cloth.

facial proportions The relationship of one feature of a face to another feature.

faraway Viewers feel they are standing faraway from the scene.

fiber Thin, thread-like material generally used to make yarn and woven fabrics.

flowing rhythm Rhythm that repeats curved lines or shapes.

focal point The area of an artwork that is emphasized.

foreground The part of the picture plane that appears closest to the viewer.

form Any object that can be measured in three ways: height, width, and depth.

formal balance A way of organizing a design so that equal or very similar elements are placed on opposite sides of an imaginary, central dividing line.

found materials Any items found in your home, school, or outdoor environment that can be used to create new works of art.

free-form (shape) An irregular and uneven shape. Any shape that is not geometric.

freestanding (sculpture) A three-dimensional sculpture that has empty, negative space all around; a type of sculpture that is surrounded by space on all sides.

freestanding assemblage A type of assemblage that has space all around it. Freestanding assemblage is meant to be viewed from all sides.

frozen motion When one action is frozen in time.

functional form Objects created by artists for use in daily life.

Futurists Early twentieth-century Italian artists who arranged angular forms to suggest motion. They called the forces of movement dynamism.

G

geometric A math shape, such as a circle, triangle, rectangle, or square.

geometric form A three-dimensional figure that has precise measurement and can be described in mathematical terms, such as a sphere, a cube, or a pyramid.

geometric shape A figure that has precise measurements and can be described in mathematical terms, such as a circle, a square, a triangle, or a rectangle.

gesture An expressive movement.

gesture lines Lines quickly drawn to capture the movement of a person, animal, or object in a painting or drawing.

gesture sketch A quick sketch to capture movement or action of an object.

Gothic Artistic style developed in western Europe between the twelfth and sixteenth centuries. Gothic cathedrals used pointed arches and flying buttresses to emphasize upward movement and featured stained-glass windows. Sculpture and painting showed humans realistically.

gradation A gradual change of one value to another.

green ▬▬▬

guidelines Lines that help an artist place things in a work of art.

H

harmonious When things seem to go together.

harmony The principle of design that creates unity by stressing similarities of separate but related parts; a pleasing relationship between parts of an artwork.

hatching A shading technique using a series of repeated parallel lines.

height How tall something is.

hexagon A six-sided shape.

highlight Small area of white used to show the very brightest spot on an object.

horizon line The point at which the earth and sky meet.

horizontal A line that moves from side to side.

hue Another word for color.

I

images The things you see in an artwork.

imitated texture A kind of visual texture that imitates real texture by using a two-dimensional pattern to create the illusion of a three-dimensional surface.

implied line A series of points that are connected by the viewer's eyes.

Impressionism Style of painting started in France in the 1860s. It captured everyday subjects and emphasized the momentary effects of sunlight.

informal balance A way of organizing parts of a design so that unlike objects have equal visual weight.

intensity The brightness or dullness of a color.

interior designer An artist who designs the insides of buildings and their furnishings, such as carpeting, furniture, and drapes.

intermediate color One of six colors that are made when a primary color is mixed with a secondary color.

intermediate hue Made by mixing a primary hue with a secondary hue. Another name for *intermediate color.*

invented texture A kind of visual texture that does not represent a real texture, but creates the sensation of one.

isolation When an object is placed alone and away from all the other objects in an artwork.

J

jeweler An artist who designs and makes jewelry.

jewelry Three-dimensional art that is made for people to wear.

L

lighter Having more white in a color.

line A mark drawn by a tool such as a pencil, pen, or paintbrush as it moves across a surface.

line variation Changes in the look of a line.

line variety Lines may be short or long, thick or thin, rough or smooth.

linear perspective A way of using lines to show distance and depth.

location When the eyes are naturally drawn toward the center of an artwork.

M

mandala A radial design divided into sections or wedges, each of which contains an image.

Mannerism European sixteenth-century artistic style featuring highly emotional scenes and distorted figures.

mask Three-dimensional art form of a sculpted face, often made to be worn over the face.

matte Textured surfaces that reflect a soft light, with an almost dull look.

Medieval Related to the *Middle Ages.*

Middle Ages Period of roughly one thousand years from the destruction of the Roman Empire to the *Renaissance.* Culture centered around the Church. The Middle Ages are also called the Dark Ages (because few new ideas developed) and the Age of Faith (because religion was a powerful force).

middle ground Area in a picture between the foreground and background.

minimal detail Very little detail in a drawing.

mola An artwork in reverse appliqué when layers are cut away after stitching, and is sometimes added to clothing.

monochromatic Using one color plus all the tints and shades of that color.

monochromatic color scheme A color scheme using one color plus all the tints and shades of that color.

mood How an artwork makes you feel.

mosaic A picture made by setting small pieces of colored tile, glass, or stone side by side.

motif Shape or object that is repeated.

movement The look of constant motion in a work of art.

mural A large work of art painted on a wall.

N

negative space The empty space that surrounds objects, shapes, and forms in an artwork.

Neoclassicism New classic. French artistic style developed in the nineteenth century after the *Rococo* style. It used *classical* features and was unemotional and realistic.

neutral color scheme A color scheme using only neutral colors.

neutral colors Black, white and gray.

New Realism Twentieth century artistic style in which artists tried to create the impression of movement on the surface of paintings with hard edges, smooth surfaces, and mathematical planning.

nonobjective painting A painting with no recognizable subject matter.

O

observation brush drawing A preliminary sketch done with brush and watercolors.

observation drawing A drawing made while looking at a person or object.

octagon An eight-sided shape.

one-point perspective One way of using lines to show distance and depth, with all lines that move back into space meeting at one point.

Op Art Optical art. Twentieth century artistic style in which artists tried to create the impression of movement on the surface of paintings with hard edges, smooth surfaces, and mathematical planning.

orange

outline A line that marks the outside of an object

overlap When one object covers part of a second object.

P

painting A type of art in which paint is applied to a flat surface, such as paper, canvas or silk.

parallelogram A shape with four sides; opposite sides are parallel and equal in length.

pattern The use of shapes, colors, or lines repeated in a planned way.

pentagon A five-sided shape.

perception The act of looking at something carefully and thinking deeply about what is seen.

perspective techniques Techniques used by artists to create the feeling of depth on a flat surface.

photographer Artist who takes pictures with a camera.

picture plane The surface of a drawing or painting.

point of view The position from which the viewer looks at an object.

Pop art Artistic style used in the early 1960s in America featuring subject matter from popular culture (mass media, commercial art, comic strips, and advertising).

portrait A picture of a person.

position Placement of elements in a work of art.

positive space The area in a work of art that shapes and objects fill.

Post-Impressionism French painting style of the late nineteenth century that used basic structures of art to express feelings and ideas. The Post-Impressionism movement, which immediately followed *Impressionism,* was led by Paul Cézanne, Vincent van Gogh, and Paul Gauguin.

Prehistoric Period before history was written down.

primary color One of the three basic colors: red, yellow, and blue.

Primary colors cannot be made by mixing other colors.

primary hue One of the three basic hues: red, yellow, and blue. Primary hues cannot be made by mixing other hues.

printing Pressing a shape from one thing to another many times.

profile proportions The relationship of one feature of a face to another feature when looking from the side view.

progressive To change or move forward.

progressive motion When a scene or motif changes a little each time it is repeated.

progressive reversal When an object starts out as one object or form and slowly changes into another object or form.

progressive rhythm When a motif changes each time it is repeated.

proportion Principle of art concerned with the size relationships of one part to another.

purple Also known as violet.

R

radial balance When the elements in a design come out from a central point.

radiate To come out from a central point.

rainbow Red, orange, yellow, green, blue, and violet curved into a semicircle.

random rhythm Motifs that appear in no apparent order and have irregular spaces between them.

ratio A comparison of size between two things.

real texture Texture you can feel.

Realism Mid-nineteenth-century artistic style in which artists turned away from the style of Romanticism to paint familiar scenes as they actually were.

realistic scale Where everything seems to fit together and make sense in size relation in a work of art.

Realists Artists in the nineteenth century who portrayed political, social, and moral issues.

rectangle A four-sided shape in which opposite sides are parallel and equal in length, and each corner forms a right angle.

red

Regionalists Artists who painted the farmlands and cities of America realistically.

regular rhythm Visual rhythm that is created by repeating the same motif with equal amounts of space in between.

relief assemblage A type of assemblage where objects stick out from one side only.

relief print A technique in which the design to be printed is raised from the background.

relief sculpture A type of sculpture from which objects stick out of a flat surface.

Renaissance The name given to the period of awakening at the end of the *Middle Ages.* French for "rebirth." Interest in *Classical* art was renewed. Important Renaissance artists are Leonardo da Vinci, Michelangelo, and Raphael.

repeated lines Lines that are repeated give the feeling of movement or motion.

repeated shapes Shapes that are repeated several times give the feeling of motion.

repetition When an artist repeats lines, colors, or textures.

rhythm The repetition of lines, shapes, or colors to create a feeling of movement.

Rococo Eighteenth-century artistic style that began in the luxurious homes of the French aristocracy and spread to the rest of Europe. It stressed free, graceful movement, a playful use of line, and delicate colors.

Romanesque Style of architecture and sculpture developed during the Middle Ages in western Europe that featured massive size; solid, heavy walls; wide use of the rounded Roman arch; and many sculptural decorations.

Romanticism Early nineteenth-century artistic style that was a reaction against *Neoclassicism*. It featured dramatic scenes, bright colors, loose compositions, and exotic settings. It also emphasized the feelings and personality of the artist.

rough Texture that reflects light unevenly.

rough line An uneven, bumpy line.

S

sarcophagus A mummy case.

scale Size as measured against a standard reference.

sculptor An artist who makes sculpture.

sculpture A three-dimensional work of art.

secondary color The mixture of two primary colors. Orange, green, and violet are secondary colors.

secondary hue Orange, green, or violet. Another name for *secondary color.*

shade Any dark value of a color.

shading A technique for darkening values by adding black or darkening an area by repeating several lines close together.

shadows Shaded, or darker, areas in a drawing or painting.

shape A flat, two-dimensional figure.

shape reversal When a shape or positive space starts out as one image and then, in another image, turns into the negative space.

shiny Texture that reflects a bright light.

silhouette The shape of a shadow.

simplicity A method of creating unity by using only one color, shape, or texture in a work of art.

simulated texture A kind of visual texture that imitates tactile texture by using a two-dimensional pattern to create the illusion of a three-dimensional surface.

slanted line A line moving at an angle to the picture plane, not horizontal or vertical.

smooth Texture that reflects light evenly.

smooth line A line that has an even surface, free from irregularities.

solid form A three-dimensional object, having height, width, and depth.

solid (line) An unbroken line.

space The element of art that refers to the area between, around, above, below, and within an object.

spectral color One of the six colors of the rainbow. Red, orange, yellow, green, blue, and violet are spectral colors.

spectral color scheme A color scheme using the colors of the spectrum.

square A shape with four equal sides that form right angles.

still life Collection of objects that do not move.

stippling A shading technique using dots. The closer the dots, the darker the area.

stitchery Technique for decorating fabric by stitching fibers onto it.

Stone Age Period of history during which stone tools were used.

straight line A line that does not curve or bend.

subject What the artwork is about.

subtractive sculpture A type of sculpture made from carving a form. The original material is taken away, or subtracted.

Surrealism Twentieth-century artistic style in which dreams, fantasy, and the subconscious served as inspiration for artists.

swirling line A line that curves in a circular motion and creates a sense of movement in a work of art.

symmetry A type of formal balance in which two halves of an object or composition are mirror images of each other.

T

tactile texture The element of art that refers to how things actually feel when you touch them.

tessellation A type of shape reversal that changes quickly and fits together like a puzzle.

texture The element of art that refers to how things feel, or look as if they might feel, if touched.

thick (line) A wide line.

thin (line) A narrow line.

three-dimensional (3-D form) Something that can be measured by height, width, and depth.

tint Any light value of a color.

trapezoid A shape with four sides, only two of which are parallel.

triangle A three-sided shape.

Trompe l'oeil French for "deceive the eye." Style of painting in which painters try to give the viewer the illusion of seeing a three-dimensional object so that the viewer wonders whether he or she is seeing a picture or something real.

two-dimensional (shape) A flat figure that can only be measured by height and width.

U

unity The feeling of wholeness or oneness that is accomplished by properly using the elements and principles of art.

unrealistic scale When size relationships do not make sense in a work of art.

V

value The lightness or darkness of a color or object.

vanishing point The point on the horizon line where all the lines moving back into a space seem to meet.

variety The use of different lines, shapes, and colors in artwork.

vertical (line) A line that moves up and down.

violet ▬▬▬ Also called purple.

visual movement Visual rhythm that pulls the viewer's eyes through a work of art.

visual pattern Pattern created by the repetition of shapes, colors or lines.

visual rhythm Rhythm created by the repetition of shapes, colors or lines.

visual texture The way something looks like it might feel if you could touch it.

visual weight Weight of elements in a work of art seen with your eyes.

W

warm color Color that seems to move toward the viewer and suggests warmth and energy. Red, orange, and yellow are warm colors.

warm hues Yellow, orange, and red. Another name for *warm colors.*

warp threads Vertical threads attached to a loom.

weaving Creating fabric by criss-crossing.

weft threads Threads that are woven over and under the warp threads.

white ○

width How wide something is.

Y

yellow ▬▬▬

Z

zigzag (line) Diagonal lines that connect and change direction sharply.

PROGRAM INDEX

Items referenced are coded by Grade Level and page number.

ART ACROSS THE CURRICULUM INDEX

Items referenced are coded by
Grade Level and page number.

T48